Anonymous

Watertown Records

Vol. VII

Anonymous

Watertown Records
Vol. VII

ISBN/EAN: 9783337143732

Printed in Europe, USA, Canada, Australia, Japan

Cover: Foto ©ninafisch / pixelio.de

More available books at **www.hansebooks.com**

WATERTOWN RECORDS

COMPRISING

East Congregational and Precinct Affairs

1697 to 1737

ALSO

RECORD BOOK OF THE PASTORS

1686 to 1819

PREPARED FOR PUBLICATION

BY THE

HISTORICAL SOCIETY

BOSTON
DAVID CLAPP & SON, PRINTERS
291 Congress Street
1906

PREFACE.

THIS, the fourth published volume of Watertown Records, comprises the only two volumes specially devoted to ecclesiastical affairs now extant. The records of congregational and precinct affairs are in the one book, entered the one at the beginning, the other at the end of the book which has been reversed. The pastors' records are those of a book kept by the Rev. John Bailey, Henry Gibbs, Seth Storer, Daniel Adams, Richard R. Elliot and Convers Francis. The many pages of the record devoted by Pastor Bailey to his pious meditations, ejaculations and hints upon Bible texts, the Committee has not deemed to be of sufficient present interest to be now reproduced. Of the many pages occupied with his remarks made at Communion services, only a few selected portions are given, to indicate their general character. As he intended them to serve only as private memoranda, he wrote them in a much abbreviated form, using the common abbreviation of "y" in place of "th" with most all words beginning with those two letters, using the Greek "X" *i.e.* "Ch" for Christ, "I. X." for Jesus Christ, and "H. G." for Holy Ghost, and others then readily understood by him at least.

BENNETT F. DAVENPORT,
CHARLES F. FITZ,
Committee of Publication.

[WATERTOWN RECORDS.

East Precinct Congregational Affairs.]*

---

[2] At a great and Genll Court, or afsembly for his majesties Province of Mafsachufets-Bay in New-England, began & heild at Boston upon Wednesday the 29th of May 1700—and Continued by feverall Prorogations untill Wednesday the 12th of February following, for accomodateing and Ifsuing the differrences relating to the fupport of the miniftrey in the middle and easterly parts of Watertown, Refolved and Ordered that there be a fubfscription throwout the whole town of Watertown, The farmers excepted, In order to the fupport of the miniftre in the old and new meeting-houfe, that there Perfons & Eftates who fubfcrib for fupport of the miniftrey at the Old meeting-houfe be liable to be afsefed thereto and no where elfe, and that there Perfons and eftates who fubfcribe for fupport of the miniftre to the middle-meeting-houfe be liable to be afsefsed thereto and no where elfe, that fuch who refufe to fubfcribe to the miniftre at either meeting-houfe shall be liable to pay to the miniftrey of the meeting-houfe ftanding within the bounds of the military Precinct where thay dwell, that each fociety be Impowred to Choofe a certaine number of men to afsefs them, and thofe to be upon oath that the feverall fubfcribers shall enter their names at or before the twentieth of may next before Samll Hayman and Tho: Brown Esqrs two of his majesties Justices within the County. Sd Justice Hayman to appoint the time and Place in fd: town to take the fubfcribtion of such the Inhabitants as shall be prevented of subfcribing at the time, or times fo to be appointed as aforesd by reafon of their being then ought of town, or detained by ficknefs, shall have liberty to subfcribe before the town Clarke at any time before the twentieth Day of August next coming, that this order Continue in force untill the end of feven years next, or untill the Inhabitance of both faid parts of the town shall mutually agree to fupport the miniftre in any other manner, and that all actions suets & controverfies Relating to the meeting-houfes, or miniftre in the faid town of Watertown Doo ceafe untill the accomplifhment of fuch fubfcribtions confented to.

Isaac Addington Secretary. William Stoughton.

* See vote of Oct. 20, 1701, on p. [11] concerning keeping records.—Eds.

[3]

Decembr 9th 1685. At a Genll town meeting. Voted that Endeavours should be ufed to hier an houfe for the minister, Voted, That the selectmen with Corpll Bond fr shall be a comitte to fearch ought a Place that may be hired for the minister and make return to the town.

A true copie taken ought of Watertown third Booke of Records.

pr Munings Sawin town clerk of Watertown.

Febr 12th: 1685. The town being called together by order of the comitte abovesd The town did then Declare by a vote, That, if a number of Perfons would build a convenient houfe to entertaine the minister in neer to this meetinghoufe, that then the town will pay them that build it Rent for the sd houfe, untill the town doe agree and have actually Removed this meetinghoufe, or built another in the Room of this more convenient for the Inhabitants fomewhere else where the town shall agree upon.

A true copie taken of Watertown third Booke of Records. [p. 28.]

pr Munings Sawin town Clerk for Watertown.

Alfo it was agreed by a vote of the town that that Peace of town land lying between Old Goodman Sawin's land upon the east, and the Path leading from Pastor Sherman's houfe to the burying Place on the west, and between the two highways north and south shall be to fet the aforesd houfe upon, the builders allowing the town refonable sattisfaction for it out of the Rent of the houfe, the fd land being about five acres more or lefs.

A true copie taken of Watertown third Booke of Records. [p. 28.]

pr Munings Sawin Clerk for Watertown.

Paid by	lb	s	d		lb	s	d
Mr William Bond Esqr	13	09	01	Stephen Coolidg	03	12	00
John Bond	04	09	00	William Shattuck	04	03	09
John Morfe	03	01	00	Joseph Hastings	01	06	06
John Woodward	03	03	00	John Traine fenr	02	12	06
Jonathan Brown	07	08	00	John Perry	01	09	06
John Sawin				Tho Traine	01	19	00
William Goddard fenr	04	04	00	Sergt Jno Coolidg	08	07	03
Gregory Cooke	04	18	03	Wido Mary Smith	02	10	00
Nathan Fiske fenr	03	15	00	Jno Knop fenr	05	19	00
Samuell Eddy fen	03	18	06	Micael Barstow	03	05	06
Capt Jno Sherman	00	13	00	Widow Eliz: Faning	02	14	00
Cornt Jno Hammont	11	10	06	Capt Natll Barsham	05	07	07
John Kimbol	02	01	04	Deacon Wm Bond	03	18	00
Nethaniel Bright	03	14	05	Nethaniell Coolidg	05	19	03
Marten Townend	02	19	00	Ensn Samll Thatcher	05	04	05
John Chenry	03	02	02	Caleb Grant	01	17	06
Elliz Barron	02	16	00	Jofeph Grant	02	06	00
Mr Jno Bisco	05	01	09	Christopher Grant	01	16	00
Tho: Bisco	02	11	00	Mr Ric Norcrofs	06	09	11

Deacon Jno Bright - -	06	16	11	Deacon Jno Stone -	04	12	10
Joſeph Maſon - - - -	03	12	03	John Straton ſenr -	06	13	11
David Church - - -	02	13	06	Nicolas Wyeth - -	01	06	11
Corpll Roger Wellington	04	04	00	Simon Stone ſen -	06	09	01
Samuell Livermore - -	06	06	04				
Jonathan Coolidg - -	02	16	00				

[4]

At a Genll town meeting by adjornment the 14th of October, 1690: The town by there vote did manifest their earnest deſire that Mr. Henry Gibbs might be treated witn in order to his being a conſtant help to the town, not only for the Preſent, but for the futer alſo, so that thay might not be deſtitute of the word nor Ordinances of Christ if god shall pleas to Continue him amongst us.

Voted by the town that the Deacons together with Capt Sherman & Leut. Bond shall treat wth mr Henry Gibbs, and to Returne his anſwer at the Genll town meeting next enſuing.

A true copie taken out of Watertown third booke of Records. [p. 42]

pr me Munings Sawin Town Clark for Watertown.

At a Genll town meeting Novembr the 3d 1690: At this meeting Capt Sherman & Leiut Bond together with the Deacons being sent to treat with Mr Henry Gibbs about his being a help to the town in the worke of the miniſtrey and his anſwer is as followeth to wit. that he locketh upon it as a call from god, that hath Inclined the town to be ſo unanimus in their calling of him, and therefore is willing to attend the ſd. worke as god shall enable him, The town alſo accepts his anſwer herein, and did by a vote of the town declare that this Day his time began as unto his ſallerry, as is above written.

A true copie taken of watertown third booke of Records.

pr Munings Sawin Town Clerk for Watertown.

At a Genll town meeting by adjornment the 16th of Novembr 1691. Voted at this meeting that the town doe renew their call unto the Reverend Mr Gibbs That he would Continnue to carry on the worke of the miniſtrey amongſt us, according unto there former Call, as appeares upon Record. The town by their vote, chooſe Mr William Bond, Capt Warren, Simon Stone, for to treat with the Revd Mr Henry Gibbs to come amongſt us to carry on the miniſtrey.

A true Copie taken out of Watertown third booke of Records. [p. 45.]

pr Munings Sawin town Clarke for Watertown.

Perſuant to a vote of the town Paſsed at A Gen^ll town meeting the 4th of February 1695/6 legally warned, wherein wee the ſubſcribers wer deſired to provide a miniſter to Preah the word of God in the new-meeting-houſe, and treat Mr Henry Gibbs in the first place for his acceptance, wee have accordingly treated the Rev^nd Mr Henry Gibbs once and againe, and he hath Refuſed to preach with us as o^r miniſter, or ſo much as one day as other miniſters did afterwards. Dan^ll Warren, ſen^r Caleb, Church, and Phillip Shattucke.

A true Copie taken of Watertown third book of Records for Watertown [p. 111.]
p^r Munings Sawin town Clerk for Watertown.

Voted at a Gen^ll town meeting the 20th ot Decemb^r, 1695, legally warned, it was voted by the town that wee doe Renew our Call to the Revd Mr Henry Gibbs. In order to his being fixed amongſt us, in the worke and office of the miniſtrey for the town, to officiate in the new-meeting-house, according to the advice and determination of the hon^d Committee, bareing date May 18th 1693.

A true Copie taken of Watertown third Book of Records. [p. 107.]
p^r Munings Sawin town Clerk for Watertown.

[5]

In anſwer to the Propoſals made in thoſe votes Preſented to me by Capt Warren, Isaac Mixer j^r and Benjamin Gearfield one the 23^d December 1695.

Being ſensible that there is great diſsatisfaction in the town with Refferrence to the meeting wherein thoſe votes wer paſsed, I feare it might prove uncomfortable should I accept my Compliance therewith and accordingly I am adviſed to decline the matter, till ſuch time as caer be taken to remove the ſd diſsattisfaction, not doubting, but that this being effected which I earnestly pray that god would in his own time grant it would much conduce to the mutuall comforte and advantage. Watertown february the 4th 1695/6. By Henry Gibbs.

A true Copie taken of Watertown third booke of Record. [p. 108.]
p^r Munings Sawin town Clerk for Watertown.

[6, 7 & 8] Blank.

[9]

Jan^r 8th: 1696/7 The Brethren and Inhabitants of the east end of Watertown, being aſsembled did by Vote make Choice of Simon Stone to keep a Record of all votes that paſsed that Day, and ſo from time to time of what might be voted in after meetings by the above s^d Company.

Item. Voted at the fame meeting that thay would ftill continue to maintaine the Revd Mr Henry Gibbs, as thay did for the last year, Provided he will continue with them in the worke of the Miniftrey in order unto a fettlement with them in the office of a Paftor (as foon as God in his Providence Shall make way for the fame) in the old Meeting-houfe.

Item: It was Voted in order to the promoteing of a fettlement, that fome Perfons be Chosen & Impowred to act for the s^d^ Society in moveing to the Neighbour Churches for advice & affiftance, and any fower of thofe Prfons to call a meeting when they shall fe occation, the Prfons fo chofen were, Capt Nathaniel Barsham, Lieu^t^ John Hammonde, Mr Richd Norcrofs, Dr Palsgr. Wellington, Jofeph Sherman, Nat^ll^ Bright, and Simon Stone.

Octob^r^ 1697 At a meeting of the fubfcribers to the maintenance of Mr Henry Gibbs, Jofeph Sherman, Nat^ll^ Bright, and Serg^t^ Thatcher wer Chosen to be affefsors for Mr Gibb's salary, and alfo Robert Goddard was Chofen Commifion^r^ to take their Invoice.

Item. It was voted at the fd Meeting that every Poll should be Rated at 12^lb^. Cattle according to the Countrey Invoice, Plowing land and Mowing land at ten shillings p^r^ acre, Houfing ye highest not exceeding fower pounds, the lowest not lefs than ten shillings.

Item. It was voted that 12^lb^ be allowed for wood for Mr Gibbs, and that fuch as brought in wood fhould be allowed for walnut eight shillings, and for oak feven shillings p^r^ Cord.

Item. It was voted at s^d^ Meeting that every one bring in his money by Contribution Paper^d^, and that all lofe money should be Reconed for the ufe of the fociety when thay shall call for it.

Octo^r^ ye 5th 1698. At a meeting of the Inhabitants of the Easterly part of Watertown vizt Thofe who fubfcribed to the maintenance of the Miniftrey there.

Simon Stone was Chofen moderato^r^ for fd Meeting.

Item. A fallary of fixty five pounds besides houfeing & fireing was Granted to Mr Gibbs according to agreem^t^ for the Enfuing year.

Item. Mr Nathaniel Bright. Serg^t^ Thatcher, and Corp^ll^ Sherman wer Chofen afsefsors, alfo Robert Goddard was Chofen to take their Invoice.

Item. It was voted that the 65^lb^ aboves^d^ fhould be paid by Contribution and that every on should put in their money paper^d^, and that what money came in Loofe or unpaper^d^ Should be to the ufe of the Society.

Item. Capt Barsham & Serg^t^ Bond wer Chofen Collecto^rs^.

Item. It was voted at s^d^ Meeting that 12^lb^ Should be added to the 65^lb^ aboves^d^ to Provide Mr Gibb's with wood and to be put in the rate therewithall.

Item. That the aboves^d^ fumms should be proportioned according to the Rules obferved the last year.

Item. It was voted at the aboves^d^ meeting that one fixt part of s^d^ fums be p^d^ by ye middle of next November.

Feb: 4. 1700/1 Item: Then paid in to Mr Henry Gibbs in full of what was granted to him for the carriing on the work of the ministrey for the year begining October the fift 1698, being sixty five pound with housing & firewood according as is above granted.

Novembr the 7th 1698. At a meeting of the Subscribers abovesd, Voted that Joseph Grant should mend the glass, and Joseph Child the Casements of the meeting house, and bring in their accounts at the next meeting and that the Society would se them paid for the same.

Item: At the sd meeting there was granted to Sergt Chadwick for looking after the Meeting-house for the year past and ensuing three pounds.

Novembr ye 16th 1698 At a Meeting of the Inhabitants of the east end of Watertown.

Voted, First that we will elect appoint and authorize, some Prsons from among orselves to transact such matters as relate to our further settlemt wth respect to maintaining of the publick worship at the old meetinghouse which Persons shall have power either to Petition on our behalfe, when & to whome they shall se needfull, or to answer in or name to any such Petitions, or complaints which may be offered & exhibited to our disadvantage.

Item: We Elect, appoint & authorize for ye ends abovesd Capt Barsham, Corpll Sherman, Wm Shattuck, Dr Wellington, Lieut Bond and Nathanll Bright.

[10]

Octobr ye 4th 1699 At a meeting of the Inhabitants of the east end of Watertown to agree upon the way of gathering Mr Gibb's maintenance there being granted to him as his sallary & for wood 77lb There was then Chosen Simon Stone Moderator. Chosen to take an Invoice Nathan Fiske, Chosen assessors. Nathan Fiske, Sergt Beeres and Sargt Thatcher, chosen Collectors Deacon Barsham and Deacon Bond.

Item. Voted that the meeting be adjourned untill monday the 23d Instant that care may be taken for the Pastors wood, and to agree how to raise the sd Rate, and take account of the Collectors of the money pd into the Pastor the year Past.

Novembr ye 27th 99 At a meeting of the Inhabitants of the east Congregation in Watertown for the raising of the ministers Sallary It was voted that every head should pay six shillings.

Item: That the rate should be raised as to Chattles & lands as it was the two former years.

April 19th 1700 Then pd to the Revd. Mr Henry Gibbs: for his carriing on of the work of ye ministrey as it was granted October the 4th 1699 the sum̄ of sixty five pounds, with sufficient fire wood which was in full according as it was granted.

Octob^r^ 2^d^ 1700 At a meeting of the Inhabitants of the east-end of Watertown to agree upon the way of gathering Mr Gibb's maintenance, Chosen moderato^r^ Simon Stone.

It^m^: Voted that we do grant to the ministers maintenance this year ensueing the sum of 77^lb^ a sixt part being for wood at the same price as formerly.

It^m^: That each head shall pay six shillings and all other rateabl estate according to the contrey Invoice.

Chosen to take the Invoice Serg^t^ Coolidg.

Chosen asessors, Serg^t^ Beeres, Ens^n^ Thatcher & Corp^ll^ Fiske.

Chosen Collecto^rs^ Deacon Barsham & Deacon Bond.

Novemb^r^ ye 27th 1700 At a meeting of the Inhabitants of the east-end Precinct by adjournment.

Voted that we will meet at the house of Serg^t^ Ric: Collidg on the 18th day of Decemb^r^ next ensuing for to have an account of the arrears of the ministers rate of the two last years, and to se what the Company will doe concerning the despoling of the lose money, and also to Chose a Clerke.

Decemb^r^ 18th 1700 At a meeting by adjournment Ens^n^ Sam^ll^ Thatcher was Chosen clerke, and the meeting adjourn^d^ untill Jan: 14th 1700/1.

Jan: 14th 1700/1 By adjorn^t^ At a meeting of the Inhabitants at the east end of Watertown, It was voted by s^d^ Society at the aboves^d^ meeting that the loose money according to ou^r^ former votes to be disposed of by the Cociety and now in the hands of the Collecto^rs^ be given to Mr Gibbs — except so much of it as to Clear the Rates of those removed, which cannot be obtained, but are certainly lost and the rates of those who appear to be certainly unable to pay the same.

Also Doct^r^ Palsgrave Wellington, Lt Jonas Bond and Corp^ll^ Nathan Fiske were Chosen & appointed to Joyn wth the Collectors to effect the disposial of s^d^ moneys according to the above written vote, and for further bisiness which may accur it was voted that the meeting be adjorn^d^ to be heild at at the house of Mr Nathaniel Bright on the second Monday in Feb^r^ 1700/1 at five of the Clock afternoon, and Capt Nathan^ll^ Barsham was Moderat^or^ of the aboves^d^ meeting.

Feb^r^ 10th 1700/1 Nathan^ll^ Bright was Chosen Moder^rr^ and the meeting adjorned untill Feb^r^ the 17th next at six of the Clock afternoon at the house of Capt Barsham, to finish the aboves^d^ worke.

Persuant to the aboves^d^ vote Jan^r^ 14th 1700/1 Doct^r^ Palsgrave Wellington Lt Jonas Bond and Corp^ll^ Nathan Fiske wer Chosen & appointed to Joyne wth the Collecto^rs^ to examin and effect the desposall of the loose money — there returne is as follows.

An account of the desposall of the money gathered for the maintenance of the ministre of the east end of s^d^ town, both that which was loose, and that which was papered, and that which was given in by rate, and that which was given in otherwise.

[11]

Febr ye 10th 1698/9 Then paid by the abovesd Collectors, and comitte by order of sd company out of the loose money to Mr Henry Gibbs for the making up his sallary for the year past, two pounds thirteen shillings and six pence, and of the rate money sixty two pounds six shillings and six pence, which maketh sixty five pounds, which is in full sattisfaction and wood to content for said year, and there yet remaines ungathered for the use of sd companey, in arreres of sd year six pounds, ten shillings and three pence.

For the rate made in the year 1698–9 for the maintenance of the ministry in the east end of Watertown, was made 77lb 14s–08d and ought of the same rate was paid 60lb 5s 2d and ought of the loose money 04lb–14s–10d which maketh sixty five pounds in money and wood to full content, and there yet remaines in arrears ungathered for the use of said Companey, nine pounds thireteen shillings & fower pence.

Itm voted In exsplaination of the vote made Octobr the 2d 1700 that the rate to be made shall be raised as followeth, that Poles shall be rated at six shillings Pr head, horses at three pounds Pr head, oxen at three pounds Pr head, cowes at two pounds Pr head, swine and sheep at fower pounds Pr score. Improved land at ten shillings Pr acre and west land at five shillings Pr acre, and housing at fower pounds the highest, and the lowest not under ten shillings, and the rate to be made for mending the meeting-house glass, and the paying the sexton's sallary to be made by the assessors Chosen for the Present year.

Itm Voted, that when and so often as there shall be occation for the Inhabitants of the east end Precinct of Watertown to be called together, it shall be in the power of Mr Simon Stone, and Capt Natll Barsham to call them together.

Feb. 17th 1706–7 Paid to the Reverend Mr: Henry Gibbs in part of what was granted to him for carrying on the work of the ministrey as it was granted Octobr the 2d 1700. the sum of sixty pounds, sixteen shillings and eight pence.

Octobr ye 1st 1701 At a meeting of the Inhabitants of the easterly Precinct of Watertown, being orderly to grant a sallary for the upholding of the ministre in sd Precinct, and for the Chosiing of assessors, Collectors and other officers. Mr Simon Stone was Chosen Moderatr to cary on the worke of sd meeting.

Itm Voted that each head shall pay six shillings.

Itm: Voted, that we do grant for the ministers maintenance for the year ensuing the sum of 77lb a sixt part being for wood.

Itm. Voted, that the remainder that the heads do not amount to shall be raised by the same rules the province tax is.

Itm: Chosen for assessors Nathan Fiske, Lt Jonas Bond, and Samll Livermore.

Voted. That Capt Natll Barsham & Deacon Wm Bond be colectors for the ministers rate.

It^m: Munings Sawin Chofen Clerk for s^d fociety, John Chadwick fn^r Chofen to looke after the meeting-houfe, and to be allowed for it one pound and ten fhillings.

Voted that all thofe that will cary in wood to Mr. Gibb's doe it by the first wednesday in Novemb^r and if that do not fufficiently bring in a fupply, then the Deacons to take money out of the Salary granted and buy wood for his fefonable fupply, unless Mr Gibbs will fupply himselfe, and take the money as it comes in.

Octob^r ye 20th 1701 Voted, that Capt Barsham carry the affefsors before lawfull authority, to be fworn to the faithfull difcharge of their offices.

It^m: Voted, that the s^d Rate be p^d in as formerly, by a Conftant Contribution on every Sabbath day (only all p^rfons to come down to the table, to the box) and all money to be paper'd.

It^m: Voted, that Munings Sawin lay ought three shillings of the s^d focietie's money to purchafe a booke to keep the s^d Societies Records, and to tranfcrib there former Records into s^d Booke.

It^m: Voted, that the s^d fociety take caer and order all there youth, that at the publique worship of God on the Sabbath Days, thay fit in the feats appointed for that end, so that they may be under the infpection of the tything-men.

It^m. Voted, that this meeting be adjorned to the first monday of Decemb^r next at fower of the clock in the afternoon, to be at the houfe of Mr Nath^ll Bright, In order to heer the accompt of the Minifters Rate.

Decemb^r ye 1st 1701. At a meeting at the houfe of Mr Nathl Bright, the account of what was unpaid in the ministers rate in s^d Precinct and there remained unpd. 13^lb.

Alfo the rate made for the year enfuing was then brought and Read to the cociety, which amounted to the fum̄ of feventy five pounds, and five shillings, and it was com̄itted into the hands of the Collecto^rs to gather, vizt Deacon Nat^ll Barshan & Deacon Wm Bond, according to the vote at the meeting octob^r the 1st 1701.

Feb. 17th 1706/7 Then Paid to the Revd Mr Henry Gibbs for his carying on of the worke of the minifrey amongst us in the year. octob^r the first 1701, as it was granted, paid in part of the fume of fifty nine pounds two shillings and three pence, and in fier wood according as it was granted.

[12]

Octob^r ye 7th 1702 At a meeting of ye east-end society for the granting of the ministers sallery. Voted that we will give to the ministers maintenance 77^lb a fixt part for to provide wood.

It^m Voted, that the Rate to be raifed for s^d money shall be according to the rules the P^rvince tax was ordered to be made by (excepting heads;) which are to be fet at fix fhillings P^r head.

Lieu^t Jonas Bond, Sam^ll Livermore, and Mr Nat^ll Bright wer Chofen afsefsors to make s^d rate.

Deacon Nat^ll Barsham & Deacon Wm Bond wer Chofen afsefsors to gather s^d Rate, and pay it in to the minister of s^d Society.

Munings Sawin Chofen Cler.

Sergt Jno Chadwick Choſen to locke after the meeting-houſe, and the sd ſociety to allow him for his ſervice one pound and ten shillings.

Itm: Voted, that the youth which attend ye Publick worship of God on the Sabbath days ſtill continue to ſitt in the places appointed for that end.

Itm: Voted that there shall be a rate forthwith made of fower pounds, three pound whereof to pay ſergt Chadwick for locking after the meeting-houſe for the year past, and the year enſuing, and twenty ſhillings for the mending the meetinghouſe glaſs this Prſant year.

Itm. Voted, that the sd aſseſsors make sd rate, and comitt it to Danll Benjamen, who is choſen to gather it and pay it in for ye uſes aforesd.

Itm. Voted, that Sergt Jno Chadwick and Danll Benjamen take caer and get the meeting houſe glaſs mended and to be pd ought of the rate made for mending the glaſs, voted, that ye sd rate be pd according to the way stated the last year.

Itm Voted, that one ſixt part of the rate granted for the miniſtrey be pd in at or before the first monday of Decembr next for to provide wood.

Alſo at sd meeting Joſiah Goddard gave an account of A rate comitted to him to collect in the year 1700 as follows

Paid to Joſeph grant 01lb-07s-09d }
Paid to John Chadwick 02 -16 -11 }

Jan: ye 5th 1702/3. At a meeting of the east end ſociety, at the houſe of Mr Natll Bright.

Voted, that the Collectors should ſpake with Tho: Rider, and ſe whether he will pay the whole part of the rate due to Mr Gibbs from Watertown old Grist miln for the year begun the 6th of octobr 1701. that then the sd ſociety will baer him hearmleſs for paying to any others for sd milnse for ye abovesd.

Itm: Voted, that the rate to be made for Mr Gibbs for this prsant year, be made according to the act for makeing the Province tax this Preſant year.

Itm. Voted at sd meeting that Mr Simon Stone & Capt Natll Barsham, do on the next lectur day Post up on the old meeting-houſe door, that the Inhabitants of the easterly society of Watertown do give a meeting at said meeting houſe on the 15th day of this Instant January, at one of the Clocke in the afternoon, to take caer to repaire sd meeting houſe, and to Choſe a comitte to ſe the worke done.

Jan: ye 15th 1702/3 At a meeting of ye east end cociety at the old meeting-houſe in Watertown. Voted that Mr Simon Stone should be moderatr for sd Meeting.

Itm. Voted, that we will grant a rate, a quarter part of the ſum of ſeventy ſeven pounds, towards the repairing the old meeting-houſe in sd town, and that there be forthwith a rate made, at or before the 25th of march next enſuing by the Prſant aſseſsors.

Itm: Voted, at sd Meeting that Capt Natll Barsham Doct:

Paslgrave Wellington. Sergt Ric: Coollidge are chosen a comitte to se that the sd worke be sesonably and well don.

Itm; Sergt Jabez Beeres was chosen Collector to demand and gather in the sd rate and pay it in to the abovesd comitte by the 25th of march aforesd for the end abovesd and no other.

Itm: Voted, at sd meeting that all the loose money that is given in on the sabbath days Contrebutions for the maintenance of the ministrey shall be given to Mr Gibbs over and above his sallary.

Febr 17th 1706/7 Paid to the Reverend Mr Henry Gibbs by the Collectors, in part of what was granted to him on october the seventh 1702. for the Carying on of ye worke of the ministrey amongst us, the sum of fifty pounds fourteen shillings and six pence, and in wood according as it was granted.

[13]

October 6th 1703. At a Genll meeting of the Inhabitants of the east end of Watertown, Mr Simon Stone was Chosen Moderator.

Item. Voted that we will give to the Ministers maintenance 77lb in money, a sixt part whereof to be to provide wood, at seven shillings Pr Cord.

Item. Voted, that the rate to be raised for sd money shall be made according to the rules this Prsant province is made by.

Item. Voted, and Choosen for assessors to make sd Rate Samll Livermore, Obadiah Coollidg and Nathan Fiske.

Item. Chosen for Collectors to gather & pay in sd Rate to the ministrey of sd end Capt Natll Barshan & Deacon William Bond.

Item. Munings Sawin Choosen Clerke, and Thomas Coollidg Choosen to looke after the meeting-house, and sweep it for the year ensuing, and to be allowed one pound & ten shillings for his service.

Item. Voted, that the contribution be still continued on the Sabbath days, and all the money to be papered, or written upon.

Item. Voted, that this meeting be adjorned to the first Wednesday in November next, to one of the clocke in the afternoon of sd day at the old meeting-house, to consider of sum way to get in the arrers that are yet unpaid to the ministrey belonging to ye east end of sd town.

Novembr ye 3d 1703. At the abovesd meeting by adjornment, In order to take caer about geting ye abovesd arreres for sd ministrey maintenance, it was adjorned to the second wednesday of sd Novembr to one aclocke of the sd day at the old meeting-house, Capt Barsham to give notice of it the next Sabbath Day after exercize.

Novembr 10th 1703. At the sd Meeting by adjournment, Capt Netll Barsham was Choosen moderator for said meeting.

Iteim. Munings Sawin was Choosen to take caer that the assessors Choosen to make the ministers rate for this present year, be sworn as the law directs.

Item Voted, that the collectors draw ought a list of ye names of all such persons as have not pd and made up their accts for there proportion of ye ministers Rate made for the year 1702. in order to comit it to the Conſtable to gather.

Item. The aboveſ^{d} meeting is adjorned to the houſe of Corp^{ll} Nat^{ll} Brights to be on the first monday of Decemb^{r} next, to five aclocke in the afternoon, to conſider further about ye arrears of the ministers rate.

Decemb^{r} the 6th 1703. At a meeting at the houſe of Corp^{ll} Nat^{ll} Brights by adjornment Corp^{ll} Bright was Chooſen Moderato^{r}.

Feb: 17th 1706/7. Paid to the Rever^{d} Mr Henry Gibbs by the Collectors, and Conſtable Samuell Jeniſon, In part of what was granted for the carying on of the worke of the miniſtrey amongst us, in october the ſixt, one thouſand ſeven hundred and three, the ſum of fifty ſeven pounds twelve ſhillings and nine pence, and in firewood in full as it was granted.

[**14**]

Augt 30th 1704. At a meeting of the Inhabitants of the easterly part of Watertown In order to take caer that the miniſters ſallary be p^{d} in according to the grant.

Item. Voted, at ſ^{d} meeting, that the rate granted for the ministers maintenance for this preſant year 1704, in the east end, have forwith a warrant affixed to it, by the preſant aſseſsors that made ſ^{d} Rate, and that the ſ^{d} rate with the warrant to it, be forthwith commited to the conſtable in ſ^{d} east end, to gather in what of ſ^{d} Rate is unpaid, to the Rever^{d} Mr Henry Gibbs, by the first wednesday of octob^{r} next hence enſuing the date hereof.

October ye 4th 1704. At a meeting of the east end Inhabitants of Watertown In order to rais a maintenance for ye miniſtry in s^{d} east end. Mr Simon Stone was Chooſen moderato^{r} for ſ^{d} meeting.

Item. Voted at s^{d} meeting, that we will give to the maintenance of the ministrey in ſ^{d} end for the year enſuing 77^{lb} in money, a ſixt part whereof to be for to provide wood, at 7^{s} P^{r} cord.

Item. Voted that the rate to be raiſed for ſ^{d} money shall be made according to the rules that this p^{r}sant Province tax is made by.

Item: Voted, and Choſen for aſseſsors to make ſ^{d} Rate Sam^{ll} Livermore, Nathan Fiske and Munings Sawin.

Item. Voted, and Chooſen for Collectors to gather in ſ^{d} Rate, and pay in the ſame to the miniſter of s^{d} east end Capt Nat^{ll} Barsham and Deacon William Bond.

Item Voted, that the aſseſsors shall affix a warrant to ſ^{d} Rates and comit it to the Conſtable to gather and pay to the minister of s^{d} end, that is to ſaie what is unpaid by the first wednesday, of october next enſuing the date hereof, the collectors to give the account of what is unp^{d} to the Conſtable.

Item: Voted and Chooſen for clerke Munings Sawin, Thomas Coollidg Chooſen to to locke after the meeting houſe and ſweep it, and to be allowed for his ſervice one pound ten Shillings.

Item: Voted, that the Contributions be continued upon the Sabbath days and all money contributed to be papered, or written upon.

Item: Voted, at s^{d} meeting that the Clerke doe enter into the booke purchaſed by ſd east end of Watertown, all ſuch votes & agreements as have paſsed in ſ^{d} cociety Refering to the ſupport of the miniſtre in ſ^{d} east end of Watertown.

Feb^{r} 17th 1706/7 Paid to the Rever^{d} Mr Henry Gibbs by the Collectors, and Conſtable John Chadwick, in pat of what was granted for the ſupport of the miniſtrey amongst us: Octob^{r} the fourth one thouſand ſeven hundred and fower, the full & Just ſum̄ of fifty ſeven pounds three shillings and two pence, and firewood in full according as it was granted.

[15]

March 26th 1705. At a meeting of the east end ſociety in Watertown. Voted that for the further promoteing & carying on the worke of Repaireing the old-meeting-houſe, in ſ^{d} cocietie, we do deſire the Collector forthwith to goe to thoſe perſons that have not p^{d} equall proportion with their Neighbours, and alſo carry with him a ſubſcription that ſo all may pay there equall proportion, or otherwiſe ſubſcribe and pay as thay thinke meet.

July 23^{d} 1705. At a meeting of the east end Inhabitants of Watertown, and s^{d} meeting was adjorn^{d} to the first wednesday of october next

October ye 3^{d} 1705. At a meeting of the Inhabitants of the easterly end Inhabitants of Watertown orderly warned & met.

Mr Simon Stone was choſen Moderato^{r} for s^{d} Meeting.

Voted, at said meeting, that we will give to the maintenance of the miniſtrey in s^{d} east end societie for the year enſuing 77^{lb} in money, one ſixt part whereof to provide wood at ſeven shillings P^{r} cord.

Voted, that the aboves^{d} rate shall be made according to the rules Prescribed in the law for the making the last Province tax. Chooſen for aſseſsors at s^{d} meeting Samuell Livermore, Nathan Fiske and Munings Sawin.

Voted, that s^{d} aſseſsors shall perfix a warrant to s^{d} Rate and com̄it it to the constable to gather and pay the aboves^{d} ſum̄ to the ministrey of s^{d} east end cociety by the first wedneſday of September next.

Voted, that the Contrebution be ſtill continued on the Sabbath day and Deacon Net^{ll} Barshan and Deacon William Bond to receive s^{d} contrebution: and pay it in to the Minister of s^{d} cociety, and all s^{d} money to be Papered or written upon.

It^{m} Munings Sawin was choſen clerk at s^{d} meeting.

Thomas Coolidg chooſen ſexton to locke after the meeting houſe & to Ring the bell for the year enſuing, and s^{d} cocietie doe allow him for his s^{d} ſervice two pounds.

Voted at s^{d} meeting, that the Gen^{ll} meeting for the granting the miniſters sallery shall be as formerly on the first wednesday of october annually for s^{d} cociety, and that the clerke of s^{d} cociety post up the warning on the meeting houſe Door on the sabbath day before s^{d} meeting, and all ſuch officers as may be thought necefsary for the ends afores^d of makeing gathering & Recieving s^d Rates according to our ufuall custom.

Voted, at s^d meeting that the aboves^d afsefsors shall make the rate for the sextons sallery this year, and alfo we do defire the abovs^d Deacons to gather s^d rate, and allfo the remainder of what is due of the last years rate to the sexston, and pay it in to him.

Jun: 17th 1706 At a meeting of the Inhabitants of the easterly cociety in Watertown orderly warned and meet in order to take caer to gather in the arrears of the ministers rates and fuch other concerns as may be thought needfull.

It was voted at s^d meeting, that the constables vizt Samuell Jenifon and John Chadwick Senr forthwith gather in the arrears of the ministers rates comited to them to gather, and pay in the fame forthwith according to the warrants.

Voted at s^d Meeting, that we doe defire appoint and Impower Deacon Nathaniell Barsham and Deacon William Bond & Enfign Samuell Thatcher to gather in what of the arrears of the ministers rates, which are ungathered, before the rates wer comitted to the constables to gather.

Voted, at s^d meeting that Deacon Net^ll Barsham Deacon Wm: Bond and Mr Nat^ll Bright be a comitte to enter into said cocieties booke of Records what thay may think nedfull, by the clerk of s^d cociety.

[16]

Octob^r 2^d 1706 At a meeting of the east end Cocietie or Congregation in Watertown Orderly warned and mete.

Jonas Bond Esqr was Chofen Moderato^r.

Voted at faid meeting that we doe grant a rate of ninety Seven pounds in money for the minifters maintenance, in f^d focietie, for the year enfuing, twelve pounds of f^d fum̄: to provide wood for f^d Ministrey, at feven shillings Pr Corde, twenty pounds of s^d fum̄ which is more that our ufuall rate is in Confideration of o^r Pastures prefent Circumftances by sicknes & weeknes.

Voted at s^d meeting that ye f^d Rate be made according to the Rules in ye law for the makeing the last Province tax, with a warrant affixed to it to be comitted to the Conftable in ye east end.

Voted at s^d meeting and Chofen for afsefsors to make s^d Rate, Sam^ll Livermore, Nathan Fiske and Munings Sawin.

Voted at f^d meeting that the Contrebution be ftill Continued as ufually it hath been in f^d cociety on the Sabbath days.

Voted at f^d meeting & Chofen for Clerke for f^d society Munings Sawin. Chofen for sexton Tho: Coollidg, and to allow f^d sexton for his sallery for one yere next enfuing two pounds money, and f^d afsefsors to make a Rate and affix a warrant to it, to be gathered by the Conftable in f^d Cocietie.

Voted at f^d meeting That ther fhall be a Contrabution four times this year, that is to saie every qurter of a year on the Sabbath day, the Decons to give notice of it the Sabbath before.

Said meeting is adjorned unto the first monday in December next to one of the Clooke in the afternoon of s^d day.

At a meeting of the east end Cocietie or Congregation the 2^d day of December 1706

Capt Barsham was Chosen Moderato^r.

Voted At s^d meeting, That we doe nominate, appoint & impower Jonas Bond Esqr and Samuell Jenison to answer to what may be objected by any of said Societie neglecting to pay their ministers Rates in s^d cocietie.

Voted At s^d meeting and Chosen as an adition to the first three assessors to make s^d Rate, John Coollidg and Samuell Jenison.

Voted and Chosen at s^d meeting to treate wth the Reve^d o^r Pasto^r Mr Gibbs, In order to gaine help to Carry on the worke of the ministrey amongst us for the p^rsent, Mr Simon Stone, Deacon Barsham & Decon Bond.

December 16th 1706 the above granted rate of 97^lb was made & comited to Constable John Straton Ju^r to Collect & gather in, Pr Sam^ll Livermore, Nathan Fisk & Munings Sawin assessors.

Octo: 1: 1707 At a meeting of the east end Societie or Congregation in Watertowne, Orderly warned & met,

Capt Jonas Bond Esqr was Chosen Moderato^r for s^d meeting.

Voted at s^d meeting that we do grant a Rate of 77^lb in money for the maintenance of the ministrey in s^d Congregation for the year ensuing, twelve pounds of s^d Rate for to provide wood for the minister of s^d cocietie.

Voted That s^d Rate be made according to the rules in the law for the makeing the last Province tax, this Present year.

Voted And chosen assessors to make s^d Rate, Lieu^t Sam^ll Thatcher, Mr Palsgrave Wellington and Samuell Jenison.

Voted and Choosen Sexton for the year ensuing, Thomas Coollidg, and to be p^d by two Contrebutions on the Sabbath Days, The Deacons to give notice of it the Sabbath beforehand.

Voted And Choosen for clerke for s^d Societie for the year ensuing, Munings Sawin.

Voted That the Contribution be still Continued on the sabbath days as formerly.

Voted That the Deacons, or one of them give notice to s^d congregation the Sabbath before each quarter of s^d year is ought That so Persons may make up by Contrabution each quarter Part of s^d Rate, the next Sabbath following.

[17]

Novemb^r 12 1707. At a meeting of the Inhabitants of the easterly Congregation in Watertown, orderly warned and meet.

Voted That we do desire, nominate, appoint and Impower, these severall Gen^t to be a Comitte to Consider & advise what steps may be thought most Proper to be taken for our futer, honorable and Comfortable settlement in s^d Congregation, by Prefering a Petition to the hon^d Gen^ll Court now siting in Boston, vizt Capt Jonas Bond Esqr Leiu^t Jno Hammond, Mr Palsgrave Wellington, Mr Net^ll Bright and Capt Net^ll Barsham, are Chosen for the ends aboves^d.

Jan: 7th 1707/8 At a meeting of the Inhabitants belonging to the easterly Congregation in Watertowne orderly warned and meet together.

Capt Jonas Bond Esqr was Choosen Moderator

1 voted. By said Inhabitants that thay will Choose a Comitte to take an account of the Deacons of what is behind of the ministers rate in arrears, in those years before sd rates wer Commited into the hands of the Constables, and to make there Report of what thay find to sd Precinct at there next meeting.

2 voted. That Samuell Livermore, Richard Coollidg and Nathan Fiske be a comitte for the ends abovesd.

3 voted. That sd Meeting be adjourned unto wednesday the 14th of January Currant at one of the Clocke in the afternoon.

What is above written are the severall votes Passed at sd meeting. Attest Jonas Bond Moderator of sd meeting.

At a meeting of the east end Cocietie in Watertowne legally warned the 7th of January 1707/8

Voted. That Mr Bright be choosen Moderator.

Voted That thay would choose a committe to audate accounts between those that are charged to be behind in the ministers rates. And the Deacons from the year 1697 until 1702/3.

Voted. That Capt Jonas Bond, Samll Livermore, Richard Coollidg, Nathan Fiske, Doctr Wellington be Choosen for the ends aforesd and to take account of the Deacons of strangers money.

Voted That the meeting be adjorned untill the 11th of February 1707/8.

[18]

At a meeting of the easterly Cocietie or Congregation in Watertown Febr 11th 1707/8 Mr Netll Bright was Choosen Moderator.

The Comitte appointed to audate accounts with the Deacons Refering to the loose money, and we received an account of, 19lb–10s–10d. which money was delivered to our Reverend Pastur Mr Henry Gibbs.

Sd meeting is adjurned unto the 18th day of this Instant Febr at one of the Clocke in the afternoon.

At a meeting of the east end Cocietie or Congregation in Watertowne Febr 18: 1707/8.

Voted That the Committe Chosen Jan: 7th 1707/8 to take an account of the Deacons of what is behind of the ministers Rates in arrears, in the year beforesd Rats wer Comitted into the hands of the Constables. Doe forthwith Indeavoure to get in the remainder of the same, and also to Recon with any such as are behind in sd Rates, and also doe allow sd Comitte to abate such part of sd arrears as thay shall b sattiffyed ought to be abated, (That is to say if the same be don within three months next hence ensuing the date hereof), and if any of them that are said to be behindhand in sd Rates & arrears will give their oaths before a lawfull authority that thay have already pd a part of the whole, then the same shall be allowed pd.

At a meeting of the easterly Cocietie or Congregation in Watertown the 7th of June 1708

Capt Jonas Bond Esqr was Chosen Moderatr for sd: meeting.

1. Voted That the last Rate made for the Support of the ministrey in sd: Cocietie be forthwith Commited to Constable Nathan Fiske to gather, and he to Issue & make up his accounts of the whole of said Rate at or on the first wednesday of october next.

2. Voted and ordered that the sd: Constable give an account of what part of sd Rate is not exspended in Carrying on ye worke of the ministrey in sd cocietie to the Reverend Pastur Mr Henry Gibbs, by the abovesd first wednesday in octobr

3. Voted and Choosen to be added to the Comitte for warning of meetings in sd Cocietie Deacon William Bond and Samuel Eddy sr and what sd Comitte shall agree upon & send to the Clarke of said Cocietie in writing shall be accounted sufficient warrant for sd Clerk to post up in writing.

4. Voted That we do Desire Deacon Natll Barsham, Deacon Wm Bond, Mr Natll Bright & Samll Eddy sr to procure som Person or Persons for the carrying on of the worke of the ministrey in sd Cociety for ye next & last quarter of the present year, upon as resonable terms as may be.

[19]

5. Voted At the sd meeting, that som further steps may be taken for the more honorable & comfortable support of the Ministrey in sd Cocietie or Congregation.

6. Voted That for that end we do Desire the former Gentn Imployed as a committe for sd worke to take and use such methods for the ends abovesd as thay may thinke most proper. Vizt Capt Jonas Bond, Lieut Jno Hammond, Mr Palsgrave Wellington, Mr Netll Bright & Deacon Netll Barsham.

Octobr 6 1708 At a meeting of the easterly Cocietie, or Congregation in Watertown Orderly warned & meet.

Mr Netll Bright was Chosen Moderator for sd Meeting.

Voted 1 That we do grant a Rate of 77lb in money for the maintenance of the ministrey in sd Societie.

Voted 2 That sd Rate be made according to the ruls for making the Province tax this year.

Voted 3 And chosen for assessors to make sd Rate Lieut Samll Thatcher, Samll Jenison & Josiah Goddard.

Voted 4 And Chosen Clerk for sd Cocietie for the year ensuing Munings Sawin.

Voted 5 And Chosen for sexton to Ring the bell & sweep & locke after the meeting-house, Tho: Collidg, and to be pd by a Contribution at twice in the year.

Voted 6 That the Contrebution be still Continued on the Sabbath days.

Voted 7 That we do desire the Comitte Chosen Jan: 7th 1707/8 to take an account of what money is quite lost, with the names & sums of each Person, and bring in ye account to the next meeting.

Voted 8 That we do desire Serg^t Jno Chadwick & Dan^ll Benjamen to take caer that the glass in the meeting-house be mended, and bring in their account to the next meeting.

Voted 9 That the s^d meeting is adjorned to the first wednesday in Decemb^r next, at one of the Clock at this meeting-house.

[20]

Decemb^r 1st 1708 0 At a meeting of s^d Cocietie by Adjornment.

1 Voted at s^d meeting that we do add to ye rate granted October the sixt, 1708, eight pounds in licke money, being to make up what money is quiet lost, from the year, 1703, to the year 1708.

Voted 2 Voted that there be a contrebution to gather money on the Sabbath day for the payment of the mending of the meeting-house glass, (and if any over plus be) to be left in ye Deacons hands for the use of s^d Cocietie, the Committe to give notice for s^d Contrebution the Sabbath before.

Voted 3 That we do desire Capt Jonas Bond Esqr Deacon Net^ll Barsham, Deac: W^m: Bond, Mr Net^ll Bright, Munings Sawin, and Serg^t Jno Chadwick, To give o^r Reverend Pasto^r Mr Henry Gibbs thanks for his gift to s^d Cocietie.

Voted 4 That Mr Gibb's gift to ye s^d Cocietie be entered in ou^r Booke of Record for s^d P^rcinct.

To Jonas Bond esq^r Mr Palsgrave Wellington, Mr Sam^ll Livermore, Mr Richard Cooledg, Mr Nathan Fiske, The Comittee appointed by the Easterly Precinct of Watertown, to take acc^tt of the arrearages Due to the ministry of s^d P^rcinct.

Gentlemen, Please to inform the Inhabitants of your Precinct, That I freely Remit twenty Pounds of the Arearages due to me, for Preaching unto them: vizt eighteen pounds twelve shillings and five pence, of what was due before octob^r 8: 1703. and one pound seven shillings and seven pence, of the Rate Comitted to Constable Jno Straton, which offer of mine, if accepted by the P^rcinct let it be entered in the book of Records belonging to the same. yours to serve,

Watertown Nov: 30: 1708. HENRY GIBBS.

[21]

Octob^r 5: 1709 At a meeting of the Easterly cocietie or Congregation in Watertown Orderly warned & meet:

Voted 1 That we do grant a rate of 77^lb in money for the maintenance of the Ministrey in s^d congregation, twelve pounds of said sum to be for to provid wood for the ministrey, at seven shillings Pr Cord.

Voted 2 That s^d Rate is to be made according to the Rules for making the Province tax this Present year, and that the assessors affix a lawfull warrant to s^d rate and Deliver it to the Constable in s^d cocietie sesonably.

Voted 3 and Chosen for assessors to Make s^d rate, Corp^ll Sam^ll Jenison, Cler: Josiah Goddard & Henry Spring.

Voted 4 And Chofen for Clerk for fd cocietie or Congregation Munings Sawin.

Voted 5 And Chofen for fexton to Ring the bell and sweep and lock after the meeting-houfe Tho: Coolidg, and to be pd by two Contrebutions within the year.

Voted 7 That a contrebution be still continued on the Sabbath Days for the ministre of fd Congregation.

Voted 8 That we do appoint Deacon Nethaniel Barsham, Deacon Wm: Bond and Samll Eddy fr to be a Committe to warn meetings for fd cocietie or Congregation when & so often as there be occation.

9 Voted That we do adjorne the abovesd meeting to the first monday of Decembr next at ten of the Clock in the forenoon, To take caer for the paying for mending the old meeting-houfe glafs, and fuch other Concerns as fd meeting shall fy occation for.

At a meeting of the Easterly Precinct by adjornment the 5th of Decembr 1709.

Voted That we will have a Contribution upon the 3d Sabbath day of this Instant Decembe r in order to gather money to pay for the mending the meeting-houfe glafs, and for the mending the Bel wheel, and fom other arreers due to the fexton.

Voted That fd meeting be adjorned to the third monday of this Instant month, to take account of what money is gathered, and to pay it to the Creditors, And to se if the Cocietie will Confider of som method for placing of the meeting-houfe.

At a meeting of said societie by adjornment the 19th of Decembr 1709.

The Deacons gave account of the Contrebution	£	f	d
money	01	14	07
Pd To Ephraim Cutter Jur	00	08	00
to Joseph Coollidg	00	06	00
to Sertg Jno Chadwick:	00	01	00
to Daniel Benjamen	00	01	00
to Joseph Grant	00	18	07

Voted That we do defire the severall Gentn vizt Nethaniel Coollidg fr Samuel Eddy fenr Nethaniel Bright fr Samll Thatcher fr Joseph Sherman and William Chattuck fr to sit at the table.

Voted That we do defire Capt Bond and the Deacons to give the abovesd Gentn notice of the abovesd vote.

The abovesd meeting is Defolved by Capt Bond Moderatr.

Decemberr 20th 1709

Then Receivd of Munings Sawin in ye east-ends behalfe for the mending the meeting houfe glafs, the fum̄ of eighteen shillings and seven pence I said Received Pr me

his
JOSEPH X GRANT.
mark

[22]

Octobr 4th 1710. At a meeting of the Easterly Societie of Congregation in Watertown Orderly warned and met, Capt Jonas Bond esqr was Chofen Moderatr.

Voted 1 That we do grant a rate of seventy seven Pounds for the ſupport of the miniſtrey in ſaid Congregation for this Preſent year; Twelve pounds of sd ſeventy seven pounds to be for a ſupply for wood for the miniſtrey at ſeven shillings Pr cord, Provided it be brought in by the last day of March next, And ſuch as do not bring wood by the last day of March as aforesd that their part of ye rate shall be paid in money, or otherwiſe to the miniſters acceptance.

Voted 2 That the rate be made according to the Rules for making the Province tax for this Prsent year, And that they do affix a warrant to ſd rate according to law, And to deliver said rate to the Collector ſeſonably.

Voted 3 And Choſen for aſseſsors to make ſd Rate as abovesd Samll Jeniſon, Josiah Goddard and Henry Spring ſr.

Voted 4 And Choſen Clerk for said Cocietie, Munings Sawin.

Voted 5 And Choſen for ſexton Tho: Coolidg, to take caer of ye meeting-houſe, and to be pd for his service by two Contrebutions as formerly.

Voted 6 That the Contrebution be still Continued on the Sabbath days.

Voted 7 And Choſen for a Committe Deacon Netll Barsham, Deacon Wm Bond and Samuel Eddy ſr To warn ſd Cocietie together when & so often as their may be occation.

Voted 8 And Choſen for Collector for to gather in ſd rate Jonathan Stone.

Voted 9 And Choſen for receiver of the abovesd rate, Mr Netll Bright, to receive in and pay out said Rate for the ends and uſe for which it was granted, Rendering an account of the same to ſd Coſietie. And alſo ſaid Mr Bright is Choſen to call the late Conſtables to an account belonging to ſd Cocietie That have had the ministers Rates Comited to them to gather. That have not iſſued and made up their accounts according to their warrant And to pay in the ſame to the Reverend Mr Henry Gibbs.

Aprill 3d 1711. The abovesd Rate was made and Comitted to Mr Jonth Stone Collector to gather and pay in to Mr Nethll Bright Receiver amounting to the ſum of 77lb–12s–09d.

Pr Henry Spring
Josiah Goddard &
Samll Jeniſon aſſeſsors.

[23]

October 3d 1711. At a meeting of the easterly Cocietie or Congregation in Watertown orderly warned and meet.

Voted 1 That we do grant A rate of 80lb for the support of the ministrey in ſd Cocietie or Congregatn for the year enſuing, Twelve pounds whereof is to provide wood for the miniſtrey at eight shillings Pr cord.

Vot 2 That the sd rate be made according to the Rules Preſcribed for making the last Province tax, and that ther be a warrant affixed to ſd rate according to law, and to deliver said Rate to the Collector ſeſonably.

Vot. 3 And Chosen for assessors to make sd Rate, John Coollidg, Josiah Goddard and Nathan Fiske.

Vot: 4 That we Choose Deacon Netll Barsham, Deacon Willm Bond & Samll Eddy sr a Committe, for sd Cocietie for the year ensuing.

Vot: 5 That we do Choose Jonathon Stone Collector to gather & pay in sd Rate to the Treasurer or Receiver.

Vot: 6 for Treasurer or Receiver of sd Rate, Mr Nethll Bright, who is to receive in and pay out sd rate for the ends for which it was granted, and to render an account to the sd cocietie sesonably.

Vot: 7 That we do Choose Munings Sawin Clerk for sd cocietie for the year ensuing.

Vot: 8 That we do Choose Tho: Coollidg sexton, and to be pd by two free Contrebutions as formerly.

Vot: 9 Voted that the Collectors Shall annually make up their accounts with the Prsent Treasurer or Receiver, or his or their succesor in sd office of their severall rates.

Vot: 10 that the Contribution be still continued on the Sabbath day as formerly.

Votd 11 That we do desire Mr Netll Bright & Munings Sawin to take caer to find out how much the severall Rates did amount too that have been made of late years for the support of the ministrey in sd Cocietie or Congregation, and when sd rates wer made, and by whome, and when comited to the severall Constables, In order to the more effectuall & spedy gathering the arrears of said rates.

Voted 12 That the meeting be adjorned to the first monday of November next at on of ye Clock in ye afternoon. In order to Consider of som way to mend the Meeting-house glass, and to know the cocieties mind (whether they will add anything towards his late losses by fier) in the Prsent Rate, or whether they will give him a free contribution once or moer in ye year.

Novembr 5 1711. At a meeting by adjormt

Voted 1 That we will have a free Contrebution fower times in this Prsent year Insuing, for the Reverend Pastor Mr Henry Gibbs, for the repairing of his buildings, and such other uses as he shall se cause.

Vot: 2 that we will add twenty shillings to the abovesd rate last granted for the ministrey to mend the meeting-house glass.

Jun: 13th 1711/12 At a meeting of the easterly Cocietie or Congregation in Watertown Orderly warned and meet, for to despose of a certaine Contrebution in the hands of the Deacons.

Voted That we do freely give the sd Contrebution to our Reverend Pastor Mr Henry Gibbs.

[24]

Mar: 17 1711/12 At a meeting of the Inhabitants of the Easterly Congregation in Watertown orderly warnd and meet.

Voted 1 That the money that was over and above the Purchase of the Pastur land Purchased of Mrs. Judith Allen (being five pounds & five shillings) we desire Mr Nethaniel Bright one of the Committe, to keep it while ſuch time as the ſubſcribers ſe cauſe to call for it, if their should be a proſpect to purchaſe more land or lands.

Voted 2 That the Deed of the lands Purchaſed for the uſe of the miniſtrey in ſ[d] congregat[n] be lodged with their book of Records.

Voted. 3. In anſwer to the ſubſcription ſent from ſeverall of the Inhabitants of the middle Part of Watertown, and left with the Rever[d] M[r] Henry Gibbs, Bering date Feb[r] 1711/12 And ſome Propoſals made to them againe, which wer Read and voted at this said meeting.

Voted, 4 That we do deſire Maj[r] Jonas Bond to communicate the same.

Voted, 5 That all the Rates belonging to the estate of Benj[a] Wellington Dece[d], which wer due to the miniſtrey in y[e] aboves[d] Congregation (in the hands of any Constables untill this Preſent year be all Crost and diſcharged.

[25]

May, 26th 1712. At a meeting of the Inhabitants of the Congregation at the east-end of Watertown, orderly warned and meet together.

1. Voted. That we will Chooſe a Committe to Represent us at the Great & Gen[ll] Court, Upon the second Wednesday of their next ſeſſions, which will be y[e] 4th of June next, Being the day appointed for the hearing of the Petition of Sundrey of the Inhabitants belonging to the easterly Military & Companey of said town, Baring Date March, 17th 1711/12 And make ſuch defence against said Petition as they shall think most Proper. And alſo to Addreſs his Excellency and y[e] Great and Gen[ll] Court, for a Better & Lasting Settlement of the Congregation in the east end of s[d] Watertown.

2. Voted And Choſen for the ends afores[d] to Be a Commite to Repreſent o[r]ſelves in the ſ[d] Court, Maj[r] Jonas Bond esq[r] M[r] Joseph Sherman, M[r] William Shattuck ſ[r], M[r] Nethanial Bright, M[r] Palsgrave Wellington, M[r] Sam[ll] Livermore, M[r] Nathan Fiske, Cap[t] Nethaniel Barsham & M[r] Richard Coolidg.

[26] Blank.

[27]

Watertown, May: 29. 1711.

We the ſubſcribers, Inhabitants in s[d] town, being very ſenſible of the great want there is of better accommodations to the Miniſtrey in the East-End of s[d] town; as to Pasture land & meadow: And being alſo very free & willing to contribute for the Purchaſing of Lands; either Pasture, meadow, or both, for the accomodating of the Rev[d] M[r] Gibbs, who is our preſent Miniſter, & of ſuch as shall succead him, in the work of the Miniſtrey in s[d] Congregation: And there being now A Prospect off Purchaſing some Lands, for the ends afores[d] we do freely & voluntarily ſubſcribe, engage & promiſe to pay the ſeveral ſumms affixed to our names into the hands off Deacon William Bond, Mr William Shattock ſr and Mr Netll Bright A Comītte to be by them laid out for the ends aforesd of which ſumms we do engage to pay the one halfe within a week, and the other halfe within ſix months after the date hereof, giving to sd Persons full power as a committee to act & transact in that matter, and to Receive a Deed or Deeds, in our names, of Lands purchaſed with ye money, hereunto ſubſcribed, and said lands to be & remaine, for the uſe of the miniſtrey of said Congregation.

	£	s	d		£	s	d
Mr Henry Gibbs - - - -	02	00	00	Jonas Bond esqr - -	02	00	00
Richard Coollidg - -	01	00	00	Netll Barsham - -	02	00	00
John Biſco - - - - -	01	00	00	Samuel Thatcher -	01	10	00
John Chenery - - - -	00	12	00	Netll Bright - - -	02	00	00
Oliver Wellington - -	00	15	00	Samll Eddy ſr - - -	00	12	00
Samuel Holden - - -	00	10	00	William Shattuck -	01	00	00
Isaac Holden - - - -	00	10	00	William Bond - -	01	10	00
William Shattuck Jr -	00	10	00	Munings Sawin - -	00	15	00
Joseph Holden - - -	00	10		Nathan Fiske - - -	01	10	00
Joseph Coollidg - - -	00	10	00	Jonathan Stone - -	01	10	00
John Abbut - - - -	01	00	00	Josiah Goddard - -	00	15	00
David Stone - - - -	00	10	00	Daniel Benjamen -	01	00	00
Robert Goddard - - -	00	15	00	George Lawrance -	00	10	00
Thomas Bond - - - -	00	10	00	Josiah Perry - - -	00	10	00
Samuel Hastings - -	00	10	00	Ebenezer Stone - -	00	06	00
John Straton Jur - - -	01	00	00	Benjamin Eddy - -	00	12	00
Samuel Straton - - -	01	00	00	Joseph Sherman - -	00	05	00
Mrs Elizebeth Bond - -	00	05	00	Henry Mils - - -	00	15	00
Samuel Livermore - -	01	15	00	Palsgraue Wellington	02	00	00
Danll Smith - - - -	01	00	00	Henry Spring - -	01	00	00
Danll Livermore - - -	01	00	00	Samuel Jeniſon - -	01	10	00
Timothy Barron - - -	00	10	00				
Thomas Learnard - -	00	10	00				

[28] Blank.

[29]

October, 1. 1712. At a meeting of the Easterly Congregation or Precinct in Watertown Orderly warned and aſsembled, Mr Natll: Bright was Choſen Moderator.

Voted. 1 that we do grant a Rate for the ſupport of the Miniſtrey in ſd Congregation of 82lb. fourteen pounds of said rate to be for to provide wood for the miniſter at nine shillings Pr Cord. Provided the Genll Court do not other wiſe order the Raising of sd Rate.

Voted. 2 For aſſeſsors to make ſd Rate, Nathan Fiske, Jno: Coollidg, and Daniel Livermore.

Voted. 3 And Choſen for a Comītte for ſd Precinct Deacon Natll Barsham, Deacon William Bond and Mr Natll Bright.

Voted. 4 & Chosen for Receiver or Treasurer Mr Natll Bright.
5 Munings Sawin Chosen Clerk for sd Precinct.
6 Chosen for sexton Tho: Coollidge & to be pd for his worke by two Contrebutions as formerly.

The abovesd meeting is adjorned to the third Monday of November next, to Consider of what may then further to be acted. sd meeting to begine at two of the Clock of sd Day.

October 5. 1712. Recd of the Collectrs of the Rates for the Ministrey at the east end of Watertown and of other Persons, in full of all Dues to the Ministry from Oct, 6. 1711, to the sixt of Octr one thousand seven hundred & Twelve.

Recd ℘r me
HENRY GIBBS.

Novbr 17th 1712 At a meeting of the Easterly Congregation or Prcinct in Watertown by adjornmt: Voted at sd meeting that we do desire our former Comitte Chosen to Represent us in the affaire at the last Genll Court, to lay the Result of sd Court, before the Committe Chosen by the westerly or middle congregation in sd Watertown as soone as may be, and to desire sd committe to give us an answer of what they Intend to do in said affaire. The abovesd Genll Courts act was Read at the abovesd meeting, and was voted to know ye minds of sd easterly Congregation, who did Declare our willing submission to and compliance with sd courts sd order. Baring Date the 4th of Novembr 1712.

Febr 2d 1712/13 Watertown,

At a meeting of the Easterly Prcinct in Watertown orderly warned & meet.

Voted That we do Choose, appoint & Impower These severall Gentn following vizt Majr Jonas Bond, Capt Netll Barsham, Nethaniel Bright, William Shattuck sr Doctor Palsgraue Wellington, Richard Coolidge, Nathan Fiske and Samll Livermore To be a committe to Represent This Precinct at the meeting warned by order of the select men of this town on the fourth of this Instant: to hear the advice of the Genll Court relating to the support of the ministrey & to take effectuall care yt ye publick worship of God be honourably maintained amongst us. And at sd meeting to declare our willing submission to & compliance with the late order of the Genll Court bering date Novbr 4th 1712. Relating to the support of the ministrey in the two precincts of ye town according to what was formerly voted by us, and entered in our Booke of Records. And also at sd meeting to enter a Protest in our names (if need be) against any vote or Proposals that may ther be made, or offered to supersed, Infring, Invalidate or annull the sd order of the hond Court, or to Retard the effectuall execution of it. And further to declare in ye name of the Precinct that we Judge it an affront to the hond Court, and Injurious to the peace of the town to clogg ye execution of sd Order, or to pretend & endeavour by a Majr vote of the Enhabitants of the town to oblige or ensnare us, or any others of the town, who are desirus to submit to sd order, unto anything of a differrent Import. And furthermore we desire our Committe abovesd to Insist upon it that the assessors of the town be forthwith set on worke to assess the sum mentioned in sd order of Court for ye ends and in ye manner therein Specified. And to deliver a copie of this our vote to the moderator that may be assigned for said meeting.

[30]

Voted. That the Treasurer use the utmost of his endeavour to get in what of Arrears yet Remaine in the Constables hands by the 20th day of this Instant february, and to make report of his doings therein at our next meeting.

Voted. That we desire Majr Jonas Bond, And Mr Netll Bright, or any others that are willing to meet with Stephen Cook this day to agree wth said Cook, Reffering to sd Cooks Rates as they shall se meet.

[31]

March: 17th 1712/13 At a meeting of the Inhabitants of the Easterly Precinct or Congregation in Watertown Orderly warned & meet.

Voted 1 That we do choose Samuel Livermore to be an assessor in the stead of Daniel Livermore to make the Ministers Rate for the present year for sd Precinct, granted on the first of october, 1712.

Voted 2 That we will have a free contribution, on the first Sabbath day of may next ensuing, for to pay the arrears due to Mr Gibbs, which arrears are sumthing doubtfull to be gotten.

Voted 3 That we will Choose a comitte to Represent us at the next sitting of the Genll Court, in Order for any matters in Refferrence to the late order & advice of the Genll Court bearing Date Novembr 4th 1712.

Voted 4 That we do desire our former Comitte, Chosen the 26 of May, 1712, vizt Majr Jonas Bond, Mr. Joseph Sherman, Palsgraue Wellington, Netll Bright, Capt Barsham, Wm Shattuck, sr Samll Livermore, Nathan Fisk & Ric. Coollidg, they or the Major Part of them, to Represent us in what may be to be further acted in Refferrence to the aforesd order & advice.

Voted 5 That we are free and willing to pay our part of the Quarter of a year Sallorry. . . . . . Due to our Reverend Pastr Mr Henry Gibbs for preaching to ye whole town a quarter of a year, according to the towns votes, which Quarter began the 6th of November, 1695.

Octobr 7 1713. At a meeting of the Easterly Precinct or Congregation in Watertown Orderly warned & met the 7th of October, 1713. Majr Jonas Bond Chosen moderatr.

1 Voted that we will Choose A committe to Reprsent our selves, and to apply themselves to the select men of said Town, or else where as shall be thought needfull, To see that the Act of the honorable Genll Court, and the vote of the Town in June last past be put into effectuall execution for the Support of the Ministry in Watertown.

2 Voted that we desire the comitte Choosen the 26th of may, 1712 for the ends abovesd vizt Majr Jonas Bond, Mr Joseph Sherman. Mr Palsgraue Wellington, Mr Natll Bright, Capt Natll Barsham Mr Willm Shattuck, Mr Samll Livermore Nathan Fiske & Ric: Coollidg

3 Voted & chosen for a Comitte Capt Natll Barsham Deacon Wm Bond & Mr Natll Bright.

4 Mr Natll Bright Chosen Receiver for ye Ministers Rate.

5 Munings Sawin Chosen Clerk for said Precinct.

6 Tho: Coollidg Chosen sexton, and to be pd by two Contributions as formerly.

7 Voted that we will have a contrebution on the first Sabbath day of every month for the year ensuing, and what is gathered shall be set off in their Ministers Rate.

8 Voted that ye third Wednesday of this Instant october be appointed for such as are willing to cart wood for the ministrey of said Prcinct.

9 Voted that this meeting be adjornd to the second Wednesday of November next, and to begine at one oclock in the afternoon.

Watertown Octr 6, 1713. all Dues for the Ministrey at the East End of sd Town paid for the year Past. HENRY GIBBS.

Watertown Novembr 5th 1713 Recd of the severall collectors of the Rates for the Ministrey att the East-End of sd Town, and of Prticular Persons included in sd Rates, the full of all dues To the Ministrey of the East Congregation, From the time of their being seperated from the other part of sd Town, unto the sixt of Octr one thousand seven hundred & eleven.

Recd I say in full

Pr me

HENRY GIBBS

[32]

11: Novber 1713. At a meeting of the Inhabitants of Easterly Precinct or Congregation in Watertown the 11th of November, 1713. By adjornment.

1 Voted, that the Treasurer or Receiver for the Ministers Rate of sd Precinct do forthwith take effectual caer and Quicken up the Constables & Collectors forth with to finish & make up their accounts with the said Treasurer.

Decembr 14th 1713. At a meeting of the Easterly Precinct or Congregation in Watertown Orderly warned & meet the fourteenth Day of December, 1713.

1 Voted that we do grant a Rate of fourteen pounds for the Reverd Mr Henry Gibbs for his sallery for preaching to ye sd Congregation for two months: vizt from the 7th of October last past untill the fourth of December currant. And also we do grant fourteen shillings more to be added to the fourteen pounds for to make up sum lose in ye Rate last Committed to Jonth Stone, to gather for the said Congregation.

2 Voted, That we do Choose Nathan Fiske, John Coollidg

and Samuel Livermore affefsors o make the faid Rate and Deliver it with a warrant affixed to it, unto the Collector.

3 Voted and Choofen for Collector to gather f[d] Rate Robert Goddard.

At a meeting of the Inhabitants of the Easterly Congregation in Watertown Orderly warned & met the 6. of october 1714. Maj[r] Jonas Bond was Chofen Moderator for s[d] meeting. Chofen for the comitte for the year enfuing Cap[t] Nat[ll] Barsham, Deacon William Bond & M[r] Nat[ll] Bright. Chofen for Clerke for f[d] P[r]cinct Munings Sawin, Chofen for fexton Tho: Coollidge, and to be p[d] by two contributions as hath been formerly.

Voted that the monthly contrebution be continued for the Miniftrey of the f[d] Congregation as it was the last year.

Voted. That there be a Contrebution on the first Thanksgiving day for to Repaire the old meeting houfe in faid Town, And we do defire our Reverend Pasture M[r] Henry Gibbs to give sesonable notice of it to the s[d] Congregation.

[33]

Watertown May 24[th] 1715 Rec[d] of M[r] Robert Goddard Collecto[r] for the Easterly P[r]einct in Watertown & by his Order, in full for my Salery for the year beginning Octob[r] 6[th] 1713 to Octob[r] the, 6. 1714. Rec[d] P[r] me

HENRY GIBBS.

Rec[d] alfo on the day of the Date above written of the p[r]son aboves[d] in full for two months salery, beginning the fixt of Octob[r] 1714. Rec[d] P[r] me

HENRY GIBBS.

At a meeting of the Inhabitants of the Easterly Congregation in Watertown orderly warned and meet, the fift of October, 1715.

Voted and Chosen for a committe to warn meetings when their may be occation Deacon Barsham, Deacon Bond and M[r] Nathaniel Bright, Chofen for Clarke for fd congregation Munings Sawin, Chofen Sexton Tho: Coolidge.

Voted that the monthly contrebution be ftill continued on the Sabbath Day.

Voted that we will have a Contrebution the next Thanksgiving Day for the Repairing y[e] meeting houfe, and to be laid out by the former Committe.

[34]

At a meeting of the Easterly Congregation in Watertown Orderly warned & met together the 18th day of July 1715.

Voted & Chofen for Moderator Maj[r] Jonas Bond.

Voted that we will Chofe A comitte to Reprefent this Congregation, To wait on the Gen[ll] Court at their next fefsions, and to lay before sd. Court how thire Orders & acts wth respect to the fupport of the miniftrey in Watertown are Slighted & contemned by the other Congregation. And the greater part of thofe who are Chofen Town officers, whereby the Miniftrey do fail of their Just dues: And alfo to Addreff the faid Genll Court that in Cafe their cant be a dutifull complyance with the orders of Court and vote of the Town alredy made, That thire be a line of Divifion made & settled between us under fuch A Regulation as will tend most for peace and comfort for the futer.

Chofen for said Comitte for the ends afores[d] Maj[r] Jonas Bond, Richard Coollidg, Samuel Livermore, Samuel Thatcher, William Shattuck, Nat[ll] Bright, Nathan Fiske, Josiah Goddard John Coollidg, Robart Goddard, and Henry Spring.

[35]

At a meeting of the Inhabitants of the Easterly Congregation in Watertown Orderly warned and met together September the, 4,[th] 1716. Robert Goddard was Chofen Moderator.

1 Voted that we will Chofe A Committe to treat with fom man or men to be a conftant & certaine help for the upholding of Preaching among us while M[r] Gibbs's Bodily elness Remaines upon him, or for fuch time as they can agree for.

2 Voted, and Chofen for the comitte fore the ends afores[d] the Deacons of the Church.

3. Voted, That we will have a free Contrebution on the third Sabbath of this P[r]sent month for to help defray the charge of such as shall be procured to cary on Preaching among us

4 Voted that we do adjorn this meeting to the last monday of September Currant, at fower of the Clock in the after noone, at this Place, to met againe to hear the Report of the comitte and confider what is further to be don.

The above written votes wer past at faid meeting as attest

ROBERT GODDARD.

At a meeting of the Easterly Congregation in Watertown orderly warned & meet the 3[d] of October, 1716. Maj[r] Jonas Bond was Chofen moderator.

Voted, and Chofen for a comitte Maj[r] Jonas Bond, Deacon William Bond & M[r] Nat[ll] Bright, voted & chofen for Clerke Munnings Sawin, Chofen for Sexton Thomas Coollidg and to be pd. by two Contrebutions as hath been formerly.

Voted that the monthly Contrebution for the Miniftrey be still continued on y[e] Sabbath days.

Voted that fuch as will be pleafed to carry wood to M[r] Gibbs, do it on the first wednesday of November next enfuing.

Voted, That we do defire Ebenezer Stone to take caer & provide fastnings for the meeting-houfe windows, and to be paid his Reafonable cost out of the Contribution in Banke.

Voted, that we do defire y[e] aboves[d] Comitte to make inquiry into fom demand made by Joseph Grant, for mending fome glace for the meeting-houfe, and to make Report to the next meeting of what they find due.

[36]

At a meeting of the Easterly Congregation in Watertown Orderly warned and meet the 2ᵈ of Octobʳ 1717. Mʳ Natⁿ Bright was Chosen Moderator.

Voted. and Chosen for a Committe, Majʳ Jonas Bond, Deacon William Bond & Mʳ Natⁿ Bright.

Voted. And Chosen for Clerk Munnings Sawin, Chosen for sexton Thomas Coollidg, and to be paid by two Contrebutions, to be on the last Sabbath in Aprill next, and the last Sabbath in September next ensuing.

Voted That the monthly Contrebution be Continued for the Ministrey on the first Sabbath of every month during this year ensuing.

Voted. That we do desire Deacon William Bond & Mʳ Natⁿ Bright to Invite Deacon Nathan Fiske & Deacon John Coollidg to sitt in the Deacons Pue.

And this meeting was Disolved by the Moderatʳ, orderly.

At a meeting of the Easterly Societie or Congregation in Watertown Orderly warned & meet the second Day of June, 1718. Voted and Chosen for Moderatʳ Mʳ Nathanael Bright.

Voted And Chosen for A committe to take care to mend the Platform of the old meeting-house in sd. Town, Deacon Fiske and Deacon John Collidg, to procure & Provide materials and work men to do said worke sensonably as soone as may be, and to bring in a true account to the next meeting of sᵈ societie, and to be paid their Just Cost out of the money gathered for the end aforesᵈ

At a meeting of the East Congregation in Watertown Orderly warned and meet the 14ᵗʰ of Aprill, 1719. Mʳ Natⁿ Bright, was Chosen Moderator.

1 Voted, that we do lay down the monthly Contrebution for this presant year.

2 Voted, that we do desire the select-men would order the payment to the Rate for the Ministrey to be pᵈ Quarterly.

3 Voted, that we will have a free Contrebution Quarterly, or a subscription for to provide help to carry on the worke of the amongst us, which sd. Precinct shall Choose.

4. Voted, that we will have a free contrebution for the end aforesᵈ and to begine the first Sabbath day in may next ensuing, and to be the Contrebutions for this pʳesent year & to be quarterly.

5 Voted, that we will mend the fence of the Pasture Purchased for yᵉ Ministrey of the east Congregation,

6 Voted, That we desire Mʳ Joseph Coollidge to do the work about said Pasture and provide what fenceing stufe is wanting, and the Proprietors of sᵈ Pasture to se him paid for his cost & charges.

Said meeting is by a vote adjornᵈ to the 29ᵗʰ, of this Instant Aprill to five o'clock in the afternoon at the above sd house.

At a meeting of the easterly Congregation by adjornment in Watertown the Twenty ninth day of Aprill one thousand seven hundred and nineteen.

[37]

Watertown may 4th 1719 At a meeting of the east Congregation in ſaid Town, Orderly warned & meet.

Voted. That whereas one Article propoſed in the warning of the Town meeting, at the Newe meetinghouſe on this day att three of the Clock in the afternoone, is, to ſee what the Town will do in anſwer to an Addreſs made by ſundrey Inhabitants, as to the Towns coming together in one Congregation in ſome convenient time & place.

Wee choſe appoint & deſire Maj^r Jonas Bond, Nathanael Bright, William Shattuck, Deacon William Bond, Deacon Nathan Fiske, Lt Richard Coollidg, Josiah Goddard, Jonathan Stone & Joſeph Maſon, to be a Committee to repreſent us of the east end Congregation att said Town meeting & in our name to enter a deſent or Protest against the Towns Voting in ſd affaire as not being the proper buſineſs of our Town Meetings and to declare y^t we esteem it repugnant to the act of settlement made & established by the great & Generall Court of this Province in the year, 1712. Relating to the Maintenace of y^e Miniſtry in the two Congregations of this Town, By virtue of which act, no major Vote of the Inhabitants can determine any thing obligatory in this matter, and withall to, Declare in our name, that if the other Congregation will pleas to Chooſe & appoint a Committee to meet the $aboves^d$ P^rsons whome we have Choſen & appointed to Repreſent our ſelves at any Convenient time & place, freely & calmly to Conſult under o^r p^rsent Circumstances, about y^e things that may promote y^e Peace of the Town & the Interest of Religion Among us, which ſo much depends upon a well grounded peace, we Redely Conſent thereto. and heartily wish ſuch a conference may be under Divine direction and obtaine a good Iſſue. And that the Major part of the above named persons be rekoned a full committee for the East Congregation for ye ends above mentioned, and alſo upon any other occation of treating about ſd. affaire & what shall be Conſulted or proposed by sd. Committee to be laid before the easterly Congregation.

Jonas Bond
Nathaniel Bright
Willam Shattuck
William Bond
Nathan Fiske
Richard Coollidge
Josiah Goddard
Jonethan Stone
Joseph Maſon

At a meeting of the Inhabitants of the Easterly Congregation in Watertown Orderly warned and meet the, 7th of October, 1719. Maj^r Bond was Chooſen Moderator.

1 Voted, and Choſen for A comittee, Maj^r Jonas Bond, Deacon William Bond & Mr Nat^{ll} Bright.

2 Voted, and chofen Clark for sd. Congregation Munnings Sawin.

3 Voted, and Chofen for fexton Tho: Coollidg and to be p[d] by two Contrebutions as formerly.

4 Voted, that we will have a free Contrebution on the next Thankgiving day to be Improved for the Repairing the Personage.

5 Voted, that we will have a Contrebution Quarterly on the Sabbath days for M[r] Gibbs as was the last year.

6 Voted, that on the fecond Tuisday of November next we appoint to Cart wood to M[r] Gibbs and to be gratis.

[38]

At a meeting of the Easterly Congregation in Waterfown Orderly warned and meet the 5th of October, 1720. Maj[r] Jonas Bond was Chofen Modera[tr] for fd meeting.

1 Voted, and Chofen for a Committee Maj[r] Jonas Bond esq[r] M[r] Nat[ll] Bright and Deacon William Bond. 2 Chofen for Clerk Munnings Sawin. 3 Chofen fexton Tho: Coollidge and to be paid by two Contrebutions for his fervice as formerly.

4 Voted, that their shall be a free Contrebution once A Quarter this P[r]sent year, Towards the Defraying the Charges in carrying on Preaching under M[r] Gibbs prefent Bodily illness.

5 Voted, That the fecond Tuisday of November next be appointed for carrying of Wood to the Rev[d] M[r] Gibbs for fuch as are free & willing fo to do, and the wood that shall be fo carried to be free & gratis & not accounted any part of the fallary.

6 Voted, That on the third Sabbath in this P[r]sent month their be a free Contrebution for the Raifing of money to defray the Charge of fome neffefsary Repairs of the Minifterial place.

7 Voted, and Chofen for a committee to take care and fee the worke done Serj[t] Josiah Goddard Ebenezer Stone and William Bond Jn[r] and to give an Account of the Charge to the Congregation when the worke is done.

At a meeting of the Inhabitants of the Easterly Congregation in Watertown Orderly warned and meet the 14th of Octob[r] 1720. Voted & Chofen M[r] Nathanael Bright for Moderator.

Voted That we do Ajorne the aboves[d] meeting to the, 21st day of this Instant October to three of the Clock in the afternoon, at Old meeting-houfe in fd. Town.

At a meeting of the Inhabitants of the Easterly Congregation in Watertown by Adjornment the 21st of October, 1720. M[r] Nat[ll] Bright was Chofen Moderator.

1 Voted, that we will Chofe A committee to Addrefs the Gen[ll] Court for a fetled line or Boundary for each Precinct or Congregation in Watertown.

2 Voted, and Chofen A Comittee for the end afores[d] Maj[r] Jonas Bond Esq[r] M[r] Nath[ll] Bright, Lieu[t] Ric: Coollidg, Deacon Nathan Fiske, M[r] Jon[th] Stone, Dea: Jn[o] Coollidg, M[r] Joseph Mafon and M[r] Joseph Coollidge.

3 Voted, that they be a Comittee in our names & behalfe to addrefs f[d] Court, that a Divifional line may be established, whereby

the Ratable estates of the Town may be equally parted between the two Congregations in the Town. The Town having acted in the same affaire June 13th [illegible]. That so each Congregation may be enabled comfortably to proceed in granting and Raising money for their Respective Incidental Charges. The Salary for the Ministry to be Still levyed on ye whole Town, and equally divided according to the Order of the Great & Genl Court bearing Date November the [illegible] 1720.

2. Voted. That we leave it with sd Comittee to Advise & consider what methods they may think best for Obtaining the ends above.

To Munnings Sawin Clark of the Easterly Congregation in Watertown. Whereas Sundry of the Inhabitants of ye Congregation have made known to us the Subscribers who are the Committee to call meetings, That they desire there might be A meeting warned for sd Congregation to See what methods are best to be taken to obtaine A settled Precinct line between the Two Congregations in Sd Town.

These are therefore to desire you to Post up a warning for a Precinct or Congregation in ye words following

Viz. The Inhabitants belonging to the Easterly Congregation are Desired to give a meeting at the Old meeting-house in Sd Town on the fourteenth day of October Current at three of the Clock in the after noon, to Consider, advise & act on such methods as may be thought Proper to obtaine A Settled Precinct line between the Two Congregations in Sd Town. That each Congregation may be better enabled to Settle matters [illegible], or other wise for their good & benefit, able to Raise money if need be for ye ends above. By order of the Committee.

Jonas Bond.
Natll Bright
Willm Bond.

[39]

To Munnings Sawin Clark of the Easterly Congregation in Watertown. You are hereby Ordered to post up an order on the next Sabbath day, [illegible] in the words following.

The Inhabitants of the Easterly Congregation in Watertown are hereby Ordered to meet at the old meeting house in Sd Town, on the first wednesday of October next, at three of the Clock in the afternoon, To Chuse A Committee, A clerk, and a Treasurer, and such other Officers as Said Congregation may then see cause to. Watertown September 30th 1730.

Jonas Bond
Natll Bright } Comittee.
William Bond

Pursuant to this Order, I have Posted up the Warrant Order according to the time, place and Business therein mentioned.

Munnings Sawin Clark of sd Congregation.

At a meeting of the Easterly Congregation in Watertown, Orderly warned and meet the 5th of October, 1720. Capt. Jonas Bond esqr was Chosen Moderator for sd. meeting.

1 Voted, and Chosen for A committee, Jonas Bond esqr Mr Nathl Bright and Dea: Willm Bond.

2 Voted and Chosen for Clerk Manninge Sewis.. voted and Chosen for Sexton Tho: Coollidge, and for his service to have two Contributions.

4 Voted, that we will have four Contributions Quarterly this ensuing year towards ye defraying the Charges of preaching in the abovesd Congregation.

5 Voted, and agreed that all such that are of a willing mind to Carry wood gratis to our Revrd pastor, Mr Gibbs on the last Tuesday of November next do then attend said work.

At a meeting of ye East Congregation in Watertown October the 13 1720

By Adjournment from the third of ye Octobr which meeting was upon a desire to choose and Incourage some person to take care of the Old meeting house as a Sexton and to Desire and Appoint Some meet person to Officiate as a Clerk and to know the minds of ye Congregation as to Continue a quarterly Contribution &c:

1 Thomas Coollidge was desired to take the care of the Meeting house, and that he should be rewarded by having two Contributions in the year, at Each half years end.

2 It was Agreed there Shd be four Contributions this year to be Improved so far as that will go towards the paying of Such as do preach among us under Mr Gibbs Confinement.

3 It was Agreed that the first tuesday in Novembr next Shd be the day for cutting & Carting of wood for Mr Gibbs, for Such as See cause So to do, and to be free and not to be Accounted any part of his Sallary.

4 The former Committe are desired Still to Continue to call ye Congregation togethr when there is Occasion for it.

5 Joseph Mason is desired to be An Assistant to our present Clerk until his present illness and Indisposition and to put on or take of the Precinct book as there may be need.

Here Ends Congregational Affairs.

[40] Blank.

[41-43]

[Here follow the accounts of the assessors and the treasurer for the Easterly Precinct Affairs between the dates of March 12, 1723/4 and March 5, 1742/3. The Collector and Treasurer debit and credit accounts from 1734 to Feb. 25, 1742, having occupied the double pages 1 and 2 at the beginning of the book, preceding the general congregation affairs.—Eds.]

[44]

After the Town Was Divided and Precinct affairs ceased

Then the Town Voted this Book to be Improved ꝑ ye Treafurer in the Town Concerns

AND ACCORDINGLY

The Town Concerns begins Page 45

Which is over Leafe

[45 to 81]

[Here follow the accounts of the Treasurer of the Town Concerns between the dates of March 13, 1737/8, and June 18, 1792. At the reversed end of this book Precinct Affairs are continued. —Eds.]

[Precinct Affairs.]

[1]

Midd^{x} ss: To Mr Samuel Peirce Constable of the most Easterly Precinct in Watertowne, Greeting.

Application being this day made to me the Subscriber One of his Majesties Justices of the Peace within and for the s^{d} County of Midd^{x} By Jonas Bond Esqr and Ten other free holders and inhabitants within the Easterly Precinct in said Watertowne, Seting forth that there is great need of A Precinct meeting to be Called, (1) for to Choose A Clerk, Committe and all other Precinct Officers (2) to take Care for the Carrying on of Preaching in s^{d} Precinct, and to Come in to Some proper Method to proceed toward a full Settlement of the Gospel Ministrey in s^{d} Precinct (3) to agree how to raise Precinct meetings for the future.

These are therefore In his Maje^{s} Name to Will and require you the aboves^{d} Contables forthwith to Warne and give Notice to all the free holders and other Inhabitants Liveing within the bounds of the s^{d} Easterly Precinct at last Setled by Order of the Generall Court, Who are quallifyed according to Law to Vote in the affaires of s^{d} Precinct to meet at the Old Meeting house in s^{d} Precinct on Monday the Twenty third day of December Currant at Ten of the Clock in the forenoon: first after the Choice of A Moderator. To Choose A Precinct Clerk, Com^{tee} and all other Precinct Officers (2) To take Care for the Carrying on of Preaching in s^{d} Precinct, and to Come into Some proper Methods, to proceed toward, a full Settlement of the Gospel Ministrey in s^{d} Precinct (3) to Agree how to raise Precinct Meetings for the future,

And make Returne of your doings hereon Unto Jonas Bond Esqr one of the Principle Inhabitants of s^{d} Precinct at or before the Time prefixed for sd: meeting (for which this shall be your Sufficient Warrant) hereof you may not faile at your perrill &c.

Given Under my hand and Seale at Weston the Ninth day of December In the Tenth yeare of his Maje^{s} Reigne Anno-Domini 1723. FRA: FULLAM Justice of Peace.

[2]

At a Gen^ll Meeting of the free holders, and other Inhabitants of the Easterly Precinct in Watertowne Regularly Warned (By Virtue of a Warrant from Francis Fullam Esqr one of his Maje^s Justices of the Peace for the County of Midd^x) And Assembled for the Choice of A Precinct Clerk and other Precinct officers and Such busness as the Warrant Refered to

(1) Put to Vote and Chose Jonas Bond Esqr Moderator for s^d Meeting.

(2) Put to Vote and Chose Dea: Jno Coollidg Precinct Clerk.

(3) Put to Vote whether the Precinct will have five men to be A Com^tee to manage the Prudentials of this Precinct and the Vote past in the affirmative.

(4) Put to Vote and Chose Jonas Bond Esqr: Mr Nathanael Bright Capt Abra^m Browne Mr Jno Sterns & Mr Henry Spring to be a Com^tee for the ends above sd:

(5) Put to Vote & Choose Cor^l Henry Bright, Mr Natha^l Harris and Mr Jos: Coollidg for Assessors.

(6) Put to Vote and Chose for Collector Mr Jona^th Stone

(7) Put to Vote and Chose for a Receiver for the Precinct Dea: Nathan Fiske

(8) Put to Vote and Chose for A Com^tee to take Care the Pulpit be Supplyed for the present till the Precinct Can Come into a Settlement Dea: Wm Bond Dea: Nathan Fiske and Dea: Jno Coollidg

(9) Put to Vote whether the Precinct are Willing and agreed that the Method for the raising of Precinct Meeting for the future shall be, by the Com^tee or the Precinct Clerk in their Names Signing an Order directing it to the Constable within s^d Precinct to warne the Inhabitants to meet at place and Time appointed in Such Order and the Vote pased in the Affirmative.

Mid^x ss: Watertowne Janeuary 13th 1723/4

To Deacon John Coollidg Clerk of the Easterly Precinct in Watertowne you are hereby ordered to give out an order in the Name of the Com^tee of s^d Precinct directed to the Constable dwelling within the bounds of sd: Precinct to be in the forme and for the ends following,

Midd^x ss

To Sam^ll Peirce Constable of Watertowne Greeting, you are hereby Ordered and required to Warne all the freeholders and other Inhabitants dwelling within the bounds aud limits of the Easterly Precinct of s^d Towne to meet at the Old Meeting house in s^d Towne on the first Munday of Febrewary next Comeing at one of the Clock in the after noone of s^d day for the ends following.

1 That the Precinct may be informed of the Nomination the Church hath made at their meeting on the Tenth day of Janeuary Currant in Order to the Setling of A gospel Minister among us in s^d Precinct.

2 That then the Precinct may proceed to the Choice & Selection of one out of the afores^d Nomination the Church hath made to be Setled in the worke of the Minisftrey that we may Come to the injoyment of the Ordenances of Christ among us.

3 To Agree and determine what Incoragement to give to the Gentleman that may be Chosen both as to his Sallery & Settlement,

4 To Choose A Com^tee to treat with the perfon that may be Chofen with attefted Coppyes of the Votes that shall be made, hereof faile not and make returne of this order with your doings there in unto Some one of the Com^tee or Clerk before the time of s^d meeting by Order of the Com^tee Dated this 13th day of Janeuary Anno Domini 1723/4. JN° COOLLIDG Cler:

In obedience to this order I have Warned the freeholders and other Inhabitants to meet at time & place within mentioned according to the Tenoure of s^d Order. Jan^u 15: 1723.

SAM^ll PIERCE, Conftable
for Watertowne.

[3]

Febrewary the 3^d 1723/4 At a Meeting of the Eafterly Precinct in Watertowne being Orderly Warned and Mett

Voted 1 And Coronell Jonas Bond was Chosen Moderator of s^d Meeting.

Voted 2 And Mr Seth Storrer was Chosen to be the gospel Minifter for s^d Precinct Chosen by 56 Votes

Voted 3 To add 16: £: tot he 84:£: Ordered by the Gen^ll Court for the Support of the Minifter in f^d Precinct yearly, Which makes up Said: 84£: 100:£ which Sum of one Hundred pounds to be Mr Seth Storrers yearly Sallery.

Voted 4 To give Mr Seth Storrer one Hundred pounds towards his Settlement And He wholly to Provide a Settlement for himfelf, Or to Procure the Tenement that the Rev^nd Mr Henry Gibbs last dwelt on and improved. And to Putt the buildings and fences in good repaires. And Mr Storrer to have the improvement thereot in Lieu of f^d 100:£: Which Services He pleases to accept off.

Voted 5 And Chosen Coro^ll Jonas Bond, the three Deacons and Capt Abraham Browne to be A Committe to Treat with Mr Storrer in Order to his Acceptance of Said Call.

Voted 6 The meeting to be Adjorned to the last Munday of Febrewary Current at one of the Clock in the after Noon to heare the returne of Said Commitee.

At A Meeting of the Easterly Precinct in Watertowne on the last Munday in Febrewary by Adjornment 1723/4

Voted 1 To Choose A Com^tee of five men out of thofe in the Precinct who Neither they nor theire Predecefsors were out money in building the houseing and appurtenances where the Revd Mr John Bailye did live while he Lived in Watertowne.

Voted 2 And Chosen Mr Nath^ll Harris Mr Edward Herington

Mr John Sternes Mr Samll Peirce and Mr Ephraim Angier to be sd Comtte to Meet with the Proprietors of sd Houseing and prmesis in Order to Project Some way that Said Tenement may become the Precincts and to make report to ſd Precinct of theire doings thereon at theire next meeting by Adjornment

Voted 3 That this Meeting be Adjorned to the last Munday of March at One of the Clock in the afternoon of sd day to have a fuller Anſwer from Mr Storrer and to heare the report of sd Comtee

At A Meeting of the Eaſterly Precinct in Watertowne by Adjornment on March the 30th 1724

Voted For A Comtee to gather the money Subſcribed to repaire the Tenement the Revd Mr Henry Gibbs last dwelt on And to improve sd money for the ends propoſed, Mr Nathl Harris, Mr Edward Herington, Mr John Sternes, Mr Samuell Peirce and Mr Ephraim Angier.

Voted That the Comtee that was Choſen to treat with Mr Storrer should waite on him againe to Se if he please to Cancel the Proviſo in his Anſwer to the Church and Precinct.

Voted the meeting to be Adjorned to the last Munday of April next at 3 a Clock in the after noon of Said day.

[4]

At A Meeting of the East Precinct in Watertowne being Orderly warned & mett March the 30th 1724.

Voted 1 Coronll Jonas Bond was Chosen Moderator of sd Meeting.

Voted 2 for a Precinct Comtee for the yeare Enſuing Coronll Jonas Bond Mr Natll Bright Lent Samll Thacher, Mr Wm Shattuck, and Capt Abraham Browne.

Voted 3 for a Precinct Clerk John Coollidg.

Voted 4 for a Treaſurer Sergt Joseph Coollidg.

Voted 5 for Aſseſsors Cornt Henry Bright Sergt Joseph Coollidg & Mr Natll Harris.

Voted 6 for A Collector Mr Jno Hastings.

Voted 7 to take downe the uper Gallery in the Old meeting House and to improve the Stuft on the New Meeting house at the Schoolhouse hill.

Voted 8 To finiſh the inſide of the New meeting House Excepting what room may be thought proper to build Pews on and to be managed by the prudence of a Comtee now to be Chosen for that Purpose, And to be done by the money now to be granted for that End.

Voted 9 for Said Comitee Coronll Jonas Bond, Mr Natll Bright, Dea: Nathan Fiſke Mr Jno Sternes, Mr Thomas Larnard, Mr Jonath Stone, Mr Edw: Herington.

Voted 10 To raise Two Hundred pounds on the Precinct towards the finiſhing the New Meeting House in sd Precinct.

Voted 11 That the Aſseſsors Shall make the invoice that the last Province Tax was made by, The Rule to Aſseſs the Precinct for sd money granted Excepting what may be proper to Very from it as to perticular perfons obferveing the rules of Justice and Equity.

Voted 12 That the money granted be Collected and paid in unto the s[d] Precinct Treafurer at or before the last day of July next.

At A Meeting of the Eafterly Precinct in Watertowne on the last Munday of Aprill 1724 by Adjornment.

Voted That M[r] Storrers Anfwer to the Church and Precinct to be recorded in the Precinct Book of Records.

At a Meeting of the Com[tee] of the Eaft Precinct in Watertowne june 22nd 1724

Ordered that the Precinct Clerk do forthwith give an order in Writeing to the Conftable of s[d] Precinct to warne all the free holders & other inhabitants dweling within the bounds of s[d] Precinct who are quallifyed to Vote in Towne affairs to meet at the Old meeting houfe in s[d] Precinct on the last Munday of june Currant at three of the Clock in the afternoon for the Ends following Viz[t]:

1 To Se whether the Precinct will then agree upon a day for the ordination of M[r] Seth Storer whome they have Called & invited to Settle among us, who hath alfo accepted of s[d] Call

2 To agree upon a way & method to raife money for the defraying the Charge and Expence for the Entertaining y[e] Rev[nd] Elders, & Messengers y[t] may be sent to to Carry on y[e] work.

3 To Choose & impower A Com[tee] to take Care and provide a Suitable place to Entertaine the Elders & Mefsengers &c and all Suitable Entertainment for them, to be accountable to the Precinct when Called thereto what money they have Rec[d] & how they have improved the Same

Jonas Bond Nathanael Bright William Shattuck Sam[ll] Thacher Abraham Browne	Com[tee] for s[d] Precinct

[5]

To the Church and Congregation in the Eaftern Precinct in Watertowne.

Gentlemen,

I Thankfully acknowledge the refpect you have Manifested to me in makeing Choice of, and inviting me to Settle with you in the work of the Sacred Ministrey.

I have taken the Same into moft Serious Confideration have afked the Councill of heaven, and taken the advice of the moft Suitable perfons to Consult with on reference to Such an Affaire, who do advise me to Settle with you in this great and weighty work of the Minifiery. And I find myself Inclined thereunto in having a profpect in being inftrumentall of promoteing the glory of God, the intereft of Religion and the good of Souls among you.

I do therefore manefest my acceptance of the said Call upon those Conditions proposed Viz[t] That together with my yearly Sallery I Should have the Use of the House and improvement of the Land which were lately in the Possession of the Rev[d] M[r] Henry Gibbs, as is Specified in your Vote, Hoping that if my Circumstances Should hereafter Call for more then they do at present in order to my Comfortable maintainance and Support in the Sacret Office you will Provide Suitable for me.

I Begg you prayers for me that God who is the Lord of the Harvest would make me a painfull faithfull and Sucessfull Labourer in his Vineyard and that after I have preached to others I myself may not be a Castaway. I Commend you all to the divine Care and Conduct intreating that the God of Peace and Love would preserve Unity among you and add Continually to your Number and graces, And that ye may stand perfect and Compleat in all the Will of God, And that he would give you an inheritance among them that are Sanctified throu faith in Christ Jesus. So prayes in all Humble maner

Gentle[n] your Affectionate friend
and Humble servant SETH STORER.

Cambridge March 27th 1724

Midd[x] ss:

To M[r] Nat[ll] Bright Constable of Watertowne

S[r] These are to will & require you forthwith to warne all the freeholders and other Inhabitants dwelling within the bounds of the Easterly Precinct of s[d] Towne who are quallifyed to Vote in Towne affaires to meet at the Old Meeting in s[d] Precinct on the last Munday of june Currant at three of the Clock in the after Noone for the End following Viz[t]:

1 To See whether the Precinct will then agree upon a day for the Ordination of M[r] Seth Storer whome they have Called and invited to Settle among us who hath also accepted of s[d] invitation

2 To agree upon a way and method to raise money for the defraying the Charge and Expense for Entertaining the Rev[nd] Elders and Messengers that may be sent to for the Carrying on of Said work

3 To Choose and impower a Com[tee] to take Care and provide a Suitable place to Entertaine the Elders and Messengers &c and all Suitable Entertainment for them and to be accountable to s[d] Precinct when Called thereto of what money they have recieved and how they have improved the Same, hereof faile not and make a true return of this Order and of your doings thereon to Some one of s[d] Com[tee] or Clerk of said Precinct Six houres at least before the Time of s[d] meeting.

P[r] Order of s[d] Com[tee]
Jn: Coollidg Cler:

Watertowne June the 23rd 1724

[6]

At a meeting of the Eaſterly Precinct in Watertowne on the last Munday of June 1724.

1 Coro^{ll} Jonas Bond was Chosen Moderator of s^{d} Meeting.

2 Voted to Agree on a day for the Ordination of Mr Seth Storer.

3 Voted that the day for the Ordination of Mr Seth Storer be the 4th Wednesday of July next.

4 Voted to Choose two men to travel the Precinct to propose to the Inhabitants to Se what they will give towards the Charge of the Ordination of Mr Storer, And to take downe theire Names that will give and theire Sums and they that pay downe to Croſs theire Sums And to deliver what they Shall So receive to the following Com^{tee} Mentioned underneath.

5 Thomas Bond and Ephraim Cutter jun^{r} Chosen for s^{d} two men.

6 Voted to Choose a Com^{tee} to provide a place and Entertainment for said Affaire out of s^{d} money

7 Chosen for S^{d} Com^{tte} Jno Coollidg Serg^{t} Jeniſon Mr Spring Serg^{t} Stone Mr Sternes Serg^{t} Coollidg and Mr Harris

8 Voted that S^{d} Com^{tee} to give accompt to S^{d} Precinct of what money they receive and what they Expend when Called thereto

To Mr Jno Coollidg Clerk for the Easterly Precinct in Watertowne

S^{r}

You are hereby Ordered forthwith to give an Order to Joseph Coollidg Treaſurer or Receiver for s^{d} Precinct to pay unto the Revd Mr Seth Storrer the Sum of Twenty pounds, And to Leu^{t} Richard Coollidg the Sum of five pounds out of the forty Two pounds which was ordered by the Select men of s^{d} Towne to be paid into S^{d} Treaſurer p^{r} Conſtable Samuel Peirce out of the Towne Rate Commited to him to Collect

Watertowne Sepr 24: 1724	JONAS BOND NATHA^{l} BRIGHT Wm SHATTUCK ABRA^{m} BROWNE	Precinct Committe

At a meeting of the Precincts Com^{tte} Jany the 5th 1724/5

Mr Storrer being present it was then Agreed on that the Ministers that had preached after Decemb^{r} the 4th 1723 and the Charge of theire Entertainment Should be paid out of the 84£: Sallery for the yeare 1724 the yeare Ending Dec: the 4th 1724 and the Residue of S^{d} 84£ to be for Mr Storer in full for his preaching in s^{d} Precinct untill S^{d} 4th day of Dec: 1724.

[7]

Midd^{x} ſs

To Mr Nathanael Bright Conſtable of Watertowne,

Sr Theſe are to Will and require you forthwith to warne all the freeholders and other Inhabitants who dwell in the Eaſterly

Precinct in s^d Towne who are quallifyed to Vote in Towne Affaires to Meet at the New Meeting house in s^d Precinct on Munday the Eleventh day of Janewary Current at one of the Clock in the after noon of s^d day for the Ends following

(1) To Know the Precincts minde when they will meet at the New Meeting hous in s^d Precinct and make it the place of Pubblick Worship for ye future

(2) To Know the Precincts Minde how they would have the Old meeting house disposed of or Improved or any part of it.

(3) To Receive an Accompt from the Com^tee how they have improved the money already granted towards the finishing of the New Meeting house

(4) To See whether the Precinct will then grant money for the further finishing of s^d meeting house And the paying the Warnings of Precinct meetings: Hereof faile not and make Returne of this Order with your doings thereon unto Some one of the Com^tee or Clerk of s^d Precinct foure hours at least before the Time of s^d Meeting Dated the fifth day of Janewary in the Eleventh yeare of his Majesties Reigne Anno Domini 1724/5

℘^r Order of } Jno Coollidg
the Com^tee } Cler:

At A Meeting of the Easterly Precinct in Watertowne on Munday the Eleventh of Janewary 1724/5

(1) A Vote passed and Cor^ll Jonas Bond was Chosen Moderator

(2) Voted to Meet at the New Meeting House on the first Sabbath day of Febrewary next & then to make it the place of Publick Worship for the future

(3) Voted to take out of the old meeting House all that may be profitably improved in the New Meeting house next after the last Sabbath day in Janewary Currant

(4) To Raise Two Hundred pounds to pay what they are indebted for the New Meeting house and for the further finishing the Same and Sixteen pounds thereof to be part of Mr Storrers Sallery and for the paying for the Warning of Precinct Meetings and the makeing of Precinct Rates

(5) Voted that the former Com^tee imployed in building the New meeting house Should be the Com^tee to take out of the Old Meeting house and improve it in the New Meeting House what they think proper and Needfull, And to improve the Residue of s^d grant of 200^lb in further finishing of s^d house

[8]

Watertowne Janewary 18: 1724/5

To Deacon John Coollidg Clerk of the Easterly Precinct in Watertowne,

you Are hereby Ordered to deliver to the Assessors of s^d Precinct a Coppy of the grant of the Two Hundred pounds made by s^d Precinct at theire Meeting on the Eleventh day of Janewary

Currant for the Ends therein Mentioned, And direct them to Afsefs the Same Spedily the money being now Wanted for the defraying of Debts already Contracted And for the further finifhing of the New Meeting House, Said Afsefsors are to Committ the Rate or Afsefsment when made with a Lawfull Warrant to Collect the Same unto Mr John Hastings the present Collector and to Issue and make up his Accompts at or before the first Munday of July Next Enfuing

JONAS BOND
NATHA[l] BRIGHT } Com[tee]
W[m] SHATTUCK

Midd[x] fs.

To Mr Nathanael Bright Conftable of Watertown

S[r] Thefe are to will & require you forthwith to warn all the Freeholders and other Inhabitants who are Quallified to Vote in precinct Affairs who dwell in the Eafterly precinct to Meet at the New Meeting houfe in S[d] precinct on the Third Monday of March Next Enfuing at Two of the Clock in the after Noone to choofe precinct officers for the year Currant. Alfo to know the minde of y[e] precinct how they would have y[e] remaind[r] of y[e] old Meeting houfe Difpofed of which can not be proffitably Improved in y[e] New: hereof fail not but make a true return of this ord[r] and of Your doings thereon to Some one of y[e] Committee or Clerk of y[e] precinct four houres at Leaft before y[e] time of S[d] Meeting
Watertown Feb[r] 16: 1724/5 Per od[r] of y[e] Com[tee]

JOHN COOLLIDGE Cler.

At a Meeting of the Easterly Precinct in Watertown on March the 15th 1724/5

1 Chosen for Moderator Col. Jonas Bond.

2 Voted to Choofe three Men to be a Standing Committe for the precinct for the Year.

3 Voted and Choofe for Said Com[tee] Mr Nathanael Bright, Deacon William Bond and Coro[l] Bond.

4. Voted and Chofen Clerk Joseph Mafon.

5. Voted and Chofen Treafurer Ser[t] Joseph Coollidge

6. Voted and Chofen Afsefsors Cor[t] Henry Bright Ser[t] Joseph Coollidg & Mr Nathanael Harris.

7. Voted and Chofen Collector Mr Thomas Coollidg.

8. Voted and Chofen Sexton Mr Nathanael Sherman.

9. Voted y[t] Said Sexton Shall have two Contributions in the year for his reward, viz[t] on the first Sabbath in September Next and on the firft Sabbath in March next

10. Voted to Difpose of y[e] whole remainder of y[e] old Meeting houfe and the whole Effects thereof to be improved in the further finifhing of y[e] New Meeting houfe, and if their be any overpluss of y[e] money Afsigned for that Use it Shall be in the money granted for finifhing Said Meeting houfe.

11. Voted that the Same Commn^tee^ that hath been improved in Mannaging the building of ye New Meeting houfe, Shall be the Comm^tee^ to Difpose of the Old Meeting houfe.

[9]

To Joseph Mafon Clerk of the Eafterly Precinct in Watertown

You are hereby ordred forthwith to give an order to Mr Joseph Coollidge precinct Treafurer To pay to the Reverend Mr Seth Storer the Sum of Sixteen pounds out of the Two hundred pound Rate granted Pr Said precinct on the Eleventh Day of January in the Year 1724/5 which Sixteen pounds is for the Compleating the Sallery According to Contract.

Watertown Feb^r^ 17th 1725/6. JONAS BOND, NATHANAEL BRIGHT } Precinct Com^tee^

To Mr Joseph Coollidge Treafurer of ye East Precinct in Watertown

S^r^

You are hereby ordred to pay to the Reverend Mr Seth Storer the fum of fixteen pounds Out of the Two hundred pound Rate granted Pr S^d^ Precinct on the Eleventh Day of January in the Year 1724/5 which S^d^ Sixteen pounds is for Compleating his Sallery According to Contract.

P^r^ order of ye Precinct Committe

Watertown Feb^r^ 21. 1725/6. JOSEPH MASON Precinct Cler.

Midd^x^ fs.

To Mr Jonas Bond Junr Conftable of Watertown Greeting.

S^r^

You are hereby required forthwith to warne the Freeholders and oth^r^ Inhabitants within the Eafterly Precinct in S^d^ Town who are Quallifyed to Vote in Precinct Affaires to Meet at the Publick Meetinghoufe in S^d^ Precinct on ye fourteenth Day of March Next enfuing the Date hereof, at two of the clock in the afternoone of S^d^ day, for the ends following.

First. To choofe a Committee to mannage ye prudentials of S^d^ Precinct A Clerk and other precinct Officers which are proper to be chofen.

Secondly. To receive an Acc^t^ from the Committee wch were Imployed in finifhing the Meeting houfe, how far they have difpofed of the money already granted, Pr S^d^ Precinct for that End.

Thirdly. That the Precinct may then Mannifeft their Mindes if they fe caufe how and in what Method they will have the Vacant room und^r^ the gallireys in the Meeting houfe to be Improved.

Fourthly. To take effectual care that there be money raifed for the Minifters Sallery According to Contract, as alfo for others to whom money may be due from the Precinct.

Fifthly. To take care that the Saxstone may be Incourraged.
hereof fail not, but make return of this ord^r^ and Your Doings thereon to one of the Com^tee^ or Clerk of S^d^ Precinct at Least four hours before the time for S^d^ Meeting.

P^r^ ord^r^ of the Committee

JOSEPH MASON Cler.

Watertown Feb^r^ 21. 1725/6.

[10]

At a Meeting of the Inhabitants of the Easterly Precinct in Watertown on the 14th Day of March 1725/6. for the Election of Precinct officers, And Such oth^r^ buisness as is Set forth in the Warnind of S^d^ Meeting.

Voted and Choose for Moderator Jonas Bond Esqr.

Voted and Choose for the Standing Comm^tee^ to Mannage the prudentials of the precinct this Psent Year. Jonas Bond Esqr Dea. Nathan Fiske & Dea John Coollidge.

Voted and Choose for Precinct Clerk Mr Nathanael Harris.

Voted and Choose for Precinct Treasurer (or Receivor) Mr Joseph Coollidge

Voted and Choose for Assessors { Joseph Mason, Mr Nathanael Harris, Mr Henery Bright.

Voted and Choose for Collector Mr Edward Harrington.

Voted and Choose for Saxton Mr Nathanael Shermon.

Voted for the Incourragment & reward of s^d^ Sexton, That there Should be Two Contributions in the Year for him, vizt the first Contribution to be on the first Sabbath Day in Septemb^r^ and the Second to be on the first Sabbath Day in March.

At s^d^ Meeting the Comm^tee^ Chosen for the finishing the Meeting house, Laid their Acc^t^ before the Precinct of how much they had Disposed of the Money Granted P^r^ y^e^ Precinct toward the finishing of the Meeting house. The Acc^t^ Amounting to the Sum of £387=4=9. The s^d^ Acc^t^ was red to the Precinct. And Put to Vote whether the Precinct Do Axcept of Said Acc^t^

And the Vote past in the Affirmative.

Put to Vote whether the Precinct will At this Meeting Manifest their Minds how, the Vacancy under the Gallerys shall be Improved.

The Vote past in the Negative.

Put to Vote whether the Precinct are willing to Allow the Precinct Assessors, for Making precinct Rates Two shillings & sixpence Pr Day, and they Laying a fair Acc^t^ before the Precinct Comm^tee^ the Same be Allow'd. And the Vote past in ye Affirmative.

Put to Vote whether the Precinct are willing to Allow Constables three shillings A Meeting for Warning precinct Meetings

The Vote past in ye Affirmative.

Put to Vote whether the Precinct are Willing to Allow the Sum of fourty Shillings to Mr John Hastings for Collecting the precinct

Rates Committed to him to Collect. The Vote paſt in the Affarmitive.

Put to Vote whether the precinct are Willing (and Do Now Grant) the Sum of Twenty five pounds to Pay ye Revd Mr Storer According to Contract and the Aſseſsors & Conſtables and others to whom Money May be due from s^{d} Precinct.

The Vote paſt in ye Affarmative.

Put to Vote whether the Precinct are Willing to Allow Mr Dan^{ll} Haſtings Ten ſhillings for ringin the bell from ye 1st Sabbath in Feb^{r} to ye 2^{d} in March, 1724/5.

And the Vote paſt in ye Affarmitive

[**11**]

To Nathaniel Harris Clerk of the Easterly Precinct in Watertown, You Are Hereby Ordered to Deliver to the Aſseſsors of Said Precinct A Coppy of the Grant of the Twenty five Pounds Granted by the Precinct aforeſaid Att there Meeting on the Fourteenth Day of March Last Past; For the Ends therein Mentioned and Direct them to Aſsess the Inhabitance of s^{d} Precinct as the Law Directs Spedily and to Commit the Rate or Aſsessment to Mr Edward Harrington the Present Collector for s^{d} Precinct With a Lawfull Warrent to Collect the ſame and to Issue and Make up his Accompts at or Before ye First Monday of Octo^{br} Next Inſueing.

Jonas Bond } Com^{tee}
Nathan Fiske }

Watertown July y^{e}
11th 1726

To M^{r} Joſeph Coollidge Treaſurer of ye East Precinct in Watertown

Sr You are Hereby Ordered to Pay to the Reverend Mr Seth Storer the Sum of Sixteen Pounds out of the Twenty five Pound Rate Granted Pr S^{d} Precinct on the Fourteenth Day of March Last Past which Sum of Sixteen Pounds is for the Compleating his Sallary According to Contract.

Alſo to Pay to Your ſelf the ſum of one Pound Six Shillings and three Pence.

To Corn^{tt} Henry Bright the Sum of One Pound Eleven Shillings and three Pence.

To Dea Joſeph Maſon the Sum of Five Shillings And to Nath^{ll} Harris the Sum of One Pound Eleven Shillings and three Pence which Sums Ware Reſpectively Allowed for Makeing of Precinct Rates.

To Mr John Hastings the Sum of Two Pounds Allowed him for Collecting of Precinct Rates Committed to him. To Mr Samuel Pirce Six Shillings for Warning Two Precinct meetings in the Year 1723. To Mr Nath^{ll} Bright Nine Shillings for Warning Three Precinct Meettings in the Year 1724. To Mr Jonas Bond Junr three Shillings for Warning one Precinct Meetting in the Year 1725. To Mr Daniel Hastings the Sum of Ten Shillings for Ringing the Bell.

P^{r} order of the Precinct Com^{tee}
Watertown January the Nath^{ll} Harris Cler.
17th 1726/7

Middlesx ss:

To Mr Thomas Bond Constable of Watertown Greetting.

Sr

You are hereby Requiered forthwith to Warn the Freeholders and other Inhabitance Within the Easterly Precinct in Sd Town who are Qualified to Vote in Precinct affairs to Meet at the Publick Meeting house in sd Precinct on Monday the Thirteenth Day of March Next Insuing the Date hereof Att Two of the Clock in the afterNoon of sd Day for the Ends Following

Viz First to Choose a Precinct Committee to manage the Prudentialls of sd Precinct A Clerk and other Precinct officers Nessary and Proper to be Chosen.

Secondly, that the Precinct May Consider (And if they Please Conclude) How they will have the Vacant Room under the Galleries in Sd Meetinghouse Improved; and if it Should be agreed, and Concluded, to Build Pews Whether the Pews, Should be Built; By Perticular Persons or by Sd Precinct: and if it be there Minds Sd Precinct Should Buld them as a Precinct, then to Take Care and Raise Money for the Same.

Thirdly to Take Effectuall Care that there be Money Raised for the Ministers Sallary According to Contract and also for others to Whome Money May be Due from the Precinct, And Also to Raise Money for the Further Finishing Sd Meetting house if there Shall be Occation.

Fourthly to Take Care that the Saxstone may be incoarriged. hereof fail Not but Make Return of this order and Your Doings thereon to one of the Committee or Clerk of sd Precinct at Least Four hours Before the Time for sd Meetting.

Pr order of sd Commitee.

Watertown Febry 27th 1726/7 Nathll Harris Cler.

[12]

Att, A Meeting of the Inhabitance of the Easterly Precinct in Watertown. On Monday the 13th Day of March Anno Dom 1726/7 for the Election of Precinct Officers And Such Other Buisness as is Sett Forth in the Warning of Said Meetting.

Voted, And Chose for Moderator Colo Jonas Bond Esqr.

Voted, and Chose for a Standing Committee to Mannage the Prudentialls of sd Precinct For this Present Year Lt Richard Coollidge Mr Thomas Straith and Dea Nathan Fisk

Voted and Chose for Said Precinct Clerk Nathaniel Harris

Voted and Chose for sd Precinct Assessors { Mr Nathaniel Bright, Mr Joseph Holdin, Mr John Straton }

Voted and Chose for sd Precinct Treasurer or Receiver Mr Joseph Coollidge.

Voted and Chose For Collector for sd Precinct for this Present Year Mr Daniel Bond.

Voted and Chose for Sexstone Mr Nathaniel Shearmon.

Voted that there Should Be Two Contributions in this Present

Year for the Reward and Incourrigement of him the S^d^ Sextone (Viz) one on the First Sabbath in September and the other on the First Sabbath in March.

Put to Vote Whether it Be the minds of the Precinct at this meetting, that the Vacant Room in the Meetting houfe under the Gallereis Should Be Improved with Pews: and that Perticuliar Perfons Should Build them under Such Regulations as the s^d^ Precinct Shall agree upon; or by a Committee Appointed by s^d^ Precinct for that Purpofe; and the Vote Paft in the affirmitive

Put to Vote Whether the Precinct will Now Choofe Five men for a Committee to Mannage that affair (Relating to or) Concerning the Building of Pews under the Gallerries in S^d^ Meetting houfe and the Vote Pafsed in the affermitive.

Voted and Chose Ser^t^ Joseph Coollidge, Enf^n^ Jonathan Stone, Corn^tt^ Henry Bright Ser^t^ Ebenezer Stone & Nathaniel Harris for A Committee to Mannage that affair concerning the Pews haveing Refpect to Such Directions as they Shall hereafter Receive from s^d^ Precinct

Voted that s^d^ Committee Shall have Regard to what Perfons have Difbursted & have Bin Rated as to Reall & Personall Eftate for the Building of f^d^ meeting houfe; and to have Regard to Perfons of Honnour and UfefallNefs in S^d^ Precinct.

Voted that Whofoever Shall be admitted to Build Pews and they Shall Se Caufe to Difpofe of them or Leave them that the Precinct Paying the First Cost of Building the Pews Shall have them; and the Difpofsing of them again.

Put to Vote Whether the Precinct will Now att this Meetting Grant the sum of Twentifive Pounds to Pay the Reverend Mr Storer according to Contract; and to Pay others to Whom Money may Be due from fd. Precinct; and for the Further Finishing the Meeting houfe under the Galleries; and the Vote Pafsed in the affermitive.

Putt to Vote Whether the Precinct will adjorn this meeting to the Second Monday of Aprill Next Infuing at two of the Clock in the afternoon of s^d^ day to hear w^t^ the Comt^ee^ have done Relating to the Pews and then ye Vote Pafsed in the affermitive.

[13]

Att A Meeting, of the Inhabitance of the Easterly Precinct, in Watertown on Monday the 10th Day of Apprill, Anno Dom: 1727 by adjornment.

Put to Vote Whether the Report the Com^tee^ have Made Concerning the Building of Pews in the Meettinghoufe, be acceptable to the Precinct, and the Vote Past in the Negative.

Put to Vote Whether the Precinct, will Now Choofe a Com^tee^ to Draw a List of Forty Perfons, that thay Shall Think most Proper; to have Pews and Prefent to the Precinct for them, to Choofe Twenty out of, and the Vote Past in the Negative.

Put to Vote whether the Precinct, will Build Pews, at all, or No; Past in the Negative

Middlefex ſs.

To Mr Ephraim, Cutter Junr Conſtable of Watertown Greeting.

Sr You are Hereby Requiered Forthwith to Warn the Freeholders and other Inhabitance within sd Precinct in Sd Town who are Qualified to Vote in Precinct Affairs to Meet At the Pnblick Meeting houſe in Said Precinct on Monday the Second Day of October Next Infuing the Date hereof at Two of the Clock in the Afternoon of Sd Day for the Ends Following.

Viz: (1) To No the Minds of the Precinct Whether they will Agree Upon Purchaſing A More Convenient Place for A Perſonage or Ministeriall Place in sd Precinct.

(2) To No the Minds of the Precinct if they Should Agree to Purchaſe a more Convenient Ministeriall Place then whether the Precinct will be of the mind to sell the Preſent Ministeriall Place or any Part thereof to Pay Sd Purchaſe.

(3) To No if the Precinct Should Agree to Purchaſe & Sel as aforeſd if they will Chooſe A Comtee and Impower ſd Comtee to Mannage the affairs for and in Behalfe of ſd Precinct.

Hereof Fail Not But Make Return of this Order and Your Doings thereon to one of the Precinct Comtee or Clerk of sd Precinct At Least Four hours Before the Time of ſd Meeting.

Pr Order of the Precinct Comtee

Watertown Septm the 18th 1727 NATHll HARRIS Cler.

At A Meeting of the Inhabitants of the Easterly Precinct in Watertown on Monday the Second Day of October Anno Dom 1727

(1) Voted and Choſe for moderator Dea Nathan Fiske.

(2) Put to Vote whether the Precinct will Purchaſe a more Convenient Perſonage or Ministeriall Place for Sd Precinct & ye Vote Paſsed in the Affermitive.

(3) Put Vote Whether it Be the minds of the Precinct to Sell all the Preſent Ministeriall Place (Excepting the Marſh) to pay sd Purchaſe and the Vote Paſsed in the affermitive.

(4) Put to Vote Whether it Be the Minds of the Precinct to Chooſe A Committee to Mannage the Affair of Bying and Selling as aforeſd and the Vote Paſsed in ye affermitive.

(5) Put to Vote & Choſe for A Comtee Enſign Jonathan Stone, Mr William Shattuck Sergt Joſeph Coollidge, Dea John Coollidge, and Quartermaster Thomass Larnard.

(6) Put to Vote to no the Minds of the Precinct, if they will Impower the above sd Comtee to Sel; all the Preſent Ministeriall Place Excepting the marsh, and to Purchaſe a more Convenient Ministeriall Place for sd Precinct, Provided the Place sd Comtee Shall Purchaſe Cost not above one Hundred Pounds more then they shall Sell the Preſent Ministeriall Place for Excepting the marſh, and ye vote Paſsed in the affermitive.

[14]

To Nathll Harris Clerk of the Easterly Precinct in Watertown, You are Hereby Requiered & Ordered to Deliver to ye Aſsesors of s^d Precinct A Coppie of the Twenty-five Pounds; Granted by the Precinct Aforesd At there Meetting On the thirteenth Day of March Last Past for the Ends therein Mentioned; and Direct them to Assess the Inhabitance of S^d Precinct as the Law Directs Speedily; & to Commit the Rate or assessment, to Mr Daniel Bond the Present Collecton for S^d Precinct; With a Lawfull Warrant to Collect the Same: & to Issue & Make Up his Accompt with m^r Joseph Coollidge Precinct Treasurer or his Successor in S^d Office at or Before the First Day of December Next Insuing.

Watertown, October the 14th 1727.

THOMAS STRAIT
RICHARD COOLLIDGE } Com^tee

Middlesx

To Mr Joseph Coollidge Treasurer of the East Precinct in Watertown.

Sr You are hereby Ordered to Pay to the Reverend Mr Seth Storer the Sum of Sixteen Pounds out of the Twentyfive Pounds Rate Granted Pr S^d Precinct on the Thirteenth Day of March Anno Dom 1726/7 which is for the Compleating his Sallery According to Contract.

Also to Pay to Mr Joshua Grant Junr the Sum of Four Pounds and one Shilling. Allowed to him for Mending the Glace on the Meettinghouse in Sd Precinct.

Also to pay to Mr. Thomas Bond the Sum of Three Shillings for Warning one Precinct Meetting in the Year 1726.

Also to Pay to Mr Ephraim Cutter Junr the Sum of Six Shillings for warning Two Precinct Meeting in the Year 1727.

Also to Pay to Mr John Straton the Sum of Ten Shillings for making A Precinct Ra'

Also to Pay to Mr Nathaniel Bright the Sum of Ten Shillings for Making a Precinct Rate.

March the 11th 1727/8

₩ Order of s^d Precinct Comt^ee.
NATH^ll HARRIS Cler.

Middlesex ss

To Mr Ephraim Cutter Constable of Watertown, Greeting.

Sr You are Requiered hereby Forthwith To Warn the Freeholders and Other Inhabitance Within the Easterly Precinct in S^d Town Who Are Quallified to Vote in Precinct Affairs To Meet At the Publick Meettinghouse in S^d Precinct On Monday the Eleventh Day of March Next Insuing the Date hereof At Two of the Clock in the Afternoon of Said Day for the Ends Following.

Viz First. To Choose A Precinct Committee To Mannage the Prudentialls of s^d Precinct, A Clerk and other Officers Nessasery & Propper to be Chosen.

Secondly, to Take Effectuall Care That there be Money Raised for the Ministers Sallary According to Contract and also for others to Whom Money May Due from the Precinct.

Thirdly. To hear the Com^tees Accompt that was Chosen for the Building & Finishing the Meetinghouse, on Scoolhous hill, And if it be Needfull to Make Some Additionall Grants of Money for the Further Finishing of the s[d] Meettinghoufe.

Fourthly, to Take Care & Agree with the Sexton that May be Chofe for s[d] Precinct.

Hereof Fail Not But Make Return of this Order & Your Doings thereon to one of the Com[tee] or Clerk of s[d] Precinct at Least Four hour Before the Time for sd meeting.

P[r] Order of s[d] Precinct Com[tee]

Watertown February the 26th 1727/8. NATH[ll] HARRIS Cler.

[15]

Att A Meetting of the Freeholders & Other Inhabitance in the Easterly Precinct in Watertown, the 11th Day of March Anno Dom 1727/8 for the Election of Precinct Officers & Such Other Buifnefs as in Set Forth in the Warning of s[d] Meetting.

(1) Voted, and Chofe Deacon Nathan Fisk Moderator.

(2) Voted, and Chofe for A Standing Com[tee] to Mannage the Prudentialls of s[d] Precinct for this Prefent Year Dea Jofeph Mafon M[r] Thomas Bond, and Serg[t] Samuel Janifon.

(3) Voted, and Chofe for s[d] Precinct Clerk Nathaniel Harris.

(4) Voted and Chofe for sd Precinct Treafurer or Reciever M[r] Jofeph Coollidge.

(5) Voted and Chofe for s[d] Precinct Afsefsors { Nathaniel Bright. L[t] Richard Coolidge. Nath[ll] Harris.

(6) Voted and Chofe for Collector for s[d] Precinct for this Prefent Year Jonathan Stone Jun[r].

(7) Voted, and Chofe for Saxton for this Prefent Year M[r] Nath[ll] Shearmon.

(8) Voted, and Granted the sum of Twenty Pounds To Pay the Rev[d] M[r] Storer According to Contract & to Pay others to Whom Money May be due from s[d] Precinct.

(9) Voted & Excepted the Committees Accompt; that was Chofen for the Building & Furnishing the Meettinghoufe on Scoolhous hill So far as it is Finished.

(10) Voted & Granted the sum of Ten Pounds Two Shillings and Nine Pence to Ballance accompts with s[d] Committee for Building and Finishing s[d] Meetting houfe Together with the Arrearages that are in Collector Daniel Bonds Hands, and the arrearages in Collector John Hastingses Hand (Excepting, Seven Pounds Eighteen Shillings and Five Pence w[h] is not At Prefent Likely to be Collected.

(11) Voted & Granted the Sum of Five Pounds to Whitwash Point and Further Finish s[d] meetting houfe.

(12) Voted to Pay the Sexton by Two Contrabutions (Viz) one on the First Sabath in September Next and the other on the First Sabath in March Next.

[16]

To Nathaniel Harris Clerk of the Easterly Precinct in Watertown.

You are hereby Ordered Seafonably to Give out an order to the Conftables Dwelling Within the Limits of s[d] Precinct to Warn the Free holders And Other Inhabitance Who Are quallified to Vote in Precinct Affairs to Meet at the Publick Meettinghoufe in s[d] Precinct on the Tenth Day of June Next Infuing the Date hereof Att Eight of the Clock in the forenoon of f[d] Day for the Ends Following.

(1) To hear the Report of the Com[tee] that Ware Appointed by the Precinct to Make Sale of the Minnisterial Place that the Rev[d] M[r] Gibbs Lived in & alfo to Purchafe a More Convenient Place in Lew thereof for to be A Minnisteriall Place.

(2) To Know the Minds of the Precinct Whether the Reverend M[r] Storers Pofsession of the New Ministerial Place (Lately Bought of Dea: Jofeph Coolidge of Cambridge and M[r] Daniel Hastings of Watertown) Dureing the Time of his Being the Precincts Minister Should be Recorded on the Precincts Records & to be in Lew of the Pofsession which he had (by Agreement at his Settlement) of the Ministerial Place Lately Sold.

(3) To Know the Mind of the Precinct Whether they Will Make A Sutable Convenient Addition to the Ministerial houfe.

(4) To Know the Mind of the Precinct Whether they Esteem the Votes that Past at A Meetting of s[d] Precinct by Adjornment on the Tenth Day of Aprill 1727 Referring to the Pews Ware Good and Reguller.

SAMUEL JENIfON, } East Precinct Com[tee]
THOMAS BOND,
Watertown May the 27th 1728. JOfEPH MAfON.

Middlefex fs. To M[r] Jofeph Harrington Conftable of Watertown Greetting. S[r] You are hereby Requiered forthwith to Warn the Free holders & other Inhabitance Within the Easterly Precinct in s[d] Town Who Are Quallified to Vote in Precinct Affairs to Meet at the Publick Meetting houfe in s[d] Precinct on Monday the Tenth Day of June Next Infuing the Date hereof Att Eight of the Clock in the fore noon of s[d] Day for the Ends Following.

(1) To hear the Report of the Committee that Ware Apponted by the Precinct to Make Sale of the Ministeriall Place that the Rev[d] M[r] Gibbs Liv[d] in and alfo to Purchafe A More Convenient Place in Lew thereof to Be A Ministeriall Place.

(2) To Know the Minds of the Precinct Whether the Rever[d] M[r] Storer Pofsestion of the New Ministeriall Place Lately Bought of Dea Jofeph Coollidge of Cambridge and M[r] Daniel Hastings of Watertown Dureing the Time of his Being the Precincts Minister Should be Recorded on the Precincts Records & to be in Lew of the Pofsestion which he had by agreement At his Settlement of the Ministeriall Place Latly Sold.

(3) To Know the Minds of the Precinct Whether thay will Make a Sutable Convenient Adition to the Ministeriall houfe.

(4) To Know the Minds of the Precinct Whether they Esteem the Votes that Pafsed at a meetting of s^{d} Precint P^{r} adjornment on the Tenth Day of Aprill 1727 Refering To the Pews Ware Good & Reguliar.

Hereof Fail Not But Make Return of this order & of Your Doings thereon to one of the Comm^{tee} or Clerk of s^{d} Precinct at Least Four hours Before the Time for s^{d} Meetting.

Pr Order of the Com^{tee}
Watertown May ye 30th 1728. NATH^{ll} HARRIS Cler.

[17]

Att a Meetting of the Freeholders and Other Inhabitance of the Easterly Precinct in Watertown the Tenth Day of June Anno Dom 1728.

(1) Voted & Chofe For a Moderator Dea. Nathan Fisk.

(2) Voted & Accepted the Report the Com^{tee} Made that Ware appointed by the Precinct To Make Sale of the Ministeriall Place that the Revd Mr Gibbs Liv^{d} in and alfo to Purchafe A more Convenient One in Lew thereof, the sd Com^{tee} Reported as Followeth, that thay had Purchafed of Daniel Hastings late of Watertow^{n} and of Dea Jofeph Coollidge of Cambridge A Teniment in Watertown afore s^{d} Where Daniel Hastings Lately Dwelt Containing about Twenty one Acres of Land with the Buildings thereon, For the Sum of Four Hundred & Fifty Pounds & had Recieved a Deed of s^{d} Daniel Hastings of Two third Parts of s^{d} Place and a Deed of one third Part of s^{d} Place of Dea Jofeph Coollidge.

And, that they had Alfo Sold the Ministeriall Place that the Revd Mr Gibbs Liv^{d} in Excepting the Marfh to Doct^{r} Richard Checkley of Boston for the Sum of Three hundred & Fifty Pounds and had Given him a Deed thereof.

(3) Voted & Allowed the Com^{tee} the Sum of one Pound Five Shillings & Ten Pence for Writings in & about the Purchafing of the New Ministeriall Place.

(4) Put to Vote Whether the Precinct will allow s^{d} Com^{tee} the Sum of Seven Shillings and Six Pence for Writings in the Sale of the Former Ministeriall Place, Past in ye Negative.

(5) Voted & allowed Mr William Shattuck the Sum of Fifteen Shillings for Putting ye Sale of the Former Ministeriall Place into the Publick News Letter Three Times 5^{s} Each Time.

(6) Voted that the Rever^{d} Mr Storer Should have the Pofsestion of the New Ministeriall Place Lately Bought of Mr Daniell Hastings & Dea Jofeph Coollidge Dureing the Time of his Being the Precincts Minister in Lew of the Pofsestion which he had of the Ministeriall Place Lately Sold which he had by agreement at his Settlement.

(7) Voted that the Precinct Will Make A Sutable Adition to the New Ministeriall House.

(8) Put to Vote Whether it Be the Mind of the Precinct that the Addition to the Ministeriall houfe y^{t} was Latly Bought, Should be An End (with A Cellar Under it) Twenty four Feet in Lenth

and Eighteen feet in Breadth Faceing Easterly well Finished with a Chemney at the North End, and alfo to Raise the Leanter End to the height of the Rest of the houfe, and the Vote Pafsed in the Affermative.

(9) Put to Vote Whether the Precinct Will Choofe a Com^tee to Build & Finish s^d adition, and the Vote Paft in the Affermative.

(10) Voted And Chofe for a Com^tee to Mannage the affair of Building & Finishing the Adition to the Ministeriall houfe Lately Bought Lt Richard Coollidg Corn^tt Henry Bright & Serg^t Jonas Bond.

(11) Voted that it is the Minds of the Precinct that this Com^tee Acquaint the Proprietors Com^tee of the Ocation for Money to Make the adition to the Ministeriall houfe.

(12) Put to Vote Whether the Precinct Efteem the Votes that Past at a Meetting of s^d Precinct by adjornment on the Tenth Day of Aprill 1727 Refering to the Pews ware Good & Regaliar, and the Vote Past in the Negative.

[18]

To Nath^ll Harris Clerk of the Easterly Precinct in Watertown.

You are hereby Ordered to Diliver (or Show) to the afsefsors of s^d Precinct A Copy of the Grants of Money Made by s^d Precinct at their Meetting on the Eleventh Day of March Last Past for the Ends therein Mentioned And Direct them Speedily to Afsefs the inhabitance of s^d Precinct As the Law Directs And to Committ the Rate or Afsefsment to Mr Jonathan Stone Junr the Prefent Collector for s^d Precinct With A Lawfull Warrent to Collect the Same & to Pay in to the Precinct Treafurer Lt Jofeph Coollidge or to his Succefsor in s^d Office So as to Ifue & Make up an account of the Whole of s^d Afsefsment At or Before the Last Day or October Next Insuing ye Date Hereof.

SAMUEL JENIfON
THOMAS BOND
JOfEPH MAfON } Com^ee of the East Precinct in Watertown.

Watertown June the 12th 1728

To Nath^ll Harris Clerk of the East Precinct in Watertown. You are hereby Ordered Forthwith to Give An Order to Mr Jofeph Coollidge Treafurer of said Precinct To Pay out of the Grants of s^d Precinct Made the 11th Day of March Last Past & Committed To Mr Jonathan Stone Junr Collector to Collect Viz. To the Reverend Mr Seth Storer the Sum of Sixteen Pounds which is to Compleat his Sallary According to Contract.

To the Com^tee for Building & Finishing the Meetting houfe in s^d Precinct or their Order the Sum of Ten Pounds Two fhillings & Nine Pence To Ballance s^d Com^tees Accompts And To s^d Com^tee the Sum of Five Pounds w^h was Granted to Whitewash Point And further Finish s^d Meetting houfe.

To Conftable Ephraim Cutter the Sum of Three Shillings for Warning one Precinct Meetting.

To Joseph Harrington Constable the Sum of Three Shillings for Warning one Precinct Meetting.

To L[t] Richard Coollidge the Sum of Eight Shillings & Nine Pence To M[r] Nath[ll] Bright the Sum of Eight Shillings & Nine Pence and To Nath[ll] Harris the sum of Eight Shillings & Nine Pence it Being for their Making the Last Precinct Rate.

Watertown January 27th 1728/9 — THOMAS BOND, JOSEPH MASON } Precinct Com[tee]

To M[r] Joseph Coollidge Treasurer of the Easterly Precinct in Watertown.

S[r] You Are Hereby Ordered to Pay to the Reverend M[r] Seth Storer the Sum of Sixteen Pounds (: out of the Grants of Money Granted the 11th Day of March Last Past & Commited to M[r] Jonathan Stone Collector to Collect) which is to Compleat his Sallary According to Contract.

To the Committee for Building & Finishing the Meetting house in s[d] Precinct the Sum of Ten Pounds Two Shillings and Nine Pence to Ballance s[d] Com[tee] Accompts :- And to s[d] Com[tee] the Sum of Five Pounds which was Granted to Whitewash Point and Further Finish s[d] Meetinghouse.

To Constable Ephra Cutter the Sum of Three Shillings for Warning one Precinct Meetting.

To Constable Joseph Harrington the Sum of Three Shillings for Warning one Precinct Meeting.

To L[t] Richard Coollidge the Sum of Eight Shillings and Nine Pence To M[r] Nath[ll] Bright the Sum of Eight Shillings & Nine Pence and to Nath[ll] Harris the Sum of Eight Shillings and Nine Pence it Being for their makeing the Last Precinct Rate ℘ order of s[d] Precinct Com[tee]. NATH[ll] HARRIS Clerk.

[19]

Watertown Feb : 29th 1728/9

To Nathaniel Harris Clerk of the Easterly Precinct in Watertown.

You are Hereby Ordered to Write An Order or Warrant & Direct it to M[r] Joseph Harrington Constable for s[d] Towne Who dwells Within s[d] Precinct in the Words Following.

You are Hereby Ordered & Requiered Forthwith to Warn the Freeholders and Other Inhabitants Within the Easterly Precinct in Watertown Who Are Quallified According to Law to Vote in Precinct Affairs to Meet Att the Publick Meetting house in s[d] Precinct On Thirsday the 6th Day of March Next at one of the Clock in the Afternoon of s[d] Day for the Ends Following.

First, To Choose Such Precinct Officers as by Law Are Requiered to be Chosen in the Month of March.

Secondly to hear the Proposalls of the Com[tee] (Who ware Chosen and Impowered to Erect A New Addition to the Ministeriall house) for the makeing the Addition to the Ministeriall house More Convenient and accommodateing And to Know the

Minds of the Precinct Whether they Will Alter the Former Scheme they Layed for s[d] Addition and Come into A New Scheme for the Better Accomodateing & Makeing and making the Ministeriall houſe More Convenient.

Thirdly to hear the Pettition of Sundry of the Inhabitance of ſ[d] Precinct with Reſpect to the Vacant Room Under the Gallaries And on Both Sids the Pullpitt in the Meettinghouſe Above s[d] & to Know the Minds of the Precinct on s[d] Affair

Fourthly to Grant Such a Sum of Money as is Sofitient to Compleat the Reverend M[r] Seth Storer Sallary According to Contract & to Pay Such Perſons as y[e] Precinct Are Indebted to.

You Are Alſo Required to Notifie Such Perſons as the Precinct Are Indebted to to Bring in An Accompt of their Credit to the Precinct Com[tee] on Thursday the Forth Day of March Next at four of the Clock in the Afternoon of Said Day at the houſe of M[r] Thomas Bonds.

Sam[ll] Janiſon
Thomas Bond
Joſeph Maſon
Precinct Comt[ee]

Middleſx : ſs.

To M[r] Joſeph Harrington Constable of Watertown Greeting S[r] You Hereby Requiered forthwith to Warn the Freeholders and Other Inhabitance with in the Easterly Precinct in Watertown who Are Quallified to Vote in Precinct Affairs to Meet at the Publick Meetting houſe in s[d] Precinct on Thursday the Sixth Day of March Next at one of the Clock in the Afternoon of s[d] Day for the Ends Following (1) to Chooſe Such Precinct Officers as by Law are Required to be Choſen in the Month of March (2) To hear the Propoſalls of y[e] Comm[tee] (Who Ware Choſen & Impowered to Erect a New Addition to the Ministeriall house) for the Makeing the Addition to the ministeriall houſe more Convenient and Accommodateing and to Know the Minds of the Precinct Whether they will Alter the Former Scheme Laid for ſ[d] Addition and Come into a New Scheme for the Better Accommodateing & Makeing the Ministeriall houſe more Convenient (3) To Grant Such a Sum of money as is Sofitient to Compleat the Revend M[r] Seth Storers Sallery according to Contract and to Pay others that the Precinct are Indebted to: (4) To hear the Petition of Sundry of the Inhabitance of s[d] Precinct With Reſpect to the Vacant Room under the Gallarys & on Both ſ[d] the Pulpit in y[e] meeting houſe aboves[d] & to Know the mind of the Precinct on ſ[d] affair. You are alſo Requiered to Notifie Such Persons as y[e] Precinct are Indebted to to Bring in an Accompt of their Credits to the Precinct Com[tee] on Thirsday the Forth of march Next at the houſe of M[r] Thomas Bonds at Four of the Clock in the afternoon of s[d] Day. Hereof

[20]

Hearof Fail Not But Make Return of this Order And Your Doings Thereon to one of the Comm^tee or Clerk of s^d Precinct at Least four hours Before the Time of s^d Meetting.

Pr Order of the Comm^tee

Watertown Feb: the 19th 1728/9 NATH^ll HARRIS Clerk.

Att A meetting of the Freeholders & Other Inhabitance of the Easterly Precinct in Watertown Who ware Quallified to Vote in Precinct Affaires on the Sixth Day of March Anno Dom: 1728/9.

(1) Voted and Chofe for moderator Cornit Henry Bright

(2) Voted and Chofe for a Standing Com^tee to Mannage the Prudentialls for S^d Precinct for this Prefent Year Mr Samuel Pirce Mr John Stearns & Mr Jonas Bond.

(3) Voted and Chofe for Precinct Clerk Nath^ll Harris.

(4) Voted and Chofe for Precinct Treafurer or Reciver Lt Joseph Coollidge.

(5) Voted and Chofe for afsefsors for this Prefent Year { Jofeph Holden, Ebenezer Goddard, Henry Bond.

(6) Voted and Chofe for Collector for this Prefent Year Mr Thomas Coollidge.

Put to Vote Whether the Precinct will Choofe another Collector the Vote Pafsed in the Negative.

(7) Voted and Chofe for Saxton for this Prefent Year Mr Nath^ll Shearmon.

(8) Voted and Granted the Sum of Twenty Pounds to Pay the Revd Mr Storer to Compleat his Sallery according to Contract: and to Pay Others to Whom money may be Due from s^d Precinct.

(9) Voted that the Precinct will Come into the Propofalls of the Com^tee appointed for the Erecting an addition to the Ministeriall Houfe: the s^d Propofalls Being as Followeth,

Watertown March the 5th 1728/9

Viz: That the Frame for the addition to the Ministereall houfe be of the Following Dementions (viz) 25 feet in Length & 24 feet in Wedth the Posts be 16 Feet in Lenth the Chemney to Stand on the West Side of the Building & to have an entry Way of Seven Feet Wide Betwixt the Old Building and the New: for the accomodating the Stareway into ye Chamber, And Further it is Propofed that the Roof on the Front of the Old Building be Raifed So as to Conform to the New Building or addition (which will make a Very Hanfom and Commodious Front Both East and South, and Further that the Leantor or Kichen that is to be Raifed be Raifed to Such a heigth as to Conform to the Other Parts of the Building and to accommodate the Chamber Over the Kichen that their be Built a Small Chemney in s^d Chamber: and that the Whole be well Finished in the Moft Prudent Way and Manner With all Speed.

(10) Putt to Vote Whether the Precinct will act any thing at this meetting Relateing to the Improveing the Vacant Room Under the Gallerys and on Both fids the Pulpitt in the Meetting-houfe in s^d Precinct & the Vote Pafsed in the Affermative.

[21]

(11) Put to Vote Whether the Precinct Will Improve s^d Vacant Room With Pews and the Vote Pafsed in the Affermative.

(12) Put to Vote Whether the Precinct Will Adjorn this Meetting to Friday the 14th of March Current at Two of the Clock in the afternoon of s^d Day and the Vote Pasted in the Affermative.

Att A Meetting of the Easterly Precinct in Watertown the 14th of March Anno Dom 1728/9 by adjornment at Two of ye Clock in ye afternoon of s^d day.

(1) Fut to Vote Whether the Precinct Will Erect & build A Pew for the Reverend Mr Storer (Where he Shall Choofe the Same) & for his Succefsors in the Ministry and the Vote Pafsed in the Affermitive.

(2) Put to Vote Whether the Precinct as a Precinct Will Build Pews in the Remaining Vacancy under the Gallarys & on Each Side of the Pulpitt (Convenient Allyes Excepted) and Difpofe of them as they Shall Think Fitt: the Vote Paft in ye Negative.

(3) Put to Vote Whether it Be the Minds of the Precinct to Choofe A Com^tee of Five Men to Difpofe of s^d Vacant Room Under the Callarys & on Each fide of the Pulpitt (Convenient Alley Room Excepted as aforefaid) Pews to Perticular Perfons they the f^d Perfons Building the Same; under fuch Reftrictions & Limitations as the Precinct Shall Think Proper the Vote Pafed in ye affermative.

(4) Put to Vote Whether f^d Com^tee in the Difpofalls of s^d Room Shall have Due and Strict Regard to mens Reall & Perfonall Eftates w^h they now Pofsefs in Fee Simple Within the Bounds & Limits of s^d Precinct the Vote Pafed in ye affermative.

(5) Put to Vote Whether the s^d Com^tee Shall have A fortnight to Difpofe of the s^d Room to Perfons tht the Com^tee Shall Think they Belong to under the afores^d Limitations and that if the Perfons to Whom Pews are offered, Shall not See Caufe to Except of the Same Within a Week after they are Offered that the Com^tee Shall Give them to Perfons to Whom they Mextly Belong to and the Vote Pafsed in the Affermative.

(6) Put to Vote Whether the Perfons that Shall Except of the Refpective Placess Offered them Shall be Obliged to Build their Pews Within One Quarter of a Year and Whether if they Shall Neglect to Build them Within s^d Term the s^d Room and the Difpofall thereof shall Return to the Precinct Again the Vote Pafed in the Affermative.

(7) Put to Vote Whether that if Perfons that have Pews Shall fel & Dipofe of their Estates in s^d Precinct their Pews Shall Return to the Precinct the Vote Past in ye Affermative.

(8) Voted that thofe Perfons that Accept of A Pew & Build the Same Shall be Obliged to Set in the Same Perfonally.

(9) Voted & Chofe Five men to be a Com^tee^ to manage the affair of s^d^ Pews (Viz) Quat^r^ Thomas Larned Cor^l^ Henry Bright Jonathan Stone Junr Edward Harrington and Jofeph Holding.

(10) Voted & Chofe Mr Oliver Livermore Collector for ye year Infuing in Thomas Coollidgs ftead

(11) Voted & Granted the fum of Three Pounds to Build ye Revd Mr Storers Pew.

[22]

To Nath^ll^ Harris Clerk of the Easterly Precinct in Watertown You are Hereby Ordered to Give Out An Order to the Constable Within s^d^ Precinct to Warn the Freeholders and Other Inhabitance Within s^d^ Precinct Who Are Quallified to Vote in Precinct Affars to Meett Att the Publict Meetting houfe in s^d^ Precinct On Monday the 14th of Aprill Current At one of the Clock in the Afternoon of f^d^ Day for the Ends Following.

(Viz) 1 To Hear the Pettitions of Sundry of the Inhabitance of s^d^ Precinct Concerning the Vacant Room in the Meetting in s^d^ Precinct Under the Gallaries & On Each side of the Pulpitt that hath lately Bin Lotted into Pew Lotts; the Pettitioners Being the Perfons to Whom Pew Lotts Ware allotted to.

(2) For the Precinct to Proceed & Difpofe of the afores^d^ Vacant Room as they Shall Apprehend Will Conduce Most to the Peace and Comfort of s^d^ Precinct if they Pleafe.

Watertown Aprill the 4th 1729

JOHN STEARNS
SAM^ll^ PIRCE
JONAS BOND } Precinct Com^tee^

Middfx fs To Mr Jofiah Perrey Conftable of Watertown Greeting. Sr You are hereby Requiered Forthwith to Warn the Freeholders and Other Inhabitance Within the Easterly Precinct in Watertown Who are Quallified to Vote in s^d^ Precinct Affairs to meet att the Publict Meetting houfe in Said Precinct On Monday the 14th of Aprill Current At one of the Clock in the Afternoon of s^d^ Day for the Ends Following (Viz)

(1st) For the Precinct to hear the Pettition of Sundry of the Inhabitance of s^d^ Precinct Concerning the Vacant Room in the Meetting houfe in s^d^ Precinct Under the Gallaries & on Each fide of the Pulpitt, that hath Lately Bin Lotted into Pew Lotts the Pettititioners Being the Perfons to Whom Pew Lotts Ware Allotted to.

(2) For the Precinct to Proceed & Difpofe of the afores^d^ Vacant Room as they Shall apprehend will Conduce most to the Comfort & Peace of s^d^ Precinct if they Pleafe. Hearof Fail Not But make Return of this Order & Your Doings thereon to one of the Com^tee^ or Clerk of s^d^ Precinct At Least Four hours Before the Time of s^d^ Meetting.

℘ Order of the Com^tee^
NATH^ll^ HARRIS, Clerk.

Watertown Aprill the 4th 1719.

Watertown Aprill the 14th 1729.

Att A metting of the Freeholders & Other Inhabitance within the Easterly Precinct in Watertown Who Ware Quallified to Vote in Precinct affairs.

(1) Voted & Chofe for Moderator for sd Meetting Cornitt Henry Bright.

(2) Voted that Whereas Jonathan Stone Junr Edward Harrington & Oliver Livermore have Bin at Cost and Charge in Laying a Platform for Three Pews in the Meetting houfe in sd Precinct that if the sd Precinct Should Build Pews thereon as a Precinct or that sd Platform Should be Difpofed of to any Other Perfons that they shall have Reafonable Pay for What they have Expended On sd three Pew Lotts.

Put to Vote and Voted that the Precinct will adjorn this meetting to Monday the 21st Inftant at one of the Clock in the afternoon of sd Day.

[23]

At A Meetting of the Freeholders & Other Inhabitance of the Easterly Precinct in Watertown on the Twentyfirst Day of Aprill Anno Dom 1729 by adjornment.

Put to Vote Whether the Precinct Will Choofe A Comtee of Three or five men to Search the Lists of Rates and Find thofe Perfons that have Paid most to ye Building the Meetting houfe in sd Precinct; and that thofe Perfons Shall Draw Pews Succesively According to wt they have Paid; Allowing But Two heads or Polls to Any (one) Estate. Where it Happens that there is more; and Where the Fathers are Difcafed their Children or Nattural heirs to Draw according to What the Fathers have Paid or Caufe to Be Paid or their Estates have Paid Since their Deceafe. And the Vote Past in the Affermative.

Put to Vote Whether the Precinct Will Choofe A Comtee of Five men to Search the Lists of Rates upon the affair of the Pews as aforesd and Any three of them Agreeing to be Difcisive and the Vote Passed in the Affermative.

Voted and Chofe For A Comtee to Search the Lists of Rates Concerning the Drawing of Pews as aforsd Cort Henry Bright Dea Jofeph Mason Nathll Harris Mr Samuel Pirce and Lt Jofeph Coollidge.

Put to Vote Whether the Precinct are of the Mind that after the above Said Comtee have Searhed the Lists of Rates aforesd, and Found out thofe Persons Who Are the highest in sd Lists Who According to the Vote of the Precinct are to Draw the Pew Lotts, that if any of sd Perfons Shall not Accept of a Pew Lot that the Comtee Shall then Offer them, that then the Lot or Lotts so Refused, to be Offered by sd Comtee to the Next Highest Perfons Successively as they Stand in sd Rates; and that A Plan of the Pew Lotts be Drawn by sd Comtee and that Every Person that Accepts of a Pew Lott Shall fet his Name in the Spot he Shall Choofe and that Every Perfon that Accepts of a Pew Lot Shall be Obliged to Build his Pew Within three Months at Furthest from the Date hereof, or Forfit his Pew Lot to the Hands of the Precinct again to be Difpofed of by the aboves^{d} Com^{tee} as if s^{d} Perfons had Refused; and that Every Perfon that Accepts of a Pew Lot and Builds a Pew Shall be Obliged to fet Perfonally therein, And if any Perfon Perfons Shall See Caufe to Difpofe of his or their Pew that the Precinct Shall have the Refusall Paying the Prime Cost.

And that after the Com^{tee} have Compleated the Plan aboves^{d} according to the Votes of the Precinct that Said Plan Be Recorded in the Precinct Book of Records, as a Finall Settlement of s^{d} Pew Lotts; the Vote Past in the affermative.

Put to Vote and voted that the Negative Votes that have Pased at this Meetting Shall not Be Recorded in the Precinct Book of Records.

[24]

To Nath^{ll} Harris Clerk of the Easterly Precinct in Watertown You are hereby Ordered to Give out An order to Jofiah Perry Constable to Warn the Freeholders & Other Inhabitance who are Quallified to Vote in Precinct Affairs according to Law: to meet At the Publict Meetting houfe in s^{d} Precinct on the 5th Day of May Next at Two of the Clock in the afternoon of s^{d} Day for the Ends Following,

(1) For the Precinct to Choofe A Com^{tee} of Five Men & Impower them to go through with the Service Relating to the Difpofall of the Pew Lotts in the meetting houfe in s^{d} Precinct which the Com^{tee} that was Chofen by the Precinct Att their Meetting on the 21st of Aprill Current by adjournment Declined to Perform and go through with.

(2) That Whereas the Precinct at their meetting afores^{d} Voted that their Com^{tee} Should Scearch the Lists of Rates for Building the Meettinghoufe and that Perfons Should Draw Pews according to w^{t} they have Paid: that the Precinct would manifest w^{t} Perticular Rates they will have their Com^{tee} Scearch for their Rule to Act by, that their by they may Prevent Conterary Opinions in their Com^{tee} And Whereas by s^{d} Vote the Children of Deceafed Fathers were to Draw Pews According to w^{t} their Fatheirs have Paid: that if s^{d} Children Should not agree when a Pew Lot is Offered within a week after s^{d} Offer is made then s^{d} Pew Lot to Return to the Precinct Again for their Com^{tee} to Difpofe of to one of s^{d} Children which they shall Think ought In Justice to have the Same.

(3) For the Precinct to hear Mr Jonathan Stone Junr Accompt and Mr Edward Harringtons and Mr Olliver Livermors for Laying the Platform for Three Pews in the meetting houfe and for the Precinct to Take Care how they shall be Paid and order the Constable to Notifie Mr Jonathan Stone Mr Edward Harrington & Mr Olliver Livermore to Bring in there accompts to ye Precinct at s^{d} Meetting.

Watertown Aprill 28th 1729:

JOHN STEARNS } Precinct
JONAS BOND } Com^{tee}

Middlefx fs

To Mr Jofiah Perry Constable of Watertown Greetting. Sr You are Hereby Requiered Forthwith to Warn the Freeholders and Other Inhabitance of the Easterly Precinct in Watertown Who Are Quallified to Vote in Precinct Affairs to Meett at the Publict Meetting houfe in sd Precinct On Monday the 5th Day of May Next at Two of the Clock in the Afternoon of sd Day for the Ends Following.

(1) For the Precinct to Chofe a Comtee of Five Men and Impower them to go through with the Service Relating to the Difpofall of the Pew Lotts in the meetting houfe in sd Precinct wn the Comtee that was Chofen at the meetting of the Precinct the 21st of Aprill Current by adjornment. Declined to Perform and go through with.

(2) That Whereas the Precinct Voted At their Meetting aforesd that their Comtee Should search the Lists of Rates and thofe that stood Highest in sd Lists and had Paid Paid most to the Building the meetting houfe should Draw Pews Successively according to wt they have Paid, that the Precinct may Mennafest wt Perticuliar Lists of Rates they would have their Comte Search for their Rule to Act by that thereby they may Prevent Conterary Opinions in their Comtee and whereas by sd Vote the Children of Deceafed Fathers Should Draw Pews According to wt their Fathers have Paid that if sd children should not agree within a Weak after they have the offer of a Pew Lot and Except of the Same yt sd Pew Lot to Return to the Precinct again for their Comtee to Difpofe of it to one of sd Children wh they shall Think ought in Justice to have the same.

(3) for the Precinct to hear Mr Jonathan Stone Junr Mr Edward Harringtons & Mr Oliver Livermors accompt for laying a Platform for three Pew Lotts & to Take Care how they shall be Paid for ye fame. You are also to notifie sd Jonathan Stone, Edward Harrington & Oliver Livermore to Lay their accompts Before the Precinct at sd meetting, hearof fail not But make Return of this order and your Doings thereon to one of the Comtee or Clerk of sd Precinct at Least four hours Before the Time of sd meetting.

P order of the Comtee NATHll HARRIS Clerk.

Watertown Aprill 28th, 1729.

[25]

Att A Meetting of the Freeholders & other Inhabitance of the Easterly Precinct in Watertown May the 5th anno Dom 1729 Who were Quallified to Vote in Precinct affairs.

(1) Voted and Chofe for Moderator Mr Thomas Strait.

(2) Put to Vote Whether the Precinct Will Act upon the Warrant by wh this meetting was Warned and the Vote Past in the Affermative.

(3) Put to Vote Whether the Precinct will Act upon the First Article in the Warrent of this Meetting and the Vote Past in the Affermative.

This Alley to be 3

East Precinct in Watertown
June the 17th 1729.

Those Persons Whose Names are on this Plan and Prefixt in the Severall Pew Spotts are thee Persons that have Accepted of the Severall Pew Spotts to which they have affixed their Severall Names agreeable & Conformable to the Vote of the Precinct abovesd for Settling sd Pew Spotts

Certified Under Our Hands the Day and Date above said

and nine Inches.

Jonas Bonds

Joshua Bigelow

Thomas Lewis
Henry Bright
Joseph Mason
John Hastings
} Comm: tee

East Door

John Hunter

Three foot Alley

Gallery Stairs

Henry Bright

John Moore

Samuell Benjamin

(4) Voted and Choſe for a Comtee to go through wth the Service Relating to the Diſpoſall of the Pew Lotts in the meetting houſe in sd Precinct as Set Forth in the first article in the Warrent for sd meetting Deacon Joſeph Maſon Cort Henry Bright Sert Jonas Bond Sergt John Hastings and Quatr Master Thomas Larnard.

(5) Put to Vote Whether the aforesd Comtee Shall Search all the Lists of Rates that they Can Find for their Rule to Act by and the Vote Past in the Negative.

(6) Put to Vote Whether the Comtee aforesd Shall Search the List of Rates for Building the Meetting houſe that was Comted to Constable William Shattuck and the Two Lists of Rates Committed to Collector John Hastings to Collect: for their Rule to Act by and the Vote Past in the affermative.

(7) Put to Vote Whether the Precinct will act on that Part of the Second Article in sd Warrent Relating to the Children of Deceaſed Fathers and the Vote Past in the Negative.

(8) Put to Vote & Voted that thoſe Perſons that May have thoſe Platforms Allotted to them; that Mr Jonathan Stone Junr Mr Edward Harrington and Mr Oliver Livermore Layed upon three Pew Lotts for three Pews in the meettinghouſe: Shall Pay them (viz Jonathan Stone Edward Harrington and Oliver Livermore) Reaſonably; According to the Vote of the Precinct.

To Nathaniel Harris Clerk of the Easterly Precinct in Watertown. You are Hereby Ordered to Diliver (or ſhow) to the Aſseſsors of sd Precinct A Coppy of the Grants of Money Made by sd Precinct At there Meetting on the ſixth Day of March Last Past for the Ends therein Mentioned & Direct them Speedily to Aſseſs the Inhabitance of sd Precinct as the Law Directs and to Committ the Rate or Aſseſsment to Mr Oliver Livermore the Preſent Collector for sd Precinct With A Lawfull Warrent to Collect the ſame, and to Pay into the Precinct Treaſurer Lt Joſeph Coollidge or his ſucceſsor in sd Office So as to Iſue and Make up An Accompt of the Whole of sd Aſseſsment Att or Before the Fourth Day of December Next Inſuing the Date Hereof

Watertown November the 8th 1729

Samll Pearce
John Stearns
Jonas Bond
} Precinct Commtee

[26] [Plan of seats in meeting house.]

[27]

To Nathll Harris Clerk of the Easterly Precinct in Watertown. You Are hereby Ordered to Give Out An Order Forthwith to Lt Joſeph Coollidge Treaſurer for sd Precinct to Pay out of the Grants of Money Made by sd Precinct the ſixth Day of March Last Past and Committed to Mr Oliver Livermore Collector to Collect.

To the Reverd Mr Seth Storer the Sum of Sixteen Pounds to Compleat his Sallary According to Contract.

To Mr Joſeph Holding Mr Ebenezer Goddard & Mr Henry Bond One Pound Six Shillings And Three Pence (viz) the Sum of Eight Shillings and Nine Pence Each of them for Makeing one Precinct Rate.

To Mr Joseph Harrington for Warning one Precinct Meetting three Shillings.

To Mr Josiah Perry the Sum of Six Shillings for Warning Two Precinct Meettings.

To Mr Edward Harrington the Sum of One Pound & Ten Shillings in Part for Building the Reverd Mr Storers Pew.

To the Heirs of Thomas Larned Deceasd; the Sum of One Pound & Ten Shillings in Part for the Building the Reverd Mr Storers Pew.

To Mr Joshua Grant Junr the Sum of Two Pounds Four Shillings & Nine Pence for Mending the Glass on the Meetting house in s^d^ Precinct.

Also to Pay to Mr Joshua Grant the Sum of one Pound Two Shillings & Seven Pence out of the Grant of Money made by s^d^ Precinct on the 11th Day of March annoque Dom 1727/8 w^h^ was Committed to Mr Jonathan Stone to Collect.

Watertown January the 6th 1729/30

JOHN STEARNS
JONAS BOND
SAM^ll^ PIRCE
} Precinct Com^tee^

To Lt Joseph Coollidge Treasurer for the East Precinct in Watertown Sr You are Hereby Ordered to Pay to the Reverd Mr Seth Storer the Sum of Sixteen Pounds (out of the Grants of Money Granted the 6th Day of March Last Past and Committ^d^ to Mr Oliver Livermore Precinct Collector to Collect) w^h^ is to Compleat his Sallary According to Contract.

To Mr Joseph Holding the sum of Eight shillings and Nine Pence: to Mr Ebenezer Goddard the sum of Eight Shillings & nine Pence & Also to Mr Henry Bond the Sum of eight Shillings & nine Pence for making One Precinct Rate.

To Mr Joseph Harrington the sum of Three shillings for Warning one Precinct Meetting.

To Mr Josiah Perry the Sum of Six Shillings for Warning Two Precinct Meettings.

To Mr Edward Harrington the sum of one Pound & Ten in Part for Building the Reverd Mr Storers Pew.

To the Heirs of Thomas Larnard Deceased the sum of One Pound & Ten Shillings in Part for Building the Reverd Mr Storers Pew.

To Mr Joshua Grant Junr the sum of Two Pounds four Shillings and nine Pence for Mending the glass on the Meetting house in s^d^ Precinct also to Pay to Mr Joshua Grant the Sum of One Pound Two Shillings & Seven Pence out of the Grant of Money Made by s^d^ Precinct on the 11th Day of march anno Dom 1727/8 w^h^ was Committed to Mr Jonathan Stone to Collect.

Watertown January the 6th 1729/30

℘ Order of the Precinct Com^tee^ NATH^ll^ HARRIS Cler.

[28]

To Nath^ll Harris Clerk of the Easterly Precinct in Watertown. You Are Hereby Ordered to Give out An Order Forthwith to Mr Josiah Perry Constable of s^d Watertown to Warn the Freeholders and Other Inhabitance in s^d Precinct Who Are Quallified to Vote in Precinct Affairs to Meet at the Publict Meettinghouse in s^d Precinct on Fryday the Sixth Day of March Next at one of the Clock in the afternoon of s^d Day for the Ends Following.

Viz First, To Choose a Precinct Committee A Precinct Clerk Assessors & other Precinct Officers Nessasary to be Chosen as the Law Directs, & Requiers:

Secondly, To Grant A sofitient sum of money to Pay the Revd Mr Storer According to Contract & to Pay others to Whom Money may be Due from s^d Precinct.

Thirdly, For the Precinct to hear the Pettition of Sam^ll Barnerd John Orms and Sundry Others of the Inhabitance of s^d Precinct, Relateing to the Seatting the Meetting house in s^d Precinct and Repairing of Glase in s^d Meettinghouse and that the Precinct May Act thereupon as they shall see Meett.

Dated att Watertown afore the 20th Day of February Anno Dom 1729/30

JOHN STEARNS } Precinct
SAM^ll PIRCE } Com^tee
JONAS BOND }

To Nath^ll Harris Clerk of the Easterly Precinct in Watertown. You Are Hereby Ordered to Give out An Order Forthwith to Lt Joseph Coollidge Treasurer of s^d Precinct to Pay to Mr Joshua Grant Junr the sum of Fourteen shillings Out of the Grants of Money Made by s^d Precinct the 11th Day of March 1727/8 and Committed to Mr Jonathan Stone Collector to Collect; for mending Glase in the meettinghouse in s^d Precinct.

Watertown March the 6th 1729/30

JOHN STEARNS } Precinct
JONAS BOND } Com^tee
SAM^ll PIRCE }

To Lt Joseph Coollidge Treasurer of the Easterly Precinct in Watertown, Sr You are hereby Ordered to Pay to Mr Joshua Grant Junr the sum of Fourteen shilling out of the Grants of Money Made by s^d Precinct on the 11th Day March 1727/8 and Committed to Mr Jon^a Stone Junr Collector for s^d Precinct to Collect: it Being for mending Glase in the Meetting house in s^d Precinct.

Watertown March the 6th 1729/30

p Order of the Precinct Com^tee
NATH^ll HARRIS Cler

Middsx ss.

To Mr Josiah Perry Constable of Watertown Greetting. Sr You are hereby Ordered Forthwith to Warn the Freeholders and other Inhabitance Within the Easterly Precinct in Watertown afores^d who are Quallified according to Law to Vote in Precinct affairs to meett at the Publict meettinghoufe in s^d Precinct on Fryday the Sixth Day of March Next at one of the Clock in the afternoon of s^d Day for the Ends Following (viz): 1: to Choofe a Precinct Com^tee A Precinct Clerk Afsefsors & other Precinct Officers Nefsafary to be Chofen as by Law Requiered. (2.) To Grant A Sofitient Sum of Money to Pay the Reverd Mr Storer According to Contract & to Pay others to Whom money may be Due from s^d Precinct. (3) for the Precinct to hear the Petition of Saml Bernard John Orms & Sundry others of the Inhabitance of s^d Precinct Relateing to the feating the meettinghoufe in s^d Precinct & for the maintaining Glafe in s^d meettinghoufe in s^d Precinct y^t s^d Precinct may act thereupon as they Shall See meet:

Hereof Fail not But make Return of this Order & your Doings thereon to one of the Com^tee or Clerk of s^d Precinct at Least Four hours Before the Time of s^d meetting ꝑ order of the Precinct Com^tee NATH^ll HARRIS Clerk.

Watertown February the 21st 1729/30

[29]

Att A Meetting of the Easterly Precinct in Wattertown the 6th Day of March Anno Domini 1729/30

(1) Voted and Chofe for Moderator for s^d Meetting Dea Jofeph Mafon.

(2) Voted and Chofe for a Standing Com^tee for the Infuing year Mr Oliver Livermore Mr Samuel Brown and Mr Jonas Bond.

(3) Voted and Chofe for Clark for f^d Precinct for the year Infuing Nath^ll Harris.

For Precinct Treafurer was Chofen Jofeph Coollidge

(4) For Afsefsors for the year Infuing } Ebenezer Goddard, Nath^ll Bright, Jofeph Holding.

(5) Voted and Chofe for Collector for the Year Infuing Mr Ebenezer Chenry.

(6) Voted and Chofe for fexton Mr Ebenezer Hastings.

(7) Voted that the fexton fhould be Payed by Two Free Contributions: viz: the First on the First Sabath in September and the fecond on the First Sabath in March.

(8) Voted and Granted the fum of Twenty Pounds to Pay the Revd Mr Storer according to contract and to Pay others to Whom Money May be Due from s^d Precinct.

(9) Put to Vote Whether the Precinct Will Act on the Pettition of Sam^ll Barnard John Orms and others Relating to the feating the meettinghoufe and Repairing Glafe and the Vote Past in the Negative.

To Nath^ll Harris Clerk of the Easterly Precinct in Watertown. You are Hereby Required to Give out an order Forthwith to Mr Ebenezer Stone Conftable of Watertown aforef^d to Warn the Freeholders & other Inhabitants Within the Easterly s^d Precinct who are Quallified to Vote in Precinct affairs to Meet at the Publict Meettinghoufe in s^d Precinct on Monday the 10th Day of August

Current at Two of the Clock in the afternoon of s^d^ Day for the Ends Following.

Viz) First To Know the Minds of the Precinct Whether they will Releafe their Com^tee^ that Was Chofen to make the addition to the ministeriall houfe & Choofe a New Com^tee^ to Proceed in s^d^ Work & Finish s^d^ Houfe.

Secondly, to Know the minds of s^d^ Precinct whether they will grant a sum of money for Mannageing s^d^ work & Finishing s^d^ Ministerial Houfe & how much they will Grant.

Thirdly, to hear the Return of the Com^tee^ Chofen to fell the Former Ministeriall Place and to Purchase the Prefent Ministeriall Place & how they Will Reward them for s^d^ fervice & Whether the Precinct Will Grant Money for that Purpofe:

Alfo to Notifie the Com^tee^ Chofen to Make the addition to the Ministeriall Houfe to Bring in there Accomps of w^t^ they have Done Relateing to s^d^ Houfe.

OLIVER LIVERMORE } Precinct
SAM^ll^ BROWN } Com^tee^

Watertown August the 3^d^ 1730

[30]

Middls ss

To Mr Ebenezer Stone, Conftable of Watertown Greetting, Sr You are Hereby Requiered Forthwith to Warn the Freeholders & other Inhabitance Within the Easterly Precinct of Watertown afores^d^ Who Are Quallified to Vote in Precinct Affairs to Meet At the Publict Meetting houfe in s^d^ Precinct On Monday the 10th Current, at Two of the Clock in the afternoon of s^d^ Day for the Ends Following.

First to Know the Minds of the Precinct Whether they Will Releafe their Com^tee^ that was Chofen to Make the Addition to the Ministeriall houfe, & Choofe a new Com^tee^ to Proceed in s^d^ Work and Finish s^d^ houfe.

Secondly to Know the Minds of s^d^ Precinct Whether they Will Grant A fum of Money for the Mannageing s^d^ Work & Finishing s^d^ Ministeriall houfe and how much they will Grant.

Thirdly to hear the Return of the Com^tee^ Chofen to fell the Former Ministeriall Place And to Purchase the Prefent Ministeriall Place, and how they will Reward them for f^d^ fervice; and Whether s^d^ Precinct Will Grant Money for that Purpofe.

Alfo You Are hereby Ordered to Notifie Lt Richard Coollidge, Cor^l^ Henry Bright, & Ser^t^ Jonas Bond Who Ware A Com^tee^ Chofen for to Make the addition to the Ministeriall houfe, to Bring in An Accompt to the Precinct of their Proceedings in that affair.

Hereof Fail Not but make Return of this Order with your Proceedings thereon to one of the Precinct Com^tee^ or Clerk of f^d^ Precinct at Least Four hours Before ye Time of s^d^ Meetting.

℘ Order of the Precinct Com^tee^

Watertown August the 3^d^ 1730 NATH^ll^ HARRIS Cler.

Att A Meetting of the Inhabitance of the Easterly Precinct in Watertown, the Tenth Day of August Annoque Dom 1730

(1) Voted & Chose for Moderator for sd Meeting Dea Joseph Mason.

(2) Put to Vote and Voted that the Precinct Will Release their Comtee Chosen to Make the Addition to the Ministerial House.

(3) Put to Vote & Voted that the Precinct Will Chose a New Comtee to Proceed in sd Work and to Finish sd Ministeriall house.

(4) Put to Vote Whether it be the Minds of the Precinct to Chose three Men for a Comtee for that Purpose and the Vote Past in the Affermative.

(5) Voted and Chose for sd Comtee Dea: Nathan Fisk Mr Oliver Livermore & Nathll Harris.

(6) Put to Vote Whether the Precinct Will At this Meetting Grant A sum of Money for to Finish the Ministeriall house & the Vote Past in ye affermative.

(7) Put to Vote Whether the Precinct Will adjorn this Meetting And the Remaining Buisness of the same to FryDay Next At Five of the Clock in the afternoon of sd Day: and their New Comtee in the Mean Time to View the Materialls of sd Ministeriall house & Report to the Precinct at their adjornment wt they Are apprehensive will be Needfull for the Finishing sd Ministeriall house And the Vote Past in the Affermative.

[31]

Att A Meeting of the Easterly Precinct of the Easterly Precinct in Watertown the 14th of August Annoque Dom 1730 by adjornment.

Put to Vote Whether the Precinct Will Grant the sum of Two Hundred Pounds to Pay the Arrearages: and for the Finishing the Ministeriall house in sd Precinct And the Vote Past in the Affermative.

Voted that the assessors for sd Precinct be Directed in there Warrent to the Collector to Order that the sd Sum of Two Hundred Pounds to be Collected & Payed in to the Precinct Treasurer by the First Monday of October Next Insuing. And that there Comtee Chosen for the Finishing sd Ministeriall house be Impowered to Draw sd Money Out of the Treasury as shall be Needfull for the Finishing sd Ministeriall house and Paying the arrearages.

Put to Vote Whether the Precinct Will at this Meetting Act Any thing Upon the Third Article of the Warning of sd Meetting And the Vote Past in the Negative.

Watertown, August the 17th 1730

To Nathll Harris Clerk of the Easterly Precinct in Watertown aforesd. You are Herby Ordered Forthwith to Give to the Assessors for sd Precinct A Coppie of the Grant of Money Made by sd Precinct the 6th Day of March Last Past, also a Coppie of the Grant of Money made by sd Precinct the 14th of August Current & Direct them speedily to assess the same upon the Inhabitance and

Ratable Estates in s^d Precinct as the Law Directs; and to Committ the s^d Rate or assessment to Mr Ebenezer Chenry Precinct Collector With A Lawfull Warrent to Collect the same, and to Pay in to Leu^t Joseph Coollidg or his successor in s^d Office so as to Issue and make up an accomt of the Whole of s^d assessments at or Before the First Monday of October Next Insuing.

JONAS BOND
OLIVER LIVERMORE } Precinct Com^{tee}
SAM^{ll} BROWN

To Nath^{ll} Harris Clerk of the Easterly Precinct in Watertown. You are Hereby Ordered to Give out an order to Mr Ebenezer Stone Constable of Watertown To Warn the Freeholders and Other Inhabitants in the Easterly Precinct in Watertown Who Are Quallified to Vote in Precinct Affairs to meet att the Publict Meettinghouse in the s^d Precinct On Fryday the Twelfth Day of march Next at one of the Clock in the afternoon on s^d Day for the Ends Following.

First to Choose a Precinct Com^{tee} Clerk and Other Precinct Officers Nessasary to be Chosen in the Month of march.

Secondly, that the Precinct may Grant a sofitient sum of money to Pay the Revd Mr Seth Storrer according to Contract and to Pay other to Whom Money may be Due from s^d Precinct.

Thirdly to Choose A Saxton and Take Care how he shall be Rewarded for his Labour.

Fourthly to Know the mind of the Precinct whether they will Take any Further Care to Preserve the Glase in the meetting house and whether it be there minds to make shutters or Barrs to Preserve the same and if it be there minds to Do any thing Further to Preserve said Glass to Grant money for the Preforming the same.

and also to Notifie the Precinct Creditors to bring in there accompts to the Com^{tee} at the house of Mr Larnerds on the Fifth Day of march Next at Four of the Clock in the afternoon of s^d Day.

OLIVER LIVERMORE
Watertown Feb : 22 : 1730/31 : SAM^{ll} BROWN } Com^{tee}
JONAS BOND

[32]

To Nath^{ll} Harris Clerk of the Easterly Precinct in Watertown. You are Hereby Ordered to Give out An Order to Lt Joseph Coollidge Treasurer of the Easterly Precinct in Watertown To Pay out of the Grants of money made by the Precinct on the sixth Day of March Last Past and Committed to Mr Ebenezer Chenry Collector to Collect s^d Grant Being Twenty Pounds.

To the Revd Mr Seth Storer the sum of sixteen Pounds to Compleat his Sallary According to Contract.

To Mr Ebenezer Goddard the sum of Fifteen shillings. To Mr Joseph Holding the sum of Fifteen shillings. to Mr Nath^{ll} Bright the sum of Fiften shillings for making Precinct Rates.

To Mr Ebenezer Stone the ſum of ſix ſhillings for Warning Two Precinct Meettings.

To Mr Ephraim Cutter Junr the ſum of one Pound and Nine ſhillings for mending Glaſs in the meetting houſe it Being in Part: &

Watertown March the 5th 1730/31	OLIVER LIVERMORE SAMll BROWN JONAſ BOND	Precinct Comtee

To Lt Joſeph Coollidge Treaſurer of the Easterly Precinct in Watertown, Sr Your are Hereby Ordered to Pay out of the Twenty Pound Grant of money made by the Precinct aforesd on the ſixth Day of march Last Past and Committd to Mr Ebenezer Chenry Collector to Collect.

Unto the Reverend Mr Seth Storer the ſum of ſixteen Pounds to Compleat his Sallary According to Contract.

To Mr Ebenezer Goddard the ſum of £0-15-0 To Mr Nathll Bright the ſum of £0 15-0. To Mr Joſeph Holding the ſum of £0:15:0: for making Precinct Rates.

To Mr Ebenezer Stone the ſum of ſix ſhillings for Warning Two Precinct meettings.

To Mr Ephraim Cutter Junr the ſum of One Pound and Nine ſhillings for mending Glaſs in the meetting houſe in sd Precinct: it Being in Part &c:

Watertown March the ſixth 1730/31

℘ Order of the Comtee of ſd Precinct.

NATHll HARRIS Clerk

Middlx ſs To Mr Ebenezer Stone Conſtable of Watertown, Greetting. Sr You are Hereby Ordered and Requiered Forthwith to warn the Freeholders and other inhabitants within the Easterly Precinct in Watertown Who are Qualified according to Law to Vote in Precinct affairs to meet at the Publict meetting houſe Within the ſd Precinct on Fryday the Twelfth Day of march Next at one of the Clock in the afternoon of ſd Day for the Ends Following.

First to Chooſe A Precinct Comtee Clerk & other officers Neſsaſary to be Choſen in the month of March.

Secondly for the Precinct to Grant a ſofitient ſum of money to Pay the Revd Mr Seth Storrer According to Contract and to Pay others to Whom money may be Due from ſd Precinct.

Thirdly to Chooſe a ſexton and to Take Care how he ſhall be Rewarded.

Forthly, to Know the minds of the Precinct Whether they will Take any Further Care to Preſerve the Glaſs on the meetting houſe in ſd Precinct: and Whether it be there mind to make Barrs or ſhuters to the Windows to Preſerve the ſame: and if it ſhould be there minds to Do Any thing Further to Preſerve ſd Glaſs to Grant money to Perform the ſame.

You are alſo to Notiſie the Precinct Creditors to Bring in there accompts to the Precinct Comtee at the houſe of Mr Larnerds on the Fifth Day of march Next at Four of the Clock in the afternoon of ſd Day: Hereof Fail Not But make Return of this order &

your Doing thereon to on of the Precinct Com^tee or to the Clerk of s^d Precinct at Least four Hour Before the Time of s^d meetting Watertown February the 22^d 1730/31

p^r Order of the Precinct Com^tee
NATH^ll HARRIS Cler.

[33]

Att A Meetting of the Freeholders and other Inhabitants of the Easterly Precinct in Watertown the Twelfth Day of march: 1730/31:

(1) Voted and Chose for Modderator for said Meetting Dea John Coollidge.

(2) Voted & Chose for a Standing Com^tee to mannage the Prudentialls for said Precinct the Insuing Year: Mr Josiah Perry Lt Joseph Coollidge and Mr Joseph Child.

(3) Voted and Chose for there Clerk Nath^ll Harris.

(4) Voted and Chose for Precinct Treasurer & Reciver Nath^ll Harris.

(5) Voted and Chose for Assesors for the Insuing Year } Samuel Brown, Oliver Livermore, Ebenezer Goddard.

(6) Voted and Chose for Precinct Collector James Barnard.

(7) Voted and Chose for sexton Ebenezer Hastings.

(8) Voted to Pay s^d sexton by Two Contributions as Usiall.

(9) Voted and Granted the sum of Thirty shillings to Mr Edward Harrington and Mrs Mary Larned in Full with what they Have Had for Building the Ministeriall Pew:

(10) Voted & Granted the sum of Four Pounds Twelve shillings and Ten pense to Pay Precinct Creddítors (viz) for Ephraim Cutter Junr seventeen shillings for John Brown four shillings for Isaac Child Ten shillings: for the Com^tee Mr Oliver Livermore Mr Sam^ll Brown and Mr Jonas Bond: the sum of Ten shillings it being for Hanging the Bell in the Publick meetting house. for Mr Willm Shattuck the sum of Fifteen shillings: for the Com^tee Imployed in the sale of the Old Ministeriall Place the sum of seven shillings & six pence, for Josiah Perry three shillings for Warning one Precinct meetting. for Dea John Coollidge Twenty shillings for service in the Purchass of the Present Ministeriall Place. for Benjamin Hastings the sum of six shillings.

(11) Voted and Granted the sum of sixteen Pounds to Pay the Reverd Mr Storer to Compleat his salary according to Contract:

(12) Voted and Granted four Pounds to Pay others to Whom money may be Due from said Precinct.

(13) Voted And Granted the sum of Ten Pounds to Procure Barrs to Preserve the Glass on the Meetting House and for the Further Mending of the s^d Glass &c.

Watertown March the 19th 1730/31

To Nath^ll Harris Clerk of the Easterly Precinct in Watertown You are Hereby Ordered Forthwith to Give to the Assesors of s^d Precinct A Copie of the Grants of money Made by s^d Precinct on the Twelfth Day of this Inftant March and Direct them Speedily to afsefs the fame on the Inhabitants of fd Precinct as the Law Directs and to Committ the Rate or Afsefsments to Mr James Barnard Collector for fd Precinct with a Law full Warrent to Collect the fame and to Pay in to Nathll Harris Treafurer for fd Precinct or his fuccefsor in fd office the Whole of the fd afsefsments at or Before the First Monday of June Next Infuing.

Josiah Perry
Joseph Coollidg } Precinct Comtee
Joseph Child

[34]

To Nathll Harris Clerk of the Eafterly Precinct in Watertown. You are Hereby Ordered to Give Out An Order to Mr Samuel Thacher Conftable of Watertown aforesd Within fd Precinct to Warn the Freeholders and other Inhabitance Within fd Precinct Who Are Quallified to Vote in Precinct affairs to meett att the Publict Meetting houfe in fd Precinct On Monday the 24th Day of May at one of the Clock in the afternoon of sd day for the Ends Following.

(viz) First To Know the Mind of the Precinct Whether they are Willing the Town fhould be Divided by the Prefent Precinct Line, if fd Vote Pafses in the Negative then,

Secondly, Whether they Are Willing the Town fhould be Divided by fome Other Line that may be Projected and for the Precinct to Act and Do any other Thing or Things that they May think Needfull and Prudent Relating to fd Affair.

Josiah Perry } Precinct
Watertown May the 18th 1731 Joseph Coollidg } Comtee

Middfx fs

To Mr Samll Thacher Conftable for the Easterly Precinct in Watertown,

Sr You Are Hereby Requiered Forthwith to Warn the Freeholders and Other Inhabitants Within the Easterly Precinct in Watertown Who Are Quallified to Vote in Precinct Affairs to Meet at the Publict Meetting houfe in fd Precinct on Monday the 24th Day of May Current at One of the Clock in the Afternoon On fd Day for the Ends Following (Viz),

(1) To Know the Minds of the Precinct Whether thay Are Willing the Town fhould be Divided by the Prefent Precinct Line, and if faid Vote Pafses in the Negative then,

(2) Whether they Are Willing the Town fhould be Divided by fome Other Line that May be Projected, and for the Precinct to Act and Do any other thing or things yt they may Think Needfull and Prudent Relateing to faid affair.

Hereof Fail Not But Make Return of this Order and your Doings thereon to one of the Precinct Comtee or to the Precinct Clerk at Least Four Hours Before the Time of fd meetting,

p Order of the Precinct Comtee
Watertown May the 18th 1731 Nathll Harris Cler.

Att A Meetting of the Freeholders and Other Inhabitants of the Easterly Precinct in Watertown, Who Are Quallified to Vote in Precinct affairs the 24th Day of may 1731.

(1) Voted and Chose for Moderator for s[d] meeting Dea John Coollidge.

(2) Putt to Vote Whether the Precinct Are Willing that the Town should be Divided by the Present Precinct Line, and the Vote Pafsed in the Negative.

(3) Put to Vote Whether the Precinct are of the Mind that the Town should be Divided by some other Line (then the Present Line) that may Hereafter be Projected, and the Vote Pafsed in the affermative.

(4) Put to Vote Whether it be the Mind of the Precinct that the Town should be Divided the East Part to Have Half the Land Contained in the Town and the Vote Pafsed in the Negative.

(5) Put to Vote Whether the Precinct will Chose a Com[tee] of three men to Project some Convenient Line and make Report thereof to the Precinct at the adjornment of this meetting, and the Vote Past in the affermative.

(6) Voted and Chose for a Com[tee] to Project and Report as affores[d] Dea Nath[ll] Fisk Dea Joseph Mason and Dea John Coollidge.

(7) Put to Vote Whether the Precinct will adjorn this meetting to thursday the 27th Current at Four of the Clock in the afternoon of s[d] Day and the Vote Past in y[e] affermative.

[35]

Att A Meetting of the Inhabitants of the Easterly Precinct of Watertown the 27th Day of May Annoque Domini 1731 by adjornment.

(1) Put to Vote Whether it be the mind of the Precinct that the Dividing Line Between the East Part of the Town and the West Part should the Westerly Line of the First Divident so Runing upon a Strait Line With that Divident Line Southerly to Charles River; and also Northerly to Cambridge Line and the Vote Past in the affermative.

(2) Put to Vote Whether it be the mind of the Precinct to Choose three men a Com[tee] to addrefs the Great and Generall Court in their Behalf that (if the Hon[rd] Court se Reason to Divide Watertown into Two Distinct Townships) the above mentioned and Voted Line may be the Dividing Line and the Vote Past in the Affermative.

(3) Voted and Chose for there Com[tee] to addrefs the Generall Court as aforesd Dea, Nathan Fisk Dea, John Coollidge & Dea Joseph Mason.

(4) Put to Vote Whether it be the Mind of the Precinct; that (in Case the Great and Generall Court should see Reason to Divide the Town of Watertown into Two Distinct Towns) that there affores[d] Com[tee] addrefs the Court that Each Part be Obliged to Pay there Respective Proportion and Rateable Part to the Maintaining the Great Bridge Over Charles River in Watertown affores[d] for the Future, and the Vote Past in the affermative.

(5) Put to Vote Whether it be the Mind of the Precinct that if the Town ſhould be Devided as afforeſd; that Each Part ſhould be Obliged to Pay there Respective Parts of the Towns Debts that are alredy Contracted, and the Vote Past in the Affermative.

(6) Voted that Each Part as afore ſd be Obliged to Pay and Do there Proportionable Parts to the Maintainance and ſupport of Any Poor Perſon or Perſons that Have Heretofore Moved out of the Town of Watertown, if it ſhould ſo Happen that they ſhould Hereafter Become a Charge to Watertown by Reaſon of there Being Duly Warned out of other Towns Where they may Now Live.

Middlſx ſs

To Mr Samuel Thacher Conſtable of Watertown Greetting. Sr You are Hereby Ordered & Requiered Forthwith to Warn the Freeholders and Other Inhabitance of the Easterly Precinct in Watertown Who Are Qualified to Vote in Precinct Affairs (according to Law) to meet at the Publict meetting houſe in ſd Precinct On Monday the 13th of March Next Inſuing at one of the Clock in the afternoon of ſd Day for the Ends Following.

First to Choſe a Precinct Comtee Clerk & other Precinct Officers Neſsaſary to be Choſen in the Month of March.

(2) For the Precinct to Grant a ſofitient ſum of money to Pay the Reverd Mr Seth Storer according to Contract & to Pay others to Whom Money may be Due from ſd Precinct.

(3) To Choſe A ſexton and to Take Care how he ſhall be Paid.

(4) To Know the Minds of the Precinct Whether they will ſeat there Meetting houſe under ſuch Rules & Regulations as they agree upon.

(5) For the Precinct to hear the accompts of their First Comtee Choſen by the Precinct to make the addition to the ministeriall houſe in sd Precinct and that the Precinct may act there upon and with Relation thereunto as they ſhall ſee meet: Hereof Fail Not but make Return of this order & your Doing thereon unto one of the Comtee or Clerk of ſd Precinct at Least four hours Before the Time of ſd meetting.

pr order of the Comtee. NATHll HARRIS, Cler.

Feb: 21st: 1731/2

[36]

Att A Meetting of the Inhabitance of the Easterly Precinct in Watertown the 13th Day of March Annoque Domini 1731/2.

(1) Voted and Choſe for Moderator for ſd Meetting Den Nathan Fisk.

(2) Voted & Choſe for a Standing Comtee to Manaage the Prudentialls for sd Precinct for the Inſuing Year John Hastings Wm Williams & Oliver Livermore.

(3) Voted and Choſe for Precinct Cler Nathll Harris.

(4) Voted and Choſe for Precinct Treaſurer Nathll Harris.

(5) Voted and Choſe for Precinct Aſseſsors for ye Inſuing Year — Nathll Harris. Samuel Brown Henry Bond

(6) Voted and Chose for Collector for the Insuing Year Nath^{ll} Clark.

(7) Voted & Chose for sexton Eben^{r} Hastings.

(8) Voted that the sexton should be Paid by Two Contributions as Usiall.

(9) Voted & Granted the sum of Twenty Pounds to Pay the Revd Mr Seth Storer according to Contract and to Pay others to Whom Money may be Due from s^{d} Precinct.

(10) Put to Vote Whether it Be the Mind of the Precinct to seat there meettinghouse under such Rules & Regulations as they shall agree upon and the Vote Past in ye affermative

(11) Put to Vote Whether it be the mind of the Precinct to Chose A Com^{tee} to seat there meeting house as afores^{d} and the Vote Past in the Affermative.

(12) Voted that the Precinct Will Chose a Com^{tee} of Five men to seat the s^{d} meetting house.

(13) Voted & adjorned this meetting & the Remaining Business thereof to Monday the 20th of March Instant at Two of the Clock in the afternoon of s^{d} Day.

Att A Meetting of the Inhabitants of the Easterly Precinct of Watertown on the 20th Day of March Annoque Domini 1731/2 by adjornment.

(1) Put to Vote Whether it be the Mind of the Precinct that the Third seat Below in the Body of seats and the Fore seat in the Front Gallarys should be Equill in Dignity and the Vote Past in the Affermative.

(2) Voted that the Forth seat Below as aforesd and the Fore seats in the Side Gallaries should be Equill in Dignity.

(3) Voted that it is the mind of the Precinct that there Com^{tee} in seating the meetting house shall have Due Regard to Age: and to Persons Reall & Personall Estate in the Last Invice, Haveing Respect to but one Head or Poll to One Estate.

(4) Voted and Chose for A Com^{tee} to seat the s^{d} Meettinghouse Dea Nathan Fisk Dea John Coollidge Dea Joseph Mason, Mr John Hastings & Mr Oliver Livermore.

(5) Voted that it is the Mind of the Precinct that the Boys under 14 year of age shall set in the Hind seats under the Pews in the Galleries on the Men side: and that the Girls under foreteen year of age set in the hind seat under the Pews in the Gallaries on ye womens side.

(6) Put to Vote Whether the Precinct Will Accept of the Accompt of there First Com^{tee} Chosen to make the addition to the ministeriall house in s^{d} Precinct, & the Vote Past in the affermative.

[37]

Middsx ss: To Mr Joseph Holding Constable of Watertown Greetting, Sr You are Hereby Ordered & Requiered forthwith to Warn the Freeholders & other Inhabitance Within the Easterly Precinct of Watertown afores^{d} Who are Quallified to Vote in Precinct affairs To meet at the Publict meetting house in s^{d} Precinct on Monday the 24th Day of Aprill Current at Five of the Clock in the afternoon of ſd Day for the Ends following.

Viz First To Know the Mind of the Precinct Whether they will Grant a ſofitient ſum of Money to finish the Ministeriall houſe in ſd Precinct.

Secondly, To Know the Mind of the Precinct Whether they will Do any thing about the Meetting houſe in ſd Precinct that ſo People may in Durty ſeaſons Get to and go into ſd meetting houſe without Being Expoſed to Wade in Mudd & Water: and alſo Whether they Will Provide ſome More Conveniencys for to go up to the Bell in ſd Meetting houſe & if it be the Mind of the Precinct to Do any thing in theſe Reſpects then to Grant money to Defray the Charges of the ſame.

Thirdly, For the Precinct to hear the Report of the Comtes Choſen by the Precinct to ſeat there meetting houſe.

Forthly For the Precinct to agree upon ſome Certain Place for the Hearſe Cloath to be Keept in.

Hereof Fail Not but make Return of this Order & your Doings therein to one of the Precinct Comtee or Clerk of ſd precinct at Leaſt four hour Before the Time of ſd meetting.

Watertown aprill the 15th 1732

p^r Order of the Precinct Comtee
NATHll HARRIS Cler.

Att A Meetting of the Inhabitance of the Easterly Precinct in Watertown the 24th Day of aprill Anno Dom 1732 Being Regularly Warned &c.

(1) Voted & Choſe for moderator Nathll Harris.

(2) Put to Vote Whether it be the mind of the Precinct to Grant any ſum of money to Finish the Ministeriall houſe in ſd Precinct and the Vote Past in the affermative.

(3) Voted and Granted the ſum of Eighty Pounds to Finish the Ministeriall houſe in ſd Precinct and to make a Yard about ſd houſe.

(4) Voted that the Deacons Wives ſhould ſet in the Fore ſeat in the Body of ſeats Below.

(5) Voted that the Hearſe Cloath ſhould be Keept at the houſe of Mr John Hastings.

Middleſex ſs To Mr Joſeph Holding Conſtable for Watertown Greetting &c.

Sr You are hereby Ordered & Requiered forthwith to Warn the Freeholders and other Inhabitants of the Easterly Precinct in Watertown Who are Quallified according to Law to Vote in Precinct affairs to meet at the Publict Meetting in ſd Precinct on monday the 12th Day of March Next at Two of the Clock in the afternoon on ſd Day for the Ends Following,

(1) To Chooſe a Precinct Comtee Clerk & other Precinct officers Neſsary to be Choſen in the Month of March.

(2) for the Precinct to Grant a ſofitient ſum of money to Pay the Reverd Mr Storrer according to Contract and to Pay others to Whom money may be Due from ſd Precinct.

(3) To Choofe a fexton and to Take Care how he Will be Paid,

[38]

(4) To Know the Minds of the Precinct Whether they Will fink fome Rates of feverall Perfons in the Lifts of Rates in feverall of the Late Collectors Hands.

(5) To Know the Mind of the Precinct Whether they Will Do any thing about the meetting houfe in f^d Precinct for the more Comfortable Pafsing into f^d Meettinghoufe in Wet and Durty feafons and Whether they Will Provide any more Conveniencys to Git up to the Bell in f^d Meettinghoufe.

You are alfo Requiered to Notifie the Precinct Credditors to Bring in there Creddítts to the Precinct Com^{tee} at the houfe of Mrs Mary Larnard Inholder at four of the Clock in the afternoon on Fryday the Ninth Day of March Next Infuing.

Hereof Fail Not But Make Return of this order and Your Doings thereon at Leaft four hour Before the Time of f^d Meetting to one of the Precinct Comt^{ee} or Clerk of f^d Precinct.

February 8th 1732/3 Per Order of the Precinct Com^{tee}.

NATH^{ll} HARRIS Cler.

Att A Meetting of the Freeholders and other Inhabitance of th. Easterly Precinct in Watertown on Monday the 12th Day of March Annoque Domini 1732/3.

(1) Voted and Chofe for moderator for f^d Meetting Nath^{ll} Harris.

(2) Voted and Chofe for Precinct Com^{tee} to Mannage the Prudenshalls of f^d Precinct for the Year Infuing { Jonathan Brown, John Hastings, Eben^r Stone.

(3) Voted and Chofe for Clerk of f^d Precinct Nath^{ll} Harris

(4) Voted and Chofe for Precinct Treafurer Nath^{ll} Harris

(5) Voted and Chofe for Precinct Afsefsors { Eben^r Goddard, Samuel Brown, Henry Bond

(6) Voted and Chofe for Precinct Collector Samuel Stratton.

(7) Voted and Chofe for fexton Ebenezer Hastings

(8) Voted that the fexton be Paid by two Contributions as Ufiall.

(10) Put to Vote Whether the Precinct are Willing to fink Thomas Reads Rate amounting to the fum of £0 : 15s : 8 in the £220 Precinct Rate Committed to Mr Ebenezer Chenry to Collect, and the Vote Past in the affermative :

(11) Put to Vote Whether the Precinct Are Willing to Sink Allexander Maccoys Rate being £0 : 2 : 0 : the Wd^w Elizabeth Dixes Rate Being £0 : 1 : 1 : Samuel Hancoks Rate Being £0 : 0 : 1 : and John Kings Rate : Being £0 : 1 : 5 : all Being in the List of Rates Committed to Mr Edwad Harrington to Collect : and the Vote Passed in the affermative.

(12) Put to Vote Whether the Precinct Will Allow Mr Edwad Harrington the fum of Twenty fhillings for Gathering 25^{lb} and the Vote Passed in the Negative.

(13) Put to Vote Whether the Precinct Will allow Ebenezer Chenry the ſum of £1 : 5 : 0 for Gathering £220 : 0 : 0 : and the Vote Passed in the affermative.

(14) Put to Vote Whether the Precinct Will allow M[r] Edward Harrington five ſhillings for Gathering £25 : 0 : 0 : and the Vote Past in the Negative.

[39] (15

(15) Put to Vote Whether Precinct Will ſink Nath[ll] Stratons Rate Being £0 : 4 : 10 : John Orms Rate Being £0 : 8 : 7 : Allexander Maccoys Rate Being £0 : 3 : 4 : Joſeph Shattucks Rate Being £0 : 4 : 6 : Thomas Hills Being £0 : 3 : 3 all in the List of Rates Commite[d] to Jonathan Stone Jun[r] Late of Watertown Deceaſed, and the Vote Past in the affermative,

(16) Put to Vote Whether the Precinct Will Grant the ſum of Thirty Pounds to Pay the Rev[nd] M[r] Seth Storrer according to Contract and to Pay others to Whom money may be Due from the Precinct. and the Vote Paſsed in the affermative.

(17) Put to Vote to Know the mind of the Precinct Whether they will Do any thing about the meettinghouſe in ſ[d] Precinct for the more Comfortable Paſsing into the Meetting houſe in Wet and Durty ſeaſons and alſo Provide ſome conveniency to get up to the Bell and the Vote Past in the affermative.

(18) Voted that the ſtanding Committy for the Precinct for the Preſent year be a Committy to Do What they ſhall Think Proper about the meetting houſe, for the more Comfortable Paſsing into ſ[d] meetting houſe in Wet and Dirty ſeaſons, and alſo for the more Convenient Gitting up to the Bell on ſ[d] meettinghouſe.

Watertown Aprill the 11th 1733

To Nath[ll] Harris Cler of the Easterly Precinct in Watertown, You are hereby ordered to Give to the aſſeſors for ſ[d] Precinct a Copie of the Grant of Money made by ſ[d] Precinct on the 12th Day of March Last Past and Direct them ſpeedily to aſſeſs the ſame and to Committ there Rate or aſſeſſment to M[r] Samuel Stratton Collecttor to Collect With a Lawfull Warrent to Collect the ſame and Order him to Pay in the Whole of his Collections to Nath[ll] Harris Precinct Treaſurer or his ſucceſsor in ſ[d] office : and to Issue and make up an accompt of the Whole of his Collections at or Before the First Day of July Next Inſuing.

EBEN[r] STONE } Precinct
JON[a] BROWN } Com[tee]

To Nath[ll] Harris Clerk of the East Precinct in Watertown. You are hereby Ordered Forthwith to Give out An Order to M[r] Benjamin Whitney Conſtable of Watertown and Order him therein to Warn the Freeholders and other Inhabitants of the Easterly Precinct in Watertown who are Quallified to Vote in Precinct affairs to meett at the Publict Meetting houſe in ſ[d] Precinct on Monday the 11th Day of March Next at one of the Clock in the afternoon on ſ[d] Day for the Ends Following viz.

(1) To Choofe a Precinct Com[tee] Clerk and all other Precinct Officers Nefsasary to Chofen in the Month of March.

(2) For the Precinct to Grant a foficient fum of Money to Pay the Reved M[r] Seth Storer according to Contract and to Pay others to whom Money may Due from f[d] Precinct alfo to Know the minds of the Precinct Whether they will Grant an additionall fum of money to the Revend M[r] Storer fallary.

(3) For the Precinct to Choofe a fexton and to Take Care how he may be Paid:

(4) To Hear the Precinct Treafurs accompt &c.

JONATH[n] BROWN }
JOHN HASTINGS } Precinct Com[tee]
EBEN[r] STONE }

[40]

At a Meetting of the Freeholders and other Inhabitants of the Easterly Precinct in Watertown on Monday the 11th of March: A: D: 1733/4

1) Voted and Chofe for Moderator for f[d] meetting Dea Nathan Fisk.

2) Voted and Chofe for the Precinct Com[tee] to mannage the Prudentialls for the Precinct the Infuing Year { Dea Nathan Fisk. Enf[n] Jon[a] Stone. Dea John Coollidge.

3) Voted and Chofe for Precinct Clerk Nath[ll] Harris.

4) Voted and Chofe for Precinct Treafurer Nath[ll] Harris.

5) Voted & Chofe for afsefsors { Samuel Warrin, Samuel Brown, Thomas Bisco:

6) Voted and Chofe for Collector John Whitney.

7) Voted and Chofe for fexton Ebenezer Hastings.

8) Put to Vote Whether it be the mind of the Precinct to Pay the fexton by Two Contributions one on the First Sabath in September and the other on the First fabath on March and the Vote Past in the affermative.

9) Voted and Granted the fum of Twenty Pounds to Pay the Revend M[r] Seth Storer According to Contract and to Pay others to Whom Money may be Due from f[d] Precinct.

10) Put to Vote Whether it be the mind of the Precinct to make an addition to the Revend M[r] Storers fallary and the Vote Past in the affermative.

11) Put to Vote Whether it be the mind of the Precinct to add Forty Pounds to the Revend M[r] Storers fallary for this Present year (and to Grant the fame) and the Vote Past in the affermative:

12) Voted that the Precinct will finck John Phillips Rate in Daniel Bonds List of Rates Being £0-2-5: and Alexander Maccoys Rate Being £0:2:0.

Middlefex fs. Waterlown February the 15th 1734/5,

To M[r] John Sawin of Watertown in the County of Middlefex and one of the Conftables of f[d] Watertown Greetting.

You are Hereby Ordered And Required Forthwith to Warn the Freeholders and Other Inhabitance of the Easterly Precinct in Watertown Who Are Quallified to Vote in Precinct affairs to meet at the Publict meetting houfe in f[d] Precinct on Thursday the fixth Day of March Next at Two of the Clock in the afternoon for the Ends Following (viz),

First To Choofe Precinct offices as the Law Directs,

Secondly to Grant money to Pay the Precinct Creddittor.

Thirdly to Grant fixteen Pounds w[h] makes up the fallary of the Revend M[r] Storer for the year according to Contract.

Fourthly to Know the Precincts mind w[t] addition they will make to Revend M[r] Storrers fallary for the year Current.

Fiftly to Choof a fexton.

Alfo to notifie the Precinct Credditors to Bring in their accompts to the Precinct Com[tee] on the aforefd fixth Day of March at one of the Clock in the afternoon at the abovef[d] meeting houfe.

p[r] Order of the Precinct Com[tee]

NATH[ll] HARRIS Cler

[41]

Att A Meetting of the Freeholders and Other Inhabitants of the Easterly Precinct in Watertown on Thirsday the fixth Day of march Annoque Domini 1734/5.

1) Voted & Chofe for Moderator for f[d] Meeting Jofeph Mafon Efqr

2) Voted and Chofe for a ftanding Com[tee] to mannage the Prudentialls for f[d] Precinct the Infuing Year } Jonas Bond, W[m] Williams, Oliver Livermore.

3) Voted & Chofe for Precinct Cler Jofeph Mafon Efqr

4) Voted & Chofe for Precinct Treafurer Jofeph Mafon Efqr:

5) Voted & Chofe for Precinct afsefsors } Henry Bond, Sam[ll] Brown, Nath[ll] Bright,

6) Voted & Chofe for Precinct Collector John Coollidge Jun[r],

7) Voted & Chofe for fexton Ebenezer Hastings.

8) Voted and Granted the fum of fix Pounds to Pay Precinct Credditors, for Mending of the Glafs on the meeting houfe in f[d] Precinct and for to Purchafe a Fram to fet the hour Glafs in.

9) Voted and Granted the fum of fixteen Pounds to Compleat the Revend M[r] Storers falary according to Contract,

10) Voted and Granted the fum of Forty Pounds as an addition to the Revnd M[r] Storers falary for the Year Current,

11) Voted to Pay the fexton by Two Contributions as Ufiall,

Watertown October 20th 1735.

To Joseph Mason Clerk of y[e] Easterly Precinct in f[d] Town.

You are hereby ordred to give to the Afsefsors of f[d] Precinct A Copy of y[e] Grants of Money made by the Inhabitants of s[d] Precinct on the fixth day of March laft paft. And direct them fpeedily to Afsefs the fame on the Inhabitants &c. of faid Precinct, And Commit the Afsefment to M[r] John Coollidge Jun[r] Collector for ſaid Precinct with a Lawfull Warrant to Levy and Collect the ſame and Order him to pay in the whole of his Collections to Joseph Mason Treaſurer for ſ[d] Precinct or to his Succeſsor in ſaid Office And to Iſu and make up an Acc[t] of the whole of his Collection At or upon the first day of December Next Enſuing.

Jonas Bond } Precinct
Oliver Livermore } Com[tee]

[42]

To Joseph Mason Clerk of y[e] Eaſt Precinct in Watertown,

You are hereby Ordred and Directed forthwith to give out a Notification to M[r] John Bright one of y[e] Conſtables of Watertown afores[d] And order him therein to Warn the Freeholders and other Inhabitants in ſ[d] Precinct who are Quallified to Vote in Precinct Affairs to Meet at y[e] Publick Meeting houſe in ſ[d] Precinct on Munday the Eighth day of March Next at one of y[e] Clock in the Afternoon of ſ[d] day for the Ends following.

1. To Choſe a Committee a Clerk Treaſurer and all other Precinct Officers Neceſary to be choſen in the Month of March.

2. To Grant Money to pay and Satisfye the Rev[d] M[r] Storer According to Contract, And All other Perſons to whom y[e] Precinct is indebted.

3. To know the Mind of the Precinct what ſum they will Grant as an Addition to the Rev[d] M[r] S. Storers Sallery for the preſent Year.

4. To Choſe a Sexton & to take care how he may be paid.

5. To know the Mind of the Precinct whether they will Appoint a Perſon to take the whole care of the Mending of the Meeting houſe Glaſs as there ſhall be Ocation and to be paid by the Precinct.

And ord[r] the ſ[d] Conſtable to Notify the Perſons to whom the Precinct is Indebted to bring in their Acc[ts] to the Com[tee] at ſ[d] Meeting at one of y[e] Clock.

Jonas Bond } Precinct
Watertown Feb[r] 13. 1735/6. Oliver Livermore } Comm[tee]

Midd[x]. ſs. To M[r] John Bright Conſtable of Watertown in ſd County Greeting.

You are hereby ordred and required forthwith to Warn the Freehold[rs] & other Inhabitants in the Easterly Precinct of ſ[d] Town who are Quallifyed to Vote in Precinct Affairs to Meet at y[e] Publick Meeting houſe in ſ[d] Precinct on Munday the Eighth Day of March Next at one of y[e] Clock in y[e] Afternoon of ſ[d] Day for y[e] Ends following viz[t].

1. To Choſe a Committee a Clerk & other Precinct officers Neceſsary to be choſen in the Month of March.

2. To Grant Money to pay y[e] Rev[d] M[r] Seth Storer According to Contract and all other Perſons to whom y[e] Precinct is Indebted.

3. To Know y[e] Mind of y[e] Precinct what ſume of Money they will Grant as an Addition to y[e] Rev[d] M[r] Storers Salery for this Pſent Year.

4. To Chofe a faxton and to take care how to pay him.

5. To know the Mind of ye Precinct whether they will Appoint Any Perfon to take the whole care of ye Mending the Meeting houfe Glafs as there fhall be Ocation and to be paid by ye Precinct.

And Notify fuch Perfons to whom ye Precinct is Indebted to bring in their Acc^t^ to ye Committee at f^d^ Meeting at one of ye Clock.

Hereof fail not and Make return of this Ord^r^ to ye Com^te^ or Precinct Clerk seafonably before the time Appointed for f^d^ Meeting, Dated in Watertown the 13 Day of Feb^r^ A.D. 1735/6.

p^r^ order of the Precinct Comm^tee^

JOSEPH MASON Pre^t^ Clerk

[43]

At a General Meeting of the Freeholders and other Inhabitants of the Eafterly Precinct in Watertown on Munday the 8th Day of March 1735/6

Voted and chofe Joseph Mason Esqr Moderator for f^d^ Meeting.

Voted and chofe for a Com^tee^ to Manage ye Prudentials of ye Precinct { Dea: Jno Coollidge, Mr Jonas Bond, Mr Ebenz Stone,

Voted and chofe Joseph Mason Esqr Precinct Clerk,

Voted and Chofe Joseph Mason Esqr Precinct Treafurer.

Voted and chofe for Afsefsors { Henry Bond, John Coollidge Junr, Ebenez^r^ Goddard,

Voted and Chofe Nathanael Coollidge Precinct Colletor.

Voted and Chofe Ebenez^r^ Haftings faxton, And to be paid as Ufully.

Voted and Granted ye fum of fixteen Pounds to pay ye Revd Mr Seth Storer According to Contract.

Voted and Granted to Mr Wm Williams fix fhillings & fix pence.

Voted and Granted to Jonas Coollidge to fatisfy his Acc^t^ ye Sum of Three pounds three fhillings and fix pence.

Voted and Granted the fum of four pounds to mend the Glafs on ye Meeting house; & to pay ye Afsefsors this pfent Year.

Voted and Granted the fum of fifty Pounds at an Addition to the Revd Mr Storers falery for the Prefent Year.

Voted and Granted ye fum of Twenty fhillings to purchase a Book to keep ye Treafurers Acc^ts^ in.

The Vote was put whether it is the mind of ye Precinct to Appoint any Perfon to take ye whole care of ye Mending of ye Meeting houfe Glafs as there fhall be Ocation. And ye Vote paft on the Negative.

Watertown Sepr 17th 1736.

To Joseph Mason Esqr Clerk of ye Easterly Precinct in fd Town.

You are hereby Ordered to give the Afsefsors of f^d^ Precinct a Copy of the Grants of Money Made by ye Inhabitants of f^d^ Precinct at their Meeting on the Eighth Day of March Laft past, and Direct them Speedly to Afsefs the fame on the Ratable Inhabitants & Estates of ſd Precinct & Committ the Aſseſmt to ye Collector of ſd Precinct with a Lawfull Warrant to Levy and Collect the ſame and to pay in the whole of his Collection to Your ſelf Treaſurer for ſd Precinct or to your Succeſsor in ſd Office & to make up An Acct of the whole of ſd Aſseſmt at or upon the firſt day of Decembr Next.

JOHN COOLLIDGE }
JONAS BOND } Comtee
EBENEZER STONE }

Which was Done p
J: Maſon Clerk

[44]

Middx ſs. To Mr Nathaniel Coollidge Collector for ye East Precinct in Watertown.

You are hereby Deſired to Notify the Freeholdrs and othr Inhabitants in ſd Precinct who are Quallifyed to Vote in Precinct Affairs To meet at the Publick Meeting houſe in ſaid Precinct on Munday the Twenty Eigth day of March Currant at Two of ye Clock in the Afternoon for the Ends following vizt

To Choſe a Committee to manage ye prudentials of ſd Precinct ye Pſent Year.

To Choſe a Clerk A Treaſurer and all other Precinct Officers Neceſsary to be Choſen in March.

To Choſe a Sexton; and take care how he Shall be paid.

To Grant Money to pay the Revd Mr Seth Storer According to Contract.

To Grant Money to pay Such as the Precinct are Indebted to. And to Defray other Neceſsary Charges yt may Ariſe in the Precinct.

To know the mind of the Precinct what Sum of money they will Grant As An Addition to the Revd Mr Storers Salery, for ye preſent Year.

To know the mind of the Precinct whether they will Grant a Sutable Sum of Money to be Improved in the repairing the fences belonging to the Miniſterial place in this Precinct.

To Choſe a Comtee to Improve ye money yt may be granted for ſd end.

To hear the Accts of the Comtee who were choſen to finiſh the Miniſteral house, how they have proceeded in yt Affair.

Hereof fail not and make return of this Notification and Your Doings thereon ſeaſonably to ye Precinct Clerk before the time Appointed herein for ſd Meeting.

Dated at Watertown the 19th Day of March A.D. 1736/7.

pr order of the Precinct Committee.

JOSEPH MASON Prect Clerk.

At a Meeting of the Inhabitants of the Eaſterly Precinct in Watertown Regurely Aſsembled on the 28th Day of March 1737.

Voted and Choſe Joseph Mason Moderator of ſd Meeting.

Voted and Choſe Joseph Mason Deacon John Coollidge & Capt Joseph Coollidge to be a Committee to manage ye prudentials of ye Precinct ye Pſent Year.

Voted and Chose Joseph Mason Precinct Clerk.
Voted and Chose Joseph Mason Precinct Treasurer.
Voted and Chose Deacon John Coollidge Joseph Mason & Capt Joseph Coollidge Assessors. (who were Sworn by Justice Harris at sd Meeting.)
Voted and Chose David Sanger Collector for ye Precinct.
Voted and Chose Ebenezer Hastings Sexton. Voted that there Sd be two Contributions as usal to pay the Sexton.
Voted and Granted the Sum of Sixteen pounds to pay ye Revd Mr Storer according to Contract.
Voted and Granted ye Sum of Twenty eight shillings to pay Capt Joseph Coollidge his Acct.
Voted and Granted ye Sum of Twenty three Shillings & 4d to pay Epm Cutters Acct for mending the Meeting hous Glass.
Voted and Granted the Sum of Twenty two Shillings & 8d to pay Jonas Coollidge for aladdr for ye Ministeral house.
Voted and Granted 3/6 to pay Josiah Perry for a lok.
Voted and Granted 3/ to pay John Bright for warning one meeting. And 3/ to pay Nathl Coollidge for warning this Meeting.
Voted and Granted Six pounds for Necessary Charges yt may Arise in ye Precinct,
Voted and Granted the Sum of fifty Pounds As An Addition to ye Revd Mr Storers Salery for this Psent Year.
Voted and Granted ye Sum of Twenty pounds to be Improved in repairing the fences belonging to ye Ministeral place.
Voted and chose Joseph Mason Dea John Coollidge & Capt Joseph Coollidge to be A Comtee to Improve sd money for sd Ends.
The Committee for finishing ye Ministeral House laid yr Acct before ye Precinct.
Voted their Acceptance of sd Acct & Voted and Granted ye Sum of Eight shillings & Six pence Ballance Due to sd Committee.

[43]

Middx ss. To Mr John Stowel Constable of Watertown in sd County Greeting.
You are hereby required to Warn the Freeholdrs and other Inhabitants in the Easterly Precinct of sd Town who are Quallifyed to Vote in Precinct Affairs to meet at ye Publick Meeting house in the sd Precinct on Munday the fifth day of Decembr Next at one of ye Clock in the Afternoon for ye Ends following vizt
To know the Mind of ye Inhabts of sd Precinct, whether they are willing (for ye Sake of peace in the Town) that ye Town of Watertown Sd be Divided and made two Seperat Townships Upon the following Conditions vizt
That the sd Town be Divided into Two Townships, and the Dividing Line to be as the Precinct Line Now is.
That the Great Bridge over Charles River in sd Town be maintained by Each Town in proportion as they Shall be Set in the Province Tax.

That the poor who at present are Maintained by the Town be maintained by Each Town in proportion to their Province Tax, and if any Person gone out of Town Sld be returned to Watertown and become a Charge that they be maintained by Each Town in like proportion as AforeSd.

That the Towns Stock of Arms and Ammunition be Divided in Equal proportion between Each Town.

That Watertowns part of ye Two Thousand Acres of Land Granted by the General Court to them and Weston Be divided in Equal halves as to Quantity & Quallity between the two Towns when Divided.

That the Interest of Watertowns part of ye sixty thousand pound Loan be Divided to Each Town According to their Province Tax.

That the Books and records of ye Town of Watertown be Delivered up to a Comte of ye East Town who may be Chosen and Appointed to receive the Same.

That the Debts of ye Town be paid by Each Town in proportion to yr Province Tax.

That if any Money upon Ballanceing the Treasurey Acct remain in the Treasurey it be Divided between the Towns in like proportion as aforesd.

That the Publick Ways in the Town from Masters Brook to Cambridge, line be Stated and Settled as to their Course and wydth as the Court of General Sessions of ye peace Agreeable to the reporte that be made by their Committee for that purpose Appointed Shall be pleased to Ordr, And if any Lands Now Lying as Ways or reputed as Such Shall not be included in the Ways when Stated as Ared the Same Shall be to and for the Sole Use & benefit and at the Disposal of the Town where in the Same Shall Ly: Provided however that if the Sale of any of the Lands aforesd yt have been Disposed of by the Towns Comtee (not included in the ways when Stated as Aforesd) Shall remain good And Valled to the Persons who have Purchased ye Same, Also yt Each Town Shall have the Benefit of the proceeds of ye Sale of Such of ye Land aforesd as Ly within ye Same.

That if the sd Ways when Stated as Aforesd Shall Include any Land belonging to any Perticular Person the owner of Such Land Shall have Meet recompence made him by the Town wherein the Same Lyes. Hereof fail not and make seasonable Return of this Warrant and Your Doings thereon to the Precinct Comtee or Clerk before the Time Appointed for sd Meeting. Dated at Watertown the 29th Day of Novembr A.D. 1737.

℔r Order of the Precinct Committee

Joseph Mason Precinct Cler.

[46]

At a Meeting of the Freeholdrs and other Inhabitts of ye Easterly Precinct in Watertown Regularly Convend on the 5th Day of Decembr 1737.

Voted and Chose Joseph Joseph Mason Esqr Moderator of sd Meeting.

Whereas Sundry Unhapy Differances have Arisen in Watertown for the peaceable putting and End to the Same; it is tho[t] that Dividing the Town into Two Townships May be very Conducive. And in hopes of Obtaining the Valuable Blessing of peace,

The following Vote was put. viz[t] Whether it is the Mind of the Precinct (the West Precinct in s[d] Town Petitioning y[e] General Court therefor) that the Town of Watertown be Divided into Two Townships On the Conditions and provisions following Namely

(1) That the Dividing Line be as the Precinct Line Now is.

(2) That Watertowns part of y[e] Charge of y[e] repairs & rebuilding of y[e] Great Bridge over Charles River in s[d] Town be borne by Each Town in Proportion as they Shall be Set in the Province Tax.

(3) That the poor who at present are maintained by the Town be maintained by Each Town in Proportion to y[r] Province Tax, and if any persons gone out of Town Shall be returned to Watertown and become a Charge, that they be maintained by Each Town in Like proportion as afores[d].

(4) That the Towns Stock of Arms and Ammunition be divided in Equal Proportion between Each Town. (5) That Watertowns Part of the Two Thousand Acres of Land Granted by y[e] General Court to them and Weston Be Divided in Equal halves as to Quantity and Quality between the Two Towns When Divided. (6) That the Interest of Watertowns part of the Sixty Thousand pounds Loan be Divided to Each Town in proportion to y[r] Precinct Tax (7) That the Books records and papers belonging to the Town of Watertown be Delivred up to A Com[tee] of the East Town who may be Chosen and Appointed to receive y[e] Same (8) That the Debts of the town be paide by Each Town in proportion to y[e] Province Tax. (9) That if any Money upon Ballanceing the Treasurers Acc[ts] remain in the Treasury it be Divided between the Towns in Like Proportion as afores[d].

(10) That the Publick Ways in the Town from Masters Brook to Cambridge line be Stated and Settled as to their Corse and Wydth as the Court of General Sessions of the peace Agreeable to the report that may be made by y[r] Committee for that purpose already Appointed Shal Order, And if any Land Now Lying as ways or reputed as Such Shall Not be inCluded in the Ways so Stated, the Same Shall be to and for the only Use and benefit and At the Dispose of the Town wherein the Same Shall Ly.

Provided that the Sale of any of y[e] s[d] Lands already Disposed of by y[e] Towns Com[tee] (which Shall not be included in the ways when Stated as afores[d]) Shall remain good And Valled to the Purcheser of the Same, Also that Each Town Shall have the Benefit of the proceeds of y[e] Sale of Such of the Lands before mentioned as ly within the Same. And if the Ways Stated as Afores[d] Shall Include any Lands belonging to Any Perticuler Person the owner of Such Land Shall have Meet recompence made him by the Town wherein the Same Lye.

And the Vote Past in the Affirmative

Hear Ends Precinct Affairs

The End of Precincts.

Ded. [illegible]

[47] Blank

[48] Entries of certificates from the Minifter of ye Cbch of England.

To ye Town treafurer of Watertown.

This may certify that Mr Josiah Stowel of Watertown in the County of Middlefex is a profest Member of the Church of England and Hath Submitted himfelf to me as his Minifter in Chrift Church in Boston where he has attended the worfhip of God for a confiderable time.

TIMOTHY CUTLER

Boston Sepr 7th 1754. — JOHN BAKER, ALEXr CHAMBERLAIN } Church Wardens
Recd the 23d of Sepr

To the Town treasurer of Watertown

This may certify that Mr Elijah Bond of Watertown in the County of Middlefex is a Profeft Member of the Church of England & hath Submitted himfelf to me as his Minifter in Chrift Church in Boston, where he has attended the worfhip of God for a Confiderable time.

TIMOTHY CUTLER

Boston Sepr 30. 1754. — JOHN BAKER, ALEXr CHAMBERLAIN } Church Wardens
Recd Octobr 7. 1754.

To the Town Treafurer of Watertown

This may certify that Mr Josiah Bright of Watertown in the County of Middx is a Profeft Member of the Church of England and hath Submitted himfelf to me as his Minifter in Christ Church in Boston where he has attended the worship of God for a Confiderable time

TIMOTHY CUTLER

Boston Sepr 30th 1754. — JOHN BAKER, ALEXr CHAMBERLAIN } Church Wardens
Recd October 7th 1754.

Boston October 7th 1754.

This may Certify all whom it may Concern that Mrs Elizebeth Vila of Watertown in the County of Middx and Province of ye Mafsachufetts Bay in New England is a proffefsed Member and Communicant of ye Church of England and ufually & frequently attends the Publick Worfhip of God on ye Lords Days at a Church of England in Boston in the Province aforsesd Called Kings Chapel

H CANER Minister &

Teft JAMES FORBIS, JOHN BOX } Wardens of fd Chapel

To Mr Jofeph Mafon Treafurer of the Town of Watertown aforesd.

This may Certify that Mr John Coollidge of Watertown is a profeft member of the Church of England and for many years has Attended the Publick Worship of God in Christ Church Boston where I ye Subfcriber am a Minifter and has Subjected himfelf to me as his Minifter.

TIMOTHY CUTLER
JOHN BAKER } Church
Boston, Octr 5, 1754 ALLEX^r^ CHAMBERLAIN } Wardens
To the Clerk and Treafurer of y^e^
Town of Watertown

[49]

Mr James Baily of Watertown hath for many years been a Profeft Member of the Church of England According to the Records of Chrift Church in Boston whereof I am Minister, His Daughter Elizebeth was Baptized October 10th 1731 and before and ever since that time he has been a Profeft Churchman and for a Long time has Ufualy & frequently attended the Publick Worfhip of God in Chrift Church as a Parifhioner of it.

TIMOTHY CUTLER
JOHN BAKER } Church
Boston Octo^r^ 1. 1754. ALEX^r^ CHAMBERLAIN } Wardens
To the Clerk and Treafurer of Watertown

This may Certify that Mr William Goding of Watertown is a Profeft Member of the Church of England, and has Subjected himfelf to me the Subfcriber as Minifter of Christ Church in Boston. TIMOTHY CUTLER
JOHN BAKER } Church
Boston Octo^r^ 5. 1754 ALEX^r^ CHAMBERLAIN } Wardens
To ye Clerk & Treafurer of ye Town of Watertown.

To the Town Treafurer of Watertown

This to Certify that Silas Bright of your Town is a Profeft Member of ye Church of England, and has Submitted himfelf to me as his Minifter where He has Attended the Publick Worfhip of God for two months past.

TIMOTHY CUTLER
ALEX^r^ CHAMBERLAIN } Church
Watertown Octo^r^ 23. 1754 JOHN BAKER } Wardens

This may Certify that Mr Jonathan Brown jun^r^ and Mr Jonas Bond jun^r^ both of Watertown are Profeft Members of ye Church of England and for Several months paft have frequented the Worfhip of God in Christ Church Boston and have submitted themfelves to me the Subfcriber as Minifter of s^d^ Church.

TIMOTHY CUTLER
JOHN BAKER } Church
Boston Sepr 14. 1754. ALEX^r^ CHAMBERLAIN } Wardens.
To Mr Joseph Mason, Town Treasurer of Watertown.

This may Certify that Saml Stratton of Watertown is a profeft member of ye Church of England and hath Attended the Publick Worfhip of God in Christ Church Boston ever since May Laft.

TIMOTHY CUTLER
JOHN BAKER } Church
Bofton Sepr 14, 1754 ALEX^r^ CHAMBERLAIN } Wardens.

The three following Order of Seatings in the Meetinghouse are inserted papers taken from the Town Clerk's file of Original Papers.—Eds.

[50]

The Report of the Comtee chofen to Seat the meeting houfe in East Precinct in Watertown. The Ordr of Seating in as follows.

Seated in the firft Seat below
Mr Wm Shattuck
Mr Tho : Straight
Mr Henry Spring
Mr Simon Tayntor
Mr Tho : Traine
Mr Zec Cutting
Mr Ephm Cutter

in the 2d Seat
Mr David Stone
Mr Tho : Coollidge
Mr Andw White
Lt Joseph Coollidge
Mr John Kimbal
Mr Saml Pierce
Mr John Cunningham

3d Seat
Lt John Fiske
Mr Tho : Bond
Mr Joseph Child
Mr John Holland
Mr Joseph Harrington
Mr Richd Clark
Mr Daniel Bond

4th Seat
Mr Joseph Bright
Mr Stephen Cooke
Mr Benjn Whitney
Mr Saml Parry
Mr Saml Warrin
Mr Ephm Cutter Junr
Mr Joshua Grant

5
Mr John Ormes
Mr Wm Williams
Mr Joseph Holdin
Mr David Sanger
Mr Jonan Benjamin
Mr Wm Goddin
Mr Isaac Church

6 Seat
Mr Nathl Clark
Mr Eb : Haftings
Mr Geo : Cutting
Mr John Beers
Mr Theo : Grover
Mr John Tayntor
Mr Timy Harris

7 Seat
Mr Nathl Stearns
Mr John Coollidge
Mr Benjn Chadwick
Mr Joshua Warrin
Mr John Stearns
Mr Henry Goddins

Fore Seat in the front Galy
Mr Oliver Livermore
Mr Nathl Harris
Mr Nathl Bright
Mr John Haftings
Mr John Stonel
Mr Saml Brown
Mr Danl Whitney

fore Seat in ye Side Galy
Mr Josiah Perry
Mr Eb : Stone
Mr John Bright
Mr John Bond
Mr Benjn Haftings
Mr John Maddocks
Mr Nathl Norcrofs
Mr Andw White Junr
Mr Nathl Bond
Mr Saml Hager
Mr Henry Spring Junr
Mr Saml Stratton
Mr John Whitney
Mr Henry Bond
Mr Soloman Stoddard
Mr Jonan Bemis

Front 2d Seat
Mr John Brown
Mr Nathl Coollidge
Mr Simon Coollidge
Mr Jofhua Learned
Mr Saml Clark
Mr Edmd Dix
Mr Saml Dix

Front Gallery Pew
Mr John Reed
Mr Jofiah Reed
Mr Jonan Learned
Mr David Learned
Mr Isaac Holdin
Mr Wm Goddin
Mr Tho : Bishop

Side Gallery Pew
Mr Eb: Eddy
Mr Jofiah Livermore
Mr Jonas Coollidge
Mr Nathl Haftings
Mr Edmd Livermore
Mr Henry Fiske
Mr Danl Fiske
Mr Joseph Allen
Mr Jonan Perry
Mr Wm March

In the firft Seat below on ye Womens Side
Widow Penneman
Widow Couvers
Widow Bond
& ye Gentlems wives yt are Seated in ye fore Seat

2d Seat
Mr Chary Stone
Widw Chenry
Widow Stratton
And the wives of thofe Gentlemen Seated in ye Second Seat mens Side

3d Seat
Widow Mary Haftings
Widow Elizh Benjamin
Widow Mary Grant
And ye Wives of thofe Seated in ye 3d Seat

4 Seat
All ye Wives of thofe Seated in ye fourth Seat
& ye Widow Abigail Grant

5 Seat
the Wives of thofe Seated in 5 Seat on ye men Side

6 Seat in the Same Ordr

And ye Same Ordr in ye 7th Seat

Fore Seat in ye front Gallery on ye Womens Side
Ye Wives of thofe Gentlemn Seat in the fore Seat mens front

Fore Seat on ye Side Gallery on ye Womens Side
Mrs Martha Coollidge
And ye Wives of thofe Seated in the fore Seat on ye oppofite Gallery

NATHAN FISKE
JOHN COOLLIDG
JOSEPH MASON } Comtee
JOHN HASTINGS
OLIVER LIVERMORE

Watertown April 24 : 1732

[51]

The Report of the Comtee Cohefen to Seat the Meeting House in Watertown, the Order of Seeting is as follows.

Seated in the first Seat below.
Mr Thomas Stright
Mr Henry Spring
Nathl Harris Efqr
Mr John Hunt
Doctr Jofiah Convarse
Mr Oliver Livermore
Captn Thomas Homans
Captn Jofeph Coollidg
John Kimball

in the 2d Seat
Mr David Stone
Mr Andrew White
Mr Richard Clark
Leut John Fiske
Mr Jofeph Harrington
Mr John Haftings
Mr Jofeph Child
Mr William Gooding

3d Seat
Mr Isaac Church
Mr James Baley
Mr Stephen Cooke
Mr John Whitney
En. Ebenezer Stone
Mr Jofeph Bright
Mr John Coollidge Jr
Mr Daniel Bond

4th Seat
Mr Ebenezar Thornton
Mr Josiah Perry
Mr Saml Perry
Mr Jacob Parker
Mr Nathll Norcrofs
Mr John Bond
Mr Henry Spring Junr
Mr Walter Beath

5th Seat
Mr John Bell
Mr John Becks
Mr Jona Benjamin
Mr Samll Warrin
Mr Ebenr Hastings
Mr David Sangar
Mr Joseph Whitney
Mr William Goding Jur

the Sixth Seat Below
Mr Edmond Livermore
Mr Benjamin Whitney
Mr Henery Goding
Mr Nathll Bond
Mr Joshua Warrin
Mr Jofeph Stearns
Mr Samll Nutting

7th Seat
Mr Nathll Stearns
Mr John Stearns
Mr Ifaac Holding
Mr Samll Stovell

Side Gallery Pew
Mr Nath Stone
Mr Samll Child
Mr James Dix
Mr Joseph Mafon Jr
Mr David Livermore
Mr James Hackiton
Mr Isreal Meed
Mr Phinias Holding
Mr John Gleason
Mr Richard King
Mr Nathan Parrey

Front Pew
Mr Samll Warrin Jr
Mr Thomas Stovell
Mr Josiah Stovell
Mr David Gleason

In the first Seat Below on the Womens Side
Widow Rebecak Train
And ye Gentlemens Wives that are Seated in the fore Seat

2d Seat
Widow Mary Graut
And the wives of those Gentlimen Seated in the Seckond Seat

3d Seat
Mrs Martha Coollidge
And the Wives of those Gentimen Seated in the third Seat

4th Seat
Widow Elizabeth Cutting
And the Wives of those Gentimen Seated in ye forth Seat

fore Seate in ye front Gallry
Mr Daniel Whitney
Mr John Stovell
Mr John Bright
Mr John Taintor
Mr Jona Bemis
Mr Jofeph Willington
Mr Benjimin Haftings
Mr Andrew White Junr

fore Seat Side Gallery
Mr Samll Hager
Mr Henry Boud
Mr Thomas Saltmarsh
Mr John Brown
Mr Crifterpher Grant
David Learned
Jona Church
Mr Simon Coollidge
Mr Samll Stratton
Mr Joshua Learned
Mr Samll Fiske
Mr Amos Bond
Mr Nathll Bright
Mr David Coollidge
Mr Samll Prentice
Mr John Velah

Front 2d Seat
Mr Jonathan Child
Mr Stephen Sawin
Mr Isaac Sanderfon
Mr William Lawrence
Mr Samll Cooke
Mr Samll Whitney
Mr James Grimes
Mr Josiah Perry Junr

And the Gentlemens Wives Seated in the other Seats in the Same order

OLIVER LIVERMORE
JOHN TAYNTER
JONATHAN CHURCH
HENRY BOND
} Comte

Watertown June ye 15th 1741.

[52] Blank.

[53]

Watertown June 10th 1748

We the Subscribers being a committee appointed by the town of Watertown at a General town meeting on the sixteenth of January last in order to Seat the meeting houſe have Seated it as follows (viz)

In the fore Seat below
Doc^r Josiah Convers
Mr John Kimball
Mr Richard Clark
Mr James Bailey
Mr Joseph Harrington
Mr Joseph Child
Mr Stephen Coock
Mr John Bright

In the Second Seat below
Capt John Tainter
Henry Spring Junr
John Whitney
Andrew White
En. Ebenz^r Stone
Joseph Bright
Saml Hagar
Benjn Hastings

In the third Seat below
Ebenz^r Thorington
Thomas Saltmarsh
Saml Parry
Saml Warrin
Josiah Perry
John Coollidge J^r
Joseph Whitney
Saml Nutting

In the fore Seat in the front
Saml Fisk
Nathl Harrington
Nathl Bright
Amos Bond
Jonas Coollidge
William Coollidge
David Larnard
W^d Elizabeth Larnard

In the forth Seat below
David Coollidge
David Sangar
Saml Prentice
Saml Stratton
William Godding
Henry Godding
Joseph Stearns
Simon Coollidge
Chriſtopher Grant

In the fore Seat in the long Gallirey
Jon^a Stone Junr
Jon^a Brown Junr
Nathl Stone
Seth Hastings
Nathan Perry
Edmund Foul
James Dix
Smith Prentice
Saml Coock
David Livermore
Bezalal Larnard
Saml Whitney
Jon^a Stone tartus
Jacob Calwell

In the fifth Seat below
John Vels
Joshua Warring
Henry Bond
Jon^a Child
Saml Child
Uriah Clark
Saml Warring Junr
William Lee
John Clark

In the Second Seat in ye front
Isaac Sanderſon
Josiah Stowell
Henry Larnard
John Young
Will Gamage
Benjn Whitney
Isreal Mead
Henry Spring tartus

In the hind Seat in the Long Galliery
Joseph Hastings
Nehemiah Mason
Saml Coollidge
Phenihas Holden
Elias Mason
Nathan Stone
Eliſha Coollidge
Ephrim Warrin
Daniel Bond Junr
John Gale
Eben^r Stone Junr

In the hind Seat in ye front
Daniel Pierce
Jabez Harrington
Joseph Chiles Junr
Stephen Stearns
John McCollifter
Charles McCollifter

These Persons who have Wives their Wives are placed in the Oppifite Seats to their Hufbands in the Womens Seats

NATHl BRIGHT
JONATHAN BEMIS
DANIEL WHITNEY
ANDREW WHITE
THOs SALTMARfH
Comtee

[54] Blank.

[55]

To the Freeholders & other Inhabitants of Watertown afsembled at their annual meeting March 2d 1746/7

Gentlemen, Whereas by Reafon of the finking Value of our Paper Currency, the Sums of money annually granted for my Support in the Work of the Miniftry, together with all the Advantages I make by the Miniftry, have for many Years paft, fallen very much fhort of being fufficient to defray the necefsary Charges of my Family: I do hereby requeft you to take the fame into your ferious Confideration, & to do what you may in your Wifdom and Goodnefs, think proper to be further done for the Support of a Gofpel Minifter, who is

Your Affectionate & faithful Paftor

SETH STORER.

Watertown March 2d, 1746/7

To the Moderator of faid meeting to be Communicated.

[56 & 57]

Plan of Watertown Meeting House Lore floor.
See Town Records 1755. Book V, p. 134

[58]

At a General Town Meeting of the Freeholders & other Inhabitants of Watertown qualified to vote in Town affairs regularly afsembled at the Publick Meeting house on Monday the second Day of June AD 1755. By Adjournment.

Put to vote whether it is the mind of the Town that those Persons who injoyd Pews in the former Meeting house should have Pews in the present Meeting house in the same places where their Pews were in sd former Meeting house under the regulations and upon the Terms other Pews shall be disposd of. And the Vote past in the Negative.

Put to vote whether it be the mind of the Town that the Pews should be settled upon Real & Personal Estate and one Head, And the Vote past in the Affirmative.

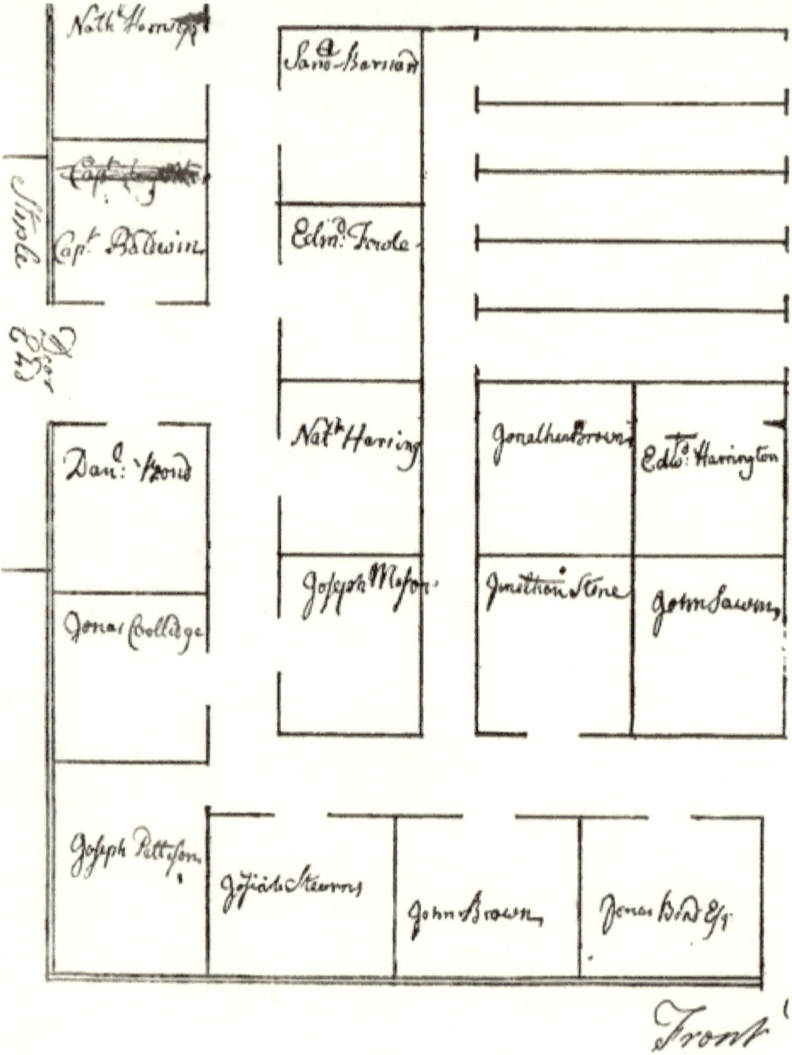

Nath. Harrington

Sam. Barnard

Capt. Baldwin

Stiple

Door

Edw. Forde

Nath. Harring

Jonathan Brown

Edw. Harrington

Dan. Bond

Joseph Mason

Jonathan Stone

John Sawens

Jonas Coollidge

Joseph Pattison

Josiah Stearns

John Brown

Jonas Bond Esq.

Front

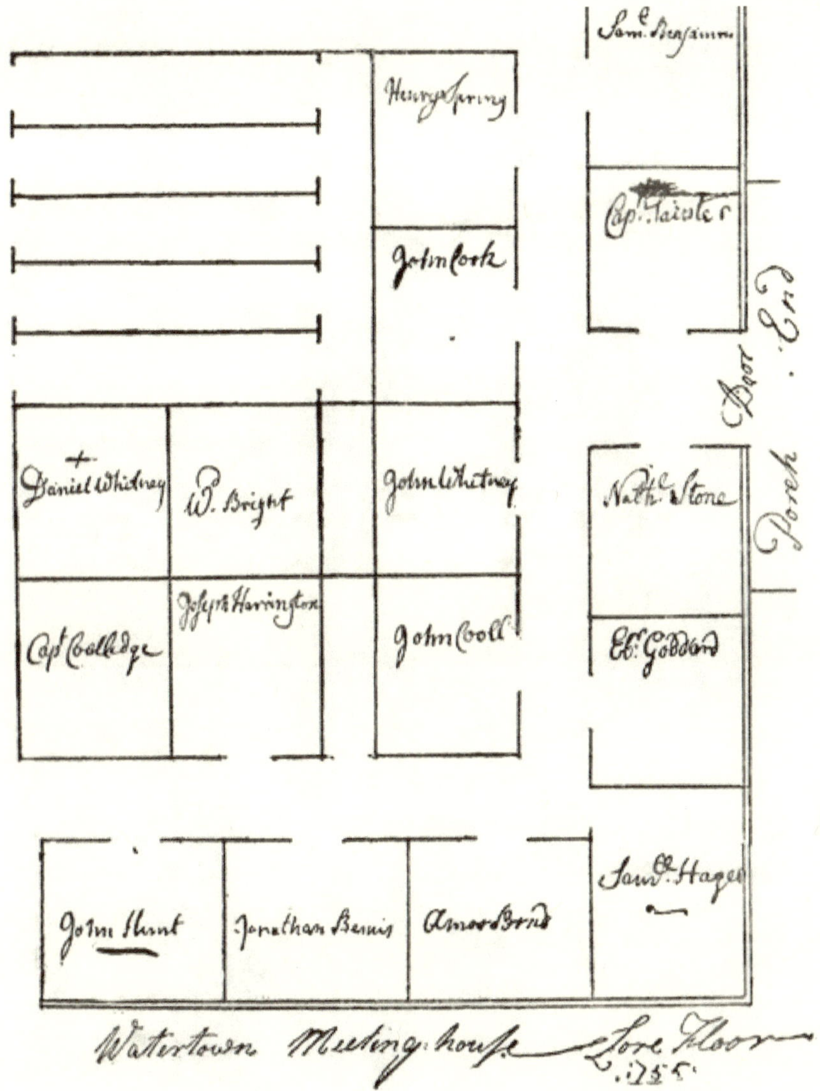
Saml. Benjamin
Henry Spring
John Cook
Door
Porch
End
Daniel Whitney
W. Bright
John Whitney
Nathl. Stone
Joseph Herrington
Capt Coolidge
Ebr. Goddard
Saml. Hager
John Hunt
Jonathan Bemis
Amos Bond
Watertown Meeting-house Fore Floor
1755

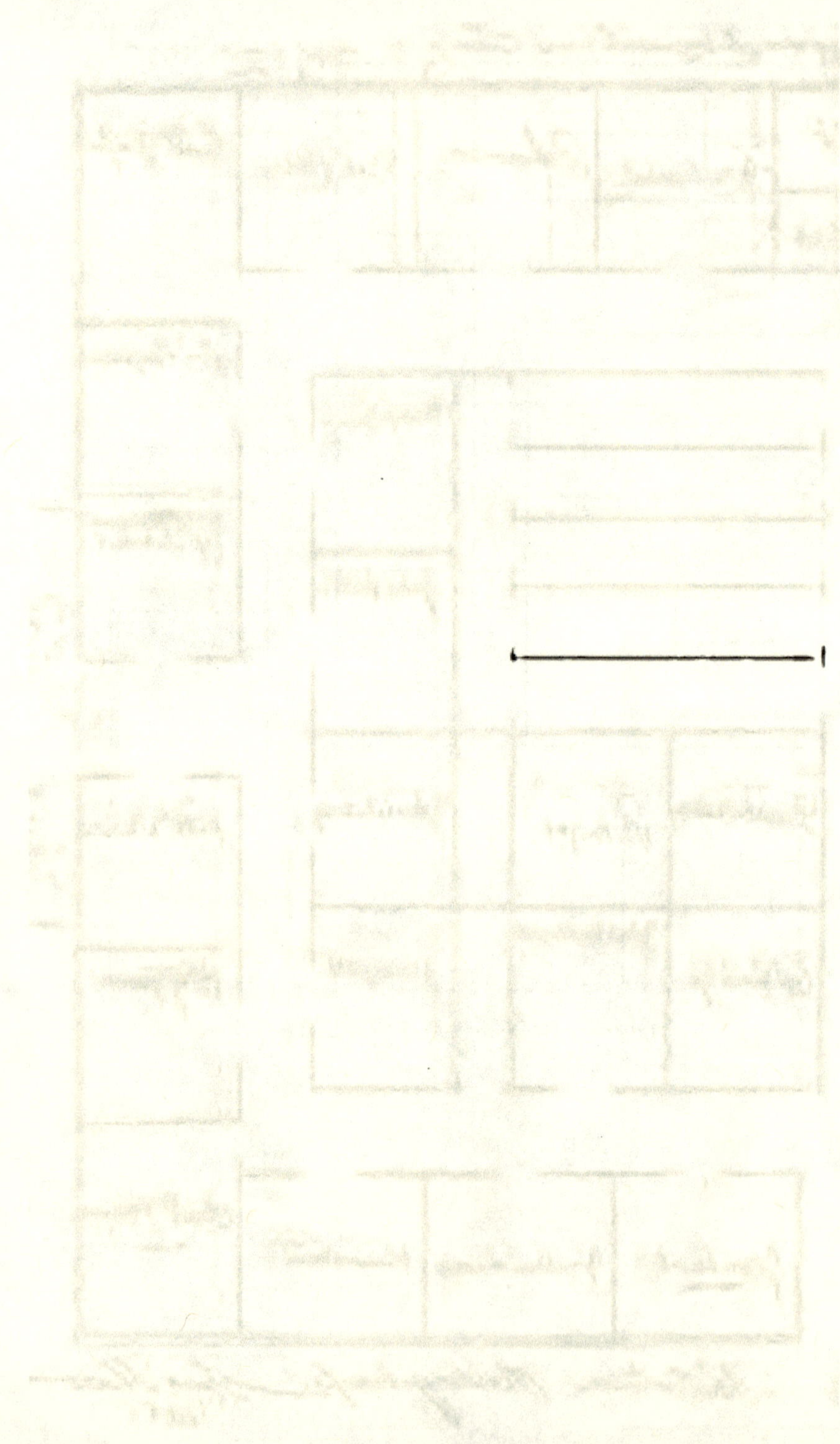

Put to vote whether it is the mind of the Town that the Valuation by which the Rate was made for building the Meeting house be the Rule by which the Pews shall be despos[d] of, And the Vote past in the Affirmative.

Voted that the Persons to whom the Pews shall be granted or who shall draw the Pews, personally set in them usually with their Families or s[d] Pews shall revert to the Town.

Voted that when any Persons shall see cause to sell their Pews the Town shall have the refusal of s[d] Pews paying the Money rais[d] on s[d] Pews.

Voted that if any Persons sell their Estates and move out of Town their Pews shall revert to the Town. The Town paying or reimbursting to them the money paid by them for s[d] Pews.

[59]

Voted that those Persons who are reputed Members of the Church of England have a chance for drawing Pews and enjoy the Pews they shall draw as long as they pay their proportion to the Meeting house & Support of the Minister in this Town. Which if they refuse to do s[d] Pews shall revert to the Town for the Town to dispose of as they shall see fit.

Voted that the Afsefsors be the Committee to make the Adjustment of the Charge to be laid upon the Pews, And to offer the Pews to Persons according to their pay, the highest payer first and so on succefsively.

L[t] Edward Harrington's Pew Afsefs[t]. £25-4-11 Old Tenor
A true Copy from Records

NATH[l] R. WHITNEY, Town Clerk.

Watertown Dec[r] 23[d] 1793.

See Bk. V. p 134.

I am of Opinion that Edward Harrington did not convey his Pew in Watertown Meeting House to his Sons by his deed of Gift of his Real Eftate to them in his life time, And that the fame Pew by his Death Defcended to his Heirs at law.

[Record Book of the Pastors.
1686 to 1819.]

---

[i]

John Balye's Booke
Pretium o—6—8 Dublin Dec: 29. 1668:
By the Gift of Mrs Sufannah Baily.
becoms Henry Gibb's Booke Nov. 24, 1698

[ii]

An Account of all ye Mariages I folemnized in New E ye first of which was on ye 10th of Auguft 1686 &c And fo ye reft as you find y^{m} putt down

The Church Book
containing various Matter's,
"Which we from former Registers
"Of Antient Times have known,
"And our Forefather's pious Care
"To us has handed down.
"That Generations yet to come
"Should to their yet unborn Heirs
"Religiously transmit the fame
"And they again to their's."

[iii]

Upon Aug. 10: 1686. I marryed in my own houfe in Watertown (it was ye first time) Rich. Norcrofs, & Rofe Woodward in y^{r} parents full confent being legally publifhed

This was returned by Mr Bond at Cambridge Oct. 19. 86.

Upon January ye 4th 1686/7 I maryed at Watertown Mill Samuel Haftings (ye fon of Thomas Haftings ye deacon of ye church in Watertown) & Lidia church, ye daughter of mr Caleb Church, wth y^{r} parents full confent being legally published

Upon ye 1st of February 1686/7 I maryed in my own houfe in watertown Solomon Johnfon widower of Sudbury, & Hannah Grefte of Natomy being legally publifhed

Upon ye 11th of March 1686/7 I maryed Abraham Prenfe & Ifsabell Whitherfpoon in my Brothers houfe in Bofton being legally publifhed

Upon ye 25th of March 1687 I maryed Danyell Benjamin (ye fone of John Benjamin) & Elizabeth Brown (ye daughter of Jon. Brown) both of Watertown, in my houfe they being legally publifhed, & y^{r} parents fully confenting

Upon yᵉ 25th of March 1687 at my houfe in Watertown I maryed James Begalow (yᵉ fon of John Begalow Sergᵗ) & Patience Brown (yᵉ daughter of Jon. Brown) wth their Parents full confent, yᵉ being legally publifhed

Upon yᵉ 31th of March 1687 at my houfe in Watertown I maryed William Hager) yᵉ fone of widdow Hager) & Sarah Benjamin (yᵉ daughter of John Benjamin) wth their parents full confent, yᵉ being legally publifhed

Upon yᵉ 31 of March 1687 at my houfe in Watertown I maryed Benjamin Whitney (yᵉ fon of John Whitney) & Abigail Hager (yᵉ daughter of widdow Hager) wth yʳ parents confent, yᵉ being legally publifhed

Upon yᵉ 5th of May 1687 at my houfe in Watertown I maryed Jofeph Allen (yᵉ fon of John Allen of Sudbury) & Abigaill Myricck (yᵉ daughter of John Miriack, of charlftown, wth their parents confent, being legally publifhed

Upon yᵉ 24th of May 1687 I maryed near yᵉ Mill bridge in Bofton Edward Taylor Juniour (his Father lodged at Mʳ W. Gibbins) & Rebekah Humphreys (who came lately from Antigo, but her Mother fully confenting her father witnefsing it) be'g Licenfed

[iv]

Upon yᵉ 25th of May 1687 I maryed in my Brothers houfe in Bofton William Clargett, & Mary Neggres, both of yᵐ dwelling in Mʳ Jo. Adams houfe in Boston, they being Licenfed &c i—e. yᵉ having a fpeciall Licence

Upon yᵉ 25th of May 1687 I maryed in yᵉ Almfhoufe on yᵉ common in Bofton James Cornifh Junioʳ, & Mary Kay yᵉ daughter of Thomas Kay yᵉ being legally publifhed

All thefe Eleven laft were returned to yᵉ Court at Cambridge by Mʳ William Bond Seniʳ Justice of peace, this 7th day of June 1687.

Upon yᵉ 20th of June 1687 I maryed in my houfe at Watertown Nathanaell Norcrofse (yᵉ fon of Richard Norcrofse) & Mehetabell Hager (yᵉ daughter of Widdow Hager) both of Watertown wth yᵉ full confent of their parents yᵉ being legally publifhed

Upon yᵉ 4th of July 1687 I maryed in yᵉ houfe of Goody Mefsenger in Bofton Richard Leckey, & Ann Greenfield he having a fpeciall Lycence

Upon yᵉ 4th of July 1687 I maryed Ebenezer Mefsenger & Rofe Collins both of Bofton (in his Mothers houfe) wth yᵉ confent of friends, yᵉ being legally publifhed

Upon yᵉ 11th of Auguft 1687 I maryed in my houfe at Watertown Eliezer Whitney (yᵉ fon of Thomas Whitney of Watertown) now living in Sudbury, & Dorothy Rofse yᵉ daughter of James Rofse of Sudbury wth yᵉ consent of parents, being legally publifhed

Upon yᵉ 17th of Auguft 1687 I maryed in my houfe at Watertown Thomas Fenton & Elizabeth Bafset both of Bofton, being legally publifhed (I having their cirtificutt) & friends confenting

All thefe 5 laft couples were returned to yᵉ Quarter fefsions at Charlftown by William Bond Senioʳ Juftice of peace this 6 day of September 1687

As for any other Mariages y[t] may afterwards be you may look for them on y[e] 2 page, All thefe hitherto being faithfully returned as above faid

[1] [This page occupied by meditations upon Bible texts.]

[2] Mariages Solemized by me, whilft I lived in Watertown

1687

Upon y[e] 18th of October 1687 I maryed in my houfe at Watertown William Feris, Taylor of Watertown & Abigaill Avered widdow of dedham being publifhed according to law

Upon y[e] 3[d] of November 1687 I maryed in my houfe John Garfield of Watertown, & Deborah Holman of Cambridge, wth y[e] confent of parents, they being publifhed according to law

Upon y[e] 22[d] of November 1687 I maryed Peter Barbour, taylor, & coufin Sarah Willy in her chamber in Bofton, parents confenting y[e] having a fpecial Lycenfe

Upon y[e] 24th of November 1687 I maryed Jofeph Winfhipp y[e] fon of Lt. Edward Winfhipp of Natomys, & Sarah Harrington y[e] daughter of Robert Harrington of Watertown in his houfe wth y[e] confent of Friends, y[e] being publifhed according to law

All thefe 4 laft couples were returned to y[e] Court at Cambridge by M[r] William Bond Juftice of Peace this 6th day of December 1687

Upon y[e] 15 of December 1687 I maryed in my houfe George Blanchard & Sarah Bassett both of charlftown with y[e] confent of Friends y[e] being publifhed according to law

Upon y[e] 2[d] of January 1687 I maryed in my houfe Nathanaell Coolidge (y[e] fon of Nathanaell Coolidge) & Lidia Jones (y[e] daughter of Jofiah Jones) both of Watertown, wth y[e] confent of Friends, y[e] being publifhed according to law

Thefe 2 laft Mariages were returned to y[e] Court at Charlftown by M[r] William Bond Juftice of peace this 6th day of March 1687/8

Upon y[e] 10th of Aprill 1688 I maryed in my houfe in Watertown John Whitney (y[e] fon of Jonathan Whitney) & Mary Hapgood (y[e] daughter of Shadrach Hapgood) both of Sherborn, wth y[e] confent of friends, y[e] being publifhed according to law

Upon y[e] 26th of Aprill 1688 I maryed in my houfe in Watertown James Smith & Prudence Harrifon widdow, both of Bofton, having a fpeciall Lycence

Upon y[e] 30th of May 1688 I maryed in my houfe in Watertown Thomas Woodward of Muddy river & Tryphena Fairfield of wth y[e] confent of friends being publifhed according to law

[3]

Marriages folemnifed by me whilft I lived in Watertown

N. E. 1688.

Thefe 3 laft Marriages were returned to y[e] Court at Cambridge by M[r] William Bond Juftice of y[e] peace this 5th day of June 1688

Upon y[e] 24th of Auguft 1688 I maryed in my houfe in Watertown Jonatan Fairbanks of Lancaſter & Mary Haward of Concord wth ye conſent of Friends ye being publiſhed according to law.

This laſt Marriage were returned to ye Court at Charleſtown by Mr William Bond Juſtice of peace ye 4th of September 1688.

Upon ye 19th of September 1688 I maryed in my houſe at Watertown Thomas Knop & Mary Grout of Sudbury wth ye conſent of friends ye being publiſhed according to law

Upon yt 26th of September 1688 I maryed in my houſe at Watertown Richard Bloſse of Watertown & Ann Cutler of Cambridge Farmes wth ye conſent of Friends, ye being publiſhed according to law.

Upon ye 7th of November 1688 I maryed in my houſe at Watertown Joſeph Harrington & Joanna Mixer both of Watertown with ye conſent of Friends, ye being publiſhed according to law

Theſe 3 laſt Marriages were returned to ye Court at Cambridge by Mr William Bond Senr Juſtice of peace ye 4th of December 1688

Upon ye 21st of February 1688/9 I maryed in my houſe at Watertown Ephraim Riſe of Sudbury & Hannah Livermore of watertown wth ye conſent of Friends, ye being publiſhed according to law

This Single mariage were returned to ye court at Charleſtown by Mr W. Bond Juſtice, the 5th of March 1688/9

Upon ye 13th of March 1688/9 I maryed in my houſe at Watertown Abraham Watſon & Mary Butterfield both of Cambridge with ye conſent of Friends, ye being publiſhed according to law.

Upon ye 20th of March 1688/9 I maryed in my houſe at Watertown Joſeph Pearſe junir & Ruth Holland both of Watertown wth ye conſent of friends, being publiſhed according to law

Upon ye 5th of Aprill 1689 I maryed in my houſe at Watertown John Earl of Boſton (a ſeaman) & Mary Lawrence (ye daughter of George Lawrence of Watertown, but ſhe now living in Boſton) with ye conſent of Friends, ye being publiſhed according to law—

[4]

Marriages ſolemnized by me in Watertown.

1689.

Upon ye 26th of September 1689 I maryed in my houſe at Watertown Benjamin Flagg & Experience Child wth ye conſent of Freinds ye being publiſhed according to law

Upon ye 31st of December 1689 I maryed in my houſe at Watertown William Ward & Abigail Spring both of Cambridge village, wth ye conſent of Friends, ye being publiſhed according to law ye Deputy Governour Danforth was preſent

Upon ye 8th of January 1689/90 I maryed in my houſe at Watertown John Moſse, & Elizabeth Gooding (ye daughter of Gregory Cooke wife by a former husband) wth ye conſent of Friends, ye being publiſhed according to law

There is now an end of my Marrying, N. E being in ſome meaſure reſtored to its old way, for wch I deſire heartily to bleſs gd—the Magiſtrats now marry, its very well, Vale conjugium,

Upon ye 22th of December 1690 I maryed in my houſe at Watertown Alexander Bulman & Margarett Taylor with ye conſent of Friends ye being publiſhed according to law

This next above mentioned couple I were much adoe prevailed wth to marye them, ptly for my own ſake, bsc I wid not give offence (tho I hope I ſhall not) & ptly for their ſake, bec its good doing what is done on a good foundation & wth Authority. I was much importuned by friends, ſhe is one of my Ireland friends, & was once my ſervt, it hath been practiſed, I leave it wth g^d, oh y^t I was maryed to J. X.

Upon ye 5th of March 1690/1 I maryed in my houſe (*i. e.* in my study at Watertown) Peter Allen & Mary Smethurſt wth ye conſent of Friends ye being publiſhed according to law

This above couple were my countrey Folk who by their Importunity prevailed wth me I am not forbidden to marry, y^{e}fore I do it only on ſpeciall occaſions

[5]

Mariages Solemnized by me in Boſton, in N. E.

1692

There was by ye Generall Aſsembly ſitting in October & November 1692 an order made for Miniſters marying as well as Juſtices of the peace. wch hath encouraged me to do it at ye importunity of Friends

Upon ye 8th of November 1692 I maryed Joſhua Corniſh & Suſanah Bennet both of Boſton (at her fathers houſe) with ye conſent of Friends, ye being publiſhed according to law.

This above named Mariage was returned & recorded ye 21st of Feb. 1692/3 by Mr Webb ye T^n. Clarke, Mr Wilkins went to him

Upon ye 9th of May 1693 I maryed in my houſe in Boſton Simon Taintor & Joanna Stone both of Watertown with ye conſent of Friends ye being publiſhed according to law

Muning Sawin was ye Clark, & teſtifyed it publickly.

This above named mariage was recorded in ye later end of May or begining of June 1693 by Mr Webb, Mr Wilkins went wth it to him, I gave him 3 black doggs

Upon ye 14th of September 1693 I maryed (in Capt. Leggs houſe) Capt John Barrett & Sabella Legg both of Boſton with ye conſent of Friends ye being publiſhed according to law

This next above named mariage was recorded ye 4th of October 1693 by Mr Webb, I went wth it myſelf & payd him.

Upon ye 5th of October 1693 I maryed in my houſe John Child & Hannah French both of Watertown wth ye conſent of Friends ye being publiſhed according to law

Upon ye 19th of October 1693 I maryed in Capt. Checkly's John Adams & Hannah Checkley both of Boſton wth ye conſent of Friends ye being publiſhed according to law

The 2 above mentioned mariages was recorded by Mr Webb ye 20th of October 1693, I delivered y^m myſelf unto him

Upon ye 16th of November 1693 I maryed in my houſe in Boſton

Samuel Capen & Ann Stone both of Doracester (tho she belongs to Watertown) wth ye content of Friends ye being published according to law

This above mentioned mariage was given to Mr Webb to be recorded by Mr Wilkins ye 12th of December 1693 wth ye money due to him for so doing

[6]

Mariages solemnized by me in Boston in N. E. 93. 94.

Upon ye 13th of December 1693 I maryed in my house in Boston Daniel Collins & Rebekah Clemens both of Boston wth ye consent of Friends ye being published according to law

This above mentioned mariage was given to Mr Webb to be recorded by Mr Wilkins ye 5th of January 1693/4

Upon ye 26 of April 1694 I maryed in my house in Boston William Brown Esq of Salem, & Sister Rebekah Bailey in Boston, ye being published according to law, wth ye consent of friends

Upon ye 17th of May 1694 I maryed in Boston Jabez Beers & Elizabeth Barber both of Watertown wth ye consent of Friends ye being published according to law.

Deacon Allen was present.

These 2 above mentioned mariages was given by Mr Wilkins to Mr Webb to be recorded ye 18th of May 1694.

Upon ye 29th of May 1694 I maryed in my house in Boston Mathew Poole & Sarah Blake of Boston ye being published according to law

This above mentioned mariage was given by Mr Wilkins to Mr Webb to be recorded ye 13th of June 1694.

Upon ye 3^d^ of July 1694 I maryed in my house in Boston Thomas Gray of Plymouth, & Anne Little of Marshfield with ye consent of Friends they being published according to law

This above mentioned mariage was given by M^r^ wilkins to Mr Webb to be recorded ye 24th of July 1694

Upon ye 9th of August 1694 I maryed Francis Thresher & Elizabeth Hicks both of Boston (widow in her house in Boston) ye being published according to law.

This above mentioned marriage was given by M^r^ wilkins to Mr Webb to be recorded ye 29th of August 1694

Upon ye 14th of August 1694 I maryed in my house in Boston a couple of Negros, ye mans name was George, living wth Sam. Gray, ye womans name was Hager living wth Mrs Sweet, al y^t^ belonged to y^m^ gave y^m^ free & full consent, ye were not published, for such use not to be as ye say

This mariage was given by Mr Wilkins to Mr Webb to be recorded ye 16th of January 1694/5

[7]

Mariages Solemnized by me in Boston in N. E.–94–& 95–

Upon ye 15th of September 1694 I maryed in my house in Boston Benjamin Watson & Ann Drue both of Boston wth ye consent of Friends ye being published according to law

This above mentioned mariage was given by Mr Wilkins to Mr Webb to be recorded ye 18th of Oct. 1694

Upon ye 28 of November 1694 I maryed in Mr Peter Butlers houfe Mr George Jafferyes of Pifcataqua & Mrs. Anna Porter of Bofton they being publifhed according to law

This above mentioned mariage was given by Mr Wilkins to Mr Webb to be recorded by him ye 18th of January 1694/5

Upon ye 7th of February 1694/5 I maryed in Mr Chriftophers houfe in Bofton John Wiett & Hannah Garratt both of Bofton ye being publifhed according to law

This above mentioned mariage was given by Mr Wilkins to Mr Webb to be recorded by him ye 14th of March 1694/5

Upon ye 4 of Aprill 1695 I maryed in my houfe Mr Robert Fitzhugh & Mrs Hannah Man both of Bofton ye being publifhed according to law

This above mentioned mariage was given by Mr Wilkins to Mr Webb to be recorded by him ye 23 of April 1695

Upon ye 2^d^ of May 1695 I maryed in my houfe in Bofton Robert Hanna & Hannah Macfon both of Bofton ye being publifhed according to law

This above mentioned mariage was given by Mr Wilkins to Mr Webb to be recorded by him ye 11th of June 1695

Upon ye 10th of June 1695 I maryed in my houfe in Bofton William Briggs & Rebekah Dyer both of Bofton, being publifhed accordng to law

Upon ye 27th of June 1695 I maryed in old Mr Pembertons houfe Mr Jonathen Elliston & Mis Elizabeth Wisondonk both of Bofton, ye being publifhed according to law

Thefe 2 above mentioned mariages was given by Mr Wilkins to Mr Webb to be recorded by him ye Firft of July 1695

Upon ye 26th of July 1693 I maryed in my houfe in Bofton Richard Thomas & Mary Mafon both of Bofton ye being publifhed according to law

This above mentioned Mariage was given by Mr Wilkins to Capt. Savage to be recorded by him (whofe work it is at prefent) ye 22 of Auguft 1695

Upon ye 15th of Auguft 1695 I maryed a couple of Mr Gibbins Negros in his houfe viz Toby & Jane, ye confented to it, & there were many witnefses

[8]

Mariages Solemnized by me in Bofton in N. E. 1695 1696–

Upon ye 25 of October 1695 I maryed in my houfe in Bofton Humphrey Richards & Sufanna Wakefield both of Bofton with ye confent of Friends, ye being publifhed according to law

Upon ye 11th of December 1695 I maryed in my houfe in Bofton Nathanael Pitman & Mary George both of Bofton wth ye confent of Friends ye being publifhed according to law

Thefe 2 above mentioned Mariages given by Mr Wilkins to Capt. Ephraim Savage to be recorded by him ye 26th of December 1695

Upon ye 4th of February 1695/6 I maryed in my houſe in Boſton Elias Maverick & Sarah Smith both of this town ye being publiſhed according to law

Upon ye 13th of February 1695/6 I maryed in old Mr Pembertons Houſe Major Read Elding & Hannah Pemberton of Boſton ye being Legally publiſhed

Upon ye 9th of April 1696 I maryed in my houſe in Boſton Thomas Stevens & Sarah Place both of Boſton being legally publiſhed

Upon ye 9th of April 1696 I maryed in my houſe in Boſton William Hannah of Boſton & Martha Clark of Roxbury ye being legally publiſhed

Theſe 4 above mentioned mariages was given by myſelf to Capt. Ephraim Savage to be recorded by him ye 11th of Aprill 1696

Upon ye 24th of March 1697 I maryed in Capt. Legs houſe Samuel Weaver & Eliz Cravath both of Boſton, being legally publiſhed

This above mentioned mariage was given by myſelf into ye hand of Mr William Grays (to whom now it appertains) to record it viz this 31 of May 1697 wn I dined at Mr Isaac Tay's

Upon ye 29 of July 1697 I maryed at ye Bowling Green Joſeph Royall & Eliz Coleman both of Boſton being legally publiſhed

[9] [Record of those who owned ye Covenant.]

1724/5.	January. 27.	Oliver Livermore
	Feb. 14.	Jonathan Stone Junr
	21.	George Lawrence Junr
	March. 7.	Joſhua Warren Junr
	28.	Nathll Bond & Ann Bond
	April. 25.	Hephzibah Bond
	July. 18.	Ebenezer Chenery & Ruth his wife, Samll Hager & Hannah his wife
	Nov. 14.	Hannah Stone
1725/6.	Feb. 6.	Daniel Haſtings & Sarah his wife
	March. 27.	Jabez Stratton & Tabitha his wife
	May 1.	Jonth Harrington
	Aug. 21.	Isaac Barnard
	Sept. 11.	Samuel Jenniſon Junr
1726/7	Jan. 15.	Samuel Benjamin & Mary his wife
1727.	April 9.	Edward Jackſon & Abigail his wife
	Nov. 5.	Charles Chadwick & Sarah his wife
	19.	Hannah Cutler made publick Confeſsion of her sin & owned ye Covenant.
	Dec. 3.	John Dix, Samuel Dix & Mary Dix
	31.	Simon Coolidge owned ye Covenant, and Caleb Benjamin & Abigail his wife made publick Confeſsion
1727/8.	Jan. 14.	Caleb Benjamin, Suſanna Benjamin, Abigail Benjamin & Abigail Dix
	Feb. 11.	Judith Sawin
1728.	Aug. 11.	John Coollidge & Mercy his wife made publick Confeſsion of their sin & owned ye Covent.

1728/9,	Feb. 23.	Phebe Palfrey.
1729.	May 17.	Nathanael Jennifon & Abigail his wife made publick Confefsion of their fin & owned y[e] Covenant.
	31.	Sufanna Whitney.
1731.	March. 28	Peter, a Negro man of M[r] Stone's entered into Covent.
	April. 11.	Jofhua Learned & Elizabeth his wife made publick Confefsion of their fin & he owned y[e] Coven[t].
	Dec[r] 5	Sufanna Holdin made publick Confefsion of her fin & owned y[e] Covent.
1731/2	Feb. 27.	Ruth underwood made publick Confefsion of her fin & was rec[d] into Favour
1732.	July 16.	Edward Harrington & Anna his wife made publick Confefsion of their fin & owned y[e] Covenant
	Aug[st] 13.	William Goddin Jun[r] & Martha his wife
1732/3.	Feb. 25.	Allen Brown made publick Confefsion of his fins and Ruth Brown Made Confef-sion
	March. 18.	Hephzibah Berry made publick Confefsion of her fin
	April. 29.	Allen Brown
	May. 13.	John Brown
1734.	Sep[t] 8.	Henry Bond Jun[r] & Mary Bond made publick Confefsion of y[e] sin and on 22. Day they owned y[e] Covenant.
	Oct[r] 20.	Joseph Wellington & Dorcas Wellington owned y[e] Covenant

[10]

1734.

	Nov[r] 24.	Sufanna Cutting
1734/5	Feb. 9.	Ebenezer Wellington made Confefsion of his fin w[e] was accepted, & y[n] he was difmifsed to y[e] C[hh] in Stoughton.
	16.	Samuel Barnard
		Margaret Wafson made confefsion of her sin & then owned y[e] Covenant.
1734/5	Jan[ry] 26.	John Lawrence
	Feb. 8.	Stephen Sawin

[11]

The Following Persons have Owned y[e] Covenant since I was ordained.

DAN[l] ADAMS

1778

May 17th	Will[m] Warren and his wife Robe
June 28th	Mofes Cooledge & Hannah his wife
June 28th	Sufanna y[e] wife of Nath[l] Bright

[12]

The following persons have owned the Covenant since I was ordained. R. R. Eliott, Viz

1780

Nov[r]	Lucy & Elizabeth Bond

1781

March 10th	Benj[n] Capan & his Wife Elizabeth

1782

July 29th	Moses Warren & his Wife
Feb[y] 17.	John Bullard & his Wife
Nov[r] 3.	Will[m] Beals & his Wife
17	Hugh Mason & his Wife

1783

Aug[t] 24	Andrew Stimpson & his Wife
Nov[r] 16	Abijah Stone & his Wife
30.	Daniell Jackson
Dec[r] 7	Joseph Bright & his Wife

1784

Feb[y] 1.	Lucy the Wife of Daniel Jackson
May 2.	Nathaniell Bemifs & Wife
Oct[r] 17	Jonathan Stone
Dec[r] 26	Joseph Coolidge & his Wife

1785

Aug[t] 21	Francis Faulkner & his Wife
Oct[r] 30	Thomas Vose & his Wife
Nov[r] 6	Susana the Wife of John Cooke Jun[r]

1786

Aug[t] 7.	Lydia the Wife of Nathan Porter

1787

March 4.	Kate the Wife of Stephen Harris Jun[r]

1788

July 27	Thomas Clarke & his Wife
Nov[r] 23	Benjamin Hastings & wife

1789

Oct[r] 11	John George

1792

March 4	Moses Mason

1793

June 2	Kathy Wife of Ezekiel Whitney Jun[r]
	Charles Bond & Wife

1794

March 9	John Vinal

[13]

1794

March 30 Sarah Saunders

1795

June 21 Sukey Norcrofs
Oct[r] 16 Elizabeth Coolidge Freeman

1796

July 17 Joshua Underwood & wife
Sep[t] 11 Peter Clark & wife
Oct[r] 2 Joshua Grant & wife

1797

June 4 Sarah Wife of Isreal Cooke

1798

Jan[y] 7 John Durant & wife
May 13 Phinehas Hovey & wife
June 24 Luke Bemis

1801

June 7 John Tucker & Wife
Joseph Pierce & wife
July 12 William Bond & wife
James Simmons & wife
Aug[t] 2 Jonathan Alden & wife

1803

Oct[r] 2 Elisha Livermore & wife
23 Luther Coolidge & Wife

1805

Sep[r] 6 Jofeph Russell & Wife
Paul Kendal & wife
Nov[r] 10 Andrew Blackmer & wife

. 1808

May 14 Jonathan Robbins

[14]

May 22 Tyler Bigelow & Wife
Henry Dalrymple & Wife
June 19 Nathaniel R. Whitney Jun. & Wife
Oct[r] 1 Charles Whitney & Wife
23 Afa Stone & wife and Luther Barrett

1809

Oct[r] 29 Jonathan Child & Wife
Nov[r] 5 Isaac Patten & Wife

1810

June 3 Levi Thaxter
Nov[r] 4 Thaddeus Cole & Wife

1811

	Jany 20	Seth Bemis & wife
	June 23	John Trull & Wife
	July 26	Anna Bent
	Sepr 22	Nathaniel Harrington & wife

1812

	Jany 5	Joseph Bird & wife
1813	Nov 14	Phebe S. Stone
1814	Sepr 18	Mary Rand, Sophia Leath
1815	July 16	Mary Robbins
	30	Sarah Robbins
1816	April 21	Jonathan Stone Junr & wife
		Julianna Wife of Charles Stone

[Pages **15** to **41** inclusive blank.]

[42] Marriages

Novr 23^d 1780. Phineas Stearnes & Efther Sanderson were married
Decr 7th 1780 John Sangar & Ame Trask were marr^d
Decr 28. 1780 Isaac Parkhurst & Lucy White were married

The following account of persons baptized by the Revd Mr Seth Storer was soon after his Decease, transcribed from his interleaved Almanaks by his Nephew Eben^r Storer Esqr. An account of the persons baptized by Mr Storer previous to the 18th of April 1773 is entered in this Book. See page [**222.**]

1773

May 23	Susanna Daughter of John Hunt Junr
July 25	Phineas Son of Thomas Learned
Augt 8	Katherine Daugh^t of Nathl Sparhawk at Cambridge Village
Sep^t 30	Elizabeth Daughter of Samuel Soden
Octr 17	Parnel Daugh^r of Jonathan Learned Junr
	Lucy Daugh^r of John Stratton
31	Elisha Son of Amos Livermore

[43]

Novr 21	Susannah Daughter of Joshua Kendall

1774

Feby 20	Frances Daughter of William Fuller
	Christopher. Son of Christopher Grant Junr
27	Thomas Son of Daniel Cornwall
March 13	Elizabeth Daughter of Josiah Bright
	Lois Daughter of Josiah Bright
	James Son of William Leaned
	Israel Son of Israel Whitney

20. Rhoda Daughter of David Coolidge
27 Lydia Daughter of Henry Sanderson
May 8 David & Susana Twins of Jonas Barnard
15 William Son of Nathaniel Rogers }
Abigail Daughter of Phineas Robbins } at Newton
June 12 Lucy Daughter of Penuel Park
26 Grant Son of Jedediah Learned
Joseph Son of Jonathan Whitney
July 10 Grace Daughter of Elkanah Wales
31 Kezia Daughter of Zachariah Shed
Edmund Son of Edmund Fowle

[44]

Aug. 14 Nathaniel Son of John Tainter Junr
Moses Son of Josiah Norcrofs
21. Daniel & John the Sons }
Sarah & Hannah the Daughters of } of Daniel Bond
28 Relief Daughter of John Wellington
Sep^t^ 11. Hannah Daughter of Amos Bond
Octr 2. John Son of Ezekiel Hall
Mary Daughter of Joseph Gardner
23 Benjamin Son of Phineas Jinnison
Sybill Daughter of Wm Chenery
Novr 6 Aaron Son of Wm Sanger
Abner Son of Abner Craft
Rebecca Daughter of Eyris Tainter
Lucy Daughter of Stephen Whitney

[45]

The following account of persons rec^d^ into full communion by the Revd Mr Storer was also transcribed from his interleaved Almanacks

1773

May 23 Charity Capen
July 25 Josiah Bisco
Decr 19 Samuel Barnard & Elizabeth Barnard

1774

April 17 Jonas Barnard & Abigail Barnard
Mary Coolidge & Dorothy Coolidge
24 Amos Bond
May 22 Mercy Coolidge
June 5. Sarah, Elizabeth, & Mary Fisk

See page **[304.]**

[46]

Form of the Covenant to be administered to those who join in full Communion with the Church.

You do now in the presence of the great God, and this christian Afsembly, profefs your belief in the holy Scriptures, that they are the word of God, and the only rule of our faith and obedience, You believe that the Lord Jesus Christ, is the Son of God and the only Mediator between God and Man, and with all your heart, you desire to give up yourself to God, in an everlasting covenant, and to accept of Jesus Christ as your Saviour and Redeemer, in the way prescribed in the Gofpel, and solemnly promise [47] that by the help of divine grace, you will fincerely endeavour to conform to the rules & precepts of our holy religion, to forsake the sins and vanities of this evil world, and to approve yourself a true diciple of Jesus Christ, in all good behaviour, towards God and towards man. And, particularly, you promise, that you will endeavour to walk with this Church, while you have opportunity, in the exercise of christian affection, in conforming to the regulations, and submitting to the discipline of the Church, in all things, agreeably to what you do know, or may hereafter know, to be your duty.

Do you make this profession, and take upon you the obligation of this Covenant? I then declare you to be a Member in [48] full Communion with the Church of Christ, and we who are members of the Church, do promise and engage, that by the help of the divine Spirit, we will make it our fincere aim and endeavour, to treat you in every respect, as a member of the fame body with ourselves, watching over you and that for your good, with a spirit of meeknefs, love and tendernefs, earnestly praying, that the Lord God, the great Head of the Church, would dwell among us, that his blessed Spirit, may be upon us, and that his glorious kingdom may be advanced by us. Amen.

[49]

Form of the Covenant to be administered to those who own the Covenant.

You do now in the presence of the great God, and this christian Assembly, profefs your belief in the holy Scriptures, that they are the word of God, and the only rule of our faith and obedience: You believe that the Lord Jesus Christ is the Son of God, and the only Mediator between God and Man, and with all your heart, you desire to give up yourself to God, in an everlasting Covenant, and to accept Jesus Christ as your Saviour and Redeemer, in the way prescribed in the Gospel, and you folemnly promise, that by the help of divine grace you will fincearely endeavour to conform to the rules and [50] precepts of our holy religion, to forsake the sins and vanities of this evil world, and to approve yourfelf a true disciple of Jesus Christ in all good behaviour towards God, and towards man, And you likewise fubmit to the government and discipline of Christ in his Church, and engage to walk in all things, agreeably to what you do know, or may hereafter know, to be your duty.

Do you thus profefs and promise? I then declare you to be entitled to all the privileges which are usually given by this Church, to those, who take upon them the obligations of this Covenant.

[51 to 61 inclusive] all blank.

[62]

An Epitaph upon my Dear Wife's Tomb Stone in Watertown in N. E. made by Mr Moodey:

Pious Lydia made and given by God
As a moft meet help to John Bailey
Minifter of ye Gofpel—
Good betimes, Beft at laft,
Lived by Faith, Dyed in peace
Went off singing, Left us weeping,
Walked wth God till tranflated in y^e^
39 yeare of her age April 16, 1691
Read her Epitaph in Prov. 31, 10, 11, 12, 28, 29, 30, 31.

[See page 292]

[63]

Epitaph upon 2 or 3 pfons I were acquainted with, Brother Thomas and my D^r^ wife Lydia.

An Epitaph upon Mr Sherman in Watertown in N. E. In my time, my Honorable predeceffor, made by Mr Willard.

"Johannis Shermanni, Maximæ Pietatis, Gravitatis, & Candoris Viri
In Theologia plurimum verfati, In concionando vere Chryfoftomi,
In Artibus Liberalibus præcipue Mathematicis incomparabilis;
Aquitamenfis Ecclefiæ in Nova Anglia fideliffimi Paftoris,
Collegii Harvardini Infpectoris & Socii,
Qui poftquam annis plus minus XLV Chrifto fuit
YIIIPETHS [i.e. under rowers ye fteer ye fhip towards heaven,]
in Ecclesia Fidus—Morte Matura tranfmigravit
et a Christo palma Decoratus eft,
A.D. MDCLXXXV, Augusti. 8.
Ætatis. Suæ LXXII.
Memoriæ."

This is better written in ye end of my Concordance.

An Epitaph upon my Brother Thomas Tomb Stone,
In Watertown in N. E. Made by Mr Moody.

"Here lyes ye precious duft of
Thomas Bailey,

A painful preacher,	A Moft defirable neighbour,
An Exemplary Liver,	A pleafant Companion,
A Tender Hufband,	A Common Good,
A Careful Father,	A Cheerful doer,
A Brother for Adverfity,	A patient Sufferer,
A Faithful Friend,	Lived much in a little time.

A Good Copy for all Survivors,
Aged 35 years
Slept in Jesus 21 of January 1688."

[Epitaph in the Granary Burial Ground of Boston,

"Here lyeth interred the Body of the
Reverend and Faithful Minister
Of the Gospel in Boston
M[r] John Bailey
aged 54 years who
Deceased the 12 of December 1687"]

[64] Blank

[65]

A Legacy being left, by M[rs] Ann Mills late of Watertown to the Church in the East part of this Town, which Legacy consisted of Two Hun[d]. Eighty Three p[ds] 10[s]. The Church chose a Committee to let the same out upon Interest; which Interest was to be paid to the Minister & Deacons to be disposed of by them according to the last will of y[e] s[d] M[rs]. Mills.

The account of what has been received, & to what objects of Charity disposed of, follows.

1730.		£	s	d
May. 13.	Received of the Churches Comittee which was disposed of to the following Persons Viz.	7.	11.	3
	To M[rs] Chamberlain 40/	2.	00.	00
	To the widow Sarah Perry. 20/	1.	00.	00
	To the wife of Sam[ll] Warren 20/	1.	00.	00
	To Martha Whitney 20/	1.	00.	00
	To the widow Ruth Coollidge	1.	01.	3
	To M[r] Tho[s] Coollidge for the widow Webb	1.	10.	0
		£7.	11.	3

Dec. 13

Received of the Churches Comittee which was given to the following persons viz.	£9 : 00 : 0
To the wife of Ebenezer Biggelow	3 : 00 : 0
To M[r] Eph. Cutter Sen[r]	1 : 05 : 0
To his wife Bethiah Cutter	1 : 05 : 0
To Martha Whitney	1 : 00 : 0
To M[r] Benj[a] Chadwick	1 : 05 : 0
To widow Ruth Coollidge	1 : 05 : 0
	£9 : 00 : 0

1731.

July 26.	Received of the Churches Comittee Eighteen pounds five Shillings & fix pence	18. 05. 6
	of w^c^ was given To ye widow Sufanna Benjemin	3. 00. 00
	To Ep. Cutter Senr	1. 00. 00
	To Martha Whitney	1. 00. 00
		£5. 00. 00

1732/3

March.	5th	Rec. of the Churches Committee, by ye Minifter & Deacons.	14. 12. 1
		To Eph. Cutter	00. 18. 0
March.	5.	To Margrett Warren	01. 10. 0
		Sam^ll^ Warrens Wife	1. 10. 0
		Martha Whitney	2. 00. 0
		Benj^a^ Chadwicks Wife	3. 00 0
		Wm Goddin Senr	1. 5. 5
		Widow Sufanna Benjamin	2. 00. 0
			£12. 3. 5

[66 to **77]** Occupied with the continued account of this fund.

[78] Blank

[79] 1798

A List of the persons who have contributed towards the fupport of the Communion Table, in Watertown with the fums by them respectively paid. Viz—

John Remington	£0 3 0
Josiah Mixer	2 3
Ruth Stone	1 6
Easter Cook	9
Daniel Sawin	1 6
Jedediah Leathe	3 0
Daniel Whitney	3 0
Samuel White	3 0
Richard Clark	1 6
Moses Coolidge	3 0
Susanna Bond	1 6
Eunice Coolidge	1 6
Mary Stearnes	1 6
Sarah Clark	1 6
Sibil Livermore	1 6
Amos Bond	3 0
Joanna Cook	9

[80 to **85]** occupied with continuation of this list.

[86 to 89] Blank.

[90 to 119] "Texts."

[120 to 127] Blank.

[128]

At a meeting of the Church belonging to the East part of Watertown January. ye 22nd 1728/9

The Following votes were pafsed vizt

Voted. 1. Wether the Church be of the mind to chufe a Committee to receive what is due to this Church by vertue of the last Will and Testamont of Mrs Anne Mills, late of Watertown deceafed. It pafsed in the affirmative.

Voted. 2. That Lieu^t Sam^ll Stearns, Deacon John Coollidge Deacon Joseph Mafon, Lieu^t Joseph Coollidge & Mr Nath^ll Harris be the Church's Comittee to act on their behalf in referrence to the aforsaid Legacy.

Voted. 3. Whether the Church doth invest the faid Comittee with full Power to recover and receive, in their behalf, the whole that is or fhall be due to this Church by virtue of the aforsaid last Will and Testament of Mrs Anne Mills, of the Executors of faid Will, or of fuch of them as fhall be furviving, and in the name of the Church to give faid Executors a Difcharge or Difcharges

It pafsed in the affirmative.

Voted. 4. Whether the Church doth empower the aforesaid Comittee to let out upon Lawful Interest, they having fuch Security as they think fufficient. that part of the eftate of the abovesaid Anne Mills, which doth or fhall belong to this Church, which Interest fhall be paid in yearly to the Minister or Ministers and Deacons. It pafsed in the affirmative.

Voted. 5. That if the Minister or Ministers and Deacons of this Church fee need to call for part or all of the Principal of the above mentioned Eftate, as well as for the interest of it we do acknowledge that they have full power to do it, and their receipt shall be the Comittee's Difcharge for fuch Sum or Sums as they receive of them. Atteft. SETH STORER Paftor.

[129]

At a Meeting of The Church belonging to the Eaft part of Watertown. October 13th 1731.

1. Put to vote, whether the Church be of the mind that Daniel Whitney, (he having explicitly owned the Covenant among, and fubmitted himself to the Watch and Difcipline of thofe who acted as a third Church in Watertown, and having a Child baptized by Mr Robert Sturgeon after the Refult of the Council of Churches met at watertown on May 1. 1722,) could juftly claim the privilege of Baptifm for his Children, before he had made Satisfaction.

It pafsed in the negative.

2. Put to Vote whether the Church do leave it with the Minister and Deacons to receive fuch Satisfaction, from s^d whitney, as they shall think fufficient, and that in behalf of the Church.
It pafsed in the affirmative.

July. 15. 1736.
At a meeting of the Church of Chrift in the Eaft part of Watertown in order to make choice of fome fuitable Perfon to the office of a Deacon in faid Church, the Bretheren voted & chofe Mr Jofeph Mafon to faid office, and he declared his acceptance thereof.
Atteft. SETH STORER Paftor.

May. 29. 1741.
At a meeting of the Church of Chrift in Watertown in Order to make Choice of fome fuitable perfon to the office a Deacon in faid Church, the Bretheren voted & chofe Mr Joseph Coollidge to faid office, who accepted thereof.
Atteft. SETH STORER Paftor.

June 27th 1749.
At a meeting of the Church of Chrft in Watertown in Order to make Choice of fome fuitable Perfon to the office of a Deacon in faid Church, the Bretheren voted & chofe Mr Samuel Fifk to faid office & he accepted thereof
Atteft. SETH STORER Paftor.

[130]

July. 14th 1749.
At a Meeting of the Church of Chrift in Watertown An account was exhibited to faid Church by fome of the faid Committee, chofen to let out on Intereft Mrs Ann Mills's Legacy to faid Church, of their difcharging the Truft repofed in them as the Churches Committee for the Time paft; after reading whereof it was put to vote, vizt

Voted. 1. Whether the Church be fatisfied with the account given unto the Church by faid Committee?
It paft in ye Affirmative.

Voted. 2. Whether the Bretheren of the Church give their Thanks to faid Committee for their faithful Care in the Difcharge of their office as the Churches Committee?
It paft in ye Affirmative.

Voted. 3. Whether the Church be of the mind to chufe two perfons to fupply the vacancies made in the Churches Comittee to let out Mrs Ann Mills's Legacy, in the Room of two of faid Committee removed by Death? It paft in ye Affirmative.

Voted. 4. Voted & chofe Deacon Samuel Fifk to be one of the Churches Committee to let out the Legacy left to this Church by Mrs Ann Mills. Atteft SETH STORER Paftor

Voted. 5. Voted & chofe Capt. John Tainter to be one of the Churches Committee to let out on Intereft the Legacy left to this Church by Mrs Ann Mills. Attest. SETH STORER Paftor.

June 12. 1761. At a Meeting of the Church of Christ in Watertown in order to make choice of some suitable Person to be a Deacon in said Church, the Bretheren voted & chose Cap[t] John Tainter to said office; and he declared his acceptance thereof.

Attest SETH STORER Pastor.

Voted. 2. Whether the Church be of the Mind to chuse a Person to supply the vecency made in the Churches Comittee to let out M[rs] Ann Mills's Legacy. in the Room of Nath[l] Harris Esq[r] removed by Death. It past in the affirmative.

Voted. 3. Voted & chose Nath[r] Stone to be one of y[e] Churches Comittee for the service aforesaid.

Attest SETH STORER Pastor.

[131]

June 12th 1761. At a Church Meeting, Deacon Samuel Fisk rendred An Account of the Churches Comittee's Discharge of their Trust in letting out M[rs] Ann Mills' Legacy to said Church & their receiving the Interest due thereon to the middle of last July, which was accepted by the Bretheren.

Voted. The Bretheren of the Church voted sd Comittee Thanks for their faithful discharge of their office.

Attest SETH STORER Pastor

1777. Nov[r] 22[d]. M[r] Nathaniel Stone was Chosen to the office of Deacon in the Church, of which he accepted.

The Same Day M[r] Sam[ll] White was Chosen one of the Com[tee] to take care of the Legacy Left to this Chh: by M[rs] Ann Mills.

Att[t] SAM[ll] FISK Moderator

1780 Oct[r] 27th

At a meeting of the Chh of Christ in Watertown The following Votes were passed, Viz.

Vote 1[ly] That all Confessions & acknowledgements for Crimes committed should hereafter be mad before the Chh and not before the Congregation.

Vote 2[d]. That all persons who have stood propounded the usual time & against whom no objections have been offered, should be received into the Chh by the Pastor without an express Vote of the Chh they publickly assenting to the holy Covt.

Attest RICHARD R. ELIOT Pastor

[132]

1793

April 3. At a meeting of the Chh of Christ in Watertown the following Votes were passed Viz—

Voted. That a Committee of the Chh be chosen to take care of the monies belonging to the Chh, to collect any Debts which may be due to the Chh, to receive any monies belonging to the Chh which may now be in the hands of any person or persons,— & apply them for the use of y[e] Chh in such a manner as they may think proper, unless they are the procedes of certain donations heretofore made to the Chh. in which Case the Committee are to apply the money to ſuch uses as have been expreſsly pointed out by the Donors.

Voted. That Deacon Leathe, Dea^n^ Whetney & Mr Soden be a Commit^e^ to act in behalf of the Chh, in respect to the Matters which are mentioned in the preceeding vote—

at^t^ RICHARD R. ELIOT Pastor

[133]

1795
June 28. At a meeting of the Chh of Ch^t^ in Watertown

Voted. That Roger Adams & his Wife be dismissed from this Chh, & be recommended to the Church under the pastoral Care of the Rev. Mr Greenough of Newton. They having signified to the Chh that it is their desire to receive ſuch a Dismission.

At a meeting of the Church of Christ in Watertown on Monday the 21^t^ of Oct. 1799, the following Votes were passed Viz.

1. Voted, that all persons who have or shall hereafter own the Covenant shall enjoy the Privilege of having their Children Baptized.

2. Voted, that all the Flagons & other pewter vessells belonging to the Church, shall be ſold as ſoon as may be & that two Silver Tankards shall be purchased for the use of the Church, with the money belonging to the Church which has not been otherwise appropriated. & that Dea^n^ Leathe & Dea^n^ Whitney be requested to purchase them.

[134]

Vote 3^d^. Voted, that in all future Contributions of the Church for the ſupply of the Communion Table, the Members of the Chh present shall contribute 25 Cents each, & that the money then contributed be paid into the hands of the Deacons.

4. Voted That whenever the ſums of money which have been contributed for the supply of the Communion Table shall have been expended, an account of such expenditure shall be rendered to the Pastor by the Deacons, & that a time be appointed by the Pastor for another Contribution to be held by the Church.

5. Voted that in all future Contributions of the Church, for the ſupply of the Communion Table, which may be appointed by the Pastor, the amount of the ſums thus Contributed be afsertained by the Pastor, & an account thereof be kept by him.

[135]

At a meeting of the Church of Christ in Watertown Feby 10th 1802, in order to make choice of some ſuitable person to the office of a Deacon in said Church—the Brethren Voted & chose Col. Moses Coolidge to said office. At the same meeting of the Church the following Votes were passed. Viz

Vote 1. That Dea^n^ Coolidge be empowered to act as an agent in behalf of the Church, to ſettle with the administrator of the Estate of Dea Daniel Whitney, relative to any sum or sums of money which may have been deposited in his hands, belonging to the Church, & which he had not an opportunity of appropriating to the use for which it had been committed to his care.

Vote 2d. That Col. Amos Bond be empowered in the Name & behalf of the Church

[136]

to take the pewter Vessels belonging to the Church, of the persons who have the care of them, & to dispose thereof to the best advantage in behalf of the Chh.

That the Sacrament of the Lord's Supper be administered in the Church on the first Sabbath of the month of april next, & on the first Sabbath of the seven following Months & that the administration of the sacrament be omitted, during the Space, intervening between the first Sabbath in Novr & the first Sabbath in aprill, annually.

At a meeting of the Church of Christ in Watertown August 7th 1805—held for the purpose ot choosing fome fuitable Person to fill the office of a Deacon in faid Church, the Brethren voted by written votes, upon counting of which it appeared that Col. Amos Bond was unanimously chosen to faid office.

[137]

At a meeting of the Church of Christ in Watertown Decr 21st 1814, the following votes were passed, Viz.

Vote 1 That the Sacrament of the Lords-Supper be administered in future on the first Sabbath of every month in the year.

Vote 2 That a Sacramental Lecture on each Friday preceeding the first Lords-Day of the following month, Viz, January March, May, July, September & November

Vote 3 That the Treasurer of the Church be requested, to obtain a renewal of all the Notes belonging to the Church now in his pofsession as foon as may be after the first of January next.

Vote 4. That the Treasurer be requested to adjust his account, as foon as may be, & give a Note upon Interest for the ballance, & keep the fame on file, with the other Notes belonging to the Church.

[138]

At a meeting of the Church of Christ in Watertown on the 18th of Decr 1815 they pafsed the following Vote, Viz—

That whenever any three members of the Church desire that a meeting of the Church be holden, they shall agree upon the time & place of such meeting & fhall make application to the Pastor, to furnish them with a notification for the purpose, & shall proceed to notify all the members of the Church accordingly.

At a meeting of the Church of Christ in Watertown on the 17th of Novr 1817, in order to make choice of some fuitable person to the office of a Deacon in said Church the meeting was opened with Prayer the Brethren voted & chose Mr John Tucker to said office.

[139 to **161]** Blank.

[162 & **163]** [Meditations upon Bible texts.]

[164]

1800 March 17th

Deacon Jedediah Leathe to the Chh in Watertown	Dr.
To Cash contributed by sundry Persons & deposited in your hands	£11-13-7-
To Cash paid by the Chh.	1-5.-0-
	£12-18-7

1800 March 17

Deacon Daniel Whitney to the Chh in Watertown	Dr
To cash contributed by sundry Persons and deposited in your hands	£12-7-11
To Cash paid by the Chh	—9-11
	£12-17-11

[165]

1800 March 17th

	Cr
By sundry payments & expenditures in behalf of the Chh	£12-18-7
By sundry payments & expenditures in behalf of the Chh	£12-17-11

[166-187] Blank.

[188] [Religious Thought.]

[189]

To full communion in the church at Watertown was admitted, 1637 (or previously) Capt Patrick, once of the prince of orange's guards and made a member of the church in order to receive the rights of a freeman and be qualified to take the command of the Massachusetts men in the Pequod War—see Hutchinson Vol. 1 p 76.

[190]

Such as I admitted in Watertown to ye Lds supper.

Ye 5 of December 86. I admitted 9 to full comunion, mr Samuell Thacher & his wife Mary, Sarah Sawin, & Judith Sawin (ye wives of Muning & John) Margret Taylor (my maid)—Joseph Underwood, mis Train, Joseph Whitney's wife viz Martha, & Joanna Stone. Before yr Admission, I sd 3 things to all present, (1) I showed wt made ym worthy & yt before Gd, & men, as to yr former only grace did, & as to ye later both knowledge, & a blameless life (2) yt all these were able to give me a particular account of gds dealing wth yr soules-(3) yt I had desired ym all to say something if ye could at yr Admission for ye edification of others but ye being neither able nor free, I told y^m all I durſt not Impoſe it on y^m having no warrant for it—y^n I read briefly w^t had paſsed betwixt y^m & me as to y^r grace—y^n called for ye vote of ye ch & had it, & y^n ye pmiſed to cary becomingly, & ye were Admitted, & after y^t briefly adviſed to ſomethings, eſp to y^r family, & tongue Govern^t

Y^e 30th of January 1686/7 I admittted 11, viz Tho. Whitney, Eliz. Fiſk, Eliz. Baſham, Eliz. Goffe, Ann Stone, John Edy, Nich. With & his wife, young James Corniſh, Eliz. Barnard, Rebekah Farnworth [Remarks made at admissions from here on generally omitted]

Y^e 27th of March 1687 I admitted 14 (wch was remarkable) viz Sarah Philips, Mary Philips, Elizabeth Underwood, Mr Abiah Sherman, Joſeph Maſon, Mr Wil. Bond, (Justice of peace) old M^r Jo. Biſcoe, Thomas Ryder, George Lawrence, Anna Livermore, Elizabeth Decks, Judith Jenningſon, Sarah Warren, & Sarah Mixer

Y^e 8th of May 87. I admitted 6, viz Lidia Bowman, (ye wife of young Francis Bowman) Thomas Strait, Benjamin Pearſe & his wife Hannah, Mrs Grace Sherman, & Sarah Whitney, ye wife of Nathanael Whitney this day Nat. Holland openly acknowledged his lye

Y^e 19 of June 87, I admitted 6, viz Eliz. Tanter (ye wife of Tanter) Margret Warren, Eliz. Lawrence (ye wife of George Lawrence) Abia Sanders (ye wife of Jon. Sanders) Richard Cutting, & Jo. Bacon. I hinted at Cor. 8. 5

[191]

Such as I baptized in Watertown 1686.

Y^e 6 of October 1686 I was ſolemnly ſett y^t for ye Paſtorall work at Watertown, wthout Impoſition of Hands. I am ſick of it, & unfitt for it, but ye many particulars y^t attend this work I wholly omitt

Oct. 17. 86. I baptized 3 viz Iſraell Pierce, ye child of Joſeph Pierce, about a year old. And Mercy Begulah ye child of John Begulo, a young child. And Thomas Milling a young man who Pfeſsed his Faith in X & obed to him

Y^e 24 of Oct. 86. I baptized 10 all of y^m under a year old Samuell Livermores child called Nathanaell. William Bonds called Diliverance. John Parkis called George. Juſtinian Holden's called Elizabeth. Tho. Hamon's, called Thomas. John Cutting's called George. Michaell Flegs called Abigall. Thomas Bonds called Sarah all theſe related to the church, but ye other 2 were not, only formerly Mr Sherman baptized their children, viz Samuell Thacher's called John, & Theophilus Philips, called Mary

Y^e 7 of November 86, I baptized 6 viz Stephen Willis child (who belongs to ye church in Brantrey) viz Benjamin, & Jonathan Stimpſons child viz Rebecca, & Tho. Williams child (who at preſent lives in Wooborn his wife formerly lived in this town & owned ye Covenant) viz Damaris, all of y^m under a year old.

Alfo I baptized James Knopp a young man, & John Price a young man, & alfo Mary Price his Sifter, but fhe is maryed & her hufband from her above thefe 2 yeares, ye Ld blefs this ord to ym

Ye 14th of November I baptized 3 children, viz Abraham Geals child (who is a member ye church) viz Ebenezer, it was young. & Abigall Townfends child (her hufbands name I know not) viz Martin. & John Bonds child, called Abigall, not a fortnight old

Ye 21. of November 86 I baptized 12, viz Tredaways child called Jofiah, & John Chinerys child (who owned yr Covt) called Sarah, & 5 of old Simon Millings children, viz Simon, Richard, Mary, James, & John. & David Fifks wife viz Elizabeth (in order to Admifsion) & her child David. & George Adams wife Martha who owned ye Covt, & her child called George. & Mary Adams who is his Sifter, who owned ye Covt

Ye 28 of Nov. 86 I baptized 9 viz 4 children of Tho. Underwood (who owned ye Covt privately, & his wife publickly) viz Thomas, Jonathan, Mary & Elizabeth. And Jonathan Smithes wife viz Jane. And Sarah Jane and her child Jonathan, & Widow Fifks daughter viz Elizabeth. And Sarah Sanders, viz William Sanders daughter. And Samuell Severn ye widows fon

Ye 5 of December 86. I baptized 7, viz 6 of John Aplin who owned ye Covt, viz John, Thomas, Mary, Hannah, Bafhuah, Abiah. & Benjamin Davis who owned ye Covt

[192]

Such as were Admitted by me to Full Communion In Watertown—1687

Ye 31 of July 1687 I admitted 6, viz Tho. Cutler, Thomas Millings, Benjamin Goddard, Sarah Cuttings, Abiah Leafon, & Elizabeth Willington, I fpent fome time in a word in Benj. Goddards relation, viz a child of ye Covnt, oh yt gd wid blefse it for much good. Eliz. Willington is ye wife of Jofeph Willington

Ye 13th of November I admitted 7, viz Philip Shattock, Benjamin Flegg, Jonathan Stimfon, Abigaill Townfend (ye wife of Martin Townfend) Elizabeth Chinery (ye wife of John Chinery) Sufanna Grout (ye wife of Jofeph Grout) Elizabeth Nevenfon (ye wif of John Nevinfon, whom I admitted wthout a Relation her hufband who is of ye church of England wid not fuffer it, but ye church was fatiffyed in her wthout it), I hope gd will blefse ym, & make ym blefsings

Ye 8th of January I admitted 3, viz Mr William Goddard, Abigail Fox (ye wife of Ifaac Fox, of Miftick, or Medford as it is called) & Bithia Satle

Y 4th March 1687/8 I admitted 3 viz Calib Church, Stephen Cook, & Abraham Brown I had faid fomething largely to ym but yt I had other matters yt day

Ye 15th of Aprill 1688 I admitted one viz Samuell Bigelow.

Y 19 of Auguft 1688 I admitted 6, viz young John Warren & his wife Elizabeth, Benjamin young Richard Child, Martha Fifk, Thomas Thornton.

Y^{e} 11th of November 1688 I admitted 4 viz John Ball & his wife, John Aplin, & Walter Taylor. now admitted by me 76

Y^{e} 3^{d} off February 1688/9 I admitted 7 viz John Whitmore of Mistick, young Henery Spring, Susannah Cook (viz Gregory Cooks wife) Samuell Stearnes, John Child (who was baptized by me a year ago) Elizabeth Gale (ye wife of John Gale) & Mary Grant, who was baptized by me not long a gon—now 83.

Y^{e} 17th of March 1688/9 I admitted 6 viz Rebeka Shattuck (i.e Philips wife,) Hepzibah Bond, (i. e young Williams wife) Elizabeth Stimson (i. e Jonathans wife) Benjamin Taylor, Danyell Stone & his wife, to whom I s d something.

[193]

Such as were baptized by me in Watertown. 1686.

Upon ye 26 of December 86 I baptized 13, viz Joseph Grants child (who owned ye Cov^{t} some old businefs brought againft him, but nothing proved) viz Mary. Ebenezer Stones child who lives in Cambridge village, viz Ebenezer, & Allin Fleggs child (who owned ye Cov^{t}) viz Sarah, & Sarah Thropp, & Mary Throp, & Elizabeth Goodwin, & Margaret Fisk, & Elizabeth Dill, all wch owned ye Covenant & Joseph Masons wife, y^{t} both of y^{m} stood acknowledging & taking shame to y^{m}selves for her name was Mary, baptized 2 of y^{r} children viz Mary & Hester. I baptized John Knop, & his child Sarah, he & his wife also stood as it were in ye stool of repentance for ye same Folly, much was sd to y^{m} wch I now pass by

Y^{e} 2^{d} of January 86/7 I baptized 3. viz Nathanell Brights child called Nathanaell, & Muning Sawins child called Abigall, & Mary Gregg who owned ye covenant.

Y^{e} 9 of January 86/7 I baptized 4 children viz Tho. Cutlers (who had formerly owned ye covent) viz James, & 2 of Jo. Harringtons (who now owned ye covenant, viz John, & Hannah, & one of Nat. Bonds whose wife owned ye covenant, viz Nathanaell.

Y^{e} 16 of January 86/7 I baptized 9, viz 5 of Joseph Whitney's (she lately Joyning herself to ye c^{h}) viz Joseph, John, Isaac, Abigall, & Martha. also I baptized ye wife of Daniell Pierse viz Elizabeth, & 3 of her children, viz John, Hannah, & Benjamin, he viz Danyell Pierse owned ye cov^{t}.

Y^{e} 20th February 86/7 I baptized one, viz a grand child of Simon Stone, she lives at Dedham, her husbands name is Comfort Starr, ye childs name was Mary

Y^{e} 27th of February 86/7 I baptized one, viz Hannah Johnson y^{t} lived at Mr Bonds, I hope a good girle.

Y^{e} 20th of March 86/7 I baptized 5 young persons (ye Ld blesse it unto y^{m}) viz Henery Stretcher who lives wth Mr Bridge, & Hester Sanders, ye daughter of Edward Sanders, & Hester Bullard ye daughter of Jonathan Bullard, & Bethia Meatox, & Mary Meatox ye daughters of Danyell Meatox.

Y^{e} 10th of Aprill 86 I baptized 4 children of Abiah Leason (ye wife of young William Leason) who owned ye cov^{t}, y^{r} names were

William, Joseph, John, & Elizabeth. I sd something to y[m] from Mark 10. 14

Y[e] 17 of Aprill 87 I baptized 3, viz 2 of Jo. Fisks children who owned y[e] covenant viz Abigall, & Elizabeth, & also I baptized Ruth Garfield y[e] daughter of widdow Garfield. she also owned y[e] Cov[t].

[194]

Such as was admitted to y[e] Lds Supper, or to full Comunion in Watertown in my time. A. D. 1689.

Y[e] 18 of August 1689 there was admitted 2 women viz Mary Mason i. e. Josephs wife, & Mary Tufts i. e. Johns wife of Mistick.

Y[e] 29 of September 1689 there was only one admitted viz Elizabeth Flegg, y[e] wife of Allin Flegg.

Y[e] 20[th] of October 1689 I did in y[e] name of y[e] church admitt Deacon Stephen Cooke to full comunion w[th] us being a member of y[e] church of X in Mendon, he being cast by Pr[d]ence here, & had his dismission from thence.

Y[e] 2[d] of February 1689/90 I admitted 2 viz M[r] Edw. Procter of Boston, (he being my countreyman had y[e] advantage others had not. I grtly rejoyce I shid be usefull to him, oh y[t] Lancashire might live in y[e] light.) & Sarah Wait, y[e] wife of Thomas Waite. I hope y[t] wth y[e] rest will walk worthy.

Y[e] 27 of Aprill 1690 I admitted 4, viz M[r] Hen. Gibbs who hath some time preached for me here & now this quarter of a yeare liveth w[th] me, Phebe Cutler (who publickly owned her aggravated sin before y[e] congregation, Amos Merrett, & Mehetabell Child who at present lives w[th] me as a serv[t]. Here have an hundred save one given vp y[m]selves to y[e] Ld since my comeing hither.

Y[e] 22[th] of June 1690 there were 5 Admitted, viz Thomas Flegg (& oh w[t] a mercy & wonder of mercy is it y[t] ever I shid see him thus presenting of himself, often was I affrayed to heare of his drowning or hanging of himself, but I see y[e] foundation of gd standeth sure, & he is a prayer hearing gd. it was worth my coming for N. E but to convert such a man I hope much good was don at y[e] reading of his Relation, & by those words y[t] were occasionally dropt by me. Blessed be gd, Let all say Amen & Amen) & Isaac Stearnes, & Abigail Stratten (y[e] wife of young John Stratton my Neighbour) & Bithia Merrett, (y[e] wife of Amos Merrett) & Sarah Fanning &c. Now 104

Y[e] 3[d] of August 1690 there were 5 admitted, viz Mary Flegg (who publickly took shame to herself before y[e] Ld & his people for her sin & Freely offered herself thus publickly to give glory to gd, & not only so, but desired full comunion wth this church she had so offended & grieved, & obtained it). & Tho. Hammond, & Samuel Whitmore of Cambridge Farmes

[195] Such as were Baptized by me in Watertown 1687.

Y[e] 24 of Aprill 87 I baptized 10, viz Philip Shattocks child, called Joseph, & Jonathan Coolidge child called Mary, & y[e] child of Susannah Grout (Joseph Grouts wife) who owned ye Covt, it was called Jonathan. I likewise Sarah Mosse & her child called James, she is ye wife of Jeremye Mose. she owned ye covt. John Garfield, & Mercy Garfield ye children of Widdow Garfield, ye both owned ye Covt. William Rowe, who lives at Phil. Shattocks, & Elizabeth Child, & Mary Child, who owned ye Covt ye are ye children, i. e. ye young daughters of John Childs, their mother is now maryed to Nath. Fisk.

Ye First of May 87. I baptized 3 children of Jonathan Philips viz Sarah, Elizabeth, & Ruth

Ye 22 of May 87 I baptized 9, viz 2 children of Danyell Harrington who owned ye Covt, viz Danyell & Robert — & a child of Rich. Childs, viz John, & a child of John Fisks viz John, & a child of George Adams viz Mathew — & 4 young folks who gave vp ymselves to ye Ld, viz John Johnson, Thomas Johnson, Mary Johnson, & John Child

Ye 5th of June 87 I baptized 9, viz 3 of Tho. Chadwicks children, (who owned ye covnt, & tho he had committed folly at ye first long agon, yet Satisfaction was given to ye church at Newbury, where he had 4 children baptized since, & I could not but think once Satisfaction is enough for one fault) viz Elizabeth, Lidia, & Richard. I baptized 4 of Nathanaell Fisks (who also owned ye covenant) viz Nathanaell, John, Hannah, & Sarah. I baptized also one of his wives children by a former husband, viz Danyell Child, ye vndertook for ye bringing it of it up. I also baptized Joseph Childs child, viz Mary

Ye 19 of June 87 I baptized 14. viz 6 of John Decks children, viz Elizabeth, John, Edward (or Edmond) Joseph, Abigaill, & Debora, a child of Josiah Jones who owned ye Covenant (he never did it have before) viz John, and 2 children of John Gale's, (she having formerly owned it) viz Anna & Abigaill, I baptized Danyell Stone's wife (who owned ye Covenant) viz Joanna, & her 3 children viz Danyell, David, & Dorcas. I also Baptized a child of John Harringtons viz Mary

Ye 10th of July 87 I baptized 11, viz 4 of Caleb Church his children (who solemnly owned ye Covt), viz Caleb, Joshua, Isaac, & Rebekah, also a child of Jo. Balls called Abigaill, also I baptized Isaac Lamb, Abigaill Sanders & Mary Laurence, all wch 3 owned ye Covent, I baptized 3 of George Dills children, (he himself taking shame to himself for his sin) his children were called Thomas, Sarah and James

[196]

Such as were admitted to Full communion in Watertown N. E by me Anno domoni 1690

Sarah Edy, & Hannah Johnson.

Now 109

Ye 1st of March 1690/1 I admitted one, viz Thomas Underwood, yr was John Bond and wife also, but he was buryed just 3 houres (or yrabouts) before he was to be admitted, stupendious Providence, he dyed of yᵉ small pox. He was a thriving man both as to this world & another, & likely to have been of grᵗ vſe to this ch & town, he dyed comfortably, I formerly ſtirred him vp to this duty, but his feares & Tempᵗ kept him, & now was eager vpon it. He ſent me word to warn all others by him yᵗ yᵉ looſe no opportunity putt into yʳ hands, for now he wld but muſt not ptake of ye ord This thing this evening I largely ſpoke to (wᶜʰ now I paſse by) ye Ld bleſse it

Yᵉ 12 of Aprill 1691 I admitted 5, viz John Woodward, an ancient man of 70 yeares, John Bemis, John Moſse, Rich Bloſse, & Grace Bond, i. e, yᵉ wife of Jonas Bond Now 116 wᵗʰ John Bond & his wife who were as good as admitted.

I had thought to have ſd ſomething here further as to it, but my Dᵗ Lyddy is dead & ſo am wholly indiſpoſed to everything.

Yᵉ 24 of May 1691 I admitted 2 viz Roſe Norcroſse i. e young Richards wife, & Elizabeth Berſham I took an occaſion to take leave of ch members, & gave ſome ſerious hints from 2 Tim. 2. 19. I ſuppoſe I ſhall admitt no more 118

[197]

Such as were Baptized by me in Watertown 1687

Yᵉ 17 of July 87. I baptized 11, viz a child of Joſeph Shermans called Elizabeth, 2 children of Thomas Biſcoe's (who owned yᵉ covnᵗ) called John, & Elizabeth, 2 children of Jonathan Tanters called Jonathan & Benjamin, a child of Nathanaell Whitney's called Samuell, a child of Jonathan Smiths called Zechariah, & 2 young women, viz Lidia Corley yᵗ owned yᵉ covenant, ſhe lived yⁿ wᵗʰ John Ball, & Lidia Smith, who formerly was called Zipparah, ſhe lives at Father Satle I wiſh ſhe may have yᵉ New name indeed

I have now already baptized an Hundred Forty-nine

Yᵉ 31 of July 87 I baptized 2 children, viz Sam. Livermor child called Lidia, & John Stratten (vp in yᵉ town) child, called Mercy

Yᵉ 14 of Aug., 87 I baptized William Shattocks child, called Benjamin

Yᵉ 21 of Auguſt 1687 I baptized 2 children of Joſeph Willingtons (his wife being lately admitted) called Thomas, & Elizabeth

Yᵉ 28 of Auguſt 87 I baptized a child of Danyell Harington's (who formerly owned yᵉ covᵗ) called David

Yᵉ 4 of September 87 I baptized a child of Samuell Stearnes (his wife Mehetabell folmely owning yᵉ Covnᵗ) called Samuell

Yᵉ 11ᵗʰ of September 87 I baptized 3 children, viz Joſeph Pearſse child called Elizabeth, & Joſhuah Bigulows child called Elizabeth, & Thomas Harringtons child (his wife Rebekah who ſolemnly owned yᵉ Covenant) called Ebenezer

Yᵉ 2ᵈ of October 1687 I baptized 2, viz John Rowe who owned yᵉ Covnᵗ, he lives wᵗʰ his Father in yᵉ Farmes of Cambridge, & yᵉ child of Enoch Satle called Suſannah, his wife Suſannah owned yᵉ Covnᵗ

Y^e^ 16 of October 87 I baptized ye Mother & child, viz ye wife of Samuell Shattock who owned ye covenant, called Abigaill, & her child was called Abigaill

Y^e^ 23 of October 1687 I baptized 5, viz Elizabeth Beamis (who solemnly owned ye covenant) ye wife of Ephraim Beamis, & her 4 children, viz Elizabeth, Sarah, Rebekah & Abigaill

Y^e^ 6 of November 1687 I baptized a child of David Church (who had owned ye covn in Mr Shermans time) called John

Y^e^ 4th of December I baptized 7, viz 5 of Joseph Smith's (who had owned ye Covn^t^ in Mr Shermans time) viz Joseph, John, Danyell, Hanah & Rebekah & 2 of John Hastings, viz Elizabeth & Hephzibah he had formerly owned ye Cov^t^

[198] Admissions to full Communion in ye East Chh of Watertown p H. Gibbs.

1697.

Dec. 12. David Stone
19. Samll Eddy
Febr. 6. Elizabeth Eddy, Abigail Benjamin
13. Elizabeth Stone

1698.

May. 29. Edward Goddard, Benjamin Eddy
Septr. 18. Rebecka Train
Jan. 8. Mary Hasting Mary Rice Susanna Fisk

1699.

June 25. Sarah Chadwich
Oct. 15. Josiah Goddard, Nathan Fisk, John Coolidge, Sarah Fisk
Decr 10. Nathaniell Coolidge jun^r^ Lydia Coolidge, his wife, Abigail Bacon, Rachel Goddard
Febr. 4. Nathaniell Bright. Mary Bright. Rebecca Barstow. Martha Whitney

1700.

Apr. 7. Lydia Spring
May 26. Hephzibah Stone
July 28. Elizabeth Train
Jan. 5. Mr Jonas Bond
12. Timothy Barron

1701.

Apr. 27. Susanna Goddard
Aug. 27. Deliverance Eddy

[199]

Such as were Baptized by me in Watertown—1687.

Y^e^ 11th of Dec. 87. 2 children, viz Serj. Garfields called Mehatabell, & a child y^t^ Jo. Flegg adopted, I suppose a bastard of Matthew Humsteds, called Jabez

Ye 25th of Dec. 87 ye child of John Bacon, called Mary

Ye 22 of Jan. 1687/8 4 young psons, viz Joseph Memory who lives wth Martin Townsend who vndertook for him, wth ye other 3 Owned ye Covenant, viz Mary Memory who lives wth Lt Winship, & Mary Grant who lives wth Mr Goddard, & Ann Leason, who lives wth her Mother

Ye 29th of January 1687/8 John Mosse child, called Nathanaell

Ye 5th of February 1687/8 a child of Thomas Bond's called William

Ye 12th of February 1687/8 a child of Joseph Vnderwood called Sarah

Ye 4th of March 1687/8 a child of Benjamin Willingtons called Mehetabell

Ye 18th of March 1687/8 a child of Joseph Grant called Sarah

Ye 8th of Aprill 1688 2 young Psons who owned ye covenant, viz William & Hannah Sanderson, ye children of William Sanderson

Ye 15th of Aprill 1688 7, viz 4 of Stephen Cooks called Stepheen, Isaac, John, & Mary. John Parkis child called Samuell. & Samuell Bigulows child called Abigaill, & Nathanaell Fisks child called Lydia

Ye 22 of Aprill 1688 a child of John Winters called Sarah

Ye 29th of Aprill 1688 3 viz a child of Benj. Pearse called Sarah, & one of Martin Townsends called Jonathan, & one of young John Warrens called Jonathan

Ye 6th of May 1688 4, (viz) a child of Sam. Thacher called Anna, one of James Begulow's called James, one of Henery Springs called Lidia, & one of Jeremy Mosse called Jonathan

Ye 20th of May 1688 3 children, a child of Samuell Jennisons called Lidia. & 2 of Sarah Sandersons (ye wife of William Sanderson) who owed ye Covenant, viz Joseph & Lidia

Ye 17th of June 1688 3 children & a Melotto, a child of Tho. Cutler called Jonathan, a child of Tho. Hammond called Elizabeth, & a child of Comfort Starrs of Dedham called Lidia—& Melotto called Walter Taylor, living wth Capt, Wade living at Mistick

Ye 24th of June 1688 I baptized a child of Jon. Stimson called Joseph

Ye 8th of July 1688 2 children, viz one of Theophilus Philips called Theophilus, & one of John Aplins called Mehetabell

[200] Blank.

[201] Such as were baptized in Watertown 1688

Ye 29th of July 1688 a child of Jonathan Tanters called Joseph

Ye 19th of Aug. 1688 2 children, viz one of my Brother Thomas Bayly's called Thomas, & one of John Chinery's called Sarah

Ye 26th of August 1688 a child of Joseph Garfield called Grace

Ye 2d of Sept, 1688 a child of John Bond's called Sarah

Ye 14th of October 1688 a child of Joseph Mason called Joseph

Ye 21th 1688 a child of John Tufte's of Mistick called Mary, both he & his wife owned ye Covenant

Ye 25th of November 1688 a child of John Fiſk called Jonathan

Ye 9th of December 1688 a child of Joſeph Willingtons called Mary

Ye 23 of December 1688 a child of William Jones called Caleb

Ye 6th of January 1688/9 a child of Joſiah Tredway's called Severanna

Ye 13th of January 1688/9 Mary Sanderſon ye daughter of William Sanderſon, ſhe owned ye Covenant

Ye 27th of January 1688/9 a child of Stephen Cooke called James

Ye 3d of February 1688/9 a child of John Knops called John

Ye 3d of March 1688/9 11 children, viz one of Philip Shattucks called Nathanaell, one of Tho. Harringtons called Suſannah, 4 of Iſaac Fox his children (of Miſtick) called Iſaac, John, Abigaill, & Samuell, & 5 of John Beamis (who acknowledged his ſin in ye publick, & owned ye Covenant both he & his wiſe) called Joſeph, John, Suſannah, Bethia, & Mary

Ye 10th of March 1688/9 2 children, viz one of Nathanaell Whitneys called Hannah, & of George Adams called John

Ye 17th of March 1688/9 Danyell Benjamins child called Danyell

Ye 31th of March 1689 a child of Michaell Flegs called Michaell

Ye 7th of Aprill 1689 5 children, viz one of Jonathan Coollidge called Jonathan, one of Nathanaell Bright's called John, one of Thomas Chadwicks called Danyell, one of Jonathan Smiths called Elizabeth, & one of Samuell Shattucks called Samuell

[202] Blank.

[203] Such as were baptized by me in Watertown in N. E.

1689

Ye 14th of Aprill 1689 2, viz a child of Danyell Harringtons called Jonathan, & a young woman one Sarah Grant who lived at Mrs Shermans, ſhe owned ye Covenant

Ye 21st of Aprill 1689 a child of Abraham Gales called Marah

Ye 28th of Aprill 1689 a child of Enoch Satle called Richard

Ye 12st of May 1689 a child of widdow Hannah Biſco's who owned ye Covent (her huſband Tho. Biſcoe being lately dead) called Thomas

Ye 14 of July 1689 6 children, viz one of John Chadwicks called Benjamin, one of Francis Bowmans called John, one one of Jonathan Sanders called Hannah, one of widdow Gales (viz Johns) called Abiah, one of Ephraim Beamis called James, & one of Allen Fleggs called Mary

Ye 28 of July 1689 a child of young John Strattens (who owned ye covenant) called John

Ye 4th of Auguſt 1689 a child of Jonathan Philips called Sarah

Ye 18th of Auguſt 1689 6 children, viz 4 of Ephraim Cutters (who owned ye covenant) viz Ephraim, Jonathan, Bethia, & Mary, a child of Muning Sawings called John, & one of Joſeph Childs called John

Y^{e} 1st of September 1689 3, viz a child of Joseph Shermans called Martha, & a child of young John Warrens called Danyell, & a young woman y^{t} lives wth Philip Shattucks called Elizabeth Danyells, she owned ye Covenant

Y^{e} 8th of September 1689 a grand child of ye wife of Ellis Barron called Benoni, his Father lives at Sherburn, viz Moses Adams

Y^{e} 6th of October 1689 one child, of David Churche's, called Sarah

Y^{e} 13 of October 1689 one child, of John Deex called Jane

Y^{e} 20th of Oct. 1689 a child of Danyell Stone called Hannah—tho I feare in hast I called Joannah

Y^{e} 27th of October 1689 a child of Joseph Grout called Mehetabell

Y^{e} 3^{d} of November 1689 a child of Joshuah Biggulo's called Jabez

Y^{e} 24th of November 1689 4 children, viz 3 of Thomas Smiths (who owned ye covn^{t} here as he had don formerly at Concord) called Samuell, Joseph, & Benjamin, & one of William Price called William, his wife a member at Brantry

[204] Blank.

[205]

Such as were baptized by me in Watertown in 1689, & also 1690

Y^{e} 1st of December 1689 a child of Isaac Foxe's called Ebenezer

Y^{e} 22 of December 1689 a child of John Fisks called Jonathan

Y^{e} 19th of January 1689/90 4 children of ye wife of Samuell Perrye (who owned ye Covenant) 3 of them by this husband, called Samuell, John, & Ebenezer, & ye other by a former husband (she being of yeares tho young owned ye Covn^{t} also) called Hester Comye

Y^{e} 2^{d} of March 1689/90 a child of John Harringtons called Lidia

Y^{e} 30th of March 1690 a child of John Bacons called John

Y^{e} 13 of Aprill 1690 3 children, one of Joseph Underwoods called Hannath, one of William Shattuck called Mary, & one of Mr Prouts called Eunice

Y^{e} 20th of Aprill 1690 3 children, one of Samuel Biggulo's called Isaac, one of Nathanall Fisks called Mary, & one of young Nathanaell Coolidge (who owned solemnly & publickly ye Covenant) called Lidia

Y^{e} 18th of May 1690 a child of Joseph Grant called Joseph

Y^{e} 25th of May 1690 3 children, one of Josiah Jones called Isaac & 2 of young Richard Norcrosse (he & his wife Rose publickly took shame for their gr^{t} sin I might have written this & many other things as y^{t} of Sarjeant Barnards, Nat, Holland, & other things by themselves but w^{t} I write is only for myself & not others) called Richard, & ye other Samuell

Ye 22th of June 1690 7 children, viz one of young John Winters (who owned ye Covent) called Hannah, & 5 of Judith Stearnes (ye wife of John Stearnes, ſhe was baptized by Mr Sherman at yeares of diſcretion, & I ſuppoſed owned ye Covnt) called George, Benjamin, Rebekah, Judith & Sarah, & one of Mary Earle's (who were baptized by me & yn owned ye Covenant) called Mary

Ye 6th of July 1690 3 children, viz one of John Bonds called Danyell, one of Jonas Bonds (who owned ye Covenant) called Sarah, & a child of one Stars of Dedham (I have formerly baptized ſome of hers) called Hannah

Ye 13 of July 1690 3 children viz one of Theophilus Philips called Jonathan, one of John Haſtings called William, & one of John Tufts called John

Ye 27 of July 1690 2 children, viz one of young William Bonds called Marah, & one of Ephraim Cutters called Hannah

[**206**] Blank.

[**207**] Such as were Baptized by me in Watertown N. E. 1690.

Ye 10th of Aug. 1690 one child (viz) of Abr-ham Pearſe, (he & his wife Iſabell came over wth me out of Ireland. I maryed them in Boſton, he was in church comunion) called Samuell. ye live at Salem

Ye 28th of Sept. 1690 2 children viz one of Samuell Thachers called Marath, & one of Jonathan Stimſons called Benjamin

Ye 23 of November 1690 5 children, viz one of Samuel Livermore's called Anna, one of Lt Ben. Garfields called Samuel, one of Tho. Hammonds called David, one of Danyel Benjamin's called John, & one of Nathanael Bonds called John

Ye 30th of November 1690 2 children one of Mr Gaſkell's called John, & one of Mary Flege called Marah, it was by Benjamin Davis

Ye 7th of December 1690 3 children, viz one of Tho. Bonds called Mary, one of young Stephen Cooks called Samuel, & one of Abiah Leaſons called Iſaac

Ye 4th of January 1690/91 a child of Benjamin Willingtons called Joſeph

Ye 1st of Feb. 1690/91 2 children one of Benjamin Fleggs called Benjamin, & one of John Chineryes called Elizabeth

Ye 10th of May 91 2 children, one of Widdow Stratton's in ye woods called Samuel, ye other of Jonathan Smith's called Eliſha

Ye 17th of May 1691 10 children, one of Jonathan Coolidg called John, one of Joſiah Tredaways called Tabitha, one of Tho. Cutler's called Samuel, one of John Parkiſse called Anna, one of Allen Fleggs called Allen, one of John Perryi's called Joſeph, one of young John Knops called James, one of John Whittamores, (ſhe was of old a member of ye church at Yarmouth, of late at Charleſtown, & now dwells where Amos Merritt did) called Daniel, one of Tho. Chadwick called Jonathan, & one of Nathanael Norcroſse (he ſolemnly owned ye Lords covenant) called Mehetabel

Y^e^ 24th of May 1691 4 children & a young woman, 3 children of Samnel Whitmore called Francis, Samuel, & Rebekah, one of Samuel Hagers called Sarah. ye young woman was Abigail Fisk who owned ye Covenant

Y^e^ 31th of May 1691 5, 3 children of young John Mosse (formerly of Groton) called Elizabeth, John, & David. one of Thomas Harringtons called Rebekah, & Mary Hawkins who solemnly owned ye Covenant

[208

Marriages Consummated p Henry Gibbs in Watertown

1697

Decr 7. Francis Pearse & Hannah Johnson, both of Watertown were married in my House

1698/9

Jan. 4. The marriage of James Stimson & Bethiah Mansfield was consummated at ye House of Deacon Barsham, both of Watert^n^

18. Benjamin Wellington & Lydia Brown, both of Watertown, were married att my House

March. 10. Timothy Barron and Rachel Jenison were joined in Marriage in my House. both of Watertown

21. Jonathan Stimson & Mehetabel Spring were Married att my House both of s^d^ Town

1699

Apr. 11. Charles Chadwick & Sarah Whitney, both of Watertown, were married in my House

Nov. 2. Samuell Jennison and Mary Stearns, both of Watertown, were joyned in marriage att my House

7. John Holdin & Grace Jennison, both of Watertown, were married by me in my House

15. The Marriage of Thomas Coolidge & Sarah Eddy was consummated att my House

Att ye Same time, was ye Consummation of ye Marriage of Jonathan Stone and Ruth Eddy all Four of Watertown

Decr 20. Sam^ll^ Stratton & Sarah Perry were Married att his Fathers House

Sam^ll^ Severns & Rebecca Stratton were Married at ye same time and place all belonging to Watertown

Jan. 2. Henry Houghton of Lancaster, and Abigail Barron of Watertown, were married at my House

16. The Marriage of John Coolidge & Margaret Bond, both of Watert^n^ was consummated at my House

1700

Apr. 2. Ebenezer Allen & Elizabeth Eddy, both of Watertown, were married att my House

4. Samuell Barnard and Mary Sherman were married att Mrs Shermans House; both of y^m^ belonging to Watertown

May. 2. Samuell Jones and Mary Woolfon, both of Watertown, were married in my Houfe

Dec. 12. Mr Hananiah Parker of Redding & Mrs Mary Bright of Watertown, were married, att her Houfe.

March 12. The marriage of Richard Barnes Senr of Marlborough & Elizabeth Stimfon of Watertown, was Solemnized at my Houfe

1701

July. 10. Sam^ll^ Haftings & Sarah Coolidge were marryed at Mr Nath^ll^ Brights Houfe, both of y^m^ of Watertown

Aug. 5. Amos Waight & Elizabeth Cutting, both of Watert^n^ were Marry'd in my Houfe

[209] Baptized ꝑ H Gibbs in Watertown

1697

Nov. 7. William & Jonathan, fons of William Bond
Samuell & Elizabeth, Children of Dan^ll^ Benjamin
Sarah, the Daughter of Henry Spring
George, the Son of Munnings Sawin
John, the Son of John Stacy

14. John, the Son of Richard Coolidge, who Owned ye Cov^t^
Ebenezer the son of John Chenery
Hannah Barftow, who being adult owned ye Covenant

21. Simon, Son of Isaac Stearns

28. Elizabeth, Daughter of Sam^ll^ Hastings, who own'd ye Cov^t^

Decr 12. Ruth Maddock, Wife of John Maddock, She owning ye Cov^t^
Sarah, Daughter of Andrew White, who Own'd ye Covenant

Jan. 16. Mercy, Daughter of Sam^ll^ Thacher

1698

Apr. 13. John, Son of James Ball, his Wife owning the Coven

May 8. Jonathan, Son of Abel Benjamin, He owned ye Cov^t^

15. Edward, Son of Edward Goddard, He owning ye Cov^t^

June 5. George, Son of George Lawrence

26. Isaac, Son of Thomas Bond

July 10. Nathaniell & John, Sons of Widow Mary Hastings, She own'd ye Cov^t^

17. Mehetabel, Daughter of Henry Spring

24. Benjamin, Son of Nathaniell Bright

Aug. 28. Joshua, Abigail, Elizabeth, children of Joseph Grant
Jonathan, Robert, Sons of William Shattuck
Abigail, Daughter of Obadiah Coolidge He owning ye Cov^t^

Oliver, Son of Daniel Livermore, He alfo owning y[e] Cov[t]
Sept[r] 18. John Train jun[r] who owned y[e] Cov[t]
Thomas, Margaret, Rebecka, Children of Jn[o] Train Sen[r] who own'd y[e] cov[t]
Abigail, Mary, Daughters of John Stratton jun[r]
Simon Beers, who own'd y[e] coven[t]
Oct. 2. John, Ruth, Mary, Sarah, Children of John Maddock
Curtis, Son of Mary Halloway
30. Henry, Son of John Maddock
Samuel, Son of Samuell Haftings
Jofeph, Son of Rachel Jennifon
Nov. 13. Jofeph, Jofiah, Sons of Jonathan Coolidge
20. Mary, Daughter of Joseph Grant
Dec. 4. Sarah, Daughter of Nathan Fifk
25. Deborah, Daughter of Thom[s] Train
Jan. 15. Henry Knop, Adult & owning y[e] Cov[t]
March. 5. Isaac, Son of Jofeph Child
26. Elizabeth, Daughter of Nathan Fifk

1699

Apr. 30. Richard, Son of Richard Coolidge
Rachel, Daughter of Josiah Goddard, He owning y[e] Cov[t]
May. 21. Hephzibah, y[e] Daughter of Deacon Bond
28. Nathaniell son of John Stone, He owned y[e] Coven[t]
June. 11. Abigail, Daughter of Widdow Anna Thare, She owning y[e] Cov[t]
18. Efther, Elizabeth, Daughters of John Kinningham, He owning y[e] Cov[t]
July. 9. Margaret My third Daughter
Mercy, the Daughter of Nicholas Wyeth
Sept. 10. Lydia, Daughter of Daniell Benjamin
Abigail, Daughter of Abel Benjamin
Oct. 8. Lydia, Sufanna, Daughters of Sam[ll] Holdin, He owning y[e] Cov[t]
22. Elizabeth, Daughter of James Ball
Dec. 3. Sarah, Daughter of Sam[ll] Thacher
Feb. 11. Samuell, Son of Munnings Sawin
Lydia, Daughter of Obadiah Coolidge
25. Sufanna, Daughter of Edward Goddard

[210] Blank.

[211] Baptisms

1700

March. 31. Samuell, Son of John Stacy
Apr. 7. Francis, Son of Francis Pearfe
May. 19. Mercy, Daughter of Nathaniell Bright
26. Sarah, the Daughter of Sam[ll] Eddy
June. 30. Timothy, Son of Timothy Barron

July. 28. Mary, Daughter of Dan Livermore
Sept. 8. Sarah, Daughter of Thomas Coolidge
22. Abigail, Daughter of Nath[ll] Coolidge jun[r]
Shadrach, Son of Jonathan Whitney
Oct. 27. John, Son of John Wellington, He owning y[e] Cov[t]
Nov. 3. Elizabeth, Daughter of George Lawrence
John, Son of John Kinningham
10. Samuell, Son of Sam[ll] Livermore, he own'd y[e] Cov
24. Benjamin, Son of Sam[ll] Hastings
Hannah, Daughter of Joseph Grant
Dec. 29. Andrew, Son of Andrew White
Jan. 19. Ebenezer, Son of Ebenezer King, He owned y[e] Coven[t]
March. 2. Abigaill, Daughter of John Chenery
16, Caleb, Son of John Maddock
Mary, Daughter of Sam[ll] Jenifon, S[d] S. Jennifon & his wife owned y[e] Cov[t]

1701

30. Jabez, Son of John Stratton
Apr. 6. Elizabeth, Daughter of Henry Spring
Elizabeth, Daughter of Ebenezer Allen
Elizabeth, Daughter of Sam[ll] Severns
Bethiah, Daughter of James Stimfon
y[e] S[d] Severns with his wife & S[d] Stimfon w[ith] his wife own'd y[e] Cov[t]
May 4. Josiah, Son of Jofiah Jones, He owned y[e] Cov[t]
June 22. Sarah, Daughter of James Ball
July. 13. Josiah, Son of Josiah Goddard
20. Nathaniell, Son of Deacon William Bond
Aug. 3. Jonathan, Son of Jonathan Whitney
17. Sam[ll] son of Sam[ll] Eddy jun[r]
Oct. 5. Samuell, son of Sam[ll] Holdin
26. Patience, Daughter of Dan[ll] Benjamin
Nov. 16. John, Sarah, Mary, Abigail, children of John Perry jun[r] He owning y[e] Covent
Dec. 7. Rebecca, Daughter of Tho[s] Train
Jan. 25. Caleb, y[e] Son of Abel Benjamin
Feb. 22. Simon, y[e] Son of Edward Goddard
March 3. Nathan, y[e] Son of Nathan Fiske
15. Nathaniel, y[e] Son of Richard Coolidge
22. Henry, y[e] first Son of y[e] Rev[d] M[r] Henry Gibbs

1702

29th Sarah, y[e] Daughter of Caleb Grant, he owning y[e] Covenant
April. 19. Sam[ll] y[e] Son of Ebenezer King
May. 31. Henry, y[e] Son of Henry Houghton of Lancafter his wife Abigail owning y[e] Covenant
July y[e] 19. Hannah, y[e] Daûter of Sam[ll] Jenifon
26. Daniel & Benjamin ye Sons of Sam[ll] Hastings

Augt 2. Peter ye Son of Timothy Barron
16. Hannah Priest was Baptized ſhe owning ye Covenant
Sep^{t} 6. Deborah, Daûter Munnings Sawin
20. Mercy, ye Daûter of Joſeph Grant
Octob. 4. Jonathan, ye Son of Jonathan Stone
11. Joanna, ye Daûter of John Maddocks
Nov. 1. Anna, ye Daûter of Jonathan Whitney, Palsgruve, ye Son of John Wellington, Hannah ye Daûter of Francis Peirce, & Abigail ye Daûter of James Ball
8. Tabitha, ye Dauter of Tho. Coollidge, & Abraham, ye Son of Jer. Mors
Decem. 6. Anna, ye Daûter of Daniel Livermore
20. William, ye Son of Andrew White

1703

Jan. 3. Rebecca, ye Daûter of John Chadwick
17. Matthew, ye Son of Sam^{ll} Livermore
31. James, ye Son of James Stimpſon
Feb. 28. John, ye Son of George Lawrence
March. 21. Mary, ye Daûter of Thos Spring
May. 2. Samuel, ye Son of Sam^{ll} Stratton, he owning ye Covenant
30. Elizabeth, ye Daûter of John Perry
June. 6. Jacob, ye Son of Jerim : Mors

[**212** to **221** inclusive Blank.]

[**222**]

I was called to the work of the Miniſtry, by the Church & Congregation in the Eaſterly Precinct in Watertown, on February ye 3rd 1723/4. and was ſolemnly ſet apart to that work by prayer & the Impoſition of the hands of the Preſbytery on July 22nd 1724.

A Record of Baptiſms p Seth Storer.

1724

Augst 30. Jonathan, Son of Jonathan Brown
October. 4. Silas, Son of Henry Bright
Enoch Son of John Haſtings
Novr 8. Eliſha and Seth, Sons of George Harrington
15. Hannah, Daûter of Sam^{ll} Peirce
Eunice Daûter of John Haſtings
29. Priſcilla Daûter of John Phillips
Lydia, Daûter of David Sanger

1724/5

Jan^{ry} 10. Phinehas, Son of Thos Bond
24. Simon, Son of Richd Beers
John, Son of David Sanger
31. Daniel, Son of Oliver Livermore
Feb. 7. Hannah, Daûter of John Tainter
14. Mary Daûter of Henry Spring jun^{r}
21. Abigail, Daughter of George Lawrence Junr

March. 7. Obadiah, Son of Daniel Bond
Mofes Son of Jofhua warren Junr
14. Grace Daûter of George Cutting
Elizabeth Daûter of Daniel Stearns
28. Ann, Daûter of Nath[ll] Bond

1725

May. 16. At Wells, Abigail Daûter of Jofeph Hill Junr
18. at Wells, it being Lecture Day, I baptized Jofeph, Son of Bro[r] John Storer
June. 13. Jonathan, Son of Jofeph Holdin
July. 18. Mary Daûter of Ebenezer Chenery
Hannah Daûter of Sam[ll] Hager
Sarah, Daû of Eben[r] Stone
Sep[t] 26. Mercy, Daûter of Thos Learned
Samuel, Son of Timothy Harris
Octo[r] 10. Thomas, Francis, Sarah & Prifcilla, Children of Nath[ll] Harris
Novr 14. Efther, Dauter of Jofeph Mafon
Ruth, Daûter of Jon[a] Coollidge
21. Jon[a] Son of widow Hannah Stone
Decr 5. Nathan, Son of Sam[ll] Warren, in private

1725/6

Jan. 2. Samuel, Son of Sam[ll] Parry
9. Lydia, Dauter of Obadiah Coollidge
Feb. 6. Elizabeth, Daûter of John Ormes
20. Lydia, Dauter of Eben[r] Wellington
March. 6. Sarah, Dauter of Dan[ll] Haftings

[223]

1726

May. 1. Elizabeth, Daûter of Jon[a] Harrington
8. Mindwell, Daûter of Jon[a] Benjamin Senr
Abijah, Son of Jabez Stratton
June 5. Mary, Dauter of John Phillips
12. Samuel, Son of And[r] White Junr
Aug. 14. Jonas, Son of Jonas Bond
21. Amariah, Son of Thos. Learned
Sep[t] 11. Stephen, Son of Daniel Sterns
18. At wells, Dauter of Gerfhom Balfton
Octr 2. Nathanael, Son of Nath[ll] Bond
16. Jofhua, Son of Jofhua Warren Jun[r]
30. Uriah, Son of Nath[ll] Norcrofs
Novem[r] 13. Hannah, Dauter of Eben[r] Stone
20. Abraham, Son of Dan[ll] Bond
27. Abraham, Son of Jon[a] Brown
Decem[r] 4. Benjamin, Son of John Stearns Senr
12. Hannah, Dauter of Thos Hamond, in private
25. Sarah, Dauter of Nath[ll] Bright

1726/7

Jan. 15. Eliſha, Son of John Haſtings
Samuel, Son of Saml Benjamin
22. Samuel, Son of Henry Spring Jur
Febry 12. Mary, Daûter of Benjamin Haſtings, in private
March. 5. Samuel, Son of Peter Oliver
Joſhua, Son of Joſhua Grant
12. Mary, Daûter of Joſeph Coollidge
26. John, Son of John Maddock
19. Milleſcient, Daûter of Henry Bright

1727

April. 9. Abraham, Jonas, Edward & Joſhua, ſons of Edward Jackſon
23. Joſiah, Son of George Cutting
May 28. Ruth Daûter of Oliver Livermore
David, Son of David Sanger
June. 11. Samuel, Son of Jonª Stone Junr
25. Nathanael, Son of Nathll Norcroſs
July. 9. At wells, Mercy, Daûter of Benjamin Hatch
Augst 27. Stephen, Son of Daniel Haſtings
Mary, Dauter of Timothy Harris
Sept 17. Oliver, Son of Samll Stratton
Octor 15. Nathaniel, Son of Nathll Clark
22. At Newton, Daniel Son of John Hamond
Novr 5. Daniel, Son of John Sawen
12. Lydia, Dauter of Joseph Maſon
Sarah, Dauter of George Harrington
Decr 3. Abijah, Son of Thomas Bond, John, Son of John Dix, Submit, Kezia & Sarah, Dauters & Abijah, Son of Charles Chadwick, Elizabeth, Dauter of Hannah Cutler
31. Dorcas, Dauter of Joſiah Perry
Eunice, Dauter of John Stratton

1727/8.

Janry 14. Abigail, Dauter of Caleb Benjamin
28. Benjamin, Son of George Lawrence Junr
Feb. 4. Isaiah, Son of Damll Stearns
March. 24. Ruth, Daûter of Andr White Junr

[224] 1728.

May. 19. Ebenezer Son of Ebenr Nutting, Moſes, Son of John Stearns Junr, Abigail, Dauter of Ebenr Chenery
June 2. Eunice, Daûter of George Cutting
July. 14. Joſiah, Son of John Bond, Suſanna, Daûter of John Tainter, James, Son of John Stowel, in private
Augst 11. Lucey, Daûter of John Coollidge
25. Elijah, Son of Jonas Bond
Sept 8. Jonas, Son of Thomas Learned
Daniel, Son of Benjamin Haſtings
22. Thomas, Son, Martha & Ruth ye Daughters of Richard Clark

Octo^{r} 6. Jonathan, Son of Nath^{ll} Bond
13. Jonathan, Son of Jon^{a} Benjamin Junr. Joſiah, Son of Nath^{ll} Norcroſs, Nathan, Son of Jabez Stratton
20. Margeret, Dauter of Eben^{r} Stone
Novr 3. Hannah, Dauter of John Coollidge
Nathaniel, Son of Isaac Child
10. Aſher, Son of John Haſtings
24. Ruth, Daûter of Sam^{ll} Pierce
Lydia, Daûter of Henry Spring Ju^{r}
Decem^{r} 8. Nathaniel, Son of Nath^{ll} Coollidge
22. Benjamin, Son of Joſhua Warren Ju^{r}
29. Lydia, Daûter of Joſhua Grant Junr

1728/9.

Feb. 9. Priſcilla, Daûter of Nath^{ll} Harris
Sarah, Daûter of Jon^{a} Benjamin Senr
23. Phebe, Palfrey was baptized, ſhe having first owned ye Covenant
March. 23. Jonas, Son of James Barnard, in private

1729.

March 30. Sarah, Daûter of Sam^{ll} Benjamin
Mary, Daûter of John Dix
June. 1. Caleb, Son of Caleb Benjamin was baptized by Rev. Emerſon, Malden.
29. Jonathan, Son of John Fisk
July 6. Mary & Rebecca, Daûters of Jon^{a} Coollidge
Augst 3. Mary, Dauter of William Ozment
17. William, Son of David Sanger
Mary Dauter of Sam^{ll} Warren in private
23. Rachel, Daûter of Oliver Livermore
Lydia, Daûter of Jon^{a} Brown
Sep^{t} 14. Mary Daûter of Nath^{ll} Clark
28. Suſanna, Daûter of Joſeph Maſon
Novr 16. Josiah, Son of Jon^{a} Stone Junr
Decr 14. Abigail, Daûter of John Stratton

1729/30.

Feb. 8. Amariah, Son of Wm Williams
Anna, Daûter of Timothy Harris
March. 15. Sarah, Daûter of John Bond
Mary, Daûter of James Nutting

1730.

Aprill. 12. Abijah, Son of John Sawen
Peter, Son of Elizabeth Gibbins
19. Jedidiah, Son of Henry Spring Junr was baptized by Revd Jeniſon
26. Elizabeth, ye Daûter of Jos. Holdin was baptized by ye Revd Warham Williams
May. 3. Moſes, Son of Eben^{r} Biggelow
10. Benjamin, Son of John Stowel

17. Josiah, Son of Nath^{ll} Jeniſon
Thomas Biſhop having first owned ye Coven^{t}
31. Suſanna, Daûter of John Whitney

[225]

June. 7. William, Son of John Maddocks
Sarah, & Martha, ye Daûters of And^{r} White Junr
21. Joſeph, Son of Simon Coollidge
Augst 9. Mercy, Daûter of Nath^{ll} Norcroſs
Sep^{t} 13. Mary, Daûter of Eleazer Biggelow
Octr 11. William Son of   Shattuck dec^{d}
25. Elias, Son of Jabez Stratton
Novr 1. Jeruſha, Daûter of John Stearns Junr
15. Mary, Daûter of John Leppington
John, Son of Eben^{r} Chenery
22. Samuel, Son of George Cutting
Decr 6. Joanna, Daûter of John Tainter by Rev. Mr Jeniſon
13. Abigail, Daûter of John Coollidge Jun.
Abigail, Daûter of Nath^{ll} Bond
20. Suſanna, Daûter of Nath^{ll} Coollidge

1730/1.

Jan^{ry} 24. Mary, Daûter of Sam^{ll} Benjamin
William, Son of David Sanger
Feb. 7. Sarah, Daûter of John Haſtings
14. Elizabeth, Daûter of Thos Dana of Cambridge
21. Samuel, Son of Sam^{ll} Peirce
Ruth, Daûter of Joſhua Grant Junr
March. 17. John, Son of John Whitney in private
21. Elizabeth, Daûter of Edmund Dix

1731.

28. Peter, negro man of Mr Jon^{a} Stone, entered into Cov^{t} & rec^{d} baptiſm
April. 11. Mary, Daûter of Nath^{ll} Bright
Moſes, Son of Isaac Child
18. Kezia, Daûter of Caleb Benjamin
25. Benjamin, Son of Nath^{ll} Harris
Mary, Daûter of John Maddocks
May. 16. Elizabeth, Daûter of Joſhua Learned
23. Thomas, Son of David Learned,
Elizabeth, Daûter of Nath^{ll} Jeniſon
June. 6. Daniel, Son of Jon^{a} Benjamin
Hopestill, Son of Eben^{r} Biggelow
July. 4. Benjamin, Son of Benjamin Haſtings
18. Mary, Daûter of Daniel Bond
Augst 1. Elijah, Son of Joſhua Warren Junr, Lydia, Daûter of John Dix, Martha, Dauter of Sam^{ll} Dix
1. Mary, Betty & Martha, Dauters of Nath^{ll} Sherman
15. Kezia, Dauter of Eben^{r} Stone
Iſaac, Son, & Sarah, Dauter of Isaac Barnard

Sep^t^ 12. Mary, Dauter of Oliver Livermore
19. Abel, Son of Sufanna Benjamin
Octr 17. Jonathan, Son of Jon^a^ Learned
24. Benjamin, Son of Nath^ll^ Clark, by Rev. Mr Cotton
Novr 21. Hannah, Dauter of Jonas Bond
Decr 12. Abigail, Dauter of Jonathan Brown

1731/2.

Jan^ry^ 2. Lydia, Dauter of Simon Coollidge
16. Hannah, Dauter of And^r^ White Junr
March. 5. Ebenezer, Son of Jofeph Mafon

1732.

Aprill. 16. John, Son of Henry Spring Junr
23. At Wefton, Jonathan, Son of Abijah Upham
30. Jonathan, Son of John Whitney

[226]

May. 7. at Marlborough, Mary, Dauter of James Brown
14. Efther, Dauter of William Williams
21. James, Son of Ruth Underwood
June. 18. at Wells, Reuben, Son of Daniel Chaney
July. 16. Richard, Son of Richard Clark
23. Uriah, Son of Nath^ll^ Norcrofs
Mary, Dauter of Edward Harrington Junr
Augs^t^ 6. Robert, Son of Jofhua Learned
13. Martha, Dauter of William Goddin
John, Son of John Tainter
Sep. 3. Silence, Dauter of Eben^r^ Biggelow
24. William, Son of Edmund Dix
Octr 8. Eliakim, Son of Samuel Gearfield
John, Son of John Stratton
29. Elizabeth, Dauter of John Haftings
Sufanna, Dauter of John Bond
Novr 5. Samuel, Son of Eben^r^ Thatcher
26. Abijah, Son of Timothy Harris
Decr 10. Mary, Dauter of Jonathan Bond
31. Hezekiah, Son of John Stowel
Ezekiel, Son of Sam^ll^ Stearns Junr

1732/3

Feb. 4. Elizabeth, Dauter of Nath^ll^ Bond
18. Anna, Dauter of Sam^ll^ Benjamin
Daniel, Son of John Coollidge Junr
Amariah, Son of Jon^a^ Learned
25. Elizabeth, Dauter of Ruth Brown
March. 25. John, Son of Adam Pattefon
David, Son of David Learned
Hannah, Dauter of Benj^a^ Haftings.

1733.

April. 15. Hannah, Dauter of Nath^{ll} Harris
Joshua, Son of Eleazer Biggelow
29. Joseph, Son and Ruth & Hannah Dauters } of Eben^r Hastings
May. 13. Abigail, Dauter of John Brown
27. Abigail, Dauter of John Dix
July. 22. Mary, Dauter of Benj^a Whitney Junr
29. Thaddeus, Son of Nath^{ll} Warren
Augs^t 5. Mary, Dauter & Daniel, Son } of Dan^{ll} Stearnes
19. Rachel, Dauter of Oliver Livermore
Lydia, Dauter of And^r White Junr
Mary, Dauter of Sam^{ll} Stratton
Sep^t 16. At Newton, Abigail, Dauter of Murdock
Nov. 4. Nathaniel, Son of David Sanger
Moses, Son of Edwd Harrington Junr
18. Isaac, Son of Dan^{ll} Bond
Lois, Dauter of Simon Coollidge
Decr 9. Ruth, Dauter of Daniel Stearns

1733/4.

Jan^{ry} 13. Jonas, Son of Josiah Reed
Feb. 17. Elizabeth, Dauter of Joshua Warren Junr
24. William, Son of Jonas Bond
Benoni, Son of Richard Clark
Sarah, Dauter of Eben^r Thatcher

1734.

Aprill. 14. George, Son of David Mc Connoughey
Eunice, Dauter of Isaac Child

[227]

May. 26. Abraham & Elijah, Sons of Eb^r Biggelow
June. 5. Lucey, Dauter of Jon^a Brown
23. David, Son of John Fisk
Ebénezer, Son of Eb^r Chenery
30. Josiah, Son of Nath^{ll} Norcross
July 14. Joseph, Son of Allen Brown
21. At Newton, Rachel, Dauter of Thos Fuller
Augst 4. Thomas & Fanning, Sons of Jon^a Learned
Sep^t 1. Ann, Dauter of John Tainter
Octr 13. Josiah, Son of Jos. Mason
17. Samuel, Son of Henry Bond jun^r
20. Mary, Dauter of Nath^{ll} Coollidge
Novr 10. Phinehas, Son of William Williams
Amos, Son of John Whitney
Samuel, Son of Sam^{ll} Jenison
17. Ephraim, Son of John Craft
Elizabeth, Dauter of Edmund Livermore

Joseph, Son of Jos. Wellington
Decr 1. Sarah, Daughter of Jabez Stratton
22. Seth, Son of Nathll Bond
Elizabeth, Dauter of Joſhua Learned

1734/5.

Janry 5. Convers, Son of Henry Spring Junr
12. At Menotomy 3 Three Children
Hubert, Son of David Dunſter
Abraham, Son of Zecharias Hill
Jason, Son of Bathrick
26. William, Son of Thos. Saltmarſh
Feb. 2d At Camb. Villige, Sarah, Dauter of John Ellis
9. Jeruſha, Dauter of John Stowel
Jedediah, Son of Andr White Junr
Phineas, Son of Joſiah Stearns
16. Sarah, Dauter of Samll Benjamin
Mary, Dauter of Jona Benjamin
Adam, Son of Adam Patterſon
Jonathan, Son of Stephen Sawen
Lethie, Dauter of Margaret Waſon
March. 2. At Menotomy three children
Aaron, Son of Jaſon Winſhip
Joſeph, Son of Ebenezer Swan
Jonathan, Son of George Cutter

1735.

30th. William Murch owned the Covenant, & Lydia his Dauter & Mercy, Dauter of Mercy Stratton & Simon, Son of Benjamin Haſtings were baptized
May 25. Edward, Son of Edwd Harrington Junr
June. 29. Stephen, Son of Nathll Harris
Suſanna, Dauter of Samll Barnard

[228]

July. 6. Stephen, Son of John Dix
20th Oliver, Son of Oliver Livermore
27th Lucey, Dauter of David Learned
Sept 21st Sarah, Dauter of John Haſtings
Samuel Stearns Junr owed ye Covent
Octobr 12th Jonathan Barnard & Hannah Barnard ownd ye Covent
19th Jonathan Son of Jona Barnard
26th Abigail & Lydia, Dauters of Joſ. Crackbone
Sarah, Dauter of Samll Stearns Junr
Novr 2. Thomas Wellington & Margaret Wellington owned ye Covt
16th James, Son of James Barnard
Decr 7th William Lawrence & Mary Lawrence owned ye Covent
Abraham, Son of John Whitney

14th Thomas, Son of Thos. Wellington Junr
21st Samuel, Son of William Lawrence

1735/6

Jan. 4. Mary, Dauter of Ebr Thatcher
Isaac, Son of Isaac Stearns } were baptized at West
Anne Dauter of Samll Fisk } Chh by S. S.
Feyry 15. Nathaniel, Son of Daniel Stearns
29. Phebe, Dauter of Jona Barnard
March. 14. Elizabeth, Dauter of Thos Wellington.

1736

April. 25th Jonathan, Son of Jonathan Bond
June. 6th. Samuel, Son of David Sanger
13th. Abigail Sawen owned ye Covent
July 4th. John Sawen Junr owned ye Covenant
Elijah, Son of Joshua Warren Junr
Silas, Son of John Coollidge were baptized
Augst 15th. Thomas, Son, & Martha Dauter of Jos. Harrington
Jonathan Church & Thankful Church owned ye Covent
29. Hannah, Sarah & Ruth, Dauters of Richd & Ab. Sawtle
Benjamin, ye Son of Benjamin Whitney
Sept 5. Mary, Dauter of Jona Church
19. Simon & Daniel, Sons }
Joanna, Abigail, Mary } of Daniel Whitney
Dorothy, Dauters }
William, Son of Wm Murch
Samuel, Son of Stephen Sawen
Ruth, Dauter of Ebr Cheany in private
Octo 3d. Samuel, Son of Edmund Livermore
Jedediah, Son of Jona Learned
17. Ruth & Elizabeth, Dauters of Jos Harrington
31. William, Son of William Godding Junr
10th Abigail, Dauter of Samll Jenison
Novr 21. Annah, Dauter of Simon Coollidge
28. Abijah, Son of Jona Brown
Decr 12. Lucy, Dauter of Andrew White junr
19. Jabez, Son of Eleazer Biggelow
Elizabeth Sawen owned ye Coven

[229]

1736/7

Janry 23rd Jonas, Son of Benja Hastings
Ephraim Perry owned the Covenant
Febry 6th Martha, Dauter of Samll Hastings
20. Anna, Dauter of John Stearns
Jonas, Son of Josiah Stearns
27. Bathsheba, Dauter of Ebr Swan of Cambridge

March. 6th Sarah, Dauter of Henry Spring Junr
Jemima, Dauter of John Stowell
Thomas, Son of Thos Saltmarsh
20. Samuel, Son of John Tainter

1737

27. Nehemiah, Son of Caleb Fuller of Newton
April. 3rd Catharine, Dauter of Jonas Bond
Elizabeth, Dauter of John Bond
Joshua, Son of Daniel Whitney
May. 22nd Fullam, Son of Nathll Harris
June. 12th Beulah, Dauter of Edwd Harrington
19. Samuel, Son of Samll Barnard
July. 3rd Jesse, Son of William Williams
24. Sarah, Dauter of John Lawrence
31. Amos, Son of Oliver Livermore
Mercy, Dauter of Joshua Learned
August. 7. Elizabeth Benjamin owned ye Covent
Rachel, Dauter of Eliza Benjamin
14. Samuel, Son of Samll Benjamin
Elisha, Son of David Learned
28. Ebenezer, Son of Ebr Thatcher
Sept 4. Jonathan, Son of John Dix
Rebecca, Dauter of Jose Wellington
11th Samuel Clark owned ye Covenant
Samuel, Son of Samll Clark
Octo. 16. Thomas Quiner & Sarah Quiner owned ye Covent
Novr 6th Eliza Bright owned ye Covent
Josiah Son } of Jose & Eliza Bright
Elizabeth, Dauter }
27. Jonathan Child & Elizabeth his Wife owned ye Covent
Anna, Dauter of Jonathan Church
John, Son of Thos Wellington Junr
Sarah, Dauter of Thos Quiner

1737/8

Janry 8 William, Son of Jonathan Benjamin
Elizabeth, Dauter of Jona Child
29th Pero, negro of Capt Bowman owned ye Covent & was baptized

[230]

Feb. 12. Francis, Son of Benja Dana of Cambridge
19 Joseph Whitney & Mary his wife owned ye Covent
Samuel, Son of Stephen Sawen
Flemming, Son of Jona Barnard
March. 5th. Sarah Tom, an Indian Woman owned ye Covenant & was baptized
Abigail, Dauter of Jos. Bright
19th Joseph, Son of Jos. Whitney
Lydia, Dauter of Samll Prentis

1738

26. Peter Stears, Mary Tainter & Mary Bemis owned ye Covent
April. 9. Margaret, Dauter of Sarah Tom, by Rev. Mr Cotton
16. Mary, Dauter of Nathll Norcrofs
John, Son of Thos Bifco
Sarah, Dauter of John Steward
30. Elizabeth Berry entred into Covent & was baptized
May. 28. Samuel, Son of Ebr Biggelow
July. 16. Pegg, Molatto Servt of Oliver Livermore entred into Covt & recd Baptifm
August. 13. Sarah, Dauter of Simon Coollidge
20. Abigail, Dauter of Andr White junr
Sept. 3rd Sufanna, Dauter of Thos Wellington
Mofes, Son of John Whitney
24th Eunice, Daughter of George Lawrence
October. 22nd William, Son of Jona Learned
Nov. 5th Sarah, Dauter of John Brown
Decr 3rd John, Son of Thos Saltmarfh
31. Henry, Son of Daniel Whitney
Jofiah, Son of Edmand Livermore

1738/9

Febry 4. Jonathan Coollidge, Son of Wm Godding
11. Efther, Dauter of John Hoar
Rebecca, Dauter of Benjn Whitney
18. Samuel, Son of Nathll Coollidge
25. Mary, Dauter of Ebenr Swan
John, Son of Zechariah Hill
March. 11. Mary, Dauter of Benja Haftings
25. Jofiah, Son of John Bowman of Lexington

1739

April 15. Mary Sawen, & Lydia Sawen owned ye Covent
29th Ann, Dauter of Ephraim Cooke } at Menotomy by S. S.
Philemon, Son of Jofeph Winship } at Menotomy by S. S.
Mary, Dauter of Jofeph Robbins } at Menotomy by S. S.
May. 13. Alpheus, Son of Henry Spring Junr
Anna, ye Dauter of Oliver Livermore
Abigail & Mercy, Dauters of Wm Lawrence
20. Zachariah, Son of Jof. Morfe, at Newton by S. S.
David, Son of James Barnard, by Revd Mr Cotton
27. Jemima, Dauter of John White
June. 10. Elijah, Son of John Coollidge
17. Mary, Dauter of David Learned

[231]

July. 1. Mary, Dauter of David Coollidge
8. Sufanna, Dauter of Ebr Thatcher
29. Sarah, Dauter of Daniel Stearns
Samuel, Son of Samuel Stratton

Sept. 2. John, Son of John Veleau
Elizabeth, Dauter of Sam[ll] Benjamin
Oct[o] 21. John, Son of Eb[r] Chenery
28. Abigail, Dautr of John Stearns
Nov. 4. Noah, Son of Josh. Warren Jun[r] by Rev. Warham Williams
18. Samuel, Son of Sam[ll] Stearns

1739/40

Feb. 3. Thomas, Son of Jon[a] Bond by Rev. M[r] Cooke
17. Paul, Son of Joshua Learned
Benjamin, Son of Stephen Sawen
March. 9. Asa, Son of Nath[ll] Norcross
Sarah, Dauter of Jon[a] Bemis
Grace, Dauter of Edw[d] Harrington
John, Son of John Gleason
16. Sarah, Daughter of John Sawen Jun[r]
23. Eunice, Dauter of Simon Coollidge
Mary, Dauter of Christopher Grant

1740

30. Jonathan, Son of Sam[ll] Hager
David, Son of John Stowel
Dorcas, Dauter of Joseph Wellington
Dorothy Gleason owned y[e] Covenant
April. 6. Daniel, Son of John Maddock
Josiah, Son of Edmund Livermore
Lydia, Dauter of Jon[a] Church
May 11. Abigail, Dauter of Thos. Saltmarsh
27. Abigail Godding owned y[e] Covenant
June. 1. Ann, Dauter of Eleazer Bigelow, by Rev. M[r] Cooke
Aaron, Son of Sam[ll] Swan } at Menotomy
Samuel, Son of Nehemiah Cutter } by S. S.
20. Josiah, Son of Tho[s] Bisco
Noah, & Aaron, Sons of Benj[a] Chadwick
Aug[st] 17. Solomon, Son of David Sanger
24. Israel Meed owned y[e] Covenant
Sept. 14. Mary, Dauter of Tho[s] Quiner
Nov[r] 23. Jonas, Son of Hephzibah Steward
30. Ephraim, Son of Ephraim Winship, at Menotomy by S. S.

1740/1

Jan[ry] 4. Anna, Dauter of John Brown
Samuel, Son of James Grimes
11. Benjamin, Son of Benj[a] Dix
25. David, Son of Joseph Whitney, by R[d] M[r] Cotton
Esther, Daughter of Jon[a] Edmunds, at Newton by S. S.
March. 1. Aaron, Son of Ephraim Cooke, at Menotomy by S. S.

1741

April. 5. Elizabeth, Dauter of Sam^ll^ Prentice
12. Ezekiel, Son of John Whitney
Hannah, Daughter of Sam^ll^ Barnard
Josiah, Son of Jonathan Barnard

[232]

April. 12. Ebenezer Bullard } Samuel Coollidge } owned the Covenant
19. Abigail, Dauter of Oliver Livermore
26. Joanna, Dauter of Wm Godding Junr
Hannah, Dauter of Jon^a^ Learned
May. 3. Andrew, Son of Andrew White Junr
10. Hannah Tainter owned ye Covenant
24. Arminna, a negro Woman owned the Covenant
31. David Gleason owned the Covenant
June. 7. William, Son of Wm Lawrence
Ruth Livermore owned the Covenant
14. Dorcas Perry owned the Covenant
28. Ephraim Mailet & Robert Crowell entered into Cov & were baptized
Daniel Livermore, Bethiah Bond & Abigail Bond owned ye Cov^t^
Mary, Dauter of Sam^ll^ Jenison
July 5. Sarah, Dauter of David Coollidge
Jonathan Stone Junr, Lois Stearns
Anna Stearns, Abigail Sawtle
Sarah Harrington & Abigail Whitney
12. Daniel Peirce, Jos Child jun^r^, Moses Stone & Hannah Hastings } owned ye Covent
19. John Cooke, Benjamin Hastings } Henry Sawtle, Ann Bond } owned ye Cov^t^
Elizabeth, Dauter of Sam^ll^ Cooke
Mary, Dauter of Sam^ll^ Child
26. Ayres, Son of John Tainter
Abigail, Dauter of Eb^r^ Goddard
Grace Bond, & Jerusha Bond owned ye Covenant
Aug^st^ 2. Seth Hastings owned ye Covenant
16. Israel, Son of Daniel Whitney
Anthony, a molatto entered into Cov^t^ & was baptized
Abijah Stearns, Hannah Godding owned ye Covenant
Octr 4. Samuel, Son of John Dix
11. Isaac, son of Isaac Sanderson
25. Joshua, Son of Josiah Perry Junr
Nov. 1. Hepzibah, Dauter of John Stearns
Decr 27. John, Son of Sam^ll^ Nutting

1741

May. 29. Joseph Coollidge was chosen to the office of a Deacon

[233]

1741/2

Jan^ry^ 3rd Simon, Son of Simon Coollidge
10. William, Son of Benj^a^ Haftings
Sarah, Dauter of David Learned
17. Jonathan, Son of Edwd Harrington
31. Elifha Biggelow and Mary Biggelow owned ye Covenant
Feb. 7. Nehemiah, Son of Nathl^l^ Norcrofs
21. Hannah Sawen owned ye Covenant
28. Marfhall, Son of Henry Spring Junr
Eunice, Dauter of Jon^a^ Bond

1742

April. 11. Lydia, Dauter of Sam^ll^ Benjamin
25. Samuel, Son of Benj^a^ Whitney
May. 9. Katherine, Dauter of John Hunt
June. 13. At Newton, Mofes, Son of Thos. Parker
July. 4. William, Son of Eb^r^ Chenery, by R^d^ War. Williams
11. Sarah, Dauter of Sam^ll^ Stratton
Aug^st^ 1. David, Son of Benj^a^ Dix
8. Peter, Son of Josiah Stearns
Sep^t^ 5. At Wefton, Ruth, Dauter of Thos Upham
Ruhamah, Son of Jofiah Wellington
12. Anna, Dauter of John Velau
Deborah, Dauter of Thos Saltmarfh
Octr 10. Joseph Mafon Junr owned the Covenant
Rachel, Dauter of Eb^r^ Goddard
Daniel, Son of John Coollidge
Grace, Dauter of Jof Mafon Junr
31. At Lexington Betty, Dauter of Daniel Tidd
Nov. 28. John, Son of Stephen Sawen
Decr 5. Mary, Dauter of Jof Wellington

1742/3.

Jan^ry^ 9. Stephen, Son of Sam^ll^ Cooke
16. Ebenezer, Son of Eb^r^ Thatcher
Abigail, Dauter of Jon^a^ Church
Feb. 6. Mary, Dauter of Daniel Searns
13. At Newton, Elifabeth Dauter of Michael Jackfon

1743

March. 27. Jonathan, Son of Oliver Livermore
Eunice, Dauter of Andrew White
April. 10. Lydia, Dauter of Daniel Whitney
Cornelius, Son of Aaron Brown
17. Jerufha, Dauter of Jona Learned
Jonathan, Son of Jos. Whitney, by Revd. W. Williams
May. 29. Jacob Caldwell owned the Covenant
June. 5. Lydia, Dauter of David Sanger
John, Son of Jacob Caldwell

July. 3. Edmund, Son of Jon^a^ Barnard
10. Margaret, Dauter of John Clark } at Newton
Mary, Dauter of Jon^a^ Trowbridge } by S. S.
24. Elisabeth, Dauter of Daniel Bond

[234]

Aug^st^ 7. James Hackleton owned the Covenant
Stephen, Son of John Whitney
John, Son of James Hackleton
Josiah, Son of Isaac Sanderson
21. Nathan, Son of Benj^a^ Hastings, by Rev. W. Williams
28. Mary Chenery owned ye Cov^t^ & Mary her Dauter was baptized
Sep^t^ 4th Josiah, Son of Josiah perry Junr, by Rev. War. Williams
Oct^o^ 2. Phineas, Son of Sam^ll^ Jenison
9. Mary, Dauter of David Coolidge
16. Josiah & Ebenezer, Sons of Eb. Goddard
30. Mary, Dauter of John Beath
Nov. 13. Hepzibah, Dauter of Simon Coollidge
Decr 11. Phineas, Son of Edward Harrington
18. Abigail, Dauter of Josh. Learned

1743/4

Jan^ry^ 8. Jonas Coollidge, James Dix & Sarah Dix owned the Coven^t^
Oliver, Son of David Learned
Sarah, Dauter of James Dix
22. Lucy, Dauter of Sam^ll^ Clark } at Camb. Village
Sarah, Dauter of Jon^a^ Fessenden } by S. S.
Feb. 5. Christopher, Son of Christopher Grant
12. Jonas, Son of Jonas Coollidge
26. Sarah, Dauter of James Grimes, by Rev. War. Williams

1744

April. 8. Elisabeth, Dauter of Wm. Coollidge
22. Hannah, Dauter of Jose Mason Junr
May. 13. Katherine, Dauter of John Hunt
June. 3. Jonathan, Son of Abijah Wheeler at Weston }
10. Dorothy, Daûter of Josiah Stearns }
July. 8. Edward, Son of Edward Park at Newton
Aug^st^ 5. Peter, Son of Wm Godding Junr
Sept. 9. Mary, Dauter of Uriah Clark
16. Sarah, Dauter of Sam^ll^ Nutting
30. Sarah, Dauter of Gershom Cutter Junr at Menotomy
Octr. 14. John, Son of Benjamin Hastings Junr
21. Rebecca, Daûter of Jacob Caldwell
28. Samuel, Son of Nath^ll^ Coollidge
Grace, Dauter of Daniel Whitney
Novr. 4. Katherine, Dauter of Thos. Saltmarsh
11. Uriah Biggelow owned ye covenant

Decr. 30. David Livermore & Abigail Livermore owned ye Covenant
Sufanna, Daûter of John Young

1744/5.

Jan^{ry}. 20. Hepzebah, Dauter of John Hackleton
27. Samuel, Son of Wm Downe
Samuel, Son of Alexander Thompfon at Camb. Village by S. S. B.
March. 3. David, Son of Stephen Sawen
Abigail, Daûter of David Livermore by R^{d} War. Williams
17. Smith Prentice owned ye Cov^{t}
Benjamin, Son of f^{d} Prentice
24. Katey, Dauter of Sam^{ll} Benjamin

[235] 1745.

April. 7. Jofiah, Son of Thos Wellington
Margaret, Dauter of John Beath
21. John, Son of John Velau
May 26. Jofeph, Son of Daniel Bond
Elijah, Son of Andrew White
July. 14. Amos, Son of Amos Bond
Aug. 11. Anna, Daûter of James Dix
25. Hannah, Dauter of Sam^{ll} Stratton
Margaret, Daûter of Jos. Wellington
Sept. 1. Kezia, Daûter of Isaac Sanderfon
15. Cornelius, Son of Jon^{a} Barnard
Henry, Son of Henry Sawtle
Octr. 20. Benjamin, Son of Jon^{a} Learned, by R. S. Cooke
27. Samuel, Son of John Hunt
Nov. 3. Elizabeth, Dauter of Eb^{r} Goddard
10. Ebenezer, Son of James Coollidge
Decr. 8. Mofes, Son of Sam^{ll} Miller at Newton by S. S.
Sarah, Dauter of Eb^{r} Thacher, by R^{d} Mr Cotton
29. Elifha, Son of James Hackleton

1745/6.

Jan^{ry}. 12. Nathaniel, Son of Oliver Livermore
Henry, Son of Benj^{a} Whitney Junr
19. Robert, Son of Sam^{ll} Cooke
Feb. 23. Benjamin, Son of Jofiah Shattuck
March. 2. Henry, Son of Henry & Sarah Bright
9. Daniel Sawen owned Covenant
23. Elifha, Son of Wm Wellington, at Menotomy by S. S.
Jefse, Son of David Learned, by R^{d} Mr Cooke

1746

30. Jonathan, Son of John Dix
April. 13. Aaron, Son of John Whitney, in private
20. Lucy, Dauter of Sam^{ll} Jenifon
Hepzibah, Dauter of David Coollidge

27. Suſanna, Dauter of Joſiah Stearns
May. 4. Jennet, Dauter of Wm Fullerton
June. 8. William, Son of John Tainter
15. Joſiah, Son of Benja Whitney
July. 6. Mary, Dauter of Henry Spring Tertius
27. Martha, Dauter of James Cutler, at Menotomy by S. S.
Suſanna, Dauter of Nathll Norcroſs, by Rd Mr Cooke
Augst. 10. Uriah, Son of Uriah Clark
24. Sarah, Dauter of Jos. Maſon Junr
Sept. 14. Eliſabeth, Dauter of Jos. Kelly
Nov. 2. Hannah, Dauter of Bezaleel Learned
16. Henry, Son of Wm Godding Jun
23. Abigail, Dauter of Benja Haſtings
30. Eliſabeth, Daûter of Jos. Whitney
John, Son of John Young
Decr. 7. Seth, Son of Thos. Saltmarſh
Anna, Dauter of Jacob Caldwell
Joſhua & Isaac, Sons, &
Hannah, Dauter, of Daniel Stearns
Nymphos, my Negro, entered into Covt & was baptized.

[236] 1746/7.

Janry 11. William, Son of Edward Harrington
18. Priſcilla, Dauter of David Livermore
Feb. 1. John, Son of John Hunt
8. Daniel, Son of Daniel Hoſmer, at Concord by S. S.
15. Mehetabel, Daûter of Simon Coollidge
22. Nathaniel, Son of Amos Bond
March. 8. Eliſha, Son of Daniel Whitney
15. Elizabeth, of Benja Cheny } at Camb. Village
Sarah, Dauter of John Cheny } by S. S.
22. Joſeph, Son of Henry Sawtle

1747

April. 19. Sarah, Daûter of Ebr Goddard
May. 10. Phinehas, Son of Sol. Robbins, at Cam : Vil : by S. S.
17. Mary, Dauter of Smith Prentice
24. Elizabeth, Daûter of Jonas Coollidge
31. Silas, Son of John Train at Weſton by S. S.
June. 28. Lydia, Daûter of Sam. Fiſk
July. 26. Hannah, Dauter of Nathan Perry
Augst 2. Eunice, Dauter of Jonas Pierce of Concord by S. S.
23. Elijah, Son of James Dix
Octo 18. Edmund Fowle owned ye Covent
Suſanna, Daûter of Samll Hager
Abigail, Daûter of Edmund Fowle
Lydia, Dauter of Benja Whitney Junr
Novr 22. David, Son of Nathll Stone
Mary, Dauter of Moſes Stone
29. Daniel, Son of Jos. White, at Brooklin by S. S.

Decr 27. Henry, Son of Jsaac Sanderfon
. Edmund, Son of Edmund Fowle

1747/8.

Jan^ry 3. Smith, Son of Benj^a Haftings
10. Nathaniel, Son of Edwd Thwing at Camb. Village by S. S.
17. Elifabeth, Dauter of John Tainter
Eunice, Dauter of Wm Coollidge
Feb. 28. Samuel, Son of Henry Bond
Sufanna, Dauter of Jofiah Shattuck
March. 6. Mary, Dauter of Wm Dana at Camb. Vil: by S. S.
13. Mary, Dauter of Sam^ll Nutting
Palfgrave, Son of Jos. Wellington

1748

April. 3. William, Son of Josiah Stearns
10. Jofeph, Son of Jon^a Barnard
17. Jerufha, Dauter of Bezaleel Learned
24. Ruth, Dauter of Uriah Clark
May. 15. Samuel Warren Junr owned ye Covenant
22. Mary, Daûter of Nath^ll Harrington
June. 5. Mary, Daûter of Sam^ll Warren Junr
12. Sarah, Dauter of Sam^ll Jenifon
Lydia, Dauter of Henry Spring Ter^ts
July. 6. Ruth, Daughter of John Whitney
Jonathan, Son of Jon^a Stone
24. Ruth, Daûter of Jon^a Stone Tertius
31. Isaac, Son of Thos Saltmarfh
Aug^st 21. Samuel, Son of James Hackleton by R^d Mr Cotton
Mofes, Son of Jofiah Greenwood at Newton by S. S.
28. Ruth, Daûter of John Hunt
Sept. 11. Mehetabel, Daûter of Sam^ll Benjamin
Daniel, Son of John Young

[237]

Oct^o 16. Nathaniel, Son of Sam^ll Stratton
Novr 6. Jacob, Son of Jacob Caldwell
20. Lucey, Dauter of Afa Warren at Waltham by S. S.
Decr 11. Sufanna, Dauter of Sam^ll Cooke
25. Jonas, Son of Jos. Mafon Junr

1748/9.

Jan^ry 29th. Lucy, Dauter of Sam^ll Hager
Feb. 26. Hannah, Daûter of Nath^ll Bright
March. 19. Thomas, Son of David Coollidge

1749

26. Mary, Dauter of Jonas Coollidge
April. 9th. Releif, Dauter of Jofiah Stearns
Amos, Son of Amos Bond
Daniel, Son of David Livermore
30. Lydia, Dauter of Daniel Bond

May. 7. Suſanna, Dauter of Joſiah Hall at Newton by S. S.
28. David, Son of Sol. Robbins at Camb. Village by S. S.
June. 4. Hannah, Dauter of Nathan Perry
11. Mercy, Dauter of Simon Coollidge
18. Moſes, Son of Moſes Stone
27. Samuel Fiſk was choſen to yᵉ office of a Deacon
July. 2. Lucey, Dauter of Daniel Whitney
Smith, Son of Smith Prentice
9. Spencer, Son of Wᵐ Godding
16. William, Son of James Dix
Augˢᵗ 13. Eliſabeth, Daûter of Abraham Cutting at Camb. Vil. by S. S.
Sept. 3. Joſiah, Son of Nathˡˡ Stone
10. Sarah, Dauter of Benjᵃ Whitney Junʳ
17. Francis, Son of Henry Spring Terˡˢ
Octᵒ 8. William, Son of Wᵐ Coollidge
Abigail, Daûter of Abigail Biſco
15. At Waltham, William, Son of Joſiah Biggelow
29. Mary Prieſt owned yᵉ Covᵗ & Sarah, her Daûter was baptized
Octᵒ 19. Jonas, Son of Daniel Knap }
yᵉ Son of Wᵐ Cheney } at Newton by S. S.
Mary, Dauter of Samˡˡ Child }
Decʳ 3. Mary, Dauter of Edmund Fowle
10. Bezaleel, Son of Bezaleel Learned
24. Anna, Dauter of Edward Harrington
Nathaniel Warren Junʳ owned yᵉ Covenant

1749/50

Janʳʸ 14ᵗʰ William, Son of John Hunt
28. At Brookline, Thankful yᵉ Daûter of Samˡˡ Gleaſon
Febʸ 4ᵗʰ Matthias Stone was diſmiſsed from this Church & recomended to the Church of Chriſt in Worceſter
11ᵗʰ Samuel, Son of Benjᵃ Haſtings
18ᵗʰ James Daſcombe entered into Covenant & was baptized
March. 4ᵗʰ Benjamin, Son of Jonᵃ Barnard
18. Joseph, Son of Samˡˡ Coollidge

1750.

April. 15. Jonas Barnard owned the Covenant
May. 20ᵗʰ Jonas White owned the Covenant
27. Abijah, Son of Jonas White
13. Suſanna, Dauter of John Warren was baptized, he & his wife Suſanna having at yᵉ ſametime owned yᵉ Covenant

[238]

June 10ᵗʰ Thankful Gearfield diſmiſsed & recomended to the Church of Chriſt in Concord, whereof the Revᵈ Mʳ Lawrence is Paſtor

July. 8th Susanna, Dauter of John Sawen Junr
Richard & Thomas, Sons of Uriah Clark
Augst 5th Nathaniel, Son of Nathll Harrington
William & Abigail, Children of Wm Gammage
Abigail, Daûter of Samll Warren Junr
19th Martha, Daûter of Jona Stone Junr
Sept. 9th Jeduthan, Son of Jos. Wellington
Daniel, Son of Wm Gammage
16th At Camb: Village Lydia, Dauter of John Dana
23d William, Son of Samll Jenison
Seth, Son of Isaac Sanderson
30th Mary, Daûter of Seth Hastings
Joshua, Son of Stephen Stearns
October. 7. William, Son of Moses Stone
John, Son of John Randall
28. Sarah, Daûter of Samll Fisk
Novr 18th Sarah, Daûter of Samll Stratton
Decr 2d Anne, Daûter of Nathll Bright
Sarah, Dauter of Jacob Caldwell
Jonathan, Son of Jona Stone Tertius
23d Daniel, Son of Nath. Stone

1750/51.

Janry 6. Lucey, Dauter of Wm Coollidge
20. Lydia, Dauter of David Livermore
March. 3. Mary, Dauter of James Hackleton
24. Abijah Stearns was dismissed & recomended to ye Chh in Lunenburgh

1751.

31. Nathan, Son of Nathan Perry
May. 5. Hannah, Daûter of Samll Cooke
Esther, Dauter of Jona Bemis Junr
June. 2. At Newton, Achsah, Dauter of John Woodward
July. 14. Thomas, Son of Amos Bond
21. At Weston Isaac ye Son of John Stratton
Hannah, Dauter of Nathll Williams
Augst 11. Deborah, Dauter of James Dix
Elisabeth Hay owned ye Covenant
18. Samuel, Son of Samll Coollidge
Sept. 15. At Waltham, Jonathan, Son of Joseph Hager
Mary, Dauter of Josiah Harrington, Mary, Dauter of Richd Cutting, Elisha, Son of Samll Harrington, Abraham, Son of Abraham Bemis, Sarah, Dauter of Elisha Livermore & Abraham, Son of Wm Lackey

[239]

Sept 29th William White Junr owned ye Covenant
William, Son of Wm White
Abigail, Dauter of James Hay

Jonathan Bond & Lydia Twitchell were diſmiſsed & recomended to ye Chh of Christ in Weſtboro, whereof ye Revd Mr Parkman is Paſtor

October. 6. Katharine, Dauter of John Hunt

20. Thomas, Son of Smith Prentice

Decr 8th Jenny, Negro Woman of Saml Parry owned ye Covt & was baptized

Nathan, Son of Jona Barnard

Nymphas, Son of Nymphas & Jenny

29. Israel, Son of Israel Meed

John, Son of John Warren

1751/2.

Janry 12th George Lawrence was diſmiſed & recommended to the Church of Chriſt in Waltham

19th Margaret, Daûter of Ebr Hinds

Feb 2d Benjamin, Son of Benja Whitney

Dorothy, Daûter of Edmund Fowle

March. 22d. Katharine, Daûter of Bezaleel Learned

1752.

April. 12. At Newton George, Son of Thos Brown Junr

26. At Camb. Village Mary, Dauter of John Stratton

May. 3d. John, Son of William Dockum of Boſton

Elizabeth, Daûter of John Randall

Moſes, Son of Joseph Peters

10th Peter, Son of Nathll Harrington

24th Daniel, Son of John Cook

June. 21st Jonas, Son of Jonas White

28th Hannah Maſon of Boſton owned the Covenant

July. 12th Benjamin, Son of Timothy Austin of Charlestown

26th At Natick Moſes ye Son of James Man

Abigail, Dauter of Enos How

Augst 2d Hephzibah, Daûter of Jos. Stevens of Boſton

9th John, Son of John White of Boſton

David, Son of David Maſon of Boſton

16th At Camb. Village Ebenezer ye Son of Ebr Storer of Boſton

23d Mary, Daûter of Edwd Harrington

Nathaniel, Son of Nathll Bright

30th Jonas, Son of Jona Learned

Samuel, Son of Wm Gammage

Uriah, Son of Uriah Clark

John Kimball Junr owned the Covenant

Joſiah Berry, John Bond & Sarah Perry were diſmiſsed & recomended to the Church of Chriſt in Worcester

Sept 24th At Waltham Aaron, Son of Isaac Brown

Lydia, Dauter of Jonathan Hammond

[240]

Oct^{o} 1st	Lydia, Dauter of Sam^{ll} Warren Junr
8th	Anna, Daûter of Wm Coollidge by Revd Mr Woodward
15th	Mary, Daûter of Jonathan Peirce
22^{d}	Abijah, Son of Nath^{ll} Stone
Novr 5th	Benjamin, Son of Benjamin Felton
12th	Mary, Dauter of Henry Bacon
	Thomas, Son of Thomas Sowen
	Sufee, Dauter of Hezekiah Allen — at Natick
	Ethel, Son of James Battle — by S. Storer
	Jacob, Son of Timothy Sparhawke
	Hannah, Daûter of Joseph Paughonot
19th	Peter Parker owned ye Covenant at Brookline
December. 17th.	Sufanna, Daûter of Nath^{ll} Coollidge Junr
	Charles, Son of Sam^{ll} Nutting
31st	Seth, Son of Jon^{a} Stone Junr

1753

Jany 7th	At Lexington, Joseph, Son of Jo^{s} Fifk
14th	At Brookline, Samuel, Son of Sam^{ll} Clark Junr
21st	Enoch, Son of Jacob Caldwell
Feb^{ry} 4th	Jonathan, Son of Mofes Stone
18th	Nymphas, Son of my Negro Man
March. 4th	At Waltham Ruth, Dauter of Stephen White
	Henry, Son of Dan^{ll} Pierce by Rev. Mr Cufhing
April. 15th	Elifabeth, Dauter of James Hay
22nd	Jofhua & Mercy, Children of Sam^{ll} Jenifon
May. 6th	Daniel, Son of James Hackleton
13th.	At Newton Amos Son of Jonas Stone
June 17th	Elifabeth, Dauter of Isaac Sanderfon
July. 1st	Mary, Dauter of Israel Meed
15th	Mofes, Son of Samuel Coollidge
	Mercy, Dauter of Smith Prentice
22^{d}	Elifabeth, Dauter of Samuel Fifk
Augst 26th	At Cambridge Village Caleb Son of Joseph Cook
Sept: 9th	John Stratton, Mary Stratton & Abigail Barnard owned ye Coven^{t}
	Jonas, Son of Jonas Barnard
October 7th	Abel Benjamin & Elizabeth Benjamin owned ye Covenant
14th	Edward, Mofes & Richard, Sons of Edwd Richardfon
21st	William, Son of William & Jane Baldwin
Novr 11th	Elifabeth, Dauter of Joseph Wellington
18th	Thomas Son of Seth Haftings by Revd Mr Cotton
	at Newton Elifabeth Dauter of Edward Durant
Decr 2.	Peter, Son of Edward Richardfon

[241] 1754.

Jan^{ry} 13th	Mary Dauter of Josiah Stearns

Febry 10th John Son of Nathll Bright
Samuel Son of Abel Benjamin
March 17th Abraham Son of Abraham Brown
24th Ebenezer Smith Son of Edmund Fowle
31st Hannah Dauter of David Livermore
Samuel Son of Henry Spring Junr
Stephen Son of John Cook
May. 5th William Son of James Hay
June 2d Thomas Son of Francis Wells at Camb. Village
23d Thankful Dauter of Jona Bemis junr
July 21st Joel, Son of Jonas White
Augst 18th Mercy Dauter of Joseph Coollidge
25. Thomas Giles & Mary Giles owned the Covenant
Sept 15th Abigail Dauter of Eb. Hinds
22nd Thomas Son of John Hunt
Samuel Son of John Randall
David Son of David Bemis
Octobr 6th Thomas Son of Thos Giles
David ye Son of Sufanna Fofter
27th Ann Rainger entered into Covenant & was baptized
Novr 24th Rebecca Dauter of Uriah & Ruth Clark
Decr 1st Ann Dauter of Samll Warren Junr
8th Mary Dauter of Nathll Coollidge Junr
22d Martha Dauter of Daniel Peirce

1755.

Janry 19th Phillis, Dauter of Nymphas a Negroe
Febry 2nd Samuel, Son of Jonas Barnard
16th John Remington & Mary Remington owned ye Covenant
23d John, Son of Israel Meed &
Efther, Dauter of John Warren
March. 2d Stephen Harris & Sarah Harris owned ye Covenant
9th John Son of John Remington
23d Nathaniel, Son of Stephen Harris
30th At Camb. Village, Nathaniel Son of Nath. Sparhawke
May. 4th Jeddediah Leath & Hannah Leath owned the Covenant
11th Sufanna, Dauter of Edwd Harrington
18th Mary, Dauter of Samuel Fifk
25. James, Son of James Hay
June. 1st At Lexington Thomas, Son of Thos Blogget

[242]

July. 27th Thaddeus, Son of Henry Bond
Augst 3rd Jonathan, Son of Jona Winchefter } at Brooklin
Solomon, Son of John Newell } at Brooklin
Elifha Gardner owned the Covenant
31st Katharine, Dauter of Nathll Harrington
Sept 14th David, Son of Smith Prentice

28th	Joseph Hay & Hannah Hay owned ye Covenant
	Hannah, Dauter of Joseph Hay
October 5th	Elizabeth, Dauter of John Hunt
Novr 16.	Elijah, Son of Sam^{ll} Hager
Decr 7.	Sufanna, Dauter of Josiah Shattuck
28th	John Tainter Junr owned the Covenant
Novr 23^{d}	Mary Shattuck owned ye Covenant

1756

Jan^{ry} 4th	Mary, Dauter of John Tainter Junr
11.	David Sanger & Lucy Sanger owned the Covenant
18th	Efther, Dauter of Joseph Patterfon
Feb^{ry} 22nd	John, Son of Edmund Fowle
	David, Son of David Sanger
March. 21st	Jonathan, Son of Abel Benjamin
28th	Molly, Dauter of Daniel Sawen
April. 4th	Amariah Learned & Hannah Learned owned ye Covenant
	Daniel, Son of Amariah Learned
11th	William Sanger & Abigail Sanger owned ye Covenant
	John, Son of Willm Sanger
	Ebenezer, Son of Eb^{r} Hinds
May. 2nd	Mary, Dauter of John Cooke
	Abigail, Dauter of Edwd Richardfon
9th	Elifabeth, Dauter of Nath^{ll} Stone
23rd	John, Son of Jedediah Leathe
30th	Lucy, Dauter of Benjamin Felton
	Daniel, Son of Nath^{ll} Coollidge Junr
June 6th	Abraham, Son of John Randall
	Samuel, Son of John Whitney Junr
	Mary Whitney owned the Covenant
27th	Mary, Dauter of James Hay
July. 18th	Edward Harrington & Anna Harrington owned ye Covenant
August. 8th	Phinehas, Son of Edwd Harrington Junr
15th	William, Son of Josiah Prieft } at Waltham
	Elifha, Son of Daniel Stearns } by S. S.
	Sufanna, Dauter of John Coffeen by R^{d} Cufhing

43]

Sep^{t} 12th	Samuel, Son of Jonas Coollidge
19th	Thomas, Son of Jedediah Spring
26th	Sufanna, Dauter of Samuel Soden
Oct^{o} 10th	Lois, Dauter of Jonas White
	Katharine, Dauter of Jon^{a} Bemis Junr
	Abigail, Dauter of Jonas Barnard
17th	Sarah, Dauter of John Hunt
31th	Jacob Boynton & Mary Boynton owned ye Covenant
	Elifabeth, Dauter of Jacob Boynton

Novr 21st Cornelius, Son of Ebenr Stone Junr
Decr 5th Daniel, Son of Danll Dana, at Camb. Village
26th Nathaniel, Son of David Bemis

1757.

Janry 16th Eliſabeth, Dauter of Joseph Coollidge
23d Abigail, Dauter of Joseph Hay
Febry 27th Abijah, Son of Wm Brown
Ebenezer, Son of Ebr Brown
Lydia, Dauter of John Stratton } Cambridge Village by S. Storer
March. 13th Tabitha, Dauter of Jonas Learned
Kate, Dauter of Nymphas (my Negro)
May 8th Daniel, Son of Danll Sawen
Anna, Dauter of Stephen Harris } by Revd S. Baldwin.
15th Samuel, Son of Samll Warren Junr
22d Jonathan, & Suſanna Raymond owned ye Covenant
Suſanna, yr Dauter baptized
29th Kezia, Dauter of John Spring of Boſton
June 5th Hannah, Dauter of Jon. Mirick at Newton by S. S.
12th Lucey, Dauter of John Remington
July. 10. Lydia, Dauter of Smith Prentice
17th Hannah, Dauter & William, Son of James Dix
24th Lucey, Dauter of Wm Park by Rev. N. Potter
Octo 9th John Son of John Cook
16th Eliſabeth, Dauter of —— Dunah at Roxbury by S. S.
23d Abraham, Son of Abraham Crawley
Nathan Son of Jacob Boynton
Novr 6th Ruth Dauter of John Warren
20th Anna Tainter owned the Covenant
28th Grace, Dauter of Benja Whitney in private
Decr 4th Deliverance, Dauter of Benja Whitney
11. Samuel, Son of John Savage

[244]

1758

Janry 1st Suſanna, Dauter of John Tainter Junr
15th Thomas, Son of David Sanger
22d Moſes Harrington & Mary Harrington owned ye Covenant
Febry 5th John Son of Abel Benjamin
12th Abigail, Dauter of Wm Sanger
26th Joſiah Norcroſs & Eliſabeth Norcroſs owned ye Covenant
Nathaniel, ye Son baptized
March. 5th Samuel, Son of Sam. White
12th Abijah, Son of Moſes Harrington
April. 2nd Sarah, Dauter of Jonas Barnard
9th Thomas, Son of James Hay
30th Mary, Dauter of Isaac Sanderſon.
May. 14th Mary, Dauter of Moſes Biggelow
21st Mary Biggelow owned ye Covenant

	Edward, Son of Edw[d] Harrington Jun[r]
June. 18th	James, Son of Nath[ll] Stone
25th	Nathaniel, Son of Nath[ll] Harris Jun[r]
July. 2nd	Lucey, Dauter of Sam[ll] Fisk
	Mary, Dauter of Amariah Learned
	Josiah Bright owned y[e] Covenant
9th	Abraham, Son of Abr. Cutting, at Camb. Village by S. S.
16th	John, Son of Edw[d] Richardson
	Isaac, Son of John Randall
23[d]	Jonathan, Son of Jon[n] Bemis Jun[r]
	Hannah, Dauter of Jedediah Leathe
August. 13th	Lucey, Dauter of Edmund Fowle
	Thomas, Son of Samuel Soden
Sep[t] 3rd	Samuel, Son of Sam[ll] Mason
17th	Jonathan, Son of John Remington
24th	Josiah & Jonathan (Twins), Sons of Josiah Bright
Oct[o] 15th	Hannah, Dauter of Josiah Thompson at Medford
Nov[r] 12th	Ephraim, Son of John Hunt
	Josiah, Son of Jonas White
26th	Isaac Sparhawk, Son of Isaac Gardner Jun[r] at Brookline

1759.

Feb[ry] 11th	John, Son of Daniel Sawen
18th	Kezia, Dauter of Joshua Jackson at Newton by S. S.
March. 25th	Nathaniel Ruggles. Son of Simon Whitney
	Abijah, Son of Abijah Brown

[245]

April. 29th	Lucey. Dauter of John Stratton of Camb. Village
May. 27th	Charles, Son of Nath[ll] Harrington
June. 24th	Elisabeth, Daûter of James Dix
July. 29th	Josiah, Son of Jedediah Spring
Aug[st] 12th	John, Son of Joseph Hay
26th	Oliver Livermore owned the Covenant
	Katharine, Daûter of Oliver Livermore
	Moses, Son of Moses Biggelow
	Matthew. Son of Matthew Johnson
Sep[t] 16th	Samuel, Son of Edw[d] Jackson at Camb. Vil: by S. S.
23[d]	Joshua, Son of Joseph Coollidge
30.	Lucy, Dauter of Sam[ll] White by Rev[d] Lawrence
Oct[o] 14th	Luke, Son of David Bemis
Nov. 25th	Susanna, Daûter of Edw[d] Harrington Jun[r]
Dec[r] 2[d]	Lucey, Daûter of John Cook
30th	Elisabeth, Daûter of Smith Prentice

1760.

Jan[ry] 6th	Susanna, Daûter of William Brown at Camb. Village
27th	Elisabeth, Dauter of Josiah Norcross
Feb. 3[d]	Benjamin, Son of Benj[a] Bridge at Brooklin

March. 9th	Sarah, Daûter of John Tainter Junr
April. 6th	Benjamin, Son of Simon Haſtings
27th	Daniel, Son of Jonas Barnard
May. 4th	Nathaniel, Son of Nath^{ll} Coollidge Junr
18th	Nathaniel, Son of David Sanger
25th	Lucey, Dauter of Sam^{ll} Warren
June 15th	James Barnard & Sarah Barnard owned ye Covenant
July. 6th	Hannah, Daûter of Stephen Harris
13th	Ebenezer, Son of Edwd Richardſon
	Lucey, Dauter of Daniel Sawen
27th	Nathaniel, Son of Nath^{ll} Stone
	Anna, Dauter of Daniel Pierce
	Jacob, Son of John Randall
	Dorothy, Dauter of Simon Whitney
Augst 10th	Abigail, Dauter of Jonas White by Rev. Meriam
17th	David, Son of James Barnard
24th	At Waltham Tabitha, Dauter of Aſa Warren
31st	Joseph, Son of Josiah Bright

[246]

Sep^{t} 28th	Sarah, Dauter of Jedediah Leathe
	Lydia, Dauter of Willm Sanger
Oct^{o} 12th	Eli, Son of Amariah Learned
	John, Son of James Hay
19.	At Cambridge Charles, Son of Thadeus Wyman
	Sarah, Daûter of Jonathan Cooper Junr
26th	Jonathan, Son of Jon^{a} Bemis Junr
Nov. 2nd	Ann, Daûter of Henry Bond
9th	Sarah, Dauter of James Bryant at Camb. Village
Decemb^{r} 21st	Jeremiah, Son of Edmund Fowle

1761.

Jan^{ry} 18th	Samuel, Son of Sam^{ll} Soden'
	Samuel Sanger & Grace Sanger owned ye Covenant
Feby 11th	Mary, Daûter of Abraham Crawley
8th	Ebenezer Maſon & Eliſabeth Maſon owned y^{t} Covenant
March. 1st	Elijah, Son of Samuel Maſon
	Samuel, Son of Sam^{ll} Sanger
15th	Ebenezer, Son of Eben^{r} Maſon
May. 3rd	Joseph Gardner owned Covenant
	Thomas, Son of Joseph Gardner
June 7th	Jonas, Son of James Dix
21st	At Weſton Samuel, Son of Isaac Whittemore
28th	At Newton Moſes, Son of Jonas Jackſon
July. 19th	Jonathan, Son of John Remington
	Abigail, Dauter of Samuel White
Augst 9th	Lucey, Daûter of Edwd Harrington
30th	Samuel, Son of Moſes Biggelow
	William Saltmarſh & Eliz^{a} Saltmarſh owned ye Covenant

Sept 13th Mary, Daûter of Simon Haſtings
20th Oliver, Son of Oliver Livermore
Octo 25th Israel, Son of John Cook
John, Son of Wm Saltmarſh
Nov. 8th Joseph, Son of Joseph Coollidge
Decembr 6th Sarah, Daûter of James Gray

1762.

Janry 10th Mary, Daûter of Simon Whitney
Febry 28th Benjamin, Son of David Sanger
Jonathan, Son of Jona Coollidge Godding
March. 7th Edward, Son of Edwd Prentice at Camb. Village
28th Lydia, Daûter of Jonas Barnard

[247]

April. 4th Joanna, Daûter of John Tainter Junr
25th Josiah, Son of Josiah Norcroſs
May 2nd Josiah, Son of Josiah Bright
9th John, Son of Jona Bemis Junr
Samuel, Son of Daniel Sawen
16th Sarah, Dauter of James Hay
30th Stephen, Son of Stephen Harris
June 13th Jonathan, Son of David Bemis
July 25th John Stearns & Martha Stearns owned ye Covenant
Katharine, Daûter of John Stearns
Augst 8th Thomas Learned owned the Covenant
Josiah & Paul, Sons of Thos Learned
22d John, Son of John Stearns
October: 10th Samuel, Son of Samll Fiſk
31st John, Son of Abraham Crawley
Joshua, Son of Smith Prentice
Elias Maſon was diſmiſsed from this Chh & recomended to the Chh of Ch in Woodſtock, ye firſt Society
Novr 14th Abijah, Son of Samll Warren
24th Martha, Daûter of John Rogers at Newton
Decr 12th William, Son of Ebr Maſon
26th Samuel, Son of Edmund Fowle
Sarah, Dauter of Joseph Gardner

1763.

Janry 2d Mercy Amelia, Dauter of Convers Spring
23rd Grace, Dauter of Samll Sanger
30th At Camb. Village John, Son of Wm Bowles
Febry 6th Achſah, Dauter of Jedediah Leathe
April. 24th William, Son of Wm Sanger
May. 22d Frederick, Son of John Remington
29th James, Son of James Bryant, at Camb: Village
June 12th Sarah, Dauter of Edwd Richardſon
Sally Dauter of Daniel Edes
July. 17th Grace, Dauter of Simon Whitney

Isaac, Son of Abijah Hammond
31st Eleanor, Dauter of Samll White by Revd Mr Cushing
Augt 21st Grace, Dauter of Nathll Coollidge
Hannah, Dauter of John Draper
Sept 4. Daniel, Son of Simon Hastings
October. 9th Katharine, Dauter of Nathll Sanger
23d Eunice, Dauter of Joseph Coollidge
2d Day, William, Son of Wm Saltmarsh
Nov. 6. Peter, Son of Jona Coollidge Godding

[248] 1764

Janry 1st Joshua, Son of John Stratton
8th Esther, Dauter of Thos Johnson
22nd Abijah, Son of Daniel Sawen
Thomas, Son of John Stearns
Daniel, Son of Oliver Livermore
Febry 12th Lois, Dauter of Jonas White
26th Amos, Son of John Thwing at Camb. Village
March. 4th Hannah, Dauter of Samll Soden
25th Spencer, Son of Nathll Sanger
April 8th Josiah Convers, Son of James Thomas of Boston
22d Lucey, Dauter of David Sanger
29th Nathaniel, Son of Josiah Norcross
Susanna, Dauter of Edwd Harrington Junr
May. 27th At Camb. Village 4 Children vizt,
Bridger, Dauter of Isaac Ridgway of Boston,
Edward· Son of Edwd Peirce of Boston
Edmund, Son of Richard Dana } of Cambridge
Mary, Dauter of Thomas Thwing Junr }
June 3rd James, Son of Jonas Barnard
Elisabeth, Dauter of Samll Jenison Junr
July. 8th Convers, Son of Convers Spring
22d Ephraim Wheeler owned ye Covenant
Elizabeth, Daûter of Ephraim Wheeler
29th Elisabeth, ye Dauter of Abraham Crawley
Augst 5th Enoch Son of Ebr Mason } by Revd Mr Cushing
Moses, Son of Moses Bigelow }
26th Moses, Son of Josiah Bright
Joshua, Son of Thos Learned
Samuel, Son of Samll Jenison Junr
Sept 2d Grace, Dauter of Daniel Fuller
Priscilla, Dauter of Samll Calderwood
Sarah, Dauter of Elisha Learned
9th Anna, Dauter of David Bemis
16th Lucretia, Dauter of Samll Fisk
October. 14th Amos Livermore owned ye Covenant
Amos, ye Son of Amos Livermore was baptized
21st Rebecca, Dauter of Wm Godding Junr
28 Abraham Brown & Mary Brown were dismissed from this Chh & recomended to ye Chh of Ct in Grafton

Novr 4. Mary, Dauter of John Remington
25th Cherry, Dauter of Jon^{a} Stone
December 2^{d} James Barnard & Sarah Barnard were dismised from this C^{ch} & recomended to the C^{ch} in Acton
9th Jonathan Learned Junr & Susanna Learned owned ye Covenant
30th Anna, ye Dauter of Jon^{a} Learned Junr

[249] 1765

March. 3rd Joseph, Son of Joseph Hay
10th Jedediah & Betty White owned ye Covenant
Diadama, Dauter &
Jedediah, Son of Jedediah White
23rd At Newton Fanny, Dauter of Parker
April. 7th Nathaniel, Son of Sam^{ll} Warren
May 5th Reuben, Son of Jedediah White by Revrd Mr Cushing
19th Rhoda, Dauter of Nathl Stone
Sarah, Dauter of Stephen Harris
June 2nd Frances, Dauter of Jedediah Leathe
Samuel, Son of John Tainter Junr
July. 14th Mary, Dauter of Thos Hovey, at Camb. Village
Augst 11th Jonathan Harrington owned ye Covenant
18th Hannah, Dauter of Benjamin Fessenden
Sep^{t} 22nd Joseph, Son of John Stearns
Elizabeth, Dauter of Wm Saltmarsh
29th Thomas, Son of Sam^{ll} Soden
Sarah Gray was dismised from this C^{hh} & recomended to the Church of Christ in Stockbridge
October. 6th Grace, Dauter of Jon^{a} Harrington
13th William, Son of Edwd Richardson by Rev. Mr Meriam
Novr 17th Hannah, Dauter of Joseph Gardner
December 8th At Roxbury, Sarah, ye Dauter of Thaddeus Partridge
29th Josiah Bisco, Wm Chenery, & Sybbil Chenery owned ye Covenant
Daniel Whitney, Son of Josiah Bisco
William, Son of William Chenery

1766

Jan^{ry} 5th Seth Son of David Sanger
26th Nathaniel, Son of Oliver Livermore
Feb^{ry} 2nd At Camb: Village Mary Dauter of Richd Dana
Rachel, Dauter of Jonathan Dana
9th Daniel, Son of Jon^{a} Stone
March. 2nd At Waltham John Son of John Pierce
At Watertown Samuel, Son of Ephraim Wheeler in private
9th Richard Coollidge, Son of John Stratton
23rd Elisha, Son of Elisha Learned
April. 6th Francis, Son of Josiah Bright

	Elifabeth, Dauter of Simon Haftings
20th	Ebenezer Stutfon & Keziah Stone } owned ye Covenant.
May. 11th	Joseph, Son of Daniel Sawen
	Abigail, Dauter of Saml Jenifon Junr
	Anne, Dauter of James Hay
25th	Benjamin Felton, Son of Ebn Stutfon
	Jemima, Dauter of Josiah Norcrofs

[250]

June. 22nd	Mary, Dauter of William Sanger
July. 6th	Samuel, Son of Abraham Crawley
	Lois & Katharine, Dauters of Phinehas Child
13th	Abraham Hews & Lucey Hewes owned ye Covenant
	David Coollidge & Dorothy Coollidge owned ye Covenant
	Abraham, Son of Abraham Hews
20th	Jonathan Whitney & Sufanna Whitney owned ye Covenant
	Sufanna, Daûter of Jona Whitney
27th	Samuel Brown & Lois Brown owned ye Covenant
Augst 3rd	Sufanna, Dauter of David Coollidge Junr
10th	Lucey, Dauter of Joseph Coollidge
17th	Jacob, Son of Saml Brown
24th	Daniel, Son of Samuel Mafon
	Silas Son of Convers Spring
	Richard Walker & Elizabeth Walker owned ye Covenant
Sept 7th	John, Son of Thomas Patten
	Jonas, Son of Jona Coollidge Godding
14th	At Camb. Village Caleb, Son of Caleb Dana Junr
21st	Josiah, Son of Saml White
	Richard, Son of Richard Walker
Octor 12th	Lizzey, Dauter of John Tainter Junr
Decr 7th	Nathan, Son of Nathaniel Coollidge by Revd Cufhing
28th	Isaac, Son of David Bemis

1767

Janry 4th	Mary, Dauter of Stephen Harris
25th	Mary, Dauter of John Draper
Febry 1st	Mary, Dauter of Jedediah Leathe.
	Anna Dauter of William Chenery
22nd	Elizabeth, Dauter of Benja Fefsenden
March. 1st	Samuel, Son of Thos Learned
29th	Lydia, Dauter of Jona Harrington
April. 5th	William & Anna Learned owned the Covenant
12.	Hannah, Dauter of Jona Learned jur
May. 17th	William, Son of Wm Learned
31st	Josiah, Son of John Stearns
June. 28th	James, Son of Ephraim Wheeler
Augst 2d	Simon Coollidge owned ye Covenant

Sept 6th Suſanna, Dauter of Eliſha Learned
Mary, Dauter of Simon Coollidge
Octo 4th Grace, Dauter of Jedediah White
Grace, Dauter of Josiah Biſco
11. Jonas Coollidge jr & Anna Coollidge owned the Covent
Sarah Saunders owned ye Covenant
Sarah, Dauter of Moſes & Sarah Saunders
Eliſabeth, Dauter of Jonas Coollidge jur

[251] [Notes upon Baptism and ye Covenant in Abraham.]
[252]

1767

October. 18th At Cambridge Village Suſanna Dauter of Benja Hill & Moſes, Son of Joshua Thomas
25th Lucey, Dauter of Simon Whitney
Novr 1st Jonas, Son of Jona Stone
15th Elizabeth, Dauter of Edwd Richardson
William, Son of Samll Warren
Decr 13. Hannah, Dauter of John Tainter junr
Jonas, Son of Jonas Barnard

1768

Janry 3d Mary, Dauter of Thos Patten
Lucey, Dauter of Amos Livermore
17th William Son of David Coollidge jur
Mary, Dauter of Jona Whitney
Febry 7th Jeſse, Son of David Sanger
14. At Camb Village Martin, Son of Jona Feſsenden jur
21. Nancy, Dauter of Josiah Bright
April. 10th Joſeph, Son of Chriſtopher Grant jur
17th Eliſabeth, Dauter of Josiah Norcroſs
24th At Waltham Betty, Dauter of Uriah Cutting
May. 1st At Newton Henry, Son of Samll Craft
22d Eunice, Dauter of Moſes Biggelow
29th Benjamin, Son of Daniel Sawen
June 12th Phinehas Stearns & Hannah Stearns owned ye Coven.
Hannah, Dauter of Phinehas Stearns
Amaſa, Son of Samll Brown
July. 17th Henry, Son of Convers Spring
Jemima, Dauter of Israel Whitney
Augst 14. Lucey, Dauter of James Hay
Octo 2. Benjamin, Son of Joseph Gardner
Nov. 6th At Camb. Village Nathan, Son of Nathl Sparhawk
13th Martha, Dauter of Wm Godding
Henry, Son of Wm Learned
27. Richard, Son of Wm Sanger

[253]

Decr 4th Eliſabeth, Dauter of Ayres Tainter
18. Isaac, Son of Samuel Maſon

1769

Jan^{ry} 8th	Lucy, Dauter of Jedediah Leathe
	Charles, Son of John Stearns
29th	Thomas, Son of Jonas Barnard
Feb^{ry} 12.	Anna, Dauter of Sam^{ll} Sanger
19th	Mary, Dauter of David Bemis
March. 5th	Rebecca, Dauter of Benj^{a} Feſsenden
	Lucey, Dauter of Thomas Learned
	Jon^{a} Stone & Martha Stone were diſmiſſed from this Church to ye 1st Church in Shrewsbury
12.	Mary, Dauter of Sam^{ll} Soden
April. 2^{d}	Lucey, Dauter of Stephen Harris
16th	John, Son of Joseph Coollidge by ye Rev^{d} M^{r} Cuſhing
30th	Andrew, Son of Jedediah White
May 7th	Lucretia, Dauter of Josiah Bright
	Spencer, Son of Jon^{a} Coollidge Godding
21.	Joseph, Son of Jon^{a} Learned ju^{r}
June. 4th	Thomas Draper & Eliſabeth Draper owned ye Covenant .
11.	John, Son of Eliſha Learned
	Hephzibath, Dauter of Simon Coollidge
	Eliſabeth, Dauter of Thomas Draper
25th	Eunice, Dauter of Sam^{ll} White } by Rev^{d} Cuſhing
	John, Son of John Draper } by Rev^{d} Cuſhing
July. 15.	Anna, Dauter of Jonas Coollidge
23^{d}	Anna, Dauter of Simon Whitney
	John Hackleton & Bethiah Hackleton owned ye Covenant
30th	Thomas, Son of Thomas Patten
Sep^{t} 10th	Thomas, Son of Joſiah Biſco
	John, Son of John Hackleton
24th	John Durant & Sarah Durant owned ye Covenant
Novr 19th	Phinehas Jeniſon & Suſanna Jeniſon owned ye Coven^{t}
26th	Suſanna, ye Dauter of Phinehas Stearns
Decr 17th	Jonathan, Son of Jon^{a} Whitney
23th	Lucey, Dauter of Edwd Richardſon

1770

Jan^{ry} 14th	Phinehas Son & Suſanna Dauter of Phinehas Jeniſon
Feb^{ry} 25th	Iſaac Son of John Stratton
	Amos, Son of William Dawes
	Mary Dauter of Iſrael Whitney
March. 4th	Abigail Dauter of Abijah Hammond
	Mary Dauter of Seth Saltmarſh
	Peter Son of David Coollidge Junr
	Seth Saltmarſh & Suſanna his Wife owned ye Covenant

[254]

April 29th	John, Son of John Tainter ju^{r}
May 6th	Joſeph, Son of Joſeph Gardner

27th John, Son of Joſiah Norcroſs
July 1st Joſeph, Son of David Sanger
8th Elijah, Son of Jonathan Bemis
Silas, Son of William Learned
22nd Eliſabeth, Dauter of Samuel Brown
29th John, Son of James Hay
August. 12th George, Son of Benjamin Feſsenden
Sep^{t} 2nd Lucey, Dauter of Ayres Tainter
16th Martha, Dauter of John Stearns
23rd Suſanna, Dauter of Daniel Sawen
30th Elijah White & Hannah White owned ye Covenant
October. 14th Lucey, Dauter of Daniel Fuller
28th Luke, Son of Convers Spring
Novembr. 4th Nathaniel, Son of Sam^{ll} Jeniſon ju^{r}
18th Hannah, Dauter of Elijah White
John Bond was diſmiſsed from ye Cth of C^{t} in Watertown & recomend to ye Cth of C^{t} in Conway
Decemb'r. 9th Eliſebeth, Dauter of John Remington
Sarah, Dauter of Josiah Bright
Eliſha, Son of William Chenery
30th Sarah, Daughter of Chriſtopher Grant jun^{r}
Stephen Whitney & Relief Whitney owned ye Covenant

1771

Jan^{ry} 6th William, Son of Phinehas Stearns
27. Stephen, Son of Stephen Whitney
Feb. 3. Josiah Warren & Abigail Warren owned the Covenant
24. Isaac, Son of Thos Patten
March. 10. Hannah, Dauter of Thos Learned
31. Josiah, Son of Josiah Warren
April. 7th Hephzibah, Dauter of Amos Livermore
21. Eliſabeth, Dauter of Sam^{ll} Sanger
Seth Haſtings & Hannah Haſtings were diſmiſsed from this Cth & recomend to ye 1st Cth of C^{t} in Cambridge.
May 31. Ann Dauter of Eliſha Learned
July 14. Eliſabeth, Dauter of Jonas Barnard
August. 4. Benjamin Shattuck Son of Joſhua Kendall
11. Simon, Son of Simon Haſtings, by Revd Merriam
25. Hannah, Dauter of David Bemis

[255] 1771

Sep^{t} 22. Suſanna, Dauter of Jon^{a} Learned jun^{r}
Oct^{o} 6. At Cambridge Village Francis, Son of George Dana
Nathan, Son of Jon^{a} Winſhip
27. Stephen, Son of Sam^{ll} Warren
Sarah, Dauter of Jos. Coollidge
Nov. 3. Moſes & Aaron, twin Sons of Simon Coollidge jun^{r}
10. Mary, Dauter of John Stratton
Samuel, Son of Phinehas Robbins

17. Dorothy, Dauter of Israel Whitney
24. Mary, Daûter of John Hunt jun[r]
Decr 15. Christopher, Son of Jedediah Learned

1772.

Jan[ry] 26. At Cambridge Village Andrew, Son of Eben[r] Seaver & John Son of Andrew Ellis
Feb. 2. Elijah, Son of Wm Learned
Dorothy, Daûter of David Coollidge
Apr. 5. Abraham, Son of William Sanger
26. Thomas, Son of Benjn Fessenden
Elias, Son of Phinehas Jenison
May. 10. At Camb. Village Thomas Son of Jon[n] Fessenden
17. Henry Saunderson & Charity Saunderson owned the Covenant
Abigail Daûter of Josiah Bright
31. Anna, Dauter of Ezekiel Hall
June 7. Hannah, Daûter of Jon[n] Coollidge Godding
28. Abigail, Dauter of Josiah Norcross
July. 12. At Camb. Village William Son of Moses Robbins
Josiah, Son of Josiah Fessenden
19. William, Son of Ayres Tainter
Jonas, Son of Jonas Coollidge
26. Francis, Son of Zacharias Shed
Sibyl, Dauter of Sam[ll] White
Charity, Dauter of Henry Sanderson
Aug[st] 2. At Newton Amasa, Son of John Murdock
16. Mary, Daûter of Edwd Richardson
23. Edmund, Son of Tho[s] Wellington
Jacob, Son of Edward Harrington ju[r]
Sep[t] 13. Henry, Son of William Godding
27. Elisabeth, Dauter of Jos. Gardner

[256]

Oct[o] 4. Abigail, Dauter of Josiah Warren, at Camb. Village
11. Anna, Dauter of Sam[ll] Brown
18. Mary, Dauter of Josiah Capen Jun[r]
Nov[r] 15. Relief, Dauter of Stephen Whitney, by Revd Cushing
Dec[r] 6. Elisabeth, Daûter of Daniel Sawin
13. William, Son of Tho[s] Patten

1773

Jan[ry] 17. Mary, Daûter of John Remington
31. Isaac, Son of Simon Hastings
Feb[ry] 26. William, Son of Phinehas Stearns, in private
28th Mary, Dauter of John & Martha Stearns
March 14. Daniel, Son of Sam[ll] Sanger
Elisabeth, Dauter of Elisha Learned
April. 4th Leonard, Son of Josiah Bisco

18th Mofes, Abigail, Jerufha & Aaron, Children of ye widow Abigail Learned, fhe being recd into Chh Fellowfhip
Elifabeth, Daughter of Convers Spring
[Continued on Page 42.]

[257] Blank.

[258]

I was called to ye work of ye Ministry by ye church and congregation in Watertown on Novbr 24th 1777, and was ordained April 29th 1778.

[He died of dysentery Sept. 16, 1778, ae. 32.]

A Record of Baptifms by Danl Adams.

1778

May 10. Saml Son of Willm Chenery
June 7th Roha, Daughter of Willm Warren
June 14th Polly, Daughter of Jona Crosby
June 28th Sufanna, wife of Nathl Bright
June 28th Eunice, Daughter of Jofiah Capen
July 12th Cate, Daughter of Danl Bond
Aug. 2d Nathl Son of Nathl Bright
Aug. 2d Sufanna, Daughter of Nathl Bright

1779

Augt 8th Saml Son of Nathl Bright, by Mr Cooke

[259]

I was called to the work of the Miniftry by the Church & Congregation in Watertown on March 13th 1780 & was Ordained June 21t 1780.

A Record of Baptisms by R. R. Eliot.

1780

Augt 20th Sally, Daughter of George Brown
Sepr 10th Hannah, Daughter, & Elijah Son of William Harrington
Sepr 10 Lucy, Daughter of Smith Adams
Nov 5th Mary Kimbal & Katharine, Daughters & Daniel fon of Daniel Whitney
Nov 26 Charles fon of Daniel Whitney
Lucy & Elizabeth Daughters of Willm Bond
Decr 17th Isaac fon & Polly Daughter of Roger Adams

1781

Jany 7th Rhoda, Daughter of Mofes Stone Jur
Jany 14. Polly, Daughter of Elijah Mead
March 4. Edward, fon of Edward Harrington Junr
March 11th Alexander, fon of Benja Capen
March 25. David, fon of Benja Capen
Charles, fon of Charles Nutting

June 24. Ruth, Daughter of William Chenery
July 1. Hannah, Daughter of Nath[l] Bright
July 29. Lucy, Daughter of Josiah Sanders
Samuel White, fon of Moses Warren
Aug[t] 12. Betsy, Daughter of Elijah Meads
Sep[t] 16. Henry Son & Hannah Daughter of Jedediah Learned

[260]

Sep[r] 30. Benjamin, Son of Phinehas Jennifon
Josiah, Son of Phinehas Jennifon
Oct[r] 21. Betsy, Daughter of Abner Craft
Nancy, Daughter of Stephen Whitney
Hephza, Daughter of Roger Adams
Oct 28. George Wafhington, fon of Phinehas Stearns
Benjamin, fon of Henry Whitney
Nov[r] 25. William, Son of William Warren
Dec[r] 9. Isaac, Son of Sam[l] Barnard
Joseph, Son of Moses Coolidge
Dec[r] 30. William, Son of William Harrington

1782

Jan[y] 6 Richard, Son of Simon Whitney
March 10th Rebecca Cooke, Daughter of Henry Bradshaw
April 21 Amos, Son of Amos Bond
June 23 Betsy, Daughter of Elkanah Wales
July 21 George, Son of George Brown
Aug[t] 25 Israel, Son of Daniel Whitney
Oct[r] 28 Mofes, Son of Moses Warren
Nov[r] 3[d] Adino Bullfinch, fon of Will[m] Beals
Dec[r] 15 Martha Clark, Daughter of Hugh Mafon
19 Samuel, Son of Sam[l] Spring

1783

Jan[y] 12 Cornelius, fon of Mofes Stone Jun[r]
Feb[y] 23. Francis, Son of Sam[l] Spring
April 6 Marcy, Daughter of Roger Adams
27. Lydia, Daughter of Amos Bond
May 4 John, Son of Josiah Mixer
11 Isaac, Son of Elijah Mead
June 6 Charles, Son of Will[m] Warren
Aug[t] 24 William, Son of Nath[l] Bright
Lucy, Daughter of Andrew Stimpson
31 Ebenezer, Son of Moses Coolidge
Sept[r] 7 Polly, Daughter of William Harrington
Oct[r] 5 Samuel, Son of Thomas Patten
12. Abigail, Daughter of William Stone
Nov[r] 16 Lucy, Daughter of Abijah Stone
30 Josiah, Son of Josiah Sanderson
Henry, Son of Daniel Jackson
Sukey, Daughter of William Beals

[261]

Decr 7 Polly, Daughter of Phinehas Stearns
Hannah, Daughter of Joseph Bright

1784

Feby 1. Nancy, Daughter of Abner Craft
15 Polly, Daughter of Nathaniel R. Whitney
March 21 Richard Clarke, Son of Hugh Mason
May 2 Samuel, Son of John Botang
David, Son of Jonathan Bemifs
June 20 Nathaniel, Son of Nathaniel Bemifs
July 11 Sally, Daughter of Eayres Tainter
Septr 5 Nathaniel Pierce, Son of Samuel Hoar
12 Dorothy, Daughter of Daniel Whitney
Samuel, Son of Elkanah Wales
19 Betsy, Daughter of Henry Bradfhaw
Octr 17 Sally, Daughter of Jonathan Stone
24 Richard Hunnewell, Son of Charles Nutting
Nov 14 William, Son of Jonas White Junr
Decr 12 William, Son of Phinehas Jennison
26 Joseph, Son of Joseph Coolidge

1785

Feb^ry^ 16 Charles, Son of George Brown
27 Carolina Matilda, Daughter of Willm Warren
Joseph, Son of Joseph Bright
May 22 Samuel, Son of Elijah Mead
29 Betsy, Daughter of Joshua Kendal
June 12 Roger, Son of Roger Adams
July 30 Mary, Daughter of Joseph Coolidge
Augt 27 Polly, Daughter of Hezekiah Metcalf
Sepr 4 Daniel, Son of Daniel Jackson
Octr 9th Moses Gill, Son of Edmund Fowle
Charles, Son of Francis Faulkner
23 Clarissa, Daughter of Shubal Downes
30 Polly, Daughter of Thomas Vose
Nov 6 Nancy, Daughter of John Bullard
John & Samuel, Sons of John Cooke Junr
13 Phinehas, Son of Charles Nutting
20 Dolly, Daughter of John Tainter
Betsy, Daughter of William Harrington
27 Josiah, Son of Abijah Stone
Decr 18 Susanna, Daughter of John Stimpson

[262]

1786

Jany 29. Anna, Daughter of Henry Bradshaw
Feby 5. Elizabeth, Daughter of Jonathan Bemifs
March 12 Katy, Daughter of Willm Beals
26 James Bradish, Son of Nathaniel R. Whitney
April 23 Caleb, Son of Caleb Cooke

May 14 Joseph, Son of Hugh Mason
June 11 Charles, Son of Abner Craft
July 23 Lucy, Daughter of Phinehas Stearns
30 Lydia the Wife & Lydia, Nabby & Nathan, the Children of Nathan Porter
Sep[r] 24 Asaph, Son of Moses Stone Jun[r]
Oct[r] 22 Ephraim, Son of Jonathan Harrington
Nov[r] 5. Hannah Stowel, Daughter of Mofes Coolidge
Samuel Mafsay, Son of Samuel Holt
19 Marcy, Daughter of Joseph Coolidge
26 Jonathan, Son of Joseph Bright
Dec[r] 31 Lois, Daughter of Josiah Mixer

1787

Jan[y] 21 Eleanor, Daughter of Mosos Warren
28 Hannah, Daughter of Roger Adams
March 11 Samuel, Son of Katharine Harris
18 Jofiah, Son of Jonas White Jun[r]
Jonathan, Son of Jonathan Stone
April 8 Rebecca Boylston, Daughter of Edmund Fowle
Francis, Son of Daniel Jackson
29 Lucy, Joel, Edward, Children of Phinehas Harrington
June 17 Charles William Henry, Son of William Warren
July 1. Naby & Lydia, Daughters of Elijah Meads
29. Grace, Daughter of Elkanah Wales
Aug[t] 5. Hannah, Daughter of Stephen Harris Jun
30 Elizabeth Swift, Daughter of Sam. Babcock
Oct[r] 7. Sally, Daughter of Thomas Vose
28 Richard, Son of William Stone
Nov 4 Isaac, Son of William Harrington

[263]

Nov[r] 4 Elizabeth, Daughter of Hugh Mafon
11. Abigail, Daughter of Abijah Stone
Dec[r] 30 Lydia, Daughter of Samuel Wellington
Eleanor, Daughter of Moses Warren

1788

Jan[y] 13 Elizabeth Thomson, Daughter of Henry Crane
Feb[y] 3. Josiah, Son of Joshua Kendal
24 Betfy, Daughter of John Stimpson
March 2 Francis, Son of Francis Faulkner
Jonathan, Son of Jonathan Bemifs
16 Nabby, Daughter of Charles Nutting
April 27 Elizabeth, Daughter of Moses Coolidge
May 25 Samuel, Son of Joseph Bright
July 6. George, Son of Abner Craft
Francis, Son of Nath[l], Ruggles Whitney
27 Sarah, Daughter & Thomas Son of Thomas Clark
Aug[t] 2 Nancy, Daughter of Joseph Coolidge

31 Lydia Stratton, Daughter of Josiah Sanderson
Aaron, Son of Mofes Stone Junr
Novr 9 John, Son of Thomas Clarke
23 Betfy, Daughter of Roger Adams
Daniel, Son of Benjamin Haftings

1789

Jany 25 Grace, Daughter of Daniel Whitney
March 22 Hephzibah, Daughter of William Stone
29 Charles, Son of Nathaniel Bemifs
April 12 Katy, Daughter of Jonathan Harrington
Charles, Son of Jonathan Stone
26 Henry, Son of Jonas White Junr
June 7 Amos, Son of Hugh Mason
July 12 Thomas, Son of Thomas Soden
Sep. 13 Mary Henshaw, Daughter of Daniel Jackson
Lucretia, Daughter of William Harrington
Sally, Daughter of Samuel Babcock

[264]

Octr 4. George, Son of William Warren
18. William Main, Son of John George
Nov. 1. Gregory, Son of Daniel Cooke

1790

Jany 10 Katy, Daughter of Samuel Wellington
17 Joseph, Son of Moses Coolidge
Charles, Son of Benjamin Hastings
Eunice, Daughter of Joseph Coolidge
31 Nathaniel, Son of Charles Nutting
Feby 14 Charlotte, Daughter of Jacob Sayer
May 9 Hannah, Daughter of Joshua Kendal
23 Polly, Daughter of Joseph Bright
Augt 15 Lucretia, Daughter of James Robbins
Sepr 26 John & Stephen, Sons of Israel Cooke
Octr 24 Patty, Daughter of Roger Adams
Novr 7 Joseph, Son of William Stone
Decr 16 Seth, Son of Josiah Sanderson

1791

Jany 6 Seth, Son of Hugh Mason
16 Hannah Bond, Daughter of Thomas Clarke
March 27 James, Son of Jonathan Bemife
April 3. Hannah Balch, Daughter of Tilly Buttrick
Elizabeth, Daughter of Benjamin Hastings
May 1 Leonard, Son of Jonathan Harrington
June 31 Samuel, Son of Jona^n Whitney
July 3 Samuel, Son of Jonathan Stone
John, Son of John George
10 Hannah, Daughter of Nathl Ruggles Whitney
31 Leonard, Son of Daniel Jackson

[265]

Sepr 4. Nathaniel, Son of Josiah Mixer
Octr 9. Daniel Parker, Son of Abner Craft
Juliana Maria, Daughter of Willm Warren

1792

Feb 19 Elisha & Kata, Son & Daughter of Joseph Bright
March 6. Moses, Isaac, Hannah, Aaron, Children of Moses Mason
April 1. Sophia, Daughter of Moses Warren
May 6 Nancy, Daughter of Moses Stone Ju^r
June 3 James, Son of Samuel Babcock
July 8 Nancy, Daughter of Nathaniel Bridge
29 Elisha, Son of Daniel Whitney
Eliza, Daughter of Stephen Crane
Sepr 16 Betsy, Daughter of William Stone
Decr 2 John Jacob, Son of John Jacob Salga
9 Nathaniel, Son of Charles Nutting
Sally Main, Daughter of John George
16 James, Son of James Robbins
Mary, Elizabeth, Samuel & George, Children of Samuel Coolidge

1793

March 31. David, Son of Joshua Kendal
June 2 Charles Bond an Adult was Bap^d having own'd the Cov^t
Samuel, Son of Charles Bond
Sally, Daughter of Moses White

[266]

June 2 Frank & Leonard, ſons of Ezekiel Whitney Junr
July 21 Lydia, Daughter of Thomas Clark
Augt 25 George Call, Son of Nathl Ruggles Whitney
Sepr 22 Richard Clarke, Son of Benj^a Haſtings
Octr 6 Susanna, Daughter of Willm Stone
Francis, Son of Jonathan Bemis
Decr 15 Henry, Son of Jonas White Junr

1794

March 9 Mary Oliver, Daug^r of John Vinal
16 Mary Little, Daughter of Tilly Butterick
30 Sally Williams, Daughter of Abner Craft
April 6 Joel, Son of Moses Stone Junr
13 Josiah, Son of Joseph Bright
May 11 Polly Goddard, Daughter of Sarah Saunders
July 6 Joseph, Son of Joseph Nison
Septr 14 Mary Ann, Daughter of John George
Sally Dorrs, Daughter of Enoch Hide
Abigail, Daughter of Ezekiel Whitney
Nancy, Daughter of Willm Barry

21 Lucy, Daughter of Daniel Jackson
Novr 16 Rebecca, Daughter of Samuel Babcock

1795

Feby 1 Rebeccah, Daughter of Jonathan Stone
15 George, Son of James Robbins
April 12 Samuel, Son of John Hunt
May 31 Mary, Daughter of Benjamin Haſtings
June 14 Eliza, Daughter of Willm Stone

[267]

June 21 Sukey, Helen, Charlotte & Polly, Children of Seth Norcroſs
July 5 Lydia, Daughter of Shubal Smith
Octr 18 Elizabeth Coolidge Freeman was Baptiz^d having this day owned the Covenant
25 William, Son of Nathl R. Whitney
Decr 6 Sally, Daughter of Charles Nutting
20 Marshall, Son of Moses Warren

1796

Jany 3 Charles, Son of Charles Bond
March 3. Mary, Daughter of Thomas Clark
May 22 Lucy, Daughter of Samuel Coolidge
June 19 Charles, Son of Joshua Kendal
Lucy, Daughter of Amos Livermore Junr
Sep^t 11 Lucy Jones, Daughter of John George
Decr 4 Joshua, Son of Joshua Grant

1797

Jany 1 Sarah, Daughter of Benj. Hastings
15. Seth, Son of Willm Stone
Feby 27 Augustus Frederick, Son of Jona. Bemis
March 5. George, Son of Shubal Smith
May 7 Joseph Watson, Son of Jonathan Stone
June 1 Francis, Son of Israel Cooke
Sepr Hannah Rawson, Daughter of Israel Cooke
Octr 1 Phinehas, Son of Charles Bond
Leonard, Son of William Winchester
Novr 5 Simon, Son of Nathl R. Whitney
Decr 18 Henry Ward, Son of John Durant

[268]

1798

March 11 Columbus Jackson, Son of Moses Stone
May 13 Unice & Sally, Daughters of Phinehas Hovey
June 3 Thomas, Son of Amos Livermore J^r
10 Josiah, Son of Thomas Clark
24 David, Son of Nathl Bemis
Robert Eddy, Son of Luke Bemis
July 15. Thomas, Samuel & Daniel, Sons of Paul Learned
23 Henry Williams, Son of Saml Coolidge

28 Sally, Daughter of Artemas Moredock
Aug[t] 12 Otis, Son of Ezekiel Whitney J[r]
26 Sarah Grant, Daughter of Peter Clark
Oct[r] 14 Patty Remington, Daughter of Daniel Jackson
28 Hepsibah, Daughter of Joshua Grant

1799

Jan[y] 20 Jane White, Daughter of James Robbins
27 Mary, Daughter of W[m] Winchester
Feb[y] 3 Mary Ann, Daughter of Shubial Smith
March 3 David, Son of David Livermore
24 Eliza Brown, Daughter of Phinehas Hovey
Ap[l] 7 John, Son of John Durant
Anna, Daughter of Joseph Bright
June 23 Everline & Caroline, Daughters of W[m] Stone
July 28 Hannah, Daughter of Charles Nutting
Aug[t] 4 Benjamin, Son of Benjamin Hastings

[269]

Dec[r] 8 Polly, Daughter of Israel Cooke
22 Horace, Son of Artemas Moredock

1800

March 9 Lucy Parkhurst, Daughter of Moses Warren
16 Luke, Son of Luke Bemis
Sibil, Daughter of David Livermore
April 6 Anna, Daughter of Jonathan Stone
June 8 Jonathan Mayhew, Son of Ebenezer Vose
July 27 Sarah, Daughter of William Winchester
Sarah Dennis, Daughter of John Durant
Aug[t] 3 Moses Davis & Aaron Davis, Children of Moses White
Hannah, Daughter of Amos Livermore Jun[r]
Hannah, Daughter of Charles Bond
Sep[t] 21 William, Son of Samuel Coolidge
29 Charles, Son of Joshua Grant
Oct[r] 20 John, Son of Nath[l] R. Whitney
Nov[r] 9 George & Eliza Wheaton, Children of James Robbins

1801

April 19. James Robbins, Son of Francis Faulkner
July 12 Mary Eddy, Daughter of Luke Bemis
Josiah Sanderson, Son of Thomas Clark
19. William Bond, a Adult
Moses, Lucy, & Hitta, Children of William Bond

[Continued upon page 320.]

[270 to 290] Some hints upon Bible texts.

[291] Blank.

[292]

My D^t^ wife dyed April 16. 1691. I wid fince her death take notice of fome things I layd out, payed, bought, fold fince y^n^.

I have & fhall forgett many.

Funerall charges.

For Gloves bought of Mr Kilenys - - - -	9- 6-0
For ye Coffin - - - - - - - - -	1-11-0
To Mrs Kay, for Candles, Tobacco, & pipes -	0- 5-3
To Mr Gibbins for Mourning - - - - -	0- 7-6
To Deacon Eliot for Man & horfe - - - -	0- 3-0
To Margaret Bulman, for bread - - - -	0- 0-8
To Mr Allifon for 8 Gold Rings - - - - -	4- 0-0
To Capt. Townfend for wine - - - - -	6-15-0
To John Knox for digging ye grave - - - -	0- 6-3
To Dearing for mourning ftockins &c - -	0- 9-0
For a Mourning hatt - - - - - - - -	1- 2-0
For Black Crape - - - - - - - -	0- 2-0
For a Mourning coat of 25^s^ p^r^ yard - -	5- 9-0
For Crape for my Hatt - - - - - -	0- 5-0
For the Bricking of her Grave or Tombe - -	0-12-0
For mourning Breeches - - - - . -	1- 3-8

For a Tombe ftone, as followes, y^t^ came one June 21 .92 from Connecticut, ye fright coft 8^s^. Carting it coft a l^s^. Carying it to ye Grave from Bofton, Something for stones & Lime 10^s^. ye building it vp was given me by Mr Willis.

The engraving of it coft me to Jof. Whittemore 12^s^. wch is but ye half of w^t^ is vfuall viz, a penny a letter, he took an halpeny a letter. W^t^ ye Epitaph was is to be found elfewhere in this book. see p. [62]

For ye Stone is fett I gave £2-5s. I payed it to Mr John Hemlin of Midleton ye 14 day of June 1693.

[293]

What things of hers I gave to friends, 1692, Aprill

Ap. 16 gave Mrs Beeres w^t^ was about her w^n^ dead, fhe wafhed & Layd her out.

April. 17 a new pair of fhoes to Mary Smith

April. 23 gave Mrs Kay a very good Crape Mantua, & petticoat, & fhift.

Ap. 25 gave Mrs Kay a good Allamode Scarfe, to Lidia Kay a Mantua & Petticoat.

Ap. 27 a paire of her Lethern gloves to Mrs Kay.

Ap. 27 I gave to Nurfe Barber a good Petticote of cloth sarg.

Ap. 27 gave Mary Smith a Rideing gown of hers.

Ap. 27 gave Mehetabel Child a good black Hood & Scarf of hers.

Ap. 27 gave Mary Smith one of her Gower hoods.

Ap. 29 gave Sifter Baily an Allamode Hood, ye best fhe had.

May 11. gave Sifter B. a new pair of her thred Gloves, fine ones.

June, I gave her Grt old Phifick book to Deacon Stones wife.

Her ftraw Hatt to Mrs Beeres, befides many other little things to others as fpoons, Lampe &c to M. Child & others. A rich neck lace to Sifter Baily.

To Lidia Kay her Silver Thimble. To Sifter Baily her beft morning Gown wch was bought in & brought from London for her.

To Benjamin Taylor I gave cloth for 2 fhirts, wch was 13^{s}.

To Ifabel Pearfe (who is very low, & a member of X) I gave her good Sarg Mantle, a good pair of yarn stockins, fome night capps & forehead clothes.

To Sifter B. a Gofe cap, her Rideing coat (or gown) of half Silk, a good one.

To Mrs Kay her Rideing hood, a good warm one.

[294] Blank.

[295] What I fold after her Death. 1691. April. N. E.

Aprill. 2 Calves to John Langdon, wch came to - - 1- 0-0

Ap. 25 Jo. Langdon fold a red cowe for me at Charlftown for - - - - - - - - - - - 2-10-0

May 12 I received of Mr Gibbs for 2 months boarding I did not defign to take it, but my ftraites forceth me. 2- 0-0

Books.

June. fold Baxters Call for 16^{s}. 2 Brafs candlefticks 15^{s} 0-16-4

June. fold Burroughs Rare Jewell wth walking wth g^{d} 5^{s}-6^{d} & sk . . . . 9^{d} - - - - - - - - - 0-14-6

June. fold a Eawer 9^{d}, botle 5^{d}, Lockyers pills 2^{s}, cheefe prefse 4-6 - - - - - - - - - - 0- 7-8

July fold Cowes for £4-10^{s}, for Barrells 5^{s}-6^{d}, old clofe, ftool 3^{s} - - - - - - - - - - 4-18-6

Sold a gr^{t} Table for 20^{s} - - - - - - - 1- 0-0

July 27 I fold my bed (y^{t} bed I have for above 19 years layd vpon wth My Dr Bedfellow, who is now in glory. I had not fold it but y^{t} I could never any more reft vpon it. It grtly greeved me to fee it caryed away, but no more of y^{t}), to Capt. Sewal for £8. 8- 0-0

a quart pott 16^{d}, Stone botle 5^{d}, two pewter difhes 8^{s} - 0- 9-9

a Tin Cullinder 6^{d}, a chaftindifh & pan 5^{s}, Stone botle 10^{d} 0- 6-4

a paire of Brafse fcales 3^{s}, an Iron chaftindifh 1^{s} - - 0- 4-0

a brafse Morter 4^{s}, Twelve Leathern chaires i. e. Rufhia £3-12^{s} - - - - - - - - - - - 3-16-0

4 Glafse bottles 16^{d}, Bees & hives 15^{s}, a jugg 4^{d}, two Stands 4^{s}-6^{d} - - - - - - - - - 1- 1-2

2 Earthen pots 1^{s}, a Limbeck £1-10^{s}, ye pott to it 6^{s}, pair bellows 2^{s} - - - - - - - - - 1-19-0

a glafse botle 2^{s}, two Juggs 1^{s}, Tuneel & pott 1^{s}, tin pan 5^{d}, 0- 4-5

Earthen pan 6^{d}, a Table 20^{s}, one blanket 6^{s}, a candleftick 4^{s}, - - - - - - - - - - 1-10-0

Ladle 1-6^{d}, driping pan 2^{s}-6^{d}, box & heater 5^{s}, pitch fork 1^{s}, 0-10-0

a Tray 2^{s}-3^{d}, two cufhings 10^{s}-6^{d}, tubbs 2^{s}-6^{d}, green curtains 2^{s}-6^{d}, - - - - - - - - - 1-15-9

a Squabb £1-8^{s}, - - - - - - - - - - 1- 8-0

To Mr Thrafher 2 fhirts for his boyes 13^{s}, for tongues 2^{s} 0-15-0

A Table 14^{s}, Hand Irons 14^{s}, a prel 2^{s} - - - - 1-10-0

Books

Barlow vpon Timothy 8s, Lee's Sol. Temple 7s, Lee's Trivmph 3s - - - - - - - - - - 0-18-0
Steeles Husbandry 3s, for other bookes £3-11s-6d . - 3-14-6
Roberts Claris 17s, Ushers divinity 5s, Ames de conscientia 2s-6d, Owen on ye 130 psalme 5s-6d, Leighs body of divinity 15s, Cartwright on Pv. 4s-6d, Ambrose work 22s
For books, viz Vrsins Catechism, & Wendelins Divinity 0- 8-0
For a warming pann 8s, for a piece of cloth 7s-6d - 0-15-6
For Bookes 9s viz Sandersons sermons 6s, Wilkins preaching 2s, praying 1s, - - - - - - - - 0- 9-0
Sold to Jo. Langdon an Hefer, it was but poor, it came to 30s, I took it out in better beefe for my winter Pvision - - - - - - - - - - - - 1-10-0
Sold to Sam. Grey ye 31 of March 1692 a Ketle - - 4- 0-0
For Bookes, Cars bible 10s, a Scotch bible 6s

[296] Blank.

[297] What I layd out in lesser things since her death, April, 1691, N. E.

Aprill, att Boston in small things 8s, to Mis Basam, a shilling - - - - - - - - - - - 0- 9-0
Apr. 23 at Boston psister B, 7s-4d, to widdow Faning for Butter 6s - - - - - - - - - - 0-13-4
Ap. to Mr Knight for ye horses 3s, for Butter 1s-6d To Betty Deex - - - - - - - - - 0-10-0
That of Betty Deex was for half a quarter, my wife gave her 10s before.
I payd Mr Thornton for a Shute of clothes for Wil. Pain, besides Hatt & shoes, but ye weeke after he had an opportunity to go for England, & I let him go tho I had need of him at present to pay for his cloths by working, but I gave him all for ye sake spy of his wife who loved, pittyed, wept, & prayed often for him. 2- 2-8

Things go but crossly wth me, let god sanctify all, & its well.

At Knights 3s 0d to Allison 1s-8d, Rum 8d, Barber 8d - 0- 6-0
To Boatman 8d, to Tho. Chadwick for working - - 0- 4-8
Att Boston 2s, To John Kimball for Barrell 6s - - 0- 8-0
May 12 I payd Mary Smith for half a years service - 1-15-0
she had receaved of my wife 15s before, my wife Pmissing her (as she sd) £5 p annum, wch is a grt deall, for this halfe year I did it. but will give no such wages, for my Dear wife' sake I now do it.
May 12 for meat 2s, to ——. C a 1s-18d, for gathering herbs 5s - - - - - - - - - - - 0- 9-8
For Rum 16d, for shoeing & other things 2s, for meat 14d. for Mault 9s-8d - - - - - - - - - 0-14-4
May 28 for some things 2s-8d, to Mis Beeres 4s-4d - 0- 7-0
May 27 I payd Sister Baily (having borrowed near £30 of her) - - - - - - - - - - - 17-0-0

May 30 I payd Sifter Bayly £3 more of w^t I owed, wch make it now £20, thire is ftill neare £7 behind - - 3- 0-0
June 4 to W. Shattock for weaving (an old bufinefs) 12^s- 6^d - - - - - - - - - - - - 0-18-0

As for this p^t, Ile Pceed no further, its enough to make a man madd to take notice of dayly expenfes. Finis.

[298]

The following perfons were received into full Communion with the firft Church of Christ in Watertown. ℣ *Seth Storer.*

1724/5

Feb. 27. Elizabeth Cunningham & Mary Childs
28th. Rebecca Tainter

1725

April. 25. Elizabeth Holden & Abigail Benjamin
June. 20. Elizabeth Shattuck & Lydia Phillips
Octob. 3. Nathaniel Harris & Joseph Holden
10th. Ephraim Cutter Senr, Mary Grant & Annabel Benjamin
Decr 5. Abigail Holden

1725/6

Jan. 25. Mary Hammond

1726.

March 31. Jonathan Stone Jun. & Huldah Coollidge
May. 15. Samuel Stearns
July 10. Elizabeth Sawtel
Sep^t 11. William Jenifon & William Ozmont
October 30. Hannah Smith
Decem^r 25. Josiah Convers, Sam^ll Coollidge & Mary Hastings

1726/7

Feb. 19. George Lawrence Junr, Mercy Stratton & Anna Stearns

1727

June. 18. Mary Jenifon, Hannah Stone & Hephzibah Bond
Decemb^r 3. Elnathan Whitney, Jonathan Brown, Sarah Hastings, Efther Barnard & Mary Church

1727/8

Jan. 28. Andrew White Junr, Sam^ll Dix, Sarah White, Kezia Spring, Eliz^a Harrington, Jane White, Joanna Tainter, Grace Coollige, Hannah Thatcher, Abigail Thatcher, Mehetabel Harris, Abigail Stearns & Abigail White
March. 17. Jabez Stratton, James Symms, Sam^ll Jenifon Junr, Jonathan Learned, Rebecca Pierce, Lydia Bond, Ann Bright, Chary Stone, Eliz^a Brown, Tabitha Stratton, Mary Dix, Sarah Bowman, Anna Cooke, Lydia Dix, Hannah White & Abigail Dix

[299]

March. 24. Joshua Warren Senr, Joshua Grant Junr, Josiah Livermore, Rebecca Warren, Eliz^{a} Ormes & Ruth Chenery

1728

April. 7th Mercy Nutting
May. 19. Benjamin Hastings & Anna Child
July. 28. Nath^{ll} Clark, dismised from & recomended by ye old Cth in Boston
Sep^{t} 1. Daniel Bond & Ruth Underwood
December. 22. Sarah Eddy & Ruth Eddy

1729

Augst 3. Richard Clark & Mary Clark

1729/30

Jan. 18. Ebenezer Thatcher, Henry Fisk, Edmund Livermore, Edmund Dix, Daniel Fisk, David Learned, Mercy Perry & Mary Mason
March. 15. Samuel Benjamin, Ebenezer Goddard & John Jenison
22. Joshua Learned, Mary Bond & Deborah Coollidge

1730

May 10. Jonathan Bond
Novem^{r} 1. Thomas Wellington & Rebecca his wife
Decr 27. Nath^{ll} Jennison

1731.

April. 4th Benj^{a} Whitney Sen
June 6th Jon^{a} Perry
13th Timothy Harris

1731/2

Jany 23. Mary Benjamin
March 12th Joseph Stearns

1732

July 2nd John Tainter

1732/3

March. 11. Nath^{ll} Harrington being dismissed & Recomended to us by ye Cth in Wells
25 Adam Patterson & Isabel Patterson

1733

Novr 18. Elizabeth Whitney

1733/4

Jan^{ry} 20. Andrew White Senr
March. 10. Joshua Biggelow, Edwd Harrington & Eleazer Biggelow being dismised & Recomended by ye west Church

[300]

1734

July. 7. Hannah Benjamin being difmifsed & Recomended to us by ye new North C^th^ in Bofton
Novr 24. Lydia Cutting & Hannah Stearns

1734/5

Feb. 9th Nathaniel Stone, Benj^a^ Dix & Sufanna Cutting

1735

April. 13. Jofiah Stearns & Sufanna Stearns
Sep^t^ 21st Isaac Holden

1736

June. 13th Peter ye Negro man of Mr Jon^a^ Stone
27. Abiah Coollidge
July. 4th Mary Stone
Oct^o^ 17. Amos Bond & Elizabeth Learned
Decr 19. Abigail Jenifon ye wife of Sam^ll^
Lydia, Abigail & Mercy Jenifon

1736/7

Feb^ry^ 13. Mehetabel Saunderfon

1737

April 3rd Nathaniel Coollidge, Ruth Haftings, Abigail Mafon & Ruth Stone
June 5th Abigail Sawen
July. 17. Sarah Stowell
Sep^t^ 18th Elizabeth Goddard
25th William Lawrence

1737/8

Jan^ry^ 8. Hannah Bright
Feb. 19th Chriftopher Grant
March. 12th Margaret Wellington

1739

July. 29th Sam^ll^ Stratton
Sep^t^ 2nd Elizabeth Child
Decemb^r^ 31. John Kimbal

1740

June. 29. Elifabeth Fifk
December 14 John Sawen Junr

1740/1

Feb^ry^ 1. Ruth Haftings

1741

April. 5. Samuel Child, Uriah Clark, Elifabeth Child & Eliz^a^ Brown
May. 29. Joseph Coollidge was chofen to the office a Deacon in this Church

May. 24. John Bond, Nehemiah Underwood, Matthias Stone, Ruth Bond, Mary Lawrence, Sufanna Cooke, Sarah Harris, Mary Perry, Mary Bemis, Mary Kimbal, Mary Parry, & Sufanna Parry
31. Dorothy Whitney & Ruth Bond
July. 19. Oliver Livermore, Samuel Whitney, Benj^a^ Bond, Ebenezer Bullard, Joanna Clark, Mary Bond, Hannah Tainter, Love Stone, Thankful Stowel, & Eunice Underwood

[301]

July. 26. Ifrael Meed, Daniel Livermore & Martha Clark
Sep^t^ 13. Sarah Chadwick, Rebecca Clark, Submit Chadwick, Sarah Harrington & Lois Stearns
20. Jon^a^ Child, John Fifk Junr, Samuel Coolidge, Elias Mafon, John Cooke & David Gleafon
Novr 8. Nehemiah Mafon, Mofes Stone, Hannah Godding & Arminna, a negro woman
15. Kezia Spring & Sarah Stowel

1741/2

Jan^ry^ 3rd Jon^a^ Stone Junr, Eunice Jenifon & Lydia Sawen
10. Abijah Stearns
Feb. 28. Jofeph Harrington & Martha Harrington

1742

March. 7. Elizabeth Barnard
April 25. Sufanna Thatcher
August 15. Mary Goodenow
22. Mary Sawen
Dec. 5th Stephen Cooke & Rebecca Gage

1743

March. 27. Hannah Fifk & Hannah Haftings

1744

April. 22. Jeremiah Beeth
August. 19. Anna Stearns

1745

July. 14. Hannah Sawen
Novr 3. Rebecca Capens

1746

April. 13. Elifha Coollidge
June 15. Ruth Hunt & Rebecca Tainter
22. Mary Stearns
Nov. 30. Samuel Stearns & Margaret Bright

1746/7

Jan^ry^ 25. Daniel Peirce
March 22. Nathan Stone

1747

May. 17. Samuel Fiſk and Lydia Fiſk
Novr 1. John Bond Junr & Abigail Bond

1747/8

Febry 28. Nathan Perry & Eliſabeth Harrington

1748

April 17. Jonn Stone Junr, Daniel Sawen, Martha Stone, Suſanna Maſon, & Ruth Clark
June. 12. David Bemis & Abigail Stowel

1749

June. 27. Samuel Fiſk was choſen to the office of a Deacon
Octo 22. Eunice Stratton & Abigail Stratton

1750

Ap. 22d Mary Kelly
Augst 5. Moſes Biggelow
Decr 2d Jonathan Bemis & Anna Bemis were admitted as members of the Church of Chriſt in Watertown being diſmiſsed & recommend to us by the Chh of Chriſt in Waltham

1751

July. 14. Anna Bemis Junr
Octr 27. Nathaniel Bright

[302]

1752

April. 9th Seth Haſtings & Hannah Haſtings
October. 15. Suſanna Tainter
Novr 5. Joseph Peters & Abigail Peters were admitted as Members with this Chh being diſmiſsed & recomended to us by the ſecond Church in Mendon.

1753

Decembr 30th Abraham Brown, Mary Brown & Eliſabeth Learned jr

1756

Janry 11. Lucey Bradford
Feby 1st. Thomas Learned & Martha Pierce
15th Lydia Baldwin
March. 28th Joanna Cooke

1757

April. 24th Lydia Coollidge
Novr 13th Simon Haſtings
Decr. 4. Nathaniel Coollidge Junr

1758

Janry 22d Simon Whitney, Mary Whitney & Mary Bemis
July. 2d Rachel Bright

Novr 19th Samuel Hager
Decr 31st Hannah Coollidge

1759

Febry 4th Abijah Brown, Nathan Coollidge, & Sarah Brown
Augst 5th Sarah Johnſon

1760

Decr 7th Mary Hunt

1761

Febry 1st Hannah Learned
April. 12th Mary Biggelow
19th Alpheus Spring
Augst 9th. Sarah Gray
Decr 27th Hannah Godding

1762

Janry 17th James Barnard & Sarah Barnard
May 9th Thomas Saltmarſh

[303]
1763

June 5th Kezia Saunderſon, Suſanna Barnard Junr & Hannah Barnard
July. 24th Abigail Walker

1764

July. 1st Grace Whitney
22. Eliſha Learned & Sarah Learned
Augst 12th Jedediah & Hannah Leathe, & Mary Hager
26th Abigail Goddard
Octr 21st Suſanna Barnard

1765

Febry 10th Ayres Tainter
April. 14th Samuel White

1767

June 10. Israel & Jemima Whitney
July 19th Joſeph Gardner & Suſanna Whitney

1768

April. 17. Samuel Hunt & John Hunt jue
Augst 14th Nathaniel Bond

1769

Febry 5th Samuel & Grace Sanger

1770

August 5th Eliſabeth Remington

1771

Janry 20th Moſes Stone june
July 31. Dorothy, Ruth, Katharine & Eliſabeth Hunt
Sept 22. Hannah Phillips

1772

March. 8th Hannah & Ann Bright
Augst 23. Edward Harrington
Sept 27. Daniel Whitney
Octo 11. Josiah Capen jun. & Mary Capen

1773

April 18th Abigail Learned

[Continued upon Page 46.]

[304]

1775

Octor 15. Solomon & Hannah Prentice, Being Dismissed & Recomd from the first Chh in Cambridge

1778

December Richard and Mary Clark, being Dismissed & Recommended from the Second Church in Cambridge

[305]

The Following Persons were Admitted into full Communion wt ye Chh of X in Watertown Per Danl Adams

1778

July 12th Nathl Bright & Susanna his wife

[306]

The following Persons were received into full Communion, with the Church of Christ in Watertown pr R. R. Eliot

1780

Augt 20. Wm Harrington & Esther his Wife
Octr 22. Danl Whitney & Mary his Wife
Novr 12th Moses Coolidge & Hannah his Wife
Decr 3. Roger Adams & Hepsibah his wife
Elijah Meads & Abigail his wife
Lucy Bond & Elizabeth Bond

1781

Feby 25th Anna Sanger
Octr 28 Hannah Whitney

1782

Novr 24th Lydia the Wife of Samuel Spring

1786

Decr 31 Thankful Harrington

1787

March 4 John Remington Junr

1788

Feby 10 Keziah, the Wife of Nathan Coolidge

[307] 1789

April 19th Samuel Soden
May 31. Abigail, the Wife of Mofes Stone Junr
July 12. Sibil White
19. Mary Stowel
Octr 4 Esther the Wife of Daniel Cooke
18. Susanna the Wife of Phinehas Jennison
25. Lucy Bowman

1790

Sepr 5. Hannah the Wife of Israel Cooke

1791

June 5 Lucy, the Wife of Bradbury Robinson

1792

Feby 12 Phinehas Jennison
Octr 7 Mary the Wife of Samuel Coolidge
Novr 4 Lucy Bond

1793

March 17 John Remington

1794

Feby 16 Hannah Soden
Novr 9 Jerusha Norcrofs

1796

Jany 10 Frederick Remington

1797

Sepr 24. Nathan Tilton

1798

Jany 7 Murriah a Negro Woman
July 15. Paul Learned & Anna his Wife
Aug. 26. Sally Coolidge

[308] 1803

June 5 Jonathan Stone & Sally his wife
26 Thomas Clarke & his Wife
Augt 7th Christopher Grant & Sarah his wife
Sepr 1t Jonathan Alden

1805

June 2 Sophia Mellen
July 7 Phineas Page
21 Mary Trowbridge
Decr 15 Daniel Jackson

1806

Sepr 28 Lucy Jackson

1807

May 3d Sarah Salter Scudder

1809

July 30 Peter Clark & Wife
Sep[r] 3 Hephzibah Grant, Elizabeth Bowes Coolidge, Hannah Stowel Coolidge & Elizabeth Mason Coolidge

[309]

1810

May 27 Mary Hunt & Sarah Postell Hunt
July 30 James Robbins was received at his own house being very sick
Aug[t] 5. Lois Robbins
Sep[r] 7 Hannah Bond at her Fathers house being very sick
Oct[r] 7 Lois Curtifs & Marthe Robbins
Nov 25 Ann Bond

1811

Jan[y] 13. Sally Tainter & Martha Chenery
April 7. Levi Thaxter
28 Elizabeth the wife of Clinton Thayer at her house, being very sick

[310]

May 19. Eleanor the Wife of Thaddeus Cole
June 2 Nathaniel Bemis & Wife, Luke Bemis & Wife, John Richardson & Wife, & Ann Richardson
23. Katharine Hunt
Oct[r] 6 Jonathan Child & Wife & Susan the Wife of Paul Kendal

1814

Feb[y] 19 Sally the Wife of Israil Whitney at her house being very sick
April 3 Nathaniel Weld & Nathaniel Ruggles Whitney & Wife
10 Thomas Learned & wife
June 5 John Tucker

[311]

Nov[r] 6. Elizabeth Babcock & Grace Winchester

1815

Jan[y] 29 Josiah Learned & Wife, Richard Sanger & Wife, Joseph Cole & Wife, Luther White & Wife & Grace Dana
Feb[y] 26 Amos Livermore Jun[r]
May 4 Sarah Russell
June 11. Eleanor Warren
25 Elizabeth Sanger & Hannah Norcrofs
Aug 6 Ann Hilliard

1816

May 5 Daniel Sawin & Daniel Bond & Wife

[312]

June 16. Jonathan Brown
Novr 3. Mary C. & Catherine M. Stearns

1817

July 15 Mary, the Wife of John Fowle, at his house, being very sick.
Sepr 16 Elizabeth Saunderson at Leonard Bond's, being dangerously sick
Novr 9th Elizabeth, the Wife of Elijah Ray
30th Nathaniel Ruggles Whitney Junr & Wife

1819

Feb 3^d Susanna Bright at her Father's House being very sick by the Rev. Mr. Ripley of Waltham

[**313** to **319**] Blank.

[**320**] [Baptisms continued from Page **269**.]

1801

Betsy, William & Simon Edgell, Children of Wm Bond
July 19 John, Sally, Ebenezer & William, Children of John Tucker
Joseph Pierce an Adult
William, John Minott & Elvira, Children of Joseph Pierce
Augt 2 Sarah & Mary, Children of James Simmons
Jonathan Alden an Adult & Sally. Nancy & Jonathan, his Children
Novr 6 William Smith, Son of Joseph Bright

1802

Feby 8 Harriot, Daughter of Moses Stone

[321]

Feby 21 Anna, Daughter of William Stone
March 7 Samuel White, Son of David Livermore
Jonathan, Son of Jonathan Alden
28 Henry, Son of Ebenezer Voce
Octr 31. Daniel, Son of William Winchester
Decr 12 Nelson, Son of Shubael Smith

1803

Jany 9 Sarah Clark, Daughter of Joshua Grant
23 Dwight Foster, Son of Francis Faulkner
Feby 13 George, Son of Charles Bond
20 Edward, Son of Jonathan Stone
March 6th Anna, Daughter of James Simmons
20 Margaret, Daughter of John George
April 24 Isaac, Son of James Robbins
May 15. Julia, Daughter of Artemas Murdock
29. Eliza, Daughter of Amos Livermore Junr

June 12. Jane, Daughter of Moses White
July 24 Martha & Hannah, Children of Luke Bemis
Sepr 25 Elizabeth Atherton & Mary Call, Children of John Tucker
Octr 23 Luther Coolidge an Adult
James Patterson & his Son
Novr 27 Joseph Nathaniel, Son of Joseph Pierce

1804

Jan 22 Susanna Thayer, Daughter of Willm Bond

[322]

May 20 Peter, Son of Peter Clarke
June 17th William, Son of Thomas Clark
June 24 Elisha, Son of Elisha Livermore
July 8. Anna, Daughter of Paul Learned
Octr 7 Addison, Son of Ebenezer Vose
Novr 4 Hannah Foster, Daughter of John Tucker
18 James, Son of James Simmons

1805

Feb. 10 Josiah, Son of David Livermore
April 14 William Emerson, Son of Francis Faulkner
June 23. Rebecca Clark, Daughter of William Winchester
30 Susan, Daughter of Charles Bond
Augt 4 Maria Bethune & Jane Lee, Daughters of Jane, the Widow of William Hunt
Hellen Maria, Sophia Ann, Daughters of Sophia the Widdow of Leonard Mellen
Octr 20 Edmund, Lucy Pierce & Charles, Children of Edmund Troubride

[323]

Octr 20 Henry Lewis, Son of Paul Kendal
Jane Ann Kendal, Daughter of Joseph Russell
Novr 17 Sally Wife & Andrew Craige, Sally Joan Turner, Eliza White, George Turner, & Roxana Richardson, Children of Andrew Blackman
Martha Blake, Daughter of Joseph Pierce

1806

Feby 2. Isaac Grant, Son of Peter Clark
16. Amos Henry, Son of Amos Livermore
Lucy, Daughter of Joseph White
April 13 Luke, Son of Luke Bemis
Augt 3. Samuel Bright, Son of Elisha Livermore
Decr 7 Stephen, Son of James Simmons
14 Nancy Daughter of William Winchester
28 Charlotte Daughter of Ebenezer Vose

1807

Jany 25 Lydia Sanderson Daughter of Thomas Clarke
Feby 8 Moses Son of Jonathan Stone

March 1 Susan Curtis Daughter to Paul Kendall
May 3 Daniel Lewis, Son of Daniel Scudder

[324]

July 5 Lucy Stimpson Daughter of Joseph Russell
Augt 16 George Washington Son of John Tucker
Novr 1 Mary Daughter of Charles Bond
15 Hannah Saunderson Daughter of David Livermore
Decr 6 Harriot Rebecca Daughter of Peter Clark
17 Abigail Jenkins Daughter of Israel Cook

1808

Feby 21 Adeline Daughter of Joseph White
May 8 Mary Daughter of Jonathan Robbins
June 5 Clarissa, Wife & Clarissa Andrews, Daughter of Tyler Bigelow
James Son of Edmund Trowbridge
William Henry, Son of Henry Dalrymple

[325]

June 26 Nathaniel Ruggles Son of Nathaniel Ruggles Whitney Junr
Octr 1. Martha Daughter of John Tucker
8 Sibil Chenery Daughter of Charles Whitney
23 Luther Gustavus Son of Luther Barrett
Novr 6 William Coolidge Son of Asa Stone
Decr 25. Jane Ann Daughter of Elisha Livermore

1809

April 9 Grace Saunderson Daughter of Amos Livermore
16 Lucretia Daughter of Ebenezer Vose
July 2 Hiram Son of Paul Kendal
Gustavus Son of Joseph Russell
Oct. 15 Rachel Daughter of Joseph White
22 Rufus Howard Son of Tyler Bigelow
Lydia Daughter of Jonathan Robbins

[326]

Octr 29. Martha Minot Daughter of Jonathan Child

1810

Feby 25 Lucretia, Wife of Isaac Patten, & Isaac his Son
March 25 Sarah Grant Daughter of Peter Clarke
April 22. Caroline Ann Daughter of Thomas Clark
May 6 Alexander Son of Nathaniel R Whitney
June 3 Lydia Ann Daughter of Levi Thaxter
July 15 Charles Son of Charles Whitney
Augt 12. Mary Daughter of Asa Stone
26 Ann Maria Daughter of Edmund Trowbridge
Sepr 30 Thomas Son of Isaac Patten
Octr 28 Benjamin Dana Son of Daniel Leverett
Novr 25 Isabella Daughter of John Frazer

[327]

Decr 9. Thaddeus Cole an Adult was Baptized
& Eleanor, Mary Ann, William, Andrew, Harriot & John his Children

1811

Jany 13. Martha Chenery an Adult
20 Jonathan Wheeler Son of Seth Bemis
April 14 George Tyler Son of Tyler Bigelow
28 George Clinton & Charles Sons of Clinton Thayer
June 2 Jonathan Stone Son of Nathaniel R. Whitney Junr
William Eaton Son of Jonathan Robbins
23. Thomas Dawes More Son of John Trull

[328]

July 21 Mary Ann Daughter of Amos Livermore Junr
28 Archibald Son of Michael Bent
Martha Daughter of Luther White
Augt 5 Eloisa Daughter of Thaddeus Cole
Eliza Carter Daughter of Paul Kendal
25 Eliza Crocker Daughter of Joseph Russell
Benjamin Robbins Son of Benjamin Curtiſs
George Son of Polly Newhall
Sepr 8. Abigail Minott & Mary Boothe, Daughters of Joseph Pierce
Sarah Wiswell Daughter of Luther Barrett

[329]

Octr 6 Hannah Saunderson, Daughter of Jonathan Child

1812

Jany 26 Marshall Bond & Joseph Sons of Joseph Bird
April 26 Hannah Bemis Daughter of John Richardson
May 24 Charles Son of David Livermore
June 14 Delia Ann Daughter of Micah Bent
28 George Howard Son of Abijah White
Sepr 20 Sarah Wheeler Daughter of Seth Bemis
Octr 4 Anna Aspinwall Daughter of Charles Whitney
25 William John Son of John Trull

1813

March 7 George Ticknor Son of Benjamin Curtiſs
May 16 Walter Son of John Fraser
July 4 George Henry Son of Asa Stone
George Son of Paul Kendall
18 James Frothingham Son of Nath R. Whitney Ju^r

[330]

July 18 Elizabeth Meriam Daughter of Joseph Bird
24 Martha Minot Daughter of Jonathan Child
Augt 1. Charles Henry Son of Tyler Bigelow

John Hosmer, Son of Jonathan Robbins
22 Mary Adeline Daughter of Thaddeus Cole
Adeline Daughter of Luther Barrett
Sepr 5 Adeline Mariah Daughter of Amos Livermore Junr
Calvin Son of Luther White
Octr 31. Richard Roswell Eliot, Son of Isaac Patten
Novr 28 Mary Bellows & Harriot Louisa, Daughters of Leonard Stone

1814

Feby 19 Sarah Barnard & Mary Ann, Daughters of Israel Whitney
April 24 Hiram Son of Micah Bent

[331]

May 22. Thomas & Edward Winship Son of Thomas Learned
June 26 Horace Son of Joseph Bird
Augt 14 Charles Henry Son of Tyler Bigelow
Lydia Daughter of Alfred Smith
Sep^t^ 25 Harriot Augusta & Elbridge Dexter, Children of Samuel Rand
Ann Geyer Daughter of John Leathe
Octr 2 Martha White Daughter of David Livermore
Novr 6 Jonas White Son of Levi Thaxter
13 Seth Son of Seth Bemis

1815

Jany 1. Joseph Russell Son of Charles Bradford
29 Joseph Cole & Elizabeth his wife
Grace wife of Caleb Dana
June 11. William Son of John Tucker
25 Elizabeth Sanger, & Hannah Norcroſs Adults

[332]

June 25. William, Richard Eliot, Anne, George Washington & Samuel Edward, Children of Richard Sanger
July 9. Edward Son of Nath R. Whitney Junr
16 Josiah Learned, Samuel, & James, Children of Joseph Cole
23 Lois Jane Daughter of Mary Robbins
Augt 27 William Son of Paul Kendall
Lucy Coolidge Daughter of Asa Stone
Octr 15 Sarah the Wife of James Robbins & Lois his Daughter
22 Mary Deneale Daughter of Isaac Patten

[333] 1816

April 28 Juliana Wife of Charles Stone, & Ann Rebecca Watson, Daughter of Jonathan Stone Junr
May 19 Francis Son of Thaddeus Cole
Mary Cutter daughter of Joseph Bird

June 2 Catharine, Eliza Ann, Jane, Edward, George & Daniel, Children of Daniel Bond
16 Jonathan Brown an Adult
July 7 George Newell Son of Thomas Learned
Augt 11. Lucy Ann Daughter of Luther Barrett
Sepr 8 Lucy White Daughter of Levi Thaxter
22 Harriot Daughter of Tyler Bigelow
Novr 17 Warren Fay Son of Joseph Stone

1817

Jany 12 Abner Foster Son of Edward Loud Junr

[334]

May 25 Harriot Louisa Daughter of Amos Livermore Junr
June 22 Martha, Daughter & Bradshaw, Son of Charles Whitney
Sepr 7 Sarah Watson Daughter of Nathaniel R. Whitney Junr
Octr 12 Juliana Danforth Daughter of Isaac Patten
Novr 16 Benjamin Franklin, Son of Paul Kendall
Decr 7 Caroline Daughter of Thaddeus Cole

1818

Feby 8th Lucy White Daughter of Levi Thaxter
March 15 Charles Banks Son of John Fraser
April 26 Samuel Sargent Son of Thomas Learned
May 10 Asa Son of Asa Stone
Aug. 9 Nathaniel Carter Son of Daniel Sanger

[335]

Octr 4th Mehetable Bond, Dauter of Joseph Bird

1819

Jan. 6th Mary Harrington an adult at her House being very sick by the Rev. Mr. Ripley of Waltham
Feb. 3 Susanna Bright an adult at her Father's House, being very sick by the Rev. Mr. Ripley of Waltham

[336-373] Blank.

[374-384] Meditations upon Bible Texts.

[384-418] Blank.

[419]

Sacramentall phrafes, or exprefsions vfed at ye L^{ds} Table in breaking & pouring out. [While at Limerick in Ireland.]

The firft facrament we ever had together was on June 15. 79. I fd much, but now have forgotton it. as oh for a broken h— its a fearfull thing to fall into y^e hands of y^e living g^d Thus wid our fines have ferved us—its precious, pleading, juftifying blood. Exhortation was given afterward to y^m.

[All from here on to page 495 omitted, alternate pages being blank.]

[495]

The 46th Sac was on Jan y^{e} 13. 8$\frac{3}{4}$ in y^{e} morning at Mr W. Jo. Currye & his wif, & Ann Collett was admitted at y^{e} Table, I ſd nothing before it, bec, I was at one of clock to preach at Mr C. in y^{e} Iriſh town, But I have now nothing to ſay to this days worke, for I was Impriſoned in y^{t} afternoon & ſo I ſuppoſe it may be ye laſt Sac, y^{t} I may give. many things were ſd at ye Table wch I now being vnder confinment forbear to ſpeake, we ſung pt of ye 118 psm—ye collection was 30—I exhorted y^{m} to prove ye things y^{t} are Acceptable to ye Ld.

[October 6 1686]

I coming for N. England, after ſome time, was ſett apt for ye church of Watertown viz on Oct. 6. 86—w^{t} out ye Impoſition of hands, I preached, others prayed &c I P'miſed to be of w^{t} vſe I could dureing my continuance amongſt y^{m} &c. ye particulars are too long &c.

The firſt Sac^{mt} by me in W. was on ye 31 of Oct. 86. many y^{r} &c. I preached on Cant. 8. 6, on ye firſt Doct &c. At ye begining I exhorted y^{m} to ye right Sanctifying of ye name of g^{d} in this Ord. w^{t} was ſd at it I have forgotten, eſp becauſe I purpoſed never more to putt down w^{t} I ſd, & w^{t} I may do for ye future ſhall be very ſhort. After ward I exh y^{m} to walk as ye redeemed of ye L^{d}, & as ſuch as had renewed y^{r} Cov & in particular theſe 3 things, viz y^{t} y^{r} wid lay in, for ſufferings, & lay vp for death, & lay out for g^{d} in ye places g^{d} had sett y^{m} & y^{n} ſpake to ye Spectators (who were very many) aſking y^{m} some Queſtions, as whether y^{r} had no need, no love, no feare, no ſhame y^{r} Father ptaking in y^{t} place, & y^{t} ye place, linnen & cups ſhid riſe vp in Judgm^{t} agnſt y^{m}, it was bleſed for much good &c we ſung ye Song of ye Lamb.

[From here to page 509 omitted.]

[509]

The 9 Sacrm^{t} we had vpon ye 20th of November '87. ye weather proving better y^{n} I thought for &c, very many y^{r}, from Dedham, Wooborn, Baſtable, Cambridge, old church in Boſton, & ye New church in Boſton, Cambridge Village, Concord, Dorcheſter, Roxbury, Newbury, Charlſtown, Waymouth, &c ye text was in Col. 3. 11. ye dayes being ſhort I only ſd before we begunn. y^{t} our work was now to Remember X, & it ought to be 2 wayes, viz wth Joy, & wth Conformity &c Gal. 6. 24. After we had donn (for I paſse by w^{t} was dropped all a long over ye Elemts) I ſpoke both to Partakers & Spectators in one, viz This was Crying blood, as all blood is, & it cryes theſe 3 wayes, (1) It cryes after y, here I ſtood vp & ſpake to ye Spectators (wch were very many on every ſide) & held ye cup in my hand, & ſd this blood cryed to y^{m}, and y^{t} for 3 things (which were preſsed) viz y^{t} ye wid Come to it, y^{t} ye wid drink of it, y^{t} ye wid waſh in it, it cryes as in Pv. 9. 2 to 8 v. I ſd, can y be ſaved wthout this blood? This bleeding X cryes come, drink, waſh & be pardoned, ſanctifyed & Saved for ever. Its ye blood of G^{d} y^{t} cryes after y all both on ye right, & left hand & before me in both Galleryes. & will y, can y, dare y refuſe this X, & his blood, y^{t} this bowll ſhall riſe vp in judgm^{t} agnſt y, & ſo ſhall alſo this good company, and y^{r} poor Miniſter &c. Is y^{r} any vnbeleeving Thomas amongſt Y, This Dear X ſaith, come & thruſt in y hands vp to ye Elbowes in my blood &c—come, oh come all Watertown to this blood, come tho ye worſt of ſinners, y are Welcome—G^{d}, X, ye H. G. Angells, Miniſters, & all good xtians bid y welcome—And if y will not come, y^{n} ye blood ſhall go for it—oh let all theſe ſeates, poſts, & galleryes bear witneſse agnſt y, & all ye old Fathers of this ancient church take notice of this 20 of Nov. 87 y^{t} I thus invited y to X, nay let all ye young folks y^{t} have been admitted of late bear witneſse y^{t} y will not come to ye blood of X—I beſeech y, nay charg y by all ye loves of X, ye beautyes of X, & his bitter Agonyes y^{t} y come in to X.

(2) This blood cryes for y, now to ye doubting communicant, tho y ſins ſpeaks high, & ſometimes y can ſay nothing for yſelf, it cryes for 3 things, viz pardon, peace, & purging &c.

(3) This blood will cry agnſt y, if ſleighted or refuſed by y, it eſp cryes agnſt 3 things (y^{t} were opened) viz Indifferency, Infidelity, & Enmity, oh ſaith X, y^{r} are ſome here y^{t} have ſlain me (i. e by y^{r} raſh & vnworthy ptaking) & others have ſleighted me, as if I were not worth ye minding—& to all y y^{t} ſleigh his ſon, & ordinances, G^{d} ſaith or may ſay My curſe be on y^{m}, & my ſons blood &c.

[511]

oh ſaith all heaven, let y^{m} never proſp in y^{r} baſkett nor ſtore, in ſoull nor body, time nor eternity y^{t} deſpiſe ſuch a matchles offer of love. Heaven, Earth, & Hell cryes out Anathema &c, let y^{m} be damned ſayn & damned for ever y^{t} ſleight ſuch blood, ye all pray as I may ſo ſay agnſt y. ye H. G. ſaith, L^{d} ſhall I never ſtrive wth y^{m} more &c, ye Angells ſaying, ſhall I go & take off y^{r} heads of theſe dead doggs, & Devills incarnatt &c—ye very Seates & galleryes crying ſhall I let y^{m} fall & break y^{r} necks, & let y^{m} go quick into y^{r} pitt, &c ye devills ſaying, let us have y^{m}, we never ſinned agnſt this blood thus, oh y^{t} I had good ground to Imagin, y^{t} y are all thinking to ſay, oh Dear Sir, y have ſd enough, ſay no more of it, we will go home & cloſe wth X & waſh in his blood &c—y^{n} will I ſay no more. But I leave all this wth I. X. to take an Anſwer from y this night, whether y will receave or reject him &c.
we ſung ye Song of ye Lamb &c.

[All from here to page 543 omitted.]

[543] [At a third from the bottom.]

VPon ye 31 of May 1691 we had our 34 Sacrm^{t} & very likely our laſt, a rayny day—at ye begining I raiſed Notes from Math, 26.29, I paſse y^{m} by tho I had no Notes, vyd Dykſon. I deſired Partakers to dept from iniquity. Spectators I reproved y^r trifling & only read Math 22- 14 & Lu. 14. 24 to y^m &c. Baptizing fome afterward, took my leave from 2 Cor. 13. 11. I did pticularly bid farewell to my houfe, old walker, all ye 3 ptes of ye town, My Afiftant Gibbs, ye Schoolm^r, Deacon, Selectmе, military Pfons, 2 Cunftables, ye burying place, my Servt y^t lived wth me formerly, this old Ch, ye 3 or 4 meetings in ye town, this neighbourhood of mine, Snts but finners efp, old but young efp, all my children wch grieved me moft, Friends and foes, ye fweet finger of Ifrael, all widdowes & fatherles familyes, all moralized pons, all y^m y^t heard me not now, ye pulpit pues, feats & galleryes, & cufhion I left as a token of my love, all my adminiftrations, him y^t digs ye graves, Neighbouring townes & ch,

[544] Adminiftrations of ye L^d fupper att y^e Eaft Chh in Watertown, Dec. 12, 1697 to Oct. 19, 1701.
[Dates of administration.]

[545-560] [Here some scattering entries, but mostly blank.]

[561-576] [An imperfectly made index of the contents of the book.]

[Finis.]

East Precinct and Pastors' Records.

Index to Persons.

Abbot, John 23
Adams, Benjamin 173
" Daniel 104, 186
" George . . 120, 123, 127
" Hannah 172
" Hepza 170
" Hepsibah 186
" Isaac 169
" John 100, 127
" Joseph 97
" Lucy 169
" Marcy 170
" Martha 120
" Mary 120
" Matthew 123
" Moses 128
" Patty 173
" Polly 169
" Roger 116, 169, 170, 171, 172, 173, 186
" Smith 169
Addington, Thomas 1
Alden, Jonathan . . 106, 187, 189
" Nancy 189
" Sally 189
Allen, Dea. 101
" Ebenezer 133
" Elizabeth 130, 133
" Hepsibah 155
" John 97
" Joseph 91, 97
" Judith 21
" Peter 100
" Susee 155
Allison, Mr. 177
Angier, Ephraim 38
Anthony (a mulatto) 146
Applin, Abiah 120
" Bashnah 120
" Hannah 120
" John . . . 120, 121, 126
" Mary 120
" Mehitable 126
" Thomas 120
Arminua (a negro) 146, 183
Austin, Benjamin 154
" Timothy 151
Avered, Abigail 98
Babcock, Elizabeth 188
" Elizabeth S. 172
" James 174
" Rebecca 175
" Sally 173
" Samuel 172, 173, 174, 175
Bacon, Abigail 125
" Henry 155
" John 126, 128
" Joseph 119
" Mary 126, 155
Bailey, Bayley, Elizabeth . . . 89
" James 89, 91, 93
" John 37
" Rebecca 101
" Sister . . 177, 178, 179, 180
" Thomas 126
Baker, John 88, 89
Baldwin, Jane 155
" Lydia 184
" Rev. S. 158
" William 155
Ball, Abigail 123, 134
" Eliza 132
" James . 131, 132, 133, 134
" John 92, 121, 123, 124, 131
" Sarah 133
Balston, Gersham 135
Barbour, Peter 98
Barker, Elizabeth 101
" Nurse 177
Barnard, Abigail . 108, 155, 157
" Benjamin 152
" Cornelius 149
" Daniel 160
" David . . . 108, 144, 160
" Edmund 148
" Elizabeth 108, 119, 167, 183
" Esther 180
" Fleming 143
" Hannah . . 141, 146, 185
" Isaac . . . 103, 138, 170
" James 71, 137, 141, 144, 160, 162, 163, 185
" Jonas 108, 152, 155, 157, 158, 160, 161, 162, 165, 166, 167
" Jonathan 137, 141, 142, 143, 146, 148, 149, 151, 152, 154, 156
" Joseph 151
" Josiah 146
" Lydia 161
" Nathan 154
" Phebe 142
" Samuel 65, 66, 104, 108, 130, 141, 143, 146, 156, 170
" Sarah 138, 158, 160, 163, 185
" Susanna . . 108, 141, 185
" Sergt. 123

Barnard, Thomas 166
Barnes, Richard 131
Barrett, Adeline 193
" John 100
" Lucy A. 194
" Luther . . 106, 191, 192, 193
" Luther C. 191
" Sarah 98
" Sarah W. 192
Barron, Abigail 130
" Benoni 128
" Elliz 128
" Peter 134
" Timothy 23, 125, 130, 132, 134
Barry, Nancy 174
" William 174
Barsham, Anna 171
" Captain 5, 6, 7
" Dea. 6, 7, 130
" Elizabeth 119, 124
" Nathaniel 2, 5, 7, 8, 9, 10, 11, 15, 17, 18, 19, 22, 23, 24, 26, 27
Bristow, Hannah 131
" Micael 2
" Rebecca 125
Bassam, Mis 179
Basset, Elizabeth 97
Bathrick, Jason 141
Battle, Ethel 155
" James 155
Beals, Adino B. 170
" Katy 171
" Sukey 170
" William . . 105, 170, 171
Beath, Beeth, Jeremiah . . . 183
" John 148, 149
" Margaret 149
" Mary 148
" Walter 91
Becks, John 92
Beers, Jabez 11, 101
" John 90
" Mis 177, 179
" Sergeant 6, 7
" Simon 132, 134
Bemis, Abigail 125
" Abraham 153
" Anna 162, 184
" Augustus F. 175
" Bethia 127
" Charles 173
" David 156, 158, 159, 161, 162, 164, 166, 167, 171, 175, 184
" Elijah 167
" Elizabeth 125, 171
" Ephraim 125, 127
" Esther 153
" Francis 174
" Hannah 167, 190
" Isaac 164
Bemis, James 127, 173
" John 124, 127, 161
" Jonathan 90, 92, 94, 145, 153, 156, 157, 159, 160, 161, 167, 171, 172, 173, 174, 175, 184, 194
" Jonathan W. 192
" Joseph 127
" Katharine 157
" Luke 106, 159, 175, 176, 188, 190
" Martha 190
" Mary 127, 144, 166, 183, 184
" Nathaniel 105, 158, 171, 173, 175, 188
" Rebecca 125
" Robert E. 175
" Samuel 149, 151
" Sarah 125, 145
" Sarah W. 192
" Seth 107, 192, 193
" Susannah 127
" Thankful 156
Benjamin, Abel 131, 132, 133, 139, 155, 156, 157, 158
" Abigail . 103, 125, 136, 180
" Anna 139
" Annabel 180
" Caleb 103, 133, 136, 137, 138
" Daniel 10, 18, 19, 23, 96, 127, 129, 131, 132, 133, 138
" Elizabeth 91, 131, 143, 145, 155
" Hannah 182
" John . . . 96, 97, 129, 158
" Jonathan 90, 92, 131, 135, 137, 138, 141, 143, 157
" Katy 149
" Kezia 138
" Lydia 132, 147
" Mary . . 103, 138, 141, 181
" Mehitabel 151
" Mindwell 135
" Patience 133
" Rachel 143
" Samuel 103, 131, 136, 137, 138, 139, 141, 143, 145, 147, 156, 181
" Sarah 97, 137
" Susannah . 103, 112, 139
" William 143
Bennet, Susanna 100
Bent, Anna 107
" Archibald 192
" Delia A. 192
" Hiram 193
" Micah 172, 193
" Michael 192
Berry, Elizabeth 144
" Hephzibah 104
" Josiah 104

Bigelow, Abigail 126
" Abraham 140
" Ann 145
" Charles H. 192, 193
" Clarrissa 191
" Clarrissa A. 191
" Ebenezer 111, 137, 138, 139, 140, 144
" Eleazer 138, 140, 142, 145, 181
" Elijah 140
" Elisha 147
" Elizabeth 124
" Eunice 165
" George T. 192
" Harriet 194
" Hopestill 138
" Isaac 128
" Jabez 128, 142
" James 97, 126
" John 97, 119
" Joseph 124
" Joshua . . 128, 140, 181
" Josiah 152
" Mary . 138, 147, 158, 185
" Mercy 119
" Moses 137, 158, 159, 160, 162, 165, 184
" Rufus 191
" Samuel 120, 126, 128, 144, 160
" Silence 139
" Tyler 106, 191, 192, 193, 194
" Uriah 148
" William 132
Bird, Elizabeth M. 192
" Horace 193
" Joseph . 107, 192, 193, 194
" Marshal B. 192
" Mary C. 193
" Mehitabel B. 194
Bisco, Abigail 152
" Daniel W. 163
" Grace 165
" Hannah 127
" Jno. 2
" John 23, 144
" Jo. 119
" Josiah 108, 145, 163, 165, 166, 168
" Leonard 168
" Thomas 2, 79, 127, 144, 145, 166
Bishop, Thomas 90, 138
Blackman, Andrew 190
" Eliza W. 190
" Roxana R. 190
" Sally J. T. 190
Blackmer, Andrew 106
Blake, Sarah 101
Blanchard, Geo. 98
Blogget, Thomas 156
Bloyse Blosse, Richard . . . 99, 124

Bond, Abigail . 120, 138, 146, 184
" Abijah 136
" Abraham 135
" Amos 92, 93, 108, 112, 117, 149, 150, 151, 153, 170, 182
" Ann 103, 135, 146, 160, 188
" Benjamin 183
" Bethiah 146
" Betsey 189
" Cate 169
" Catherine 143, 194
" Charles 105, 174, 175, 176, 189, 190, 191
" Corporal 2
" Daniel 47, 50, 51, 90, 108, 129, 135, 138, 140, 148, 149, 151, 169, 181, 188, 194
" Deacon 6, 7
" Deliverance 119
" Edward 194
" Elijah 88, 136
" Eliza A. 194
" Elizabeth 23, 105, 139, 143, 148, 169, 186
" Eunice 147
" George 189, 194
" Grace 124, 146
" Hannah 108, 139, 176, 188
" Hephzibah 103, 121, 132, 180
" Henry 57, 64, 74, 77, 80, 82, 90, 92, 93, 104, 140, 151, 156, 160
" Hitty 170
" Isaac 131, 140
" Jane 194
" Jerusha 146
" John 2, 90, 91, 108, 120, 123, 126, 129, 136, 137, 139, 143, 154, 167, 183, 184
" Jonas 7, 8, 9, 15, 17, 18, 19, 22, 23, 24, 25, 26, 27, 28, 29, 30, 31, 32, 33, 35, 36, 37, 38, 39, 41, 42, 43, 44, 45, 46, 47, 54, 57, 59, 61, 63, 64, 65, 66, 67, 69, 70, 71, 80, 81, 82, 83, 89, 124, 125, 135, 136, 139, 140, 143
" Jonathan Jona 131, 137, 142, 145, 147, 154, 181
" Joseph 149
" Josiah 136
" Leonard 189
" Lieut. 3, 6
" Lucy 105, 169, 176, 186, 187
" Lydia . . . 151, 170, 180
" Margaret 130
" Marah 129
" Mary 104, 138, 139, 181, 183, 191

Bond, Moses 176
" Nathaniel 90, 92, 103, 121, 129, 133, 135, 137, 138, 139, 141, 150, 185
" Obadiah 135
" Phineas 134, 175
" Ruth 183
" Samuel . . 140, 151, 174
" Sarah 108, 119, 126, 129, 137
" Sergt 5
" Seth 141
" Simon E. 189
" Susan 190
" Susanna . . 112, 139, 190
" Thaddeus 156
" Thomas 23, 41, 47, 50, 52, 54, 55, 56, 90, 119, 126, 129, 131, 134, 136, 145, 153
" Widow 91
" William 2, 3, 8, 9, 11, 12, 13, 18, 19, 23, 26, 27, 28, 29, 31, 32, 33, 36, 43, 97, 98, 106, 119, 126, 129, 131, 133, 140, 169, 176
Botang, John 171
" Mary E. 176
" Samuel 171
Bowen, Thomas 155
Bowles, John 161
" William 161
Bowman, Capt. 143
" Francis 119, 127
" John 127, 144
" Josiah 144
" Lydia 119
" Lucy 187
" Sarah 180
Box, John 88
Boynton, Elizabeth 157
" Jacob 157, 158
" Mary 157
" Nathan 158
Bradford, Charles 193
" Joseph R. 193
" Lucy 184
Bradshaw, Betsey 171
" Henry 170, 171
" Rebecca C. 170
Bridge, Benj. 159
" Mr. 121
" Nancy 174
" Nathaniel 174
Briggs, William 102
Bright, Abigail 143, 168
" Ann 180, 186
" Anna 153, 170
" Benjamin 131
" Elisha 174
" Elizabeth . . . 107, 143
" Francis 163
Bright, Hannah 151, 170, 171, 182, 186
" Henry 31, 38, 43, 45, 46, 48, 54, 59, 60, 63, 67, 134, 136, 149
" John 3, 81, 84, 90, 92, 93, 127, 156
" Jonathan 159
" Joseph 90, 91, 93, 105, 143, 171, 172, 173, 174, 176, 189
" Josiah 88, 107, 143, 159, 160, 161, 162, 166, 167, 168, 174
" Kata 174
" Lois 107
" Lucretia 166
" Margaret 183
" Mary . . . 125, 131, 138
" Mercy 132
" Millescient 136
" Moses 162, 163
" Nathaniel 2, 5, 6, 7, 9, 10, 12, 18, 19, 21, 22, 23, 24, 25, 26, 27, 28, 29, 30, 31, 32, 33, 36, 38, 39, 40, 41, 43, 44, 46, 47, 51, 55, 66, 69, 80, 90, 92, 93, 94, 104, 121, 125, 127, 131, 132, 135, 138, 151, 153, 154, 156, 169, 170, 183, 186
" Polly 173
" Rachel 184
" Samuel 169, 172
" Sarah . . . 135, 149, 167
" Silas 89, 134
" Susanna 104, 169, 186, 189, 194
" William 170
" William S. 189
Brown, Aaron, ... 154
" Abigail 139, 140
" Abijah 142, 158, 159, 185
" Abraham 36, 37, 38, 39, 41, 120, 135, 156, 162, 184
" Allen 104, 140
" Amasa 165
" Anna 145, 168
" Charles 171
" Ebenezer 158
" Elizabeth 96, 139, 167, 168, 182
" George 154, 169, 170, 171
" Isaac 154
" Jacob 164
" James 139
" John 71, 90, 92, 104, 140, 144, 145

Brown, Jonathan 2, 77, 78, 79, 89, 93, 96, 97, 134, 135, 137, 139, 140, 142, 180, 189
" Joseph 140
" Lois 164
" Lucy 140
" Lydia 130, 137
" Mary . . . 139, 162, 184
" Patience 97
" Ruth 104, 139
" Sally 169
" Samuel 66, 67, 69, 70, 71, 74, 77, 79, 80, 90, 164, 165, 167, 168
" Sarah 144, 185
" Susanna 159
" Thomas 1, 154
" William . . 101, 158, 159
Bryant, James 160, 161
" Sarah 160
Bullard, Eben 146, 183
" Hester 121
" John 105, 171
" Nancy 171
Bulman, Alex. 100
" Margaret 177
Butler, Peter 102
Butterfield, Mary 99
Buttrick, Hannah B. 173
" Tilly 173
Calderwood, Priscila . . . 162
" Samuel 162
Caldwell, Anna 150
" Enoch 155
" Jacob 93, 147, 148, 150, 151, 153, 155
" John 147
" Rebecca 148
" Sarah 153
Caner, H. 88
Capen, Alexander 169
" Benj. 105, 169
" Charity 108
" Elizabeth 105
" Eunice 169
" Josiah . . 168, 169, 186
" Mary 168, 186
" Rebecca 183
" Samuel 101
Chamberlain, Alex. 88, 89
" Mrs. 111
Checkley, Hannah 100
" John 100
" Dr. Richard 53
Chadwick, Aaron 145
" Abijah 136
" Benjamin 90, 111, 112, 127, 145
" Charles . . 103, 130, 136
" Daniel 127
" Elizabeth 123
" John 9, 10, 13, 14, 18, 19, 127, 134
Chadwick, Jonathan 129
" Kezia 136
" Lydia 123
" Noah 145
" Rebecca 134
" Richard 123
" Sarah 103, 125, 136, 183
" Sergt. 6
" Submit 136, 183
" Thomas 127, 129
Cheney, Chenery, Abigail 133, 136
" Anna 164
" Benjamin 150
" Daniel 139
" Ebenezer 66, 69, 70, 77, 78, 103, 131, 135, 136, 138, 140, 142, 145, 147
" Elisha 167
" Elizabeth . 120, 129, 150
" John 2, 23, 120, 126, 129, 131, 133, 138, 145
" Martha 188, 192
" Mary 135
" Ruth 103, 139, 142, 170, 181
" Samuel 169
" Sarah . . . 120, 126, 150
" Sybil 108, 163
" Widow 91
" William 108, 147, 152, 163, 164, 167, 169, 170
Child, Anna 181
" Dan'l 123
" Elizabeth . 123, 143, 182
" Experience 99
" Eunice 140
" Hannah 137
" Hannah S. 192
" Isaac 71, 132, 137, 138, 140
" John . 100, 121, 123, 127
" Jonathan 92, 93, 106, 143, 183, 188, 191, 192
" Joseph 71, 72, 90, 91, 93, 94, 127, 132, 146
" Katharine 164
" Lois 164
" Martha M. 191, 192
" Mary . 123, 146, 152, 180
" Mehitabel 122, 177
" Moses 138
" Phineas 164
" Richard 120, 123
" Samuel 92, 93, 146, 152, 182
Church, Abigail 147
" Caleb 4, 96, 120, 123
" David 3, 125, 128
" Isaac 90, 91, 123
" John 123
" Jonathan 92, 142, 145, 147
" Joshua 123
" Lydia 96, 145
" Mary 142, 180
" Rebecca 123

Church, Sarah 128
" Thankful 142
Clark, Benjamin 139
" Benoni 140
" Caroline A. 191
" Daniel 155
" Hannah B. 173
" Harriet R. 191
" Isaac G. 190
" John 93, 148, 173
" Josiah 175
" Josiah S. 176
" Lucy 148
" Lydia 174
" Lydia S. 190
" Margaret 148
" Martha 103, 136
" Mary . 137, 148, 175, 181
" Nathaniel 75, 90, 136, 137, 139, 181
" Peter 106, 176, 188, 190, 191
" Rebecca 156, 183
" Richard 90, 91, 93, 112, 136, 139, 140, 153, 181
" Ruth . 136, 151, 156, 184
" Samuel 90, 143, 148
" Sarah 112, 172
" Sarah G. 176, 191
" Thomas 100, 105, 136, 153, 172, 173, 174, 175, 176, 187, 190, 191
" Uriah 93, 148, 150, 151, 153, 154, 156, 182
" William 190
Clargett, William 97
Coffin, Coffeen, John 157
" Susanna 157
Cole, Andrew 192
" Caroline 194
" Eleanor 188, 192
" Eloisa 192
" Harriet 192
" James 193
" John 192
" Joseph 188, 193
" Josiah L. 193
" May A. 192, 193
" Samuel 193
" Thaddeus 106, 188, 192, 193, 194
" William 192
Coleman, Elizabeth 103
" Rebecca 101
Collins, Daniel 101
" Rose 97
Comyre, Hester 128
Cornish, James 97, 119
" Joshua 100
Convers, Convarse, Josiah 91, 93, 162, 180
" Widow 91
Cornwall, Daniel 107
" Thomas 107
Coolidge, Aaron 167
" Abigail . . 131, 133, 138
" Abiah 182
" Annah . 142, 155, 165, 166
" Daniel 139, 147, 157
" David 92, 93, 108, 144, 146, 148, 149, 151, 164, 165, 166, 168
" Deborah 181
" Dorothy . . 108, 164, 168
" Ebenezer 149, 170
" Elijah 144
" Elisha 93, 183
" Elizabeth 148, 150, 158, 165, 172, 174
" Elizabeth B. 188
" Elizabeth M. 188
" Eunice 112, 145, 151, 162, 173
" George 174
" Grace 162, 180
" Hannah 104, 137, 185, 186
" Hannah S. 172, 188
" Henry W. 175
" Hepzibah 148, 149
" Huldah 180
" James 149
" John 2, 15, 21, 26, 28 29, 31, 36, 37, 38, 40, 41, 42, 45, 46, 49, 71, 73, 75, 79, 80, 82, 83, 84, 88, 90, 91, 93, 103, 113, 129, 130, 131, 136, 137, 138, 139, 142, 144, 147, 166
" Jonas 148, 150, 151, 157, 165, 166, 168
" Jonathan 3, 127, 129, 132, 135, 137
" Joseph 19, 23, 29, 31, 36, 38, 43, 45, 47, 48, 49, 50, 52, 53, 54, 55, 57, 60, 63, 65, 66, 69, 71, 72, 83, 84, 90, 91, 105, 113, 132, 136, 138, 146, 152, 156, 158, 159, 162, 164, 166, 167, 170, 171, 172, 173, 182
" Joshua 159
" Josiah 182
" Kezia 186
" Lois 140
" Lucy . 136, 153, 164, 175
" Luther 106, 190
" Lydia 125, 128, 132, 135, 139, 184
" Martha 91, 92
" Mary 108, 122, 136, 137, 140, 144, 148, 151, 156, 165, 171, 174, 187
" Mehitabel 150
" Mercy 103, 108, 152, 156, 172
" Moses 104, 112, 116, 155, 167, 170, 171, 172, 173, 186

Coolidge, Nancy 172
" Nathan . . 164, 185, 186
" Nathaniel 2, 19, 82, 83, 84, 90, 98, 125, 128, 133, 137, 138, 140, 144, 148, 155, 156, 157, 160, 162, 164, 182, 184
" Obadiah 11, 131, 132, 135, 182
" Peter 166
" Rebecca 137
" Richard 7, 11, 16, 18, 22, 23, 24, 25, 26, 28, 30, 31, 47, 50, 54, 55, 67, 131, 132, 133
" Rhoda 108
" Ruth 111, 135
" Sally 187
" Samuel 93, 144, 148, 152, 153, 155, 157, 174, 175, 176, 180, 183, 187
" Sarah 131, 133, 144, 146, 167
" Sergt. 7, 41
" Silas 142
" Simon 90, 92, 93, 103, 138, 142, 144, 145, 147, 148, 150, 152, 164, 165, 167
" Stephen 2
" Susanna . . 138, 155, 164
" Tabitha 134
" Thomas 11, 12, 13, 19, 20, 21, 24, 26, 28, 29, 31, 33, 43, 57, 90, 111, 130, 133, 134, 151
" William 93, 148, 151, 152, 153, 155, 165, 176
Cook, Aaron 145
" Abigail J. 191
" Ann 144
" Anna 180
" Caleb 155, 171
" Daniel . . . 154, 173, 187
" Easter 112
" Elizabeth 146
" Ephraim 144, 145
" Esther 187
" Francis 175
" Gregory . . . 2, 99, 173
" Hannah . . 153, 175, 187
" Isaac 126
" Israel 106, 161, 166, 173, 175, 176, 187, 191
" James 127
" Joanna 112, 184
" John 105, 126, 127, 146, 154, 156, 157, 158, 159, 161, 171, 173, 183
" Joseph 155
" Lucy 159
" Mary 126, 157
" Polly 176
" R. S. 149
" Rev. Mr. 145, 150
Cook, Robert 149
" Samuel 92, 93, 129, 146, 147, 149, 153, 171
" Sarah 106
" Stephen 25, 90, 91, 120, 122, 129, 147, 156, 173, 183
" Susanna 105, 121, 151, 183
Corley, Lidia 124
Cooper, Jonathan 160
" Sarah 160
Cotton, Rev. Mr. 139, 144, 145, 149, 151, 155
Crackbone, Abigail 141
" Joseph 141
" Lydia 141
Craft, Abner 108, 170, 171, 172, 174
" Betsey 170
" Charles 172
" Daniel P. 174
" Ephraim 141
" George 172
" Henry 165
" John 141
" Nancy 171
" Sally 174
" Samuel 165
Craige, Andrew 190
" Sally 190
Crane, Eliza 174
" Elizabeth T. 172
" Henry 172
" Stephen 174
Cravath, Eliz. 103
Crawley, Abram 158, 160, 161, 162, 164
" Elizabeth 162
" John 161
" Mary 160
" Samuel 164
Crosby, John 169
" Polly 169
Crowell, Robert 146
Cunningham, Elizabeth . . 180
" John 90
Currye, Jo. 195
Curtis, Benjamin 192
" Benjamin R. 192
" Geo. T. 192
Cushing, Rev. Mr. 155, 157, 162, 163, 164, 166, 168
Cutler, Ann 99
" Elizabeth 136
" Hannah 103, 136
" James 121, 150
" Jonathan 126
" Martha 150
" Phebe 122
" Samuel 129
" Thomas . . 120, 126, 129
" Timothy 88, 89
Cutter, Bethia 111, 127
" Ephraim 19, 41, 49, 50, 54, 55, 70, 71, 84, 90,

Cutter, Ephraim. *Continued.*
111, 112, 127, 129, 180
Cutter, George 141
" Gershom 148
" Hannah 129
" Jonathan 127, 141
" Mary 127
" Nehemiah 145
" Samuel 145
" Sarah 148
Cutting, Abraham 152, 159
" Betty 165
" Elizabeth . . . 92, 131, 152
" Eunice 136
" George 90, 119, 135, 136, 138
" Grace 135
" John 119
" Josiah 136
" Lydia 182
" Mary 153
" Richard 119, 153
" Samuel 138
" Sarah 120
" Susanna 104, 182
" Uriah 165
" Zec. 90
Dalrymple, Henry 191
" Wm. H. 191
Dana, Benj. 143
" Caleb 164, 193
" Daniel 158
" Edmund 162
" Elizabeth 128, 138
" Francis 143
" George 167
" Grace 188, 193
" John 153
" Jonathan 163
" Lydia 153
" Mary 151
" Rachel 163
" Richard 162
" Thomas 138
" William 151
Danforth, Gov. 99
Dascomb, James 152
Davis, Benj. 120, 139
Dawes, Amos 166
" William 166
Dearing 177
Dill, Elizabeth 121
" George 123
" James 123
" Sarah 123
" Thomas 123
Dix, Deeks, Abigail 103, 123, 140, 180
" Anna 149
" Benjamin . 145, 147, 182
" Betty 179
" David 147
" Deborah 153
Dix, Edmund 90, 123, 138, 139, 181
" Elijah 150
" Elizabeth 77, 119, 123, 138, 159
" Hannah 158
" James 92, 93, 148, 149, 150, 152, 153, 158, 159, 160
" Jane 128
" John 103, 123, 128, 136, 137, 138, 140, 141, 143, 146, 149
" Jonas 160
" Jonathan 143, 149
" Joseph 123
" Lydia 138, 180
" Martha 138
" Mary . . . 103, 137, 180
" Samuel 90, 103, 138, 146, 180
" Sarah 148
" Stephen 141
" William . . 139, 152, 158
Dockum, John 154
" William 154
Downes, Clarissa 171
" Samuel 149
" Shubal 171
" William 149
Draper, Elizabeth 166
" Hannah 162
" John 162, 166
" Thomas 166
Drue, Ann 101
Dunah, Elizabeth 158
Dunster, David 141
" Herbert 141
Durant, Edward 155
" Elizabeth 155
" Henry W. 175
" John . . 106, 166, 175, 176
" Sarah 166
" Sarah D. 176
Earle, John 99
" Mary 129
Eddy, Benjamin 23, 125
" Deliverance 125
" Ebenezer 91
" Elizabeth 125, 130
" John 119
" Ruth 130, 181
" Samuel 2, 17, 19, 23, 132, 133
" Sarah 123, 130, 132, 181
Edes, Daniel 161
" Sally 161
Edmunds, Jonathan 145
" Esther 145
Elding, Read 103
Elliston, Jonathan 102
Eliot, Richard R. 105, 115, 116, 186
" Dea. 177
Ellis, Andrew 168
" John 141, 168
" Sarah 141

Fairbanks, Jona. 99
Fairfield, Tryphena 98
Fanning, Elizabeth 2
" Sarah 122
" Widow 179
Farnsworth, Rebecca 119
Faulkner, Charles 171
" Dwight F. 189
" Francis 105, 171, 172, 176, 189, 190
" James R. 176
" William E. 190
Felton, Benjamin . 155, 157, 164
" Ebenezer 164
" Lucy 157
Fenton, Thomas 97
Ferris, William 98
Fessenden, Benj. 163, 164, 166, 167, 168
" Elizabeth 164
" George 167
" Hannah 163
" Jonathan . 148, 165, 168
" Josiah 168
" Martin 165
" Rebecca 166
" Sarah 148
" Thomas 168
Fiske, Abigail 122, 130
" Anna 142
" Daniel . . 91, 156, 181
" David 120, 140
" Elizabeth 108, 119, 120, 122, 132, 155, 182
" Hannah 123, 183
" Henry 91, 181
" John 90, 91, 123, 127, 128, 137, 140, 183
" Jonathan . 127, 128, 137
" Joseph 155
" Lucretia 162
" Lucy 159
" Lydia 126, 150, 183
" Margaret 121
" Martha 120
" Mary 108, 128, 156
" Nathan 2, 6, 7, 8, 11, 12, 13, 17, 18, 21, 22, 23, 24, 25, 26, 28, 29, 30, 31, 36, 38, 45, 46, 47, 49, 51, 53, 68, 73, 74, 75, 79, 91, 123, 125, 132, 133
" Nathaniel . 123, 126, 128
" Samuel 92, 93, 114, 115, 142, 150, 152, 153, 155, 159, 161, 162, 183, 184
" Sarah . . 108, 125, 132, 153
" Susanna 125
Fitzhugh, Robert 102
Flag, Fleg, Abigail 119
" Allin 122, 127, 129
Flag, Benjamin . 99, 120, 129
" Elizabeth 122
" Jo. 125
" Mary 127, 129
" Michael 119, 127
" Sarah 121
" Thomas 121
Forbes, James 88
Foster, David 156
" Susanna 156
Fowle, Abigail 150
" Dorothy 154
" Ebenezer 156
" Edmund 98, 108, 150, 151, 152, 154, 156, 157, 159, 160, 161, 171, 172
" Jeremiah 160
" John 157, 189
" Lucy 159
" Mary 152, 189
" Moses G. 171
" Rebecca B. 172
" Samuel 161
Fox, Abigail 120, 127
" Ebenezer 128
" Isaac 120, 127, 128
" John 127
" Samuel 127
Frazer, Charles B. 194
" Isabella 191
" John 191, 192, 194
" Walter 192
Freeman, Elizabeth 106, 175
" Hannah 100
Fullam, Francis 35, 36
Fuller, Caleb 143
" Daniel 162, 167
" Francis 107
" Grace 162
" Lucy 167
" Nehemiah 143
" Rachel 140
" Thomas 140
" William 107
Fullerton, Jennet 150
" William 150
Gage, Rebecca 183
Gale, Abiah 127
" Abigail 123
" Abraham 120, 127
" Anna 123
" Elizabeth 120, 121
" John 93, 121
" Marah 127
Gamage, Abigail 153
" Daniel 153
" Samuel 154
" William . . . 93, 153, 154
Gardner, Benjamin 165
" Elisha 156
" Elizabeth 168
" Hannah 163

Gardner, Joseph 108, 160, 161, 163, 165, 166, 168
" Mary 108
" Sarah 161
Garfield, Benjamin . . . 4, 129
" Eliakim 139
" Grace 120
" John 98, 123
" Joseph 126
" Mehitabel 125
" Mercy 123
" Ruth 122
" Samuel 129, 139
" Serg. 125
" Thankful 152
Garrett, Hannah 102
Gaskell, John 129
George (a negro) 101
" John, 105, 173, 174, 175, 189
" Lucy 175
" Margaret 189
" Mary 102
" Mary A. 174
" Sally M. 174
" William M. 173
Gibbins, Elizabeth 137
" Mr. 102, 177
" Peter 137
" W. 97
Gibbs, Henry 3, 4, 5, 6, 7, 8, 21, 22, 24, 25, 31, 33, 37, 38, 52, 122, 125, 130, 134
" Mr. 178
Giles, Mary 156
" Thomas 156
Gleason, David . . 92, 146, 183
" Dorothy 145
" John 92, 145
" Samuel 152
" Thankful 152
Goddard, Abigail 146, 185
" Benjamin 120
" Ebenezer 57, 63, 64, 66, 69, 70, 71, 77, 146, 147, 148, 149, 150
" Edward . 125, 131, 132, 133
" Elizabeth 149, 181
" Josiah 10, 17, 18, 20, 21, 23, 28, 30, 31, 125, 132, 133, 148
" Rachel . . 125, 132, 147
" Robert . . . 5, 23, 27, 28
" Simon 133
" Susanna 125, 132
" William 2, 120
Godding, Abigail 145
" Hannah 146, 168, 183, 185
" Henry 90, 92, 93, 150, 168
" Joanna 146
" Jonas 164
" Jonathan C. 144, 161, 162, 164, 166, 168
Godding, Martha . 104, 139, 165
" Peter 148, 162
" Rebecca 162
" Spencer 151, 166
" William 89, 90, 91, 92, 93, 104, 112, 139, 142, 144, 146, 148, 150, 151, 162, 165, 168
Goffe, Elizabeth 119
Goodenow, Mary 183
Gooding, Elizabeth 99
Goodwin, Elizabeth 124
Grant, Abigail 91, 131
" Caleb 2, 133
" Charles 176
" Christopher 2, 92, 107, 145, 148, 165, 167, 182, 187
" Elizabeth 131
" Hannah 133
" Hepsibah 176, 188
" Joseph 2, 6, 10, 19, 28, 126, 128, 131, 132, 133, 134, 165
" Joshua 50, 64, 65, 90, 106, 131, 136, 137, 138, 175, 176, 181, 189
" Lydia 137
" Mary 91, 92, 121, 126, 132, 145, 180
" Mercy 134
" Ruth 138
" Sarah 126, 127, 133, 167, 187
Gray, James 161
" Samuel 101, 179
" Sarah . . . 161, 163, 185
" Thomas 101
" William 103
Grefte, Hannah 96
Gregg, Mary 121
Greenfield, Ann 97
Greenough, Rev. Mr. 116
Greenwood, Josiah 151
" Moses 151
Grimes, James . . . 92, 145, 148
" Samuel 145
" Sarah 148
Grout, Jonathan 123
" Joseph . . 120, 123, 128
" Mary 99
" Mehitabel 128
" Susanna 120, 123
Grover, Thomas 90
Hackleton, Bethiah 166
" Daniel 155
" Elisha 149
" Hepzibah 149
" James 92, 148, 149, 151, 153, 155
" John . . . 148, 149, 166
" Mary 153
" Samuel 151

Hagar (a negro) 101
" Abigail 97
" Elijah 157
" Hannah 135
" Jonathan . . . 145, 153
" Joseph 153
" Lucy 151
" Mary 185
" Mehitabel 97
" Samuel 90, 92, 93, 130, 135, 145, 150, 151, 157, 185
" Sarah 130
" Susanna 150
" William 97
Hall, Anna 168
" Ezekiel . . . 108, 168
" John 108
" Josiah 152
" Susanna 152
Halloway, Curtis 132
" Mary 132
Hamlin, John 177
Hammond, Hamont, Abigail . 166
" Abijah 162, 166
" Daniel 136
" David 129
" Elizabeth 126
" Hannah 135
" Isaac 162
" John . . . 2, 5, 15, 136
" Jonathan 154
" Mary 180
" Thomas 119, 122, 126, 129, 135
Hancoks, Samuel 77
Hanna, Hannah, Robert . . 102
" William 103
Hapgood, Mary 98
" Shadrack 98
Harrington, Abijah 158
" Anna . . . 104, 152, 157
" Beulah 143
" Betsey 171
" Charles 159
" Daniel . . . 123, 124, 127
" David 124
" Ebenezer 124
" Edward 37, 38, 45, 59, 60, 61, 62, 63, 64, 71, 77, 78, 95, 104, 139, 141, 143, 145, 147, 148, 150, 152, 154, 156, 157, 159, 160, 162, 168, 169, 170, 171, 172, 181, 186
" Elijah 169
" Elisha 134, 153
" Elizabeth 135, 142, 180, 184
" Ephraim 172
" Esther 186
" George . . . 134, 136
" Grace 145, 163
" Hannah . . . 121, 169
" Henry 130
" Isaac 172
Harrington, Jabez 94
" Jacob 168
" Joel 172
" John 103, 121, 123, 128, 163
" Jonathan 127, 135, 147, 163, 164, 172, 173
" Joseph 52, 55, 56, 64, 90, 91, 93, 99, 142, 183
" Josiah 153
" Katy 157, 173
" Leonard 173
" Lucretia 173
" Lucy 172
" Lydia 128, 164
" Martha 142, 183
" Mary 123, 139, 151, 153, 154, 158, 194
" Moses 140, 158
" Nathaniel 93, 107, 151, 153, 154, 157, 159, 181
" Peter 154
" Phineas . . 148, 157, 172
" Polly 170
" Rebecca 124, 130
" Robert 123
" Ruth 142
" Samuel . . 153, 159, 160
" Sarah . . 98, 136, 146, 183
" Seth 134
" Susanna . . 127, 156, 162
" Thankful 186
" Thomas 124, 127, 130, 142
" William 150, 169, 170, 171, 172
Harris, Abijah 139
" Anna 137, 158
" Benjamin 138
" Francis 135
" Fullam 143
" Hannah . . 140, 160, 172
" Kate 105, 172
" Lucy 166
" Mary 136, 164
" Mehitable 180
" Nathaniel 37, 38, 41, 43, 45, 46, 47, 48, 49, 50, 51, 52, 53, 54, 55, 57, 59, 60, 61, 62, 63, 64, 65, 66, 67, 68, 69, 70, 71, 72, 74, 76, 90, 91, 113, 115, 135, 137, 138, 140, 141, 143, 156, 159, 180
" Priscilla . . . 135, 137
" Samuel . . . 135, 172
" Sarah . 135, 156, 163, 183
" Stephen 105, 141, 156, 158, 160, 161, 163, 164, 166, 172
" Thomas 135
" Timothy 90, 136, 137, 139, 181
Harrison, Prudence 98

Hastings, Abigail 150
" Asher 137
" Benjamin 71, 90, 92, 93, 105, 133, 136, 138, 140, 141, 142, 144, 146, 147, 148, 150, 151, 152, 160, 173, 174, 175, 176, 180
" Charles 173
" Daniel 46, 52, 53, 103, 133, 135, 136, 162
" Ebenezer 66, 71, 75, 77, 79, 80, 82, 84, 90, 92, 140
" Elisha 136
" Elizabeth 125, 131, 139, 164, 173
" Enoch 134
" Eunice 134
" Hepzibah 125
" Hannah 140, 146, 167, 183, 184
" Isaac 168
" John 38, 45, 46, 51, 63, 74, 75, 76, 77, 79, 90, 91, 125, 129, 131, 134, 136, 137, 138, 139, 141
" Jonas 142
" Joseph . 2, 91, 140, 148
" Martha 142
" Mary 91, 125, 131, 136, 144, 153, 161, 175, 180
" Nathan 148
" Nathaniel 91, 131
" Richard C. 174
" Ruth 140, 182
" Samuel 23, 96, 131, 132, 133, 142, 152, 173
" Sarah 103, 135, 138, 141, 175, 180
" Seth . 93, 146, 153, 184
" Simon 141, 160, 161, 162, 164, 167, 168, 184
" Smith 151
" Stephen 136
" Thomas 96, 155
" William 129, 147
Hatch, Benjamin 136
Mercy 136
Haward, Mary 99
Hawkins, Mary 130
Hay, Abigail 153, 158
" Anna 164
" Elizabeth 153, 155
" Hannah 157
" James 153, 155, 156, 157, 158, 160, 161, 164, 165, 167
" John 159, 160, 167
" Joseph . 157, 158, 159, 163
" Lucy 165
" Mary 157
" Sarah 161
Hay, Thomas 158
" William 156
Hayman, Samuel 1
Hewes, Abraham 164
" Lucy 164
Hicks, Elizabeth 101
Hide, Enoch 174
" Sally D. 174
Hill, Abigail 135
" Abraham 141
" Benjamin 165
" John 144
" Joseph 135
" Susanna 165
" Thomas 78
" Zechariah 141, 144
Hilliard, Ann 188
Hinds, Abigail 156
" Ebenezer . . 154, 156, 157
" Margaret 154
Hoar, Esther 144
" John 144
" Nathaniel P. 171
" Samuel 171
Holden, Holdin, Holding, Abigail 180
" Elizabeth . . 119, 137, 180
" Isaac . . 23, 90, 92, 182
" John 130
" Jonathan 135
" Joseph 23, 47, 57, 59, 63, 64, 66, 69, 70, 75, 76, 90, 135, 137, 180
" Justinian 119
" Lydia 132
" Phineas 192, 193
" Samuel . . 23, 132, 133
" Susanna 104, 132
Holland, John 90
" Nathaniel . . . 119, 128
" Ruth 99
Holman, Deborah 98
Homans, Thomas 91
Hosmer, Daniel 150
Holt, Samuel 172
" Samuel N. 172
Houghton, Abigail 133
" Henry 133
Hovey, Eliza B. 176
" Eunice 175
" Mary 163
" Phineas . . 106, 175, 176
" Sally 175
" Thomas 166
How, Abigail 154
" Enos 154
Humphrys, Rebecca 97
Humsteds, Jabez 125
" Matthew 125
Hunt, Dorothy 185
" Elizabeth 185
" Jane 190
" Jane L. 190

Hunt, John 91, 147, 148, 149, 150, 151, 152, 154, 156, 157, 159, 168, 175, 185
" Katherine 147, 148, 154, 185, 188
" Maria B. 190
" Mary . . . 168, 185, 188
" Ruth . . . 151, 183, 185
" Samuel . . . 149, 175, 185
" Sarah 157
" Sarah P. 188
" Susanna 107
" Thomas 156
" William . . . 152, 190
Jackson, Abigail 103
" Abraham 136
" Daniel 105, 170, 171, 172, 173, 175, 176, 187
" Edward . . 103, 136, 159
" Elizabeth 147
" Francis 172
" Henry 170
" Jonas 136, 160
" Joshua 136, 159
" Kezia 159
" Leonard 173
" Lucy . . . 105, 175, 187
" Mary H. 173
" Michael 147
" Moses 160
" Patty R. 176
" Samuel 159
Jane (a negro) 102
Jeffreys, George 102
Jenny (a negro) 154
Jennison, Abigail 104, 142, 164, 182
" Benjamin 108, 170
" Elias 168
" Elizabeth . . . 138, 162
" Eunice 183
" Grace 130
" Hannah 133
" John 181
" Joseph 132
" Joshua 155
" Josiah 138
" Judith 119
" Lucy 149
" Lydia 126, 182
" Mary . . . 133, 146, 180
" Mercy 155, 182
" Nathaniel . . 138, 167, 181
" Phineas 108, 148, 166, 168, 170, 171, 187
" Rachel 130, 132
" Rev. 137, 138
" Samuel 12, 15, 17, 18, 20, 23, 51, 52, 54, 56, 103, 126, 130, 133, 140, 142, 146, 148, 149, 151, 153, 155, 162, 164, 167, 180, 182, 221
" Sarah 151
Jennison, Susanna . . . 166, 187
" Sergt. 41
" William . . . 153, 171, 180
Johnson, Esther 162
" Hannah . . . 121, 123, 130
" John 123
" Mary 123
" Matthew 159
" Sarah 185
" Solomon 96
" Thomas 123, 162
Jones, Caleb 127
" Deborah 123
" Isaac 128
" Josiah . 98, 123, 128, 133
" Lydia 98
" Samuel 131
" William 127
Kate (a negro) 158
Kay, Lydia 177, 178
" Mary 97
" Miss 177
" Thomas 97
Kelly, Elizabeth 150
" Joseph 150
" Mary 184
Kendall, Benjamin F. 194
" Benjamin S. 167
" Betsey 171
" Charles 175
" David 174
" Eliza C. 192
" George 192
" Hannah 173
" Henry L. 190
" Hiram 191
" Joshua 107, 167, 171, 172, 173, 174, 175
" Josiah 172
" Paul 106, 188, 190, 191, 192, 193, 194
" Susan C. 191
" Susanna 107
" William 193
Kimball, John 2, 90, 91, 93, 154, 179, 182
" Mary 183
King, Ebenezer 133
" John 77
" Richard 92
" Samuel 133
Kinningham, Cuningham, Elizabeth 132
" Esther 132
" John 132, 133
Knap, Knop, Daniel 152
" Henry 132
" James 120, 129
" John . . 2, 121, 127, 129
" Jonas 152
" Sarah 121
" Thomas 99
Knight, Mr. 179

Knox, John 177
Lamb, Isaac 123
Langdon, John 178
" Jo. 179
Lawrence, Abigail . . . 134, 144
" Benjamin 136
" Edmund 142
" Elizabeth 119, 133
" Eunice 144
" George 23, 99, 103, 119, 131, 133, 134, 136, 144, 154, 180
" John 104, 134, 143
" Mary . 99, 123, 141, 183
" Mercy 144
" Rev. Mr. 152, 159
" Samuel 142
" Sarah 143
" William 92, 141, 142, 144, 146, 182
Learned, Larned, Aaron . . . 169
" Abigail . . . 148, 169, 186
" Amariah 135, 139, 157, 159, 160
" Anna 163, 164, 167, 187, 190
" Benjamin 149
" Bezalel 93, 150, 151, 152, 154
" Christopher 168
" Daniel 175
" David 90, 92, 93, 140, 138, 141, 143, 144, 147, 148, 149, 181
" Edward W. 193
" Eli 160
" Elijah 168
" Elisha 143, 162, 163, 165, 167, 168, 185
" Elizabeth 93, 104, 138, 141, 168, 182, 184
" Fanning 140
" George N. 194
" Grant 108
" Hannah 146, 150, 157, 164, 167, 170, 185
" Henry 93, 165, 170
" James 107
" Jedidiah 108, 142, 168, 170
" Jerusha . . . 147, 151, 169
" Jesse 149
" Jonas 136, 154, 158
" Jonathan 90, 107, 139, 140, 142, 144, 146, 147, 149, 154, 163, 164, 166, 167, 180
" Joseph 166
" Joshua 90, 92, 104, 138, 139, 141, 143, 145, 148, 162, 181
" Josiah 161, 188
" Katherine 154
" Lucy 141, 166
" Mary . . 71, 77, 144, 159
" Mercy 135
Learned, Moses 169
" Oliver 148
" Parnel 107
" Paul 145, 161, 175, 187, 190
" Phineas 107
" Robert 139
" Samuel 164, 175
" Samuel S. 194
" Sarah 147, 162, 185
" Silas 167
" Susanna . . . 163, 165, 167
" Tabitha 158
" Thomas 23, 38, 49, 59, 63, 64, 107, 135, 136, 138, 140, 161, 162, 164, 165, 167, 175, 184, 188, 193, 194
" William 107, 144, 164, 165, 167, 168
Leason, Abiah 120, 121, 129
" Ann 126
" Elizabeth 122
" Isaac 129
" John 122
" Joseph 122
" William 121, 122
Leathe, Achsah 161
" Ann G. 193
" Frances 163
" Hannah . . . 156, 159, 185
" Jedidiah 112, 118, 156, 157, 160, 161, 163, 164, 166, 185
" John 157, 193
" Jonathan 159
" Lucy 166
" Mary 164
" Sarah 160
" Sophia 107
Leckey, Abraham 153
" Richard 97
" William 153
Lee, William 93
Legg, Capt. 100, 103
" Sabella 100
Leppington, John 138
" Mary 138
Leverett, Benjamin D. 191
" Daniel 191
Little, Anne 101
Livermore, Abigail . . . 146, 149
" Adeline 193
" Amos 107, 143, 162, 165, 167, 175, 176, 188, 189, 190, 191, 192, 193, 194
" Amos H. 190
" Anna 129, 134, 144
" Charles 192
" Daniel 23, 25, 132, 133, 134, 146, 151, 162, 183, 189
" David 92, 149, 150, 151, 153, 156, 176, 190, 191, 192, 193

Livermore, Edmund 91, 92, 141, 144, 145, 181
" Elisha . . . 100, 107, 153
" Eliza 189
" Elizabeth 141
" Grace S. 191
" Hannah . . 99, 156, 176
" Hannah S. 191
" Harriet L. 194
" Hepzibah 167
" Jane A. 191
" Jonathan 147
" Josiah 91, 144, 145, 181, 190
" Katherine 159
" Lucy 165
" Lydia 124, 153
" Martha W. 193
" Mary 133
" Mary A. 192
" Matthew 134, 139
" Nathaniel 119, 149
" Oliver 59, 60, 61, 63, 64, 66, 67, 68, 69, 70, 71, 74, 75, 80, 81, 90, 91, 92, 103, 132, 134, 136, 137, 139, 140, 141, 143, 144, 146, 147, 149, 159, 161, 162, 183
" Priscilla 150
" Rachel 137, 140
" Ruth 136
" Samuel 3, 8, 9, 11, 12, 13, 22, 23, 24, 25, 26, 27, 28, 119, 129, 133, 134
" Samuel B. 190
" Samuel W. 189
" Sarah 153
" Sibyl 112, 176
" Thomas 175
Loud, Abner F. 194
" Edward 194
Maccoys, Alex 77, 78, 79
Maddocks, Caleb 133
" Daniel 145
" Joanna 134
" Henry 132
" John 90, 131, 132, 133, 134, 136, 138, 145
" Mary 132, 138
" Ruth 131, 132
" Sarah 132
" William 138
Maillet, Ephraim 146
Man, Hannah 102
" James 154
" Moses 154
Mansfield, Bethiah 130
Mason, Aaron 174
" Abigail 182
" Amos 173
" Daniel 164, 165
" David 154
" Ebenezer 139, 160, 161, 162
Mason, Elias 93, 161, 183
" Elijah 160
" Elizabeth 160, 172
" Enoch 162
" Esther 135
" Grace 147
" Hannah 102, 148, 154, 174
" Hugh 105, 170, 171, 172, 173
" Isaac 165, 174
" Jonas 151
" Joseph 3, 30, 31, 33, 43, 44, 45, 46, 51, 52, 54, 55, 56, 60, 63, 66, 68, 73, 75, 80, 81, 82, 83, 84, 85, 91, 92, 113, 114, 119, 126, 135, 136, 137, 139, 140, 147, 148, 150, 151, 172
" Josiah 140
" Lydia 136
" Martha C. 170
" Mary . 102, 121, 122, 181
" Moses 105, 174
" Nehemiah 93, 183
" Richard C. 171
" Samuel . . 159, 160, 164
" Sarah 150
" Seth 173
" Susanna 137, 184
" William 161
Maverick, Elias 103
McCollister, Charles 84
" John 94
McConnoughey, David 140
" George 140
McKilenys, Mr. 177
Mead, Abigail 186
" Betsey 170
" Elijah 169, 170, 171, 172, 186
" Isaac 170
" Israel 92, 93, 145, 154, 155, 156, 183
" John 156
" Lydia 172
" Mary 155
" Nabby 172
" Polly 169
" Samuel 171
Meatox, Bethia 121
" Daniel 121
" Mary 121
Mellin, Helen M. 190
" Leonard 190
" Sophia 187, 190
Memory, Joseph 126
" Mary 126
Merriam, Rev. Mr. . 160, 163, 167
Merritt, Amos 122, 129
" Bethiah 122
" Daniel 129
Messenger, Ebenezer 97
Metcalf, Hezikiah 171
" Polly 171

Miller, Moses 149
" Samuel 149
Millings, James 120
" John 120
" Mary 120
" Richard 120
" Samuel 120
" Simon 120
" Thomas 119, 120
Mills, Ann 110
" Henry 23
Mixer, Isaac 4
" Joanna 99
" John 170
" Josiah . 112, 170, 172, 174
" John 170
" Lois 172
" Nathaniel 174
" Sarah 119
Moodey, Mr. 110
Morse, Abraham 134
" Daniel 130
" Elizabeth 130
" Jacob 134
" James 123
" Jeremye . . 123, 126, 134
" John . 2, 99, 124, 126, 130
" Jonathan 126
" Joseph 144
" Nathaniel 126
" Sarah 123
" Zechariah 144
Murch, Lydia 141
" William . . 91, 141, 142
Murdock, Abigail 140
" Amasa 168
" Artemas 176, 189
" Horace 176
" John 168
" Julia 189
" Sally 176
Murriah (a negro) 187
Myrick, Abigail 97
" Hannah 158
" John 97
" Jonathan 158
Neggres, Mary 97
Nevenson, Elizabeth 120
" John 120
Newell, John 156
" Solomon 156
Newhall, George 192
" Polly 192
Nixon, Joseph 174
Norcross, Abigail 168
" Asa 145
" Charlotte 175
" Elizabeth . . 158, 159, 165
" Hannah 188, 193
" Helen 175
" Jemima 164
" Jerusha 187
Norcross, Josiah 108, 137, 139, 158, 159, 161, 162, 164, 165, 167, 168
" Mary 144
" Mehitabel 120
" Mercy 138
" Moses 108
" Nathaniel 90, 91, 97, 129, 135, 136, 137, 138, 139, 140, 144, 145, 147, 150, 158, 162
" Nehemiah 147
" Polly 175
" Richard 2, 5, 96, 97, 124, 128
" Rose 124, 128
" Samuel 128
" Seth 175
" Sukey 106, 175
" Susanna 150
" Uriah 135, 139
Nutting, Ebenezer 136
" Charles 155, 169, 171, 172, 173, 174, 175, 176
" Hannah 176
" James 137
" John 146
" Mary 137, 151
" Mercy 181
" Nabby 172
" Nathaniel 173, 174
" Phineas 171
" Richard 4, 171
" Sally 175
" Samuel 92, 93, 148, 151, 155
" Sarah 148
Nymphas (my negro) 150, 154, 155, 156
Oliver, Peter 136
" Samuel 136
Orms, Elizabeth 135, 181
" John . 65, 66, 78, 90, 135
Ozment, Mary 137
" William 137, 180
Pain, Will 179
Page, Phineas 187
Palfrey, Phebe 104, 137
Park, Edward 148
" Lucy 108, 158
" Pennel 108
" William 158
Parker, Hananiah 131
" Fanny 163
" Jacob 91
" Moses 147
" Peter 155
" Thomas 147
Parkhurst, Isaac 107
Parkis, Anna 129
" George 119
" John . . . 119, 126, 129
" Samuel 126
Parkman, Rev. Mr. 154

Patrick, Capt. 118
Partridge, Sarah 163
" Thaddeus 163
Patten, Isaac . 167, 191, 193, 194
" John 164
" Juliana D. 194
" Lucretia 191
" Mary 165
" Mary D. 193
" Richard R. 193
" Samuel 170
" Thomas 164, 165, 166, 167, 168, 170, 191
" William 168
Patterson, Adam . . . 139, 141, 181
" Esther 157
" Isaac 106
" Isabel 181
" James 190
" John 139
" Joseph 157
Paughonot, Hannah 155
" Joseph 155
Pegg (a mulatto) 144
Pemberton, Hannah 103
" Mr. 102, 103
Penneman, Widow 91
Pero (a negro) 113
Perry, Parry, Abigail 133
" Dorcas 136, 146
" Ebenezer 128
" Elizabeth 134
" Ephraim 142
" Hannah 150, 152
" John . 2, 128, 129, 133, 134
" Jonathan 91, 181
" Joseph 129
" Joshua 146
" Josiah 23, 59, 61, 62, 64, 65, 71, 72, 84, 90, 91, 92, 93, 136, 146
" Mary 133, 183
" Mercy 181
" Nathan . 150, 152, 153, 184
" Samuel . 90, 91, 93, 128, 135
" Sarah . 111, 130, 133, 154
" Susanna 183
Peter (a negro) 104, 138
Peters, Abigail 184
" Joseph 154, 184
" Moses 154
Phillips, Elizabeth 123
" Hannah 185
" John 79, 134, 135
" Jonathan . . . 123, 127, 129
" Lydia 180
" Mary 119, 135
" Priscilla 134
" Ruth 123
" Sarah 119, 123, 127
" Theophilus . 119, 126, 129
Phillis (a negro) 156
Pierce, Pearse, Abigail M. . . 192
Pierce, Pearse, Abraham . . . 129
" Anna 160
" Benjamin . . 119, 121, 126
" Daniel 146, 155, 156, 160, 183
" Edward 162
" Elvira 189
" Elizabeth 121, 124
" Eunice 150
" Francis . . . 130, 132, 134
" Hannah . . . 119, 121, 134
" Henry 155
" Isabel 129, 178
" Israel 119
" John 121, 163
" John M. 189
" Jonas 150
" Jonathan 155
" Joseph 99, 106, 119, 124, 189, 190, 192
" Joseph N. 190
" Martha 156, 184
" Martha B. 190
" Mary 155
" Mary B. 192
" Rebecca 180
" Ruth 137
" Samuel 35, 36, 37, 38, 46, 57, 59, 60, 63, 64, 65, 90, 126, 129, 134, 137, 138
" William 189
Pitman, Nathaniel 102
Place, Sarah 103
Poole, Matthew 101
Porter, Anna 102
" Lydia 105, 172
" Nabby 172
" Nathan 105, 172
Preuse, Abraham 96
Prentice, Benjamin 149
" David 157
" Edward 161
" Elizabeth 146, 159
" Hannah 186
" Joshua 161
" Lydia 143, 158
" Mary 150, 159
" Mercy 155
" Samuel . . 92, 93, 143, 146
" Smith 93, 149, 150, 154, 155, 157, 158, 159, 161
" Solomon 186
" Thomas 154
Price, John 120
" Mary 120
" William 128
Priest, Hannah 134
" Josiah 157
" Mary 152
" Sarah 152
" William 157
Proctor, Edward 122
Prout, Eunice 128
Quiner, Mary 145

Quiner, Sarah 143
" Thomas . . . 143, 145
Rainger, Ann 156
Rand, Elbridge D. 193
" Harriet A. 193
" Mary 107
" Samuel 193
Randall, Elizabeth 154
" Isaac 159
" Jacob 160
" John 153, 154, 156, 157, 159, 160
" Samuel 156
Ray, Elijah 189
" Elizabeth 189
Raymond, Jonathan 158
" Susanna 158
Reed, John 90
" Jonas 140
" Josiah 90, 140
Remington, Elizabeth . 167, 185
" Frederick . . . 161, 187
" John 112, 156, 158, 159, 160, 161, 163, 167, 168, 186, 187
" Jonathan . . . 159, 160
" Lucy 158
" Mary . . . 156, 163, 168
Rice, Rise, Ephraim 99
" Mary 125, 162
Richards, Humphrey 102
Richardson, Abigail 157
" Ann 188
" Ebenezer 160
" Edward 155, 157, 159, 160, 161, 163, 165, 166, 168
" Elizabeth 165
" Hannah B. 192
" John . . . 159, 188, 192
" Lucy 166
" Mary 168
" Moses 155
" Peter 155
" Richard 155
" Sarah 161
" William 163
Ridgway, Bridget 162
" Isaac 162
Ripley, Rev. Mr. . . . 189, 194
Robbins, David 152
" Eliza W. 176
" George 175, 176
" Isaac 189
" James 173, 174, 175, 176, 188, 189, 193
" Jane W. 176
" John H. 193
" Jonathan 106, 191, 192, 193
" Joseph 144
" Lois 188, 193
" Lois A. 193
" Lois C. 188
" Lois J. 193
Robbins, Lucretia 173
" Lydia 191
" Martha 191
" Mary . 107, 144, 191, 193
" Moses 168
" Phineas 150, 167
" Samuel 167
" Sarah 107, 193
" Solomon 150, 152
" William 168
" William E. 192
Robinson, Bradbury 187
" Lucy 187
Rogers, Abigail 108
" John 161
" Martha 161
" Nathaniel 108
" Phineas 108
" William 108
Rosse, Dorothy 97
Rowe, John 124
" William 123
Royal, Joseph 103
Russell, Eliza C. 192
" Gustavus 191
" Jane A. K. 190
" Joseph . 106, 190, 191, 192
" Lucy S. 191
" Sarah 188
Ryder, Rider, Thomas . . 10, 119
Saiga, John 174
Saltmarsh, Abigail 145
" Deborah 147
" Elizabeth . . . 160, 163
" John . . . 144, 161, 163
" Katharine 148
" Mary 166
" Seth 150, 166
" Susanna 166
" Thomas 92, 93, 94, 141, 143, 144, 145, 147, 148, 150, 185
" William 141, 160, 161, 162
Sanders, Saunders, Abia . . 119
" Abigail 123
" Hester 121
" Jon. 119
" Josiah 170
" Lucy 170
" Moses 165
" Polly G. 174
" Sarah . 106, 120, 165, 174
" William 120
Sanderson, Charity 168
" Elizabeth . . . 155, 189
" Esther 107
" Hannah 126
" Henry . . . 108, 151, 168
" Isaac 92, 93, 146, 148, 149, 151, 153, 155, 158
" Joseph 126
" Josiah . . . 148, 170, 173
" Kezia 149, 185
" Lydia . . . 108, 126, 173

Sanderson, Mary . . . 127, 158
" Mehitabel 182
" Sarah 126
" Seth 153, 178
" William . . . 126, 127
Sanger, Aaron 108
" Abigail 157, 158
" Abraham 168
" Anna . . . 166, 186, 193
" Benjamin 161
" Daniel . . . 157, 168, 194
" David 90, 92, 93, 134, 136, 137, 138, 140, 142, 145, 147, 157, 158, 160, 161, 162, 163, 165, 167
" Elizabeth . . 167, 188, 193
" George W. 193
" Grace . . . 160, 161, 185
" Jesse 165
" John . . . 107, 134, 157
" Joseph 167
" Katharine 162
" Lucy 157, 162
" Lydia . . . 134, 147, 160
" Mary 164
" Molly 157
" Nathaniel . . 140, 160, 162
" Nathaniel C. 194
" Richard . . . 188, 193
" Richard E. 193
" Samuel 142, 160, 161, 166, 167, 168, 185
" Samuel E. 193
" Seth 163
" Solomon 145
" Spencer 162
" Thomas 158
" William 108, 137, 138, 157, 158, 160, 161, 164, 168, 193
Savage, Ephraim . . . 102, 103
" John 158
" Samuel 158
Sawin, Abigail . . . 121, 142, 182
" Abijah 137, 162
" Benjamin . . . 145, 163
" Daniel 112, 136, 149, 158, 159, 160, 161, 162, 165, 167, 168, 184, 188
" David 149
" Deborah 134
" Elizabeth . . . 142, 168
" George 131
" Goodman 2
" Hannah . . . 147, 183
" John 2, 79, 127, 136, 137, 142, 145, 147, 153, 159, 182
" Jonathan 141
" Joseph 164
" Judith 103, 118
" Lydia 144, 183
" Lucy 160
Sawin, Mary . . . 118, 144, 183
" Munnings 2, 3, 9, 11, 12, 13, 21, 23, 24, 26, 27, 28, 29, 31, 32, 33, 100, 127, 131, 132, 134
" Samuel 132, 142, 143, 161
" Sarah 145
" Stephen 92, 104, 141, 142, 143, 145, 147, 149
" Susanna . . . 153, 167
Sawtell, Satle, Ab. . . 142, 146
" Bethia 120
" Elizabeth 180
" Enoch 124, 127
" Hannah 142
" Henry . . . 146, 149, 150
" John 150
" Richard 127
" Ruth 142
" Sarah 142
" Susanna 124
Sayer, Charlotte 173
" Jacob 173
Scudder, Daniel 191
" Daniel L. 191
" Sarah P. 187
Seaver, Andrew 168
" Ebenezer 168
Severn, Elizabeth 133
" Samuel . . . 120, 130, 133
Sewall, Capt. 178
Shattuck, Shattock, Abigail . 125
" Benjamin . . . 124, 149
" Elizabeth 180
" John 3
" Jonathan 131
" Joseph 78, 122
" Josiah . . . 149, 151, 157
" Mary 128, 159
" Nathaniel 127
" Philip . . 4, 120, 127, 128
" Rebecca 121
" Robert 131
" Samuel . . 23, 125, 127
" Susanna 151
" William 2, 6, 19, 22, 23, 24, 25, 28, 30, 38, 39, 41, 43, 49, 53, 63, 71, 90, 124, 128, 131, 138, 180
Shed, Francis 168
" Keziah 108
" Zecariah . . . 108, 168
Sherman, Abiah 119
" Betty 138
" Capt. 2, 3
" Corporal 5, 6
" Elizabeth 124
" Grace 119
" Joseph 5, 22, 23, 25, 26, 124, 128
" Martha 128, 138
" Mary 130

Sherman, Mr. 119
" Nathaniel 43, 45, 47, 51, 57, 138
" Pastor 2
Simmons, Anna 189
" James . . . 106, 189, 190
" Mary 189
" Sarah 189
" Stephen 190
Smethurst, Mary 100
Smith, Alfred 193
" Benjamin 128
" Daniel 23, 125
" Elisha 129
" Elizabeth 127
" George 175
" Hannah 180
" James 98
" Jane 120
" John 125
" Jonathan 120, 124, 127, 129
" Joseph 125, 128
" Lydia . . . 124, 175, 193
" Mary . . . 2, 177, 179
" Mary A. 176
" Nelson 189
" Rebecca 125
" Samuel 128
" Sarah 103
" Sarah J. 120
" Shubael . . . 175, 176, 189
" Thomas 128
" Widow 129
" Zechariah 124
Soden, Elizabeth 107
" Hannah 102, 187
" Mary 166
" Samuel 107, 157, 159, 160, 162, 163, 166, 187
" Susanna 157
" Thomas . . . 159, 163, 173
Sparhawk, Isaac 159
" Jacob 155
" Katherine 107
" Nathan 165
" Nathaniel . . . 107, 156, 165
" Timothy 155
Spring, Abigail 99
" Alpheus 144, 185
" Convers 141, 161, 162, 164, 165, 167, 169
" Elizabeth 133, 169
" Francis 152, 170
" Henry 18, 20, 23, 28, 36, 90, 91, 93, 121, 126, 131, 133, 136, 137, 139, 141, 143, 144, 147, 150, 151, 152, 156, 165
" Jedediah . . . 137, 157, 159
" John 139, 158
" Josiah 159
" Keziah . . . 158, 180, 183
Spring, Luke 167
" Lydia 125, 126, 137, 151, 186
" Marshall 147
" Mary 134, 150
" Mehitable . . . 130, 131
" Mercy A. 161
" Mr. 41
" Samuel . 136, 156, 170, 186
" Sarah 131, 143
" Silas 164
" Thomas 134, 157
Stacy, John 131, 132
" Samuel 132
Starrs, Star, Comfort . . 121, 126
" Hannah 129
" Lydia 126
" Mary 121
" Peter 144
Stearns, Abigail 145, 180
" Abijah . . . 146, 153, 183
" Anna . 142, 146, 180, 183
" Benjamin 129, 135
" Catherine M. 189
" Charles 166
" Daniel . 135, 136, 140, 142, 144, 147, 150, 157
" Dorothy 148
" Elisha 157
" Elizabeth 135
" Ezekiel 139
" George W. . . . 129, 170
" Hannah 165, 182
" Hepzibah 146
" Isaac . 122, 131, 142, 150
" Isaiah 136
" Jacob 182
" John 36, 38, 57, 59, 61, 63, 64, 65, 90, 92, 129, 135, 136, 138, 142, 145, 146, 161, 162, 163, 164, 166, 168
" Jonas 142, 165
" Jonathan . . 138, 165, 166
" Joseph 92, 93, 163, 173, 181
" Joshua 150, 153
" Josiah 141, 142, 147, 148, 150, 151, 156, 164
" Judith 129
" Katharine 161
" Lois 146, 183
" Lucy 172
" Martha . 161, 166, 167, 168
" Mary 112, 130, 140, 147, 155, 168, 183
" Mary C. 189
" Mehitabel 124
" Moses 136
" Nathaniel . . . 90, 92, 142
" Peter 147
" Phineas 107, 141, 165, 166, 167, 168, 170, 171, 172
" Polly 171

Stearns, Rebecca 129
" Relief 151
" Ruth 140
" Samuel . 113, 121, 124, 139, 141, 145, 180, 183
" Sarah . . . 129, 141, 144
" Simon 131
" Stephen . . 94, 135, 153
" Susanna . . 150, 166, 182
" Thomas 162
" William . . 151, 167, 168
Stevens, Hephzibah 154
" Joseph 154
" Thomas 103
Steward, Hephzibah 145
" John 144
" Jonas 145
" Sarah 144
Stimpson, Stimson, Andrew 105, 170
" Benjamin 129
" Bethiah 133
" Betsey 172
" Elizabeth . . . 121, 131
" James . . . 130, 133, 134
" John 171, 172
" Jonathan 119, 120, 129, 130
" Joseph 126
" Lucy 170
" Rebecca 119
" Susanna 171
Stoddard, Solomon 90
Stone, Aaron 173
" Abigail 170, 172
" Abijah . 105, 155, 170, 171
" Amos 155
" Ann 101, 119, 193
" Anna 176, 189
" Asa 106, 191, 192, 193, 194
" Asaph 172
" Betsey 174
" Caroline 176
" Charles . . 107, 173, 193
" Chary 91, 180
" Cherry 163
" Columbus J. 175
" Cornelius 158, 170
" Daniel . 121, 123, 128, 153
" David, 23, 90, 91, 133, 150
" Dorcas 123, 125
" Ebenezer 23, 26, 31, 48, 66, 67, 70, 77, 78, 79, 82, 83, 90, 91, 93, 107, 121, 135, 137, 138
" Eliza 175
" Elizabeth . . 125, 157, 158
" Eveline 176
" George H. 192
" Hannah 103, 128, 135, 180
" Harriet L. 189, 193
" Hepzibath 125, 173
" Joanna . . . 100, 118, 123
" James 159
Stone, John 3, 132
" Jonas 155
" Jonathan 20, 21, 23, 30, 31, 36, 38, 49, 51, 54, 59, 60, 61, 62, 63, 64, 65, 78, 79, 93, 103, 105, 107, 130, 134, 135, 136, 137, 138, 146, 151, 153, 155, 163, 171, 172, 173, 175, 176, 180, 182, 183, 184, 190, 193
" Joel 174
" Joseph . . . 41, 175, 194
" Josiah . . . 137, 152, 171
" Johanna 107, 193
" Keziah 138, 164
" Leonard 193
" Love 183
" Lucy 170, 193
" Margaret 137
" Martha 153, 184
" Mary . 150, 182, 191, 193
" Mathias . . 152, 160, 183
" Moses 146, 150, 152, 153, 155, 169, 170, 172, 173, 174, 175, 183, 185, 187, 189, 190
" Nancy 174
" Nathan 150, 152, 153, 155, 183
" Nathaniel 93, 115, 157, 163, 182
" Phebe S. 107
" Rebecca 175
" Rhoda 163, 169
" Richard 172
" Ruth 112, 151, 182
" Sally 171
" Samuel 136
" Sarah 135
" Seth 155, 175
" Simon 3, 4, 5, 6, 7, 8, 10, 11, 12, 15
" Susanna 174
" Warren F. 194
" William 153, 170, 172, 173, 174, 175, 176, 189, 191
Storer, Ebenezer 154
" John 135
" Joseph 135
" Seth 37, 38, 39, 40, 41, 44, 46, 54, 56, 78, 94, 114, 134, 180
Stoughton, William 1
Stowell, Abigail 184
" Benjamin 137
" David 145
" Hezekiah 139
" Jemima 143
" Jerusha 141

Stowell, John 84, 90, 92, 136, 137, 139, 141, 143, 145
" Josiah 88, 92, 93
" Mary 181
" Samuel 92
" Sarah 182, 183
" Thankful 183
" Thomas 192
Stratton, Abigail 122, 132, 137, 184
" Abijah 135
" Elizabeth 138
" Eunice . . . 136, 184
" Hannah 149
" Isaac . . . 151, 153, 166
" Jabez 133, 135, 137, 138, 141, 180
" John 3, 15, 23, 103, 107, 122, 124, 127, 133, 136, 137, 139, 153, 154, 155, 158, 159, 162, 163, 166, 167
" Joshua 162
" Lucy 107, 159
" Lydia 158
" Mary 132, 140, 154, 155, 167
" Mercy . . . 124, 141, 180
" Nathan 137
" Nathaniel . . . 78, 151
" Oliver 136
" Rebecca 130
" Richard 163
" Samuel 77, 89, 90, 92, 95, 129, 130, 134, 136, 140, 144, 147, 149, 151, 153, 182
" Sarah . . . 141, 147, 153
" Tabitha . . . 103, 180
" Thomas 151
" Widow 91
Sturgeon, Robert 113
Stutson, Ebenezer 164
Swan, Bathsheba 142
" Ebenezer . . 141, 142, 144
" Joseph 141
" Mary 144
Sweet, Mrs. 101
Symms, James 180
Tainter, Tayntor, Ann . . . 110
" Anna 158
" Ayers, Eyrls 108, 146, 165, 167, 168, 171, 185
" Benjamin 124
" Dolly 171
" Elizabeth . . 119, 151, 165,
" Hannah 134, 146, 165, 183
" Joanna . . . 138, 161, 180
" John 90, 92, 93, 108, 114, 115, 134, 136, 139, 140, 143, 146, 150, 151, 157, 158, 160, 163, 164, 165, 166, 171, 181
" Jonathan 124, 126, 150, 151
" Joseph 126
Tainter, Lizzey 164
" Lucy 167
" Mary 144, 157
" Nathaniel 108
" Rebecca . . 108, 180, 183
" Sally 188
" Samuel 143, 163
" Sarah 160, 171
" Simon 90, 100
" Susanna . . 136, 158, 184
" William . . . 150, 168
Tay, Isaac 103
Taylor, Benjamin . . . 121, 178
" Edward 97
" Margaret . . . 100, 118
" Walter 121, 126
Thayer, Thare, Abigail . . . 132
" Anna 132
" Charles 192
" Clinton 188, 192
" Elizabeth 188
" George C. 192
Thacher, Thatcher, Abigail . 180
" Anna 126
" Ebenezer 139, 142, 143, 144, 149, 181
" Ensign 7
" Francis 101
" Hannah 180
" John 119
" Marath 129
" Mary 142
" Mercy 131
" Mr. 178
" Samuel 2, 7, 14, 15, 17, 28, 38, 39, 72, 74, 118, 119, 126, 129, 131, 132, 139
" Sarah . . . 132, 140, 149
" Sergt. 5, 6
" Susanna . . . 144, 183
Thaxter, Atherton 190
" Elizabeth 190
" George W. 191
" Hannah F. 190
" Jonas 193
" Levi 106, 188, 191, 193, 194
" Lucy W. 194
" Lydia A. 191
" Mary C. 190
Thomas, James 162
" Joshua 165
" Moses 165
" Richard 102
Thompson, Alexander . . . 149
" Hannah 159
" John 159
" Samuel 149
Thornton, Ebenezer . . . 91, 93
" Mr. 179
" Thomas 120
Throp, Mary 121
" Sarah 121

Thwing, Amos 162
" Edward 151
" John 162
" Mary 162
" Nathaniel 151
" Thomas 162
Tidd, Betty 147
" Daniel 147
Tilton, Nathan 187
Tobey, (a negro) 102
Tom, Sarah (a negro) 143
" Margaret (a negro) . 144
Townsend, Abigail 120
" Capt. 177
" Jonathan 126
" Martin 2, 120, 126
Train, Trayne, Deborah . . . 132
" Elizabeth 125
" John 2, 132, 150
" Margaret 132
" Rebecca, 92, 125, 131, 133
" Silas 150
" Thomas . 2, 90, 132, 133
Trask, Ame 107
Tredaway, Josiah . 120, 127, 129
" Severanua 127
" Tabitha 129
Trowbridge, Anna 191
" Charles 190
" Edmund 190, 191
" James 191
" Jonathan 148
" Lucy 190
" Mary 148, 187
Trull, John 107, 192
" Thomas 192
" William J. 192
Tucker, Ebenezer 189
" John 106, 117, 188, 189, 190, 191, 193
" Martha 191
" Sally 189
" William 189, 193
Tufts, John 126, 129
" Mary 122, 126
Twitchell, Lydia 154
Underwood, Elizabeth . . 119, 120
" Eunice 183
" Hannah 128
" James 139
" Jonathan 120
" Joseph 126, 128
" Joshua 106
" Mary 120
" Nehemiah 183
" Ruth 104, 139, 181
" Sarah 126
" Thomas 120, 123
Upham, Abijah 139
" Jonathan 139
" Ruth 147
" Thomas 147
Vila, Velah, Veleau, Anna . . 147
Vila, Velah, Veleau, John . 92, 93, 103, 145, 147, 149
Vinal, Elizabeth 88
" John 103, 174
" Mary 174
Vose, Addison 190
" Charlotte 190
" Ebenezer 176, 189, 190, 191
" Henry 189
" Jonathan 176
" Lucretia 191
" Polly 171
" Sally 172
" Thomas . . . 105, 171, 172
Wade, Capt. 126
Waight, Wait, Amos 131
" Sarah 122
" Thomas 122
Wakefield, Susanna 102
Wales, Betsey 170
" Elkanah 108
" Grace 108
" Samuel 171
Walker, Abigail 185
" Elizabeth 164
" Richard 164
Ward, William 99
Warren, Abigail . . 153, 167, 168
" Abijah 161
" Ann 156
" Asa 151, 160
" Benjamin 137
" Carolina M. 171
" Capt. 3, 4
" Charles 170, 172
" Daniel 4, 79, 128
" Eleanor 172, 188
" Elijah 138
" Ephraim 93
" Elizabeth 120, 140, 142, 165
" Esther 156
" George 173
" John 120, 126, 128, 152, 154, 156, 158
" Jonathan 126
" Joshua 90, 92, 93, 103, 135, 137, 138, 140, 142, 145, 181
" Josiah 167, 168
" Juliana M. 174
" Lucy 151, 160, 176
" Lydia 155
" Margaret 112, 119
" Marshall 175
" Mary 137, 151
" Moses 105, 135, 170, 172, 174, 175, 176
" Nathan 135
" Nathaniel . . 140, 152, 163
" Noah 145
" Rebecca 181
" Roba 169
" Ruth 158

Warren, Samuel 90, 92, 93, 111, 112, 135, 137, 151, 153, 155, 156, 158, 160, 161, 163, 165, 167, 170
" Sarah 119
" Sophia 174
" Stephen 167
" Susanna 152
" Tabitha 160
" Thaddeus 140
" William 104, 169, 170, 171, 172, 173, 174
Watson, Wason, Abraham . 99
" Benjamin 101
" Lethic 141
" Margaret 104, 141
Weaver, Samuel 103
Webb, Mr. 111
" Widow . . . 100, 101, 102
Weld, Nathaniel 188
Wellington, Abraham 141
" Benjamin 22, 126, 129, 130
" Dorcas 104, 145
" Dr. 5, 6, 7
" Ebenezer 104, 135
" Edmund 168
" Elisha 149
" Elizabeth 120, 124, 142, 155
" Jeduthan 153
" John . 108, 133, 134, 143
" Joseph 92, 104, 120, 124, 127, 129, 141, 143, 145, 147, 149, 151, 153, 155
" Josiah 147, 149
" Katy 173
" Lydia 135, 172
" Margaret . . 141, 149, 182
" Mary 127
" Mehitabel . . 126, 147, 168
" Oliver 23
" Palgrave 11, 15, 22, 23, 24, 25, 26, 134, 151
" Rebecca 143, 181
" Relief 108
" Roger 3
" Ruhamah 147
" Samuel 172, 173
" Susannah 144
" Thomas 124, 141, 142, 143, 144, 149, 181
" William 149
Wells, Francis 156
" Thomas 156
Wheeler, Abijah 148
" Ephraim . . 162, 163, 164
" Elizabeth 163
" James 164
" Jonathan 148
" Samuel 163
White, Aaron 176
" Abigail . . 144, 160, 180
White, Abijah 152, 192
" Adeline 191
" Andrew 90, 91, 92, 93, 94, 131, 133, 134, 135, 138, 139, 140, 141, 142, 144, 146, 147, 149, 166, 180, 181
" Betty 163
" Calvin 193
" Daniel 150
" Diadama 163
" Eleanor 162
" Elijah 149, 167
" Eunice 147, 166
" George 192
" Grace 165
" Hannah . . 139, 167, 180
" Henry 173, 174
" Jane 180, 190
" Jedidiah 141, 163, 165, 166
" Jemima 144
" Joel 156
" John 144, 154
" Jonas 152, 154, 156, 157, 159, 160, 162, 171, 172, 173, 174
" Joseph . . 150, 190, 191
" Josiah . . . 159, 164, 172
" Lois 157, 162
" Lucy . 107, 142, 159, 190
" Luther . . . 188, 192, 193
" Lydia 140
" Martha 138, 192
" Moses . . . 174, 176, 190
" Rachel 191
" Reuben 163
" Ruth 136, 155
" Sally 174
" Samuel 112, 115, 135, 158, 159, 160, 162, 164, 166, 168, 185
" Sarah . . . 131, 138, 180
" Sibyl 168, 187
" Stephen 155
" William . . 134, 153, 171
Whitmore, Francis 130
" John 121
" Rebecca 130
" Samuel 122, 130
Whittamore, Isaac 160
" James 129
" John 129
" Joseph 177
" Samuel 160
Whitney, Aaron 149
" Abigail 121, 142, 146, 174
" Alexander 191
" Amos 140
" Anna . . . 134, 166, 192
" Benjamin 90, 92, 93, 97, 140, 142, 144, 147, 149, 150, 152, 154, 158, 170, 181

Whitney, Bradshaw 194
" Charles 106, 169, 191, 192, 194
" Daniel 90, 92, 94, 112, 113, 116, 118, 142, 143, 144, 146, 147, 148, 150, 152, 169, 170, 171, 173, 174, 186
" David . 145, 160, 168, 171
" Dorothy 142, 183
" Edward 193
" Eliezer 97
" Elisha 150, 174
" Elizabeth 150, 181
" Elnathan 180
" Ezekiel 105, 146, 174, 176
" Francis 172
" Frank 174
" George 174
" Grace 148, 158, 161, 173, 185
" Hannah . . 127, 173, 186
" Henry . . . 144, 149, 170
" Isaac 121
" Israel 107, 146, 165, 166, 168, 170, 185, 188, 193
" James 171, 192
" Jemima, ... 165, 185
" Joanna 142
" John 79, 90, 91, 93, 97, 98, 121, 138, 139, 144, 146, 148, 149, 151, 157, 176
" Jonathan 98, 108, 133, 134, 139, 147, 164, 165, 166, 173, 192
" Joseph 92, 93, 108, 121, 143, 145, 147, 150
" Joshua 143
" Josiah 150
" Katy 105
" Leonard 174
" Lucy . . . 108, 152, 165
" Lydia 147, 150
" Martha 111, 112, 121, 125, 194
" Mary 140, 142, 143, 157, 161, 165, 166, 169, 184, 186, 193
" Moses 144
" Nancy 170
" Nathaniel 95, 106, 119, 124, 127, 159, 171, 172, 173, 174, 175, 176, 188, 189, 191, 192, 193, 194
" Otis 176
" Polly 171
" Rebecca 144
" Richard 170
" Relief 167, 168
" Ruth 151
" Sally 188
" Samuel 124, 147, 157, 173, 183, 186
" Sarah 119, 130, 152, 193, 194
Whitney, Sibil C. 191
" Simon 159, 160, 161, 165, 166, 170, 175, 184
" Stephen 108, 148, 167, 168, 170
" Susanna 104, 138, 164, 185
" Thomas 97, 119
" William 175
Wilkins, Mr. 100, 101, 102
Williams, Amariah 137
" Damaris 119
" Esther 139
" Hannah 153
" Jesse 143
" Nathaniel 153
" Phineas 140
" Thomas 119
" Wareham 137, 145, 147, 148, 149
" William 74, 80, 82, 90, 137, 139, 140, 143
Willis, Benjamin 119
" Mr. 177
" Stephen 119
Willy, Sarah 98
Winchester, Daniel 189
" Grace 188
" Jonathan 156
" Leonard 175
" Mary 176
" Nancy 190
" Rebecca 190
" Sarah 176
" William 175, 176, 189, 190
Winship, Aaron 141
" Edward 98
" Ephraim 145
" Jason 141
" Jonathan 167
" Joseph 98, 144
" Lieut. 126
" Nathan 167
" Philemon 144
Winter, Hannah 129
" John 126, 129
" Sarah 126
Wisondouk, Elizabeth 102
Witherspoon, Isabel 96
Woodward, Achsah 153
" John . . . 2, 98, 124, 153
" Rev. Mr. 155
" Rose 96
" Thomas 98
Woolson, Mary 131
Wyeth, Wiett, John 102
" Mercy 132
" Nicholas 3, 119, 132
Wyman, Charles 160
" Thaddeus 160
Young, John 149, 150, 151
" Susanna 149
" Daniel 151

Index to Places.

Acton 163
Antigo 97
Barnstable 195
Boston 1, 18, 53, 88, 89, 96, 97, 98, 99, 100, 102, 122, 129, 154, 158, 162, 179, 181, 195
Bowling Green 103
Braintree 119, 128
Brookline . 150, 152, 155, 156, 159
Cambridge 52, 73, 86, 96, 98, 99, 107, 121, 124, 138, 141, 142, 148, 149, 150, 151, 152, 156, 158, 159, 160, 161, 162, 163, 167, 168, 186, 195
Charlestown 97, 98, 99, 129, 154, 195
Concord . . 99, 128, 150, 152, 195
Conway 167
Dedham . . 98, 121, 126, 129, 195
Dorchester 101, 195
Dublin, Ireland 96
Grafton 162
Ireland 100, 194
Lancaster 99, 133
Lexington 144, 147, 156
Limerick 194
Lunenburg 153
Malden 137
Marlboro' 131, 139
Marshfield 101
Medford 120, 159
Mendon 122, 184
Menotomey 96, 98, 141, 144, 145, 148, 149, 150
Middleton 177
Muddy River 98
Mystic 122, 126, 127
Natick 154, 155
Newbury 195
Newton 108, 116, 136, 140, 143, 144, 145, 147, 148, 149, 151, 152, 153, 154, 155, 158, 159, 160, 161, 163, 165, 168
Piscataqua 102
Plymouth 101
Roxbury 103, 158, 163, 195
Salem 101, 129
Sherborn 98, 128
Shrewsbury 166
Stockbridge 163
Stoughton 104
Sudbury 96, 97
Waltham 151, 152, 153, 154, 157, 160, 163, 165, 184, 189, 194
Wells 135, 136, 139, 181
Westboro' 154
Weston 35, 139, 147, 148, 150, 160
Weymouth 195
Woburn 119, 195
Woodstock 161
Worcester 152, 154
Yarmouth 129

Index to Subjects.

Arms and Ammunition . . 85, 86
Assessment for finishing New Meeting House . . . 43
" rate of 5, 8
Auditors appointed 16
Baptism by Rev. Robert Sturgeon, irregular 113
Bailey, Rev. John's book . . 96
" bids farewell . 124, 197
" end of his marrying in N. E. 99
" pastoral work, sick of 119
" records, private memoranda only 128
" remarks on admitting to Communion certain persons . . 118, 119, 122
" daily expenses . . . 179
" death of wife 110, 124, 177
" distributes what his wife left 177, 178
" funeral expenses of wife, 177
" marriage registration fee of 3 black dogs . . . 100
Bank 28
Bell 76, 78
" wheel 19
" ringing allowance for, 13,46
" hanging of 71
Burying place 2
Certificates of attendance upon Church of England, 88, 89
Charles River 73, 84, 86
Church charity, upon whom bestowed 111
" meeting, held on desire of three 117
" England, certificate of membership . . . 88, 89
" third in Watertown . 113
" member, how received, 115
Clark 13, 15
Committee, appointed, against petition of sundry inhabitants 22
" to buy land for use of minister 22
" to wait on General Court, 27
" to obtain helper for Mr. Gibbs 28
" for conference with the other congregation 30
" upon boundary between precincts 31, 32
" for ordination of Seth Storer 39, 40
Committee on building Meeting House 55
" to take care of Church funds . . . 115, 116
Communion service administered, when 117
Communion service vessels changed, 116
Communion table, support of, 112, 116
Confessions to be made before the Church 115
Congregational affairs end . . 33
Contributions, for expenses of ordination of Rev. S. Storer, 41
" for repairing buildings of Pastor Gibbs . . 21
" to be papered, 5, 7, 9, 11, 12
Council of Churches, May, 1722, 113
Covenant, form of 109
" children of persons owning, 116
Doggs, 3 black, as marriage registration fee . . . 100
Epitaph on John Bailey . . 111
" on John Bailey's wife, 110
" on Thomas Bailey . 110
" on John Sherman . . 110
Flagons, pewter, sold; silver tankards bought . 116, 117
Full Communion, form of Covenant, 109
Funeral expenses of J. Bailey's wife, 177
Gibbs, Henry, called to ministry, 3
" " declines . . . 4
" " gift to Church . 18
" " receipt for salary, 24
Glass, repairs, 6, 10, 18, 21, 64, 66, 69, 70, 71, 80, 82, 84
Great Bridge 73, 84
Grist Mill, old 10
Hearse cloth 2, 76
Land granted 86
Legacy from Mrs. Ann Mills, 111, 112, 113, 114
Marrying, end of for Mr. Bailey in N. Eng. 99
Masters brook 86
Meeting House, repairs, 6, 10, 27, 29
" " old, 1, 5, 6, 7, 29, 38, 42, 43, 44
" " middle . . 1, 7, 24
" " new, 1, 4, 38, 42, 43, 44, 45, 56
" " on School House Hill . 38, 50, 51

Meeting House, path to . 76, 78
" " pews in, 48, 58, 59, 60, 61, 62, 63, 94, 95
" " seating of, 65, 75, 76, 90, 91, 92, 93, 94
" " shutters to windows . . . 69, 70, 71
Military precinct 1
Mills, Ann, legacy, 111, 112, 113, 114
Minister, assessment for support of, 5, 6
" Henry Gibbs chosen, 4
" support of in the east and west parts . . . 1
" advice of General Court, 24, 25
Ministeral place, 2, 37, 49, 52, 53, 55, 67, 71
" alteration and repair of, 31, 53, 55, 56, 57, 67, 68
" land and fence, 21, 22, 29, 83, 84
Notes belonging to the Church renewed 117
Ordination of Pastor Adams . 169
" " J. Bailey 119
" " Eliot . 169
" " Storer . 134
Owning the Covenant, form of, 109
" " " " "
for those children of whom to be baptized . . . 116
Pequod War 118
Pew Committee 59, 62
Pew lots, disposal of, 48, 58, 60, 61, 62, 63, 64
Precinct affairs 35, 86
" assessors, allowance of, 45
" lines 73, 74
Prince of Orange guards . . 118
Protest, town's voting in precinct affairs 30
Record book to be kept, 4, 9, 13, 14, 18, 22, 24, 39, 85, 86
" transcribed from Almanacks 107
Sacraments, when to be administered 117
Sacramental phrases and expressions of J. Bailey, 194, 195, 196
" lecture 117
Salary for Pastor, contributions for, on Sabbath days, 12, 14
" of minister, 8, 11, 18, 37, 79
" for sexton 14
Society to consider some method for placing meeting house, 19
Storer, Seth, chosen to be Gospel minister 37
" " acceptance . . 39
" " petition for increase of salary 94
Town, division of, 72, 73, 84, 85, 86
Tombstone of Mrs. Bailey . 177
Treasurer's account book . . 82
Warning for precinct meeting, 10, 31
Ways layed out 86
Wood for Pastor . . 5, 6, 10, 31

www.ingramcontent.com/pod-product-compliance
Lightning Source LLC
Chambersburg PA
CBHW021805230426
43669CB00008B/638

* 9 7 8 3 3 3 7 1 4 3 7 3 2 *